THE MITTERRAND EXPERIMENT

Europe and the International Order

Series Editor: Joel Krieger

Published

Peter A. Hall, *Governing the Economy*
Joel Krieger, *Reagan, Thatcher and the Politics of Decline*

Forthcoming

Judith Adler Hellman, *Journeys among Women*
Mark Kesselman, *The Fading Rose*
Andrei Markovits, *The West German Left: Red, Green, and Beyond*

THE MITTERRAND EXPERIMENT

Continuity and Change in Modern France

Edited by George Ross, Stanley Hoffmann and Sylvia Malzacher

OXFORD UNIVERSITY PRESS · NEW YORK
1987

Oxford University Press

Oxford   New York   Toronto
Delhi   Bombay   Calcutta   Madras   Karachi
Petaling Jaya   Singapore   Hong Kong   Tokyo
Nairobi   Dar es Salaam   Cape Town
Melbourne   Auckland

and associated companies in

Beirut   Berlin   Ibadan   Nicosia

Published by Oxford University Press, Inc.,
200 Madison Avenue, New York, New York 10016

Oxford is a registered trademark of Oxford University Press

ISBN 0-19-520608-8 (cloth)
ISBN 0-19-520612-6 (paper)

Printing (last digit): 9 8 7 6 5 4 3 2 1

To The Memory of Philip Williams

Contents

List of Contributors

Suzanne Berger	Ford International Professor of Political Science, Massachusetts Institute of Technology; Center for European Studies, Harvard University
Robert Boyer	Centre d'Etudes Prospectives d'Economie Mathématique Appliquées à la Planification; and Centre National de la Recherche Scientifique, Paris
Olivier Duhamel	Professor of Public Law, Université de Paris X
Catherine Grémion	Director, Centre de Sociologie des Organisations, Centre National de la Recherche Scientifique, Paris
Jean-Marie Guéhenno	Formerly Cultural Counsellor, French Cultural Services, New York
Peter Hall	Associate Professor of Government, Harvard University; Center for European Studies, Harvard University
Stephane Hessel	Ambassadeur de France; former member of the Haute Autorité de la Communication Audiovisuelle, Paris
Stanley Hoffmann	Douglas Dillon Professor of the Civilization of France, Harvard University; Chairman, Center for European Studies, Harvard University
Jolyon Howorth	Professor of French Civilization, University of Bath; Center for European Studies, Harvard University
John Keeler	Associate Professor of Political Science, University of Washington, Seattle
Richard Kuisel	Professor of History, State University of New York, Stony Brook
Alain Lancelot	Director, Institut d'Etudes Politiques, Paris
Marie-Thérèse Lancelot	Centre d'Etudes de la Vie Politique Française Contemporaine, Fondation Nationale des Sciences Politiques, Paris
Georges Lavau	Professor, Fondation Nationale des Sciences Politiques, Paris
Steve Lewis	Assistant Professor of Political Science, University of Wisconsin, Madison; Center for European Studies, Harvard University
Yves Mény	Professor, Sciences politique, Université de Paris II
Jean-Louis Moynot	Engineer, Thomson Electronics; President, GIP Mutations des Sociétés Industrielles, Paris

Diana Pinto	Historian, Consultant for Cultural Affairs, USIS, Paris, contributor to *Le Débat, Commentaire, Intervention* and author of *Contemporary Italian Sociology* (Cambridge University Press)
Antoine Prost	Professor, Histoire, Université de Paris I; Centre de Recherches sur l'Histoire des Mouvements Sociaux et du Syndicalisme, Paris
René Rémond	President, Fondation Nationale des Sciences Politiques; Professor, Histoire, Université de Paris X
George Ross	Morris Hillquit Professor of Labor and Social Thought, Brandeis University; Center for European Studies, Harvard University
Serenella Sferza	Ph.D. Candidate, Political Science, Massachusetts Institute of Technology; Center for European Studies, Harvard University
Alec Stone	Ph.D. Candidate, Political Science, University of Washington, Seattle

List of Acronyms

CERES	Centre d'Etudes, de Recherches et d'Education Socialiste
CFDT	Confédération Française et Démocratique du Travail
CGC	Confédération Générale des Cadres
CGPME	Confédération Générale des Petites et Moyennes Entreprises
CGT	Confédération Générale du Travail
CGT-FO	Confédération Générale du Travail-Force Ouvrière
CID-UNATI	Comité d'Information et de Défense-Union Nationale des Travailleurs Indépendants
CNPF	Conseil National du Patronat Français
ECU	European Currency Unit
EEC	European Economic Community
EMS	European Monetary System
FEN	Fédération de l'Education Nationale
FNSEA	Fédération Nationale des Syndicats d'Exploitants Agricoles
FO	*See* CGT-FO
INSEE	Institut National de la Statistique et des Etudes Economiques
OECD	Organization for European Cooperation and Development
OPEC	Oil-Producing and Exporting Countries
PME	Petites et Moyennes Entreprises
PCF	Parti Communiste Française
RPR	Rassemblement Pour la République
SFIO	Section Française de l'Internationale Ouvrière
SMIC	Salaire Minimum Interindustriel de Croissance
SNPME	Syndicat National du Patronat Moderne et Indépendant
UDF	Union Pour la Démocratie Française

Preface

The Mitterrand Experiment: Continuity and Change in Modern France originated three years ago with plans for a conference on the five years of Left rule in France from 1981–86, to be held at the Harvard University Center for European Studies. With the gracious help of the German Marshall Fund of the United States, the French Consulate in Boston, the French Cultural Services and private contributors, the conference was held in December 1985. At that moment academic analysts of French politics and society from North America and France gathered with politicians, trade unionists, business people, journalists and Civil Servants to discuss what all agreed to have been an extraordinarily interesting period in modern French history. And, everyone recognized, what was most remarkable about what had happened was how unpredictable the Left's drama and its denouement had been. When the French people voted the Left out of power in the March 1986 legislative elections they provided closure on the experiment and made us think that this book project was eminently worthwhile.

The list of people who participated in and contributed to this wide-ranging enterprise is long. The Harvard University Center for European Studies produced the original conference and the book. Abby Collins presided over and participated in both undertakings from beginning to end with incisiveness, energy, generosity and incredible skill. Guido Goldman, as always, was of inestimable help. Steve Hubbell has done great service in making the book happen. Joan Beaton, Gretchen Bouliane, Jacqueline Brown, Loren Goldner, Lucy Johnston, Trudi Koziol, Anna Popiel and Ceallaigh Reddy were professional and generous colleagues. Jean-Claude Casanova, Roland Cayrol, Michel Crozier, Georges DeMénil, Gilbert Dupin, Pierre Hassner, Pierre Héritier, Jane Jenson, Ed Kolodziej, Pierre Lellouche, Janice McCormick, Alain Minc, Michel Rocard, Ezra Suleiman, Judith Vichniac and Nick Wahl all played important roles in the conference and helped us sharpen our ideas for this volume. The French Consul General in Boston, Alain Briottet, Jean-Marie Guéhenno, the French Cultural Consul in the United States, Véronique Marteau, the French Cultural Attaché in Boston, Bernard Genton, her immediate predecessor and Christine Bolzan of the Boston Consulate were of immense help and support.

Cambridge, Mass.
GR, SH, SM.

I
Introduction

Introduction

GEORGE ROSS

One Left, radical and militant in words and program, came to power in France in 1981. Another Left, composed of the same people, but somewhat humbled and with a very different identity, abandoned power after the elections of 1986. The first Left had promised to transform the nature of French society. But such promises could not stand up to deep-rooted trends which it had underplayed, misunderstood and sometimes ignored. What followed, besides the transformation of the Left's own identity, was not simply a retreat. Important, perhaps essential, changes, occurred in France between 1981 and 1986, even if these changes were rarely those which the Left had set out to accomplish. *The Mitterrand Experiment: Continuity and Change in Modern France* will begin to unravel the complexities of this critically important moment in French development.

THE DISCONCERTING EVENTS OF MAY-JUNE 1981

On the evening of 10 May 1981, when François Mitterrand's election to the Presidency of France was officially made known, there occurred a huge *fête populaire* at the Bastille. Tens of thousands of joyful people turned out to celebrate and mingle, convinced that their country, at long last, had renewed its revolutionary heritage. Others, less joyful, watching the events on television, were afraid that this might be true. To be sure, there was cause enough for celebration on the Left. Twenty-three years of continuous rule by the Right had come to an end. Still, what had happened on 10 May was only an election, not a revolution. Moreover, it was an election which had been decided by a very small shift in votes in a country facing profound problems. There was thus a disconcerting disproportion in May-June 1981 between the extravagant hopes - and fears - of the moment and the realities of the situation.

Part of the extravagance was explainable because the events of May-June 1981 were unexpected. To begin with, the French had surprised themselves by what they had done. Elites, politicians and many French people had come to accept the Fifth Republic as an immense paradox, a democracy whose majority and political biases never changed. The Center-Right which had controlled the politics and state apparatus of this Republic since its creation in 1958 had come to believe that state power belonged to it as if by right of birth. There were also constitutional disorientations in the event. The Fifth Republic had *always* been governed from the Right. Even though *alternance* - a change in majorities - had been discussed, it had never occurred. How would the institutions hold up?

3

The Left, despite rising strength and hope in the 1970s, had not foreseen these new "events of May." As recently as 1979–80, during one of the Socialist Party's regular internal crises, many Socialists had concluded that the future President, then Party leader, was an "archaic" political anachronism who would almost certainly prevent the Left from succeeding as long as he continued to occupy center stage. At the very same moment, the Communists, without whose support Left success seemed impossible, began concentrating their considerable energies on the task of cutting the Socialists and their leader down to size rather than helping the Left more generally to win in 1981. In this atmosphere, labor leader Edmond Maire, who had a long-standing reputation for stating aloud what everyone on the Left thought quietly, announced that the Left had no chance in 1981 and that prudence dictated that organized labor make other arrangements.

May–June 1981 was unexpected from a comparative vantage point as well. The post-1974 economic crisis of advanced industrial societies had fostered strong ideological, intellectual and political movements to the Right. The terms of the post-war social compromise around consumerist economic growth, employment security, the Welfare State and Keynesian macroeconomic intervention had begun to unravel. Certainties regarded as facts of life for decades were eclipsed by each country's need to face draconian new international economic constraints. In consequence, sophisticated new neo-liberal economic ideas and not-so-sophisticated "New Right" politics had achieved prominence in debate. The interventionist state was targetted for "deregulation" and "privatization". The Welfare State was derided for its bureaucratic inefficiency and its disincentive effects on the work ethic. And the industrial relations systems which comforted trade-union power and the workers' job security were attacked as barriers to needed new "flexibility". Yet, as if to reaffirm Gallic idiosyncracy, it was at this point that the French Left came to power.

The events also had great potential significance for the Left in other advanced societies. The Left's family squabbles everywhere were usually divided between protagonists of the social democratic "politics of the possible" and those of a further Left "politics of real change". In the eyes of the harder Left, social democracy, which had often held power and had been central to constructing and maintaining the post-war compromise, was thereby tainted with compromise and had abandoned the goal of transcending capitalism. Social Democrats, of course, responded that the purists could sustain their high tone only because they had never held power. Over the years the French Left had not spared itself this kind of mutual character assassination, of course. But as it moved towards power it claimed to have transcended this dichotomy. Despite their mutual mistrust, both the French Socialists and Communists denounced meliorist social democracy and disclaimed any intention of replicating it in France, proposing instead "to break with capitalism".

There were reasons to take this seriously. The French Left had been excluded from power throughout most of the post-war economic boom. In consequence, French socialism had had no "Bad Godesberg" and had therefore never been obliged to make its peace with the reformist world which other Lefts had created and administered. In a new setting marked by severe economic crisis such temptations were likely to be absent. The French Left would probably have to be something other than social democratic after May–June 1981, therefore. Moreover, its programmatic statements, from the 1972 Socialist–Communist Common Program onwards, all promised serious change of a kind which had hardly been advocated, let alone practiced, for decades in any advanced society. Seen from the international Left, then, the events of May–June 1981 created the conditions for a long-awaited test. Was social democracy all that was possible? Or would something new come from these French politicians and intellectuals who had always claimed not only that something new was possible, but also to know what it was?

There was an "international affairs" dimension to the events as well. By the later 1970s, as the United States struggled to regain its composure after Vietnam and while the Soviet Union tried to use American uncertainty to extend its advantage, detente had given way to renewed superpower rivalry. In the face of this, France's Gaullist pretentions to relative independence from the superpowers, even in decline, would have placed the country in a delicate position. The international postures of the French Left were perhaps the least clear side of its identity in 1981, but François Mitterrand seemed to have a Gaullist side to him. More important, the Parti Socialiste (PS) was full of former *soixante-huitards* – participants in the radical mobilization of May–June 1968 – who were strongly devoted to "Third-Worldist" attitudes and "Third Way" hopes for a French role in international dealings. The kind of *tiersmondisme* which lived within the PS, with its antipathy to authoritarian regimes of the Right, sympathies for Third World progressivism and strong North–South Keynesianism had a unique logic – even when the package was presented, as it often was, as a better way of being anti-Soviet than that of the heavy-handed Americans. The Reaganite worldview in which American rearmament and diplomatic pressure would stymie the Soviets, shape up "the Alliance" and, finally, allow the reassertion of Western control over trouble-spots everywhere was not likely to sit well with such socialists. In addition, four Communists became ministers in the French government in June 1981, the first time this had happened in any major Western society since 1947.

BEHIND THE EVENTS

There were good reasons to wonder how the Left would cope with a chilling change in economic circumstances which its predecessors' behaviour had done little to confront. There were even better reasons to be perplexed about prospects for the program which the Left brought to power in May–June 1981. Finally, there were a number of profound processes going on in French society which would make the Left's ambitions and its daily life much more difficult to carry out than anyone suspected.

Crisis and inheritance

By 1981 the French economic situation had evolved in ways which would have tested the creativity and will of any administration severely. After a long and transformative post-war period of economic success France had entered a different economic world in the mid-1970s. The general situation was perhaps characterized best as a set of changes in the international system feeding back to cause new problems for national economies and, in consequence, for the social compromises which had been so carefully crafted in the post-1945 boom years. But the ways in which different national economies were situated in the international system and reacted to its changes were very important. From this point of view the Left depended very much on raw materials left by its predecessors.

Here there were huge ironies. The Giscard–Chirac tandem had initially responded to crisis after 1974 as if it were another, if rather severe, cyclical downturn like those which had earlier punctuated the post-war boom. That this was a miscalculation had become clear by 1976-77. By this point, however, Giscard and his new Prime Minister, Raymond Barre, faced a political situation which limited options severely. Giscard had won the 1974 presidential elections by a bare 1.6 per cent. By the March 1977 municipal elections, it looked as if the Left had actually become a majority. The Right managed to snatch victory from defeat in the 1978 legislative elections, largely on the strength of unexpected gifts from its newly feuding Left opponents. With its existing electoral advantage razor-thin at best and a presidential election on the horizon, however, the existing majority could not engage in serious cutbacks, redirect national income away from wages to profits and make major changes in the social service system - all measures which crisis dictated, at least to conservatives - without endangering its political survival.

Thus, rather than devising economic and industrial policies adequate to the tasks at hand, the Giscard–Barre administration had by and large postponed things. Real wages in France thus continued to rise throughout the 1970s. France's inflation levels rose more steadily and rapidly than those of most of its important trading partners, with damaging effects on France's international trade position. Raymond Barre's policy of overvaluing the franc to control international balances hurt the competitive positions of already weak French industry. The costs of social services continued to rise more rapidly than growth rates, with much of the increment borne by employers. In all, the Giscard–Barre policies intensified an already serious profits squeeze for French capital. In response, French capitalists were less and less interested in investing. And when they did invest they borrowed the money, an unattractive practice which became even more so when real interest rates began to rise.

Despite the Right's caution, however, it was unable to maintain its political hold, helping to create the circumstances which allowed François Mitterrand and the Left to win in 1981. Divisions *within* the majority, which developed in part over approaches to economic policy, played their role. Even though it was unable and/or unwilling to take the kinds of politically costly measures which might have hastened French response to the new international economic setting it was nonetheless judged responsible by public opinion for the damages of crisis. The Center-Right borrowed against France's economic future in the vain hope that this would allow it to continue running France after the all-important 1981 presidential elections. The victorious Left would be obliged to pay the outstanding bills.

Programs and politics

What was perhaps most striking about the discourse of the Left in 1981 was how closely it resembled the Left's discourse from the Resistance-Liberation period. It was as if the Left had lost its memory of the events of four complicated decades! Massive nationalizations were proposed. The economy was to be stimulated selectively and in a redistributive way to restore growth. Rising unemployment would be stopped in its tracks by this new growth, work sharing (the 35-hour week, early retirement, longer vacations, public-sector job creation) and, eventually, the restoration of French industrial dynamism by new planning and the new public sector would ensue. The firm was to be reformed and democratized, notably by the introduction of "new rights for workers". Government would be decentralized. If everything worked out, something which looked like a restoration of post-war boom conditions, only with greater social justice and democracy, would follow.

The 1981 program thus contained a catalogue of long-familiar elements plus large doses of voluntarism. If it acknowledged the coming of economic crisis – the Left Common Program of 1972, after all, had been put together before real economic troubles had emerged – it did so mainly to emphasize that crisis could be overcome if only the Left and France could generate the will to do so. If this seems mildly astonishing in retrospect, reflection on the underlying logic by which the program had emerged is a useful corrective. The program had been dictated by *political conflict*, often of a highly rhetorical kind, rather than the hard-nosed realism of potential policy-makers. The situation of the Left in the 1970s meant that things could hardly have been otherwise.

To understand this, one has first to reflect briefly on the French Left's history. What had most often been at the root of the Left's problems – its difficulties in coming to power and its failures in power (in the Popular Front and after Liberation) – and what had made the French Left unusual comparatively, was its persistent internal divisiveness. The long history of multiple social roots eventually growing into a unified social democratic trunk had not occurred in France. Instead the Left had remained divided between large rival wings of self-proclaimed "revolutionaries" and reformists, with a universe of smaller groups in and around them. Because of their persistent division each of these wings had usually pursued two simultaneous strategies, first to come to power and enact a program, and second, to gain advantage and strength over its rival(s) on the Left. In ordinary circumstances these goals were far from complementary. Thus to generate the strength needed to win power leftist groups had always had to override differences and negotiate alliances. Yet even when this had happened – rarely – persistent interorganizational rivalry had made such alliances difficult to sustain.

Perhaps most important, this constant backdrop of interorganizational rivalry created powerful incentives for "more radical than thou" debate. Over time this had perpetuated forms of radical thought and action in France long past the moment of their attenuation elsewhere. All this was not simply an esoteric and theoretical matter, for the program which the Left brought to power in 1981 was powerfully shaped by this competition and pluralism, i.e. by the logic of intra-Left politics. The difficulty here was that this logic of intra-Left politics did not necessarily create a program which would ensure Left success in power.

The most important precipitant of 1981 was the foundation of the Fifth Republic itself. Prior to 1958 and 1962 – respectively the moments of the Fifth Republic's Constitution and of a referendum establishing direct, universal suffrage presidential elections – the French Left had been fratricidally divided between a strong, unashamedly pro-Soviet Communist Party (one quarter of the popular vote, control over the most powerful trade-union organization) and a politically confused, comparatively weaker, non-Communist Left arrayed around a socialist party – the Section Française de l'Internationale Ouvrière (SFIO) – which had suffered greatly from the cold war and decolonization. The single-member constituency electoral law and presidentialism of the Fifth Republic worked, however, to accentuate Left-Right polarization in French politics, and, in consequence, strongly prodded the Left to overcome its differences. The effects of this on a pugnaciously divided Left were slow but sure in coming, aided, in the 1960s at least, by Communist willingness to make considerable short-run sacrifice to encourage alliance. It took the aftermath of May–June 1968 and the reorganization of much of the non-Communist Left into the new Parti Socialiste (PS) – finally concluded at the Epinay Congress in 1971 – to begin in earnest the drive to power which succeeded a decade later.

Two simultaneous processes worked to endow the PS and François Mitterrand with the radical program which they carried to the Elysée Palace in May 1981. First, in order to form and carry on Union de la Gauche, the Left's launching pad towards 1981, the PS and Parti Communiste Français (PCF) had to engage in mutual accommodation. The PCF, a bargaining partner of substance which, in addition, was more powerful than the PS in the early 1970s, was thus able to exercise considerable influence over the elaboration of the 1972 Left Common Program. Next, the PS itself, as it emerged from Epinay, became a federation of rival *courants* each competing for precedence and influence. The internal structure of the PS itself thus placed a premium on assertions of traditional leftism which replicated the exogenous effects of PCF pressure on the PS.

Despite the influx of *autogestionnaire* – self-management – sentiment into the PS in the mid-1970s, and even though Union de la Gauche died of a surfeit of PCF-PS rivalry after 1977, the program of the PS remained anchored in the Union de la Gauche period. This attitude undoubtedly owed much to cultural proclivities "at the base". But it was mainly due to the political strategy of François Mitterrand and his supporters. When Union de la Gauche broke down the Socialists had a choice between a posture of "unity for two", maintaining Left programmatic purity to neutralize the Communists' sectarian offensive against them, and a new "Left–Center" line of the kind advocated by Michel Rocard. Each strategy had its logic, but François Mitterrand's "unity for two" approach won out. Moreover, the intra-PS coalitional circumstances which led to Mitterrand's victory reinforced the voice of the PS's most left-wing *courant*, Centre d'Etudes, de Recherches et d'Education Socialiste (CERES), hence very radical documents like the *Projet socialiste*, published not long before the beginning of the 1981 election campaign. The PS's January 1981 election manifesto, *110 Propositions pour la France*, was but a mildly watered-down version of earlier programs.

Given the potential mismatch between program and situation it was at least a theoretical possibility that the French Left in power would disregard preelectoral rhetoric and programmatic claims, as many of its international peers on the Left had done before it. The nature of the French Left and the charge of political electricity which the first Left government in decades brought with it made this unlikely, however.

There was also the possibility that the leaders and militants of the Left, the PS in particular, would prove unusually gifted at governance and carry their program with this talent. Such talent, if it existed, was largely untried, however. The President had had a ministerial career prior to 1958, and a few Socialists had played minor roles after that. Others had served long and well in local and municipal government. And there were many *Enarques* and other high Civil Servants in Socialist ranks who were familiar with the corridors of power. Still, as of 1981, the Left as a whole had been in opposition for 23 years, a fact which would have boded ill for its success even in the absence of what seemed to be problematic programmatic commitments.

Hidden social trends

Anyone familiar with modern French history knows the great power which Left ideas and postures have had over the French intelligentsia. From the Dreyfus affair onwards there had always existed complex connivance between high Parisian intellectuals and provincial networks of *profs* to disseminate universalistic and progressive messages to "uplift the masses". And even if the "class position" of intellectuals had posed ideological problems, not least to the intellectuals themselves, politicians of the Left had long assumed the existence of alliance between workers and intellectuals who had always been considered to be auxiliaries of the political Left and honorary members of the *peuple de gauche*. Intellectuals, "on the side of the workers", had played an essential role in popularizing the Left's ideas, indeed, in conceptualizing them. In addition, intellectuals had been of primordial importance in spreading the Left's messages amongst the middle strata of French society, whether by left-leaning debate or by organizational power.

Separation, if not divorce, between the Left and the intellectuals, which had begun in the 1970s, was an important hidden social change which the Left in power would have to face. One dimension of this was the rapid triumph of anti-Sovietism and antitotalitarianism among centrally located high Parisian intellectuals. The inordinately public conversion experience undergone by former *soixante-huitards* and fellow travellers opening their eyes rather belatedly to the Gulag was a fascinating episode leading many of them to abrupt 180-degree political turns. By the later 1970s not only "existing socialism" and the Soviet model, but "Old Left" statist ideas (very often including social democratic ideas) had a much less sympathetic intellectual audience than they had had earlier. Thus there came into being a new, and socially very important, source of uncertainty about what "the Left" was about, with which the Left in power would have to cope.

There was a less spectacular, though quite as important, dimension to changing intellectual attitudes. One result of the social explosion of 1968 had been the elevation of *autogestion* to the pantheon of Left ideas, alongside the older repertories of social democracy and Communism. Beyond desiring a new decision-making environment which would place a premium on decentralization and grass-roots democracy, a desire to live in a society in which institutions incited the blooming of hundreds of flowers, and a profound rejection of virtually anything and everything about "existing socialism" (and, to a lesser degree, of the statism and centralism of "existing social democracy") *autogestion* was not a very precise vision. Whatever *autogestion* would turn out to be, the argument went, would be up to those who made it happen, as long as they went about it democratically. Its vagueness notwithstanding, *autogestion* was powerfully mobilizing. Major parts of the labor movement – the Confédération Français et Démocratique du Travail (CFDT) and beyond – Left Catholics and, of course, many, many intellectuals, were attracted by its antistatist and radically democratic appeals.

The *autogestionnaires* started out with a determination to inject their ideas into the organizational rough-and-tumble of the Left's debate. But to make a complex story very simple, however, when they did make their plays for influence in the PS, they lost. The strategic decisions made in the early 1970s, reaffirmed by the Assises du Socialisme (1974) and then in the later defeat of Michel Rocard (1979–80), were made in favour of the "Liberation, Part II" *unitaire* political program described earlier. Disaffection on the part of many *autogestionnaires* followed. The PS's politics were just too centralizing, statist and productivist to suit *autogestionnaire* tastes. By 1980, then, the *deuxième gauche* (as it was called later) had come to exist as a relatively alienated component of the Left, skeptical about the Left's electoral prospects and even more skeptical about Left policy success in the unlikely event of victory in 1981.

The Left in power would face enough criticism without the presence of a large number of skeptics within its own ranks and newly prickly intellectuals at its borders. Worse still, French organized labor was also in trouble. Periods of Left governance had everywhere and always been periods of privileged interaction between Left parties and unions. It was fairly evident, even given France's idiosyncratic and pluralist Left history, that this would be true in France as well. The lay of France's electoral land dictated that the Left would come to power, in large part, on the backs of labor voters. Once in power, the debt thus incurred would come due and, in addition, labor's support for policies and in more general terms would be important.

French labor had never had particularly strong organizations and the French economy had never been highly unionized, but French unions, which had declined dramatically after a moment of great power around 1945, had been able to rebuild considerable strength beginning in the mid-1960s. Movements toward unity on the political Left had helped this, as had the development of collaboration between the pro-Communist Confédération Génerále du Travail (CGT) and the *autogestionnaire* CFDT, but the tight labor markets and rapid economic changes of the last decade of the post-war boom were the key reasons. Thus the penultimate leg of the Left's march to power – the Union de la Gauche episode – began with a stronger, and perhaps more left-leaning, labor movement than France had known for some time.

Economic crisis and political disunity rapidly brought this happy state of affairs to an end, however. Plant closures, employment insecurity and the specific competitive problems of French "smokestack" industries (coal, steel, shipbuilding, textiles) where the most left-wing branches of French labor had their bastions of militancy, took their toll. On top of this the breakup of Union de la Gauche rapidly translated into divisive conflict between the CGT and CFDT. Union memberships, finances and capacity to mobilize had declined precipitously by 1980. Observers began to speak of a new "crisis of unionism". Whatever else happened after 1981, this "crisis" would mean that organized labor would be a much weaker and less coherent voice in support of the Left in power than it might have been earlier. After the intellectuals, yet another important part of the *peuple de gauche* was hurting badly.

Finally, there was another rather more profound dimension of French civil society – less a trend than a misunderstood aspect of French life – which was bound to make the Left's tenure in power difficult. Put simply, France pullulated with "corporatisms", old and new, collusive arrangements between the state and social groups to protect different forms of privilege. Here one had only to think of the colonization of education by the Fédération de l'Education Nationale (FEN), the domination of agricultural policy by the Fédération Nationale des Syndicats d'Exploitants Agricoles (FNSEA), or the ways in which professions were regulated. Implementing social change would involve confronting, sometimes even breaking up, such corporatisms, and many of the proposals of the Left pointed directly at this. Yet the Jacobin and statist predilections which the Left shared with much of the rest of the French political elite obscured the tenacity of such arrangements, leaving the Left ill prepared to carry out measures of reform. Attacking deep-seated corporatist arrangements would be a very difficult and resource-consuming task in the best of circumstances. To the degree to which it misperceived the field of conflict, the Left in power would have difficulty finding the best of circumstances.

CONSEQUENCES: CONTINUITY AND CHANGE IN MODERN FRANCE

In 1981 President François Mitterrand formed one of the most powerfully endowed Left governments in a major advanced industrial society in decades. The institutions of the French Fifth Republic – which gave the President extensive powers – and the existence of an absolute Left majority in the Assemblée Nationale gave it substantial resources to change the course of French development. Moreover, the Left which came to power in 1981 had great ambitions to work such change, as we have noted. Mitterrand's *110 Propositions pour la France* was one of the most radical documents to come from a serious contender for power in the recent annals of Western politics. Promises had been made to begin a "transition" to socialism, not, to be sure, of the Eastern "existing" type, nor of the classical Northern European social democratic kind, but a distinctive and democratic "Third Way".

The Left's five years in power comforted no one, as the chapters that follow demonstrate amply. There was less than a year of radical reformism – nationalizations, industrial relations reforms, decentralization, efforts at income redistribution, Keynesian demand stimulation to promote growth – energetic and dedicated efforts to carry out the Left's election program. Then, international economic problems dictated an abrupt change of course. "Keynesianism in one country" proved unworkable at a moment when the rest of the advanced industrial democratic world, led by the United States, was assiduously deflating.

From later 1982 onwards the French Left in power worked "rigorously" to reequilibrate France's international accounts, break the back of French inflation, reduce budget overruns and encourage private-sector investment. In the process it undertook a number of projects, such as the deindexation of wages from inflation and the reduction of wage shares in national income, which the Right in power had refused to try in the 1970s. Moreover, beginning in the autumn of 1983 with the government's turn towards what it called industrial "modernization", single-minded earlier efforts to contain the rise of unemployment were curtailed in the interests of major surgery on France's industrial base to enhance France's international competitive position. Thereafter, even if the Left continued to promote a variety of active labor-market measures to limit the impact of job losses, unemployment rose substantially.

In all this twisting and turning, major reforms, which had come with unprecedented speed immediately after 1981, ceased, by and large, to happen. In some cases, in fact, reforms which had already been legislated were quietly put on hold (work sharing and workweek reduction, for example). Moreover, in those rare instances when further reforms were advanced–educational reform in 1983–84 being the most important – the political consequences proved disastrous. Internationally the Left's retreat from its programmatic claims was less complex and more straightforward. In most major realms Mitterrand aligned himself more forcefully with the United States than had the right-of-center presidents of the Fifth Republic before him. Third-Worldist and Europeanist declarations of autonomy from superpower rivalry were backed by little policy substance.

The political results of all of this were predictable. The electoral shift which had brought the Left to power in May–June had been small and due as much to the internal squabbles of the Right as to enthusiasm for the Left. The political claims of the Left in its drive towards power had been ambitious: reforming France would allow a return to a post-war boom situation and make French society more equal and democratic. At least some working-class voters were likely to be alienated if these promises were not fulfilled. And many of those middle-class voters who had shifted to the Left in 1981 would likely be just as alienated if the Left actually tried to implement them.

The Left did reform things initially. But far from bringing a return to the *trente glorieuses*, it made a tenuous economic situation quite a bit worse. And when the Left's radicalism ran aground, the government turned rapidly towards policies which first seemed to punish almost everyone and then, with "modernization", gave in to a neo-liberalism which would have pleased the moderate Center and Right almost anywhere. Such policy shifting took place in an atmosphere colored by incessant attacks on the Left from the conservative opposition and by the indifference, if not hostility, of the intelligentsia. On top of this also emerged a renewal of extreme Right politics fueled in an overdetermined way by crisis and anti-immigrant sentiment. In consequence, working-class enthusiasm was dashed, along with much middle-class support. To avert a major electoral disaster the Socialists changed the electoral law to PR (proportional representation) in April 1985. Even the relative success of this strategem in March 1986 – the minimization of the Left's defeat allowed the establishment of *cohabitation* on acceptable terms for François Mitterrand – could not mask the Left's longer-term political problems. If the PS had consolidated some of its 1981 gains, the PCF seemed engaged in terminal decline. Where would any future Left majority come from?

It would be very easy to "deconstruct" this story into two classical, mirror-image readings. Seen from the Left the Mitterrand experiment constituted yet one more episode of betrayal by "procapitalist Social Democrats". From this point of view the rhetorical flourishes of the 1981 program were little more than attempts to mislead about the French Left's deeper intentions to "manage the capitalist crisis". And when the Left turned to crisis management, it did so with a vengeance, reversing many of its initial redistributive policies and helping capital to attack the labor movement. Seen from the Right the Mitterrand experiment constituted yet one more instance of the inevitable misconceptions and incompetence of Left experimentation. From this side of the mirror the programmatic claims of 1981 were all too real and had led the Left into an impasse from which hasty retreat – conducted ineptly – was the only option. France would thereby be obliged to pay the costs – long-term indebtedness, a weak currency, weakened industry and international credibility – of ill-prepared and misguided politicians who had been unable to recognize the constraints of the real world.

The subtitle of this volume, *Continuity and Change in Modern France*, is deliberately chosen to transcend the banality of both classic readings. The Left years in France – from the events of May–June 1981 to 16 March 1986, when the Right–Center again constituted a parliamentary majority – represent *both* continuity and change, but *neither* in such completely predictable ways. There were some sequences, as in foreign policy, where continuity was the rule, of course. There was undeniable continuity as well in the longer-term development of the political and economic constraints, both domestic and international, which the Left was obliged to face after 1981. And, equally undeniably, the program of change which the Left brought to power was in many ways ill conceived as a response to such constraints. What is most interesting about the Left's tenure in power has not been described adequately, however, with the reiteration of propositions about a naïve Left stymied by cold realities and forced back onto predictable paths.

The Left in power, in fact, undertook a whole set of major measures which its right-of-center "realistic" predecessors refused to work. These *real changes* in economic, industrial and social policy were undertaken at considerable political and ideological costs to the Left itself, however. Voted out of office in March 1986, the Socialists – the Communists having abandoned ship with the turn to modernization in 1984 – were unable to develop the kinds of appeals to different social groups which would have given them the legitimacy and electoral support needed to return.

Real changes, again of a kind that could not be anticipated in 1981, also occurred in the political realm. The experience of power abruptly shattered a Left political discourse which had dominated prior to 1981 and which had barely changed since the Resistance–Liberation period. Here change turned out to be both dramatic and open-ended. If, in 1986, the PS was the overwhelmingly preponderant force on the Left and the largest party in France, despite defeat, it had become quite unclear about its own identity and purpose. More generally, after five years of Mitterrand's France, observers were hard put to understand where the French Left stood and where it was going. The PCF was an exception to this, proferring strident restatements of the old discourse as it declined, but the abruptness of the PCF's decline despite its experience in government was yet another index of change.

The phenomena of changing political discourses with the Left in power extended beyond the Left, as demonstrated by the rapid rise of neo-liberalism on the Center and Right. This new liberalism of deregulation, "destatizing" and "returning to the market" remained to be tested in the heat of power, of course. But with the conceptual vocabulary of much of the Left dramatically modified and strong prospects for something similar occurring on the Right, the Socialist experiment in France could turn out, in historical retrospect, to be an important switchpoint. Had the twin – and somewhat complicit – political ideologies of the Resistance and Liberation, Gaullism and "Old Leftism" begun to give way to something new? Much in the social atmosphere of the Left's five years indicated that this was possible. It would be ironic indeed if the Left were ultimately remembered for having presided over the decline of Colbertism and Jacobinism and the resurrection of individual entrepreneurism. It would be even more remarkable if the French Left, so different from other Lefts in doctrine and practice as of 1981, had presided over a set of changes which left France and the French a little less Gallic and a little more like everyone else.

Underlying all this was another set of changes which transcended France in its scope and importance. It may no longer be possible to pursue the kinds of politics and provide underlying social groups with the kinds of rewards which social democracy had come to take for granted during the long post-war economic boom. The power of trade unions is in a retreat which seems much more than cyclical. A degree of social dualism (pockets of quasi-permanent disadvantage tied to employment insecurity) seems on the horizon. Centralizing and statist responses to perceived social problems are both unpopular and inefficient. International factors severely limit the capacities of any national state, let alone those of a middle-sized one, to choose original policy options. The French Left in power provides a biographical history of the recognition of such issues.

In this biography there are essential trends and lessons for the parliamentary Left in all advanced industrial democracies. In the years following World War II the Left had played a central role in negotiating a new domestic social compromise which had allowed a long period of stable growth, relative employment security and an unprecedented rise in living standards. By the 1980s agendas had clearly begun to change, however. Governments, Left or Right, henceforth had to concern themselves as a priority with facilitating the successful and competitive insertion of their national economies into the newly constraining international market and division of labor. Renegotiating the terms of domestic social compromise upward had therefore to come second. In such an unprecedented setting it was not surprising that older political discourses began to give way. The painful experiences of the French Left in power reflected all this. The issues discussed in this volume thus transcend by far the empirical specificities of France.

II
The Difficult Economics
of French Socialism

Introduction

Little can be understood about the Left's experiment in France without first knowing something of recent French economic history. The Left came to power in 1981 at a moment of great economic uncertainty. The long post-war boom, which had touched and changed virtually every aspect of French life, had ended. Yet the nature of the post 1974–5 economic setting – domestic and international – remained quite unclear. The program which the Left brought to power had been drafted before this great break in economic circumstances. The dilemmas of economic policy which the Left faced after 1981 as it attempted to implement this program were to demonstrate how much the world had really changed. These dilemmas, in turn, became the linchpin of the Left's subsequent efforts to rule and reform France. Underlying economic processes obliged the Left to reconsider its original goals and forced it to adapt. The complexities of this adaptation, in turn, created the unpredictability which made the Left experiment so interesting.

Since so much revolved around the economic dilemmas the Left faced, it is therefore appropriate for our volume to start with a discussion of their origins. The economic background of much Left thought and of many of the problems that the Left was called upon to face was built in the post-war boom. Richard F. Kuisel thus provides a historical overview of these boom years, which carefully distinguishes the specifically French from the more general and international. Robert Boyer then undertakes the formidable task of mapping the causes, structures and implications of the unpredictable years of "crisis" after 1974, which prepared the immediate terrain which the Left had to face after May–June 1981. Finally, Peter A. Hall provides us with a chapter reviewing and evaluating the economic policies of the Left in power between 1981 and 1986.

1

French Post-war Economic Growth

A Historical Perspective on the *Trente Glorieuses*

RICHARD F. KUISEL

The historian's task is to identify and explain long-term trends, basic discontinuities and perennial problems. I want here to address all these aspects of French post-war economic growth. The first question to ask is how this period fits into the overall pattern of modern French economic history. In the context of the last century, does the performance of the French economy from 1950 to 1974 appear as a continuation of long-term trends or represent a break with the past? Historians are adept at finding antecedents for every phenomenon, and one could easily marshal evidence that proves the post-war years were foreshadowed by the 1920s or even the 1900s. Yet what is most striking to this historian is discontinuity. The *trente glorieuses* were unprecedented. Even if there were certain aspects of the years 1900–29 (for example the growth rate of industry, investment levels, the rural exodus) which anticipated the boom following World War II, the resemblance is not close. Many of the most important features of the post-war boom, such as productivity rates or sectoral shifts in industry, were visible only in the later period. Thus the post-war boom was a rupture with the past. It is no exaggeration to contend that France developed a new economy in the post-war period.

DIMENSIONS OF THE POST-WAR RUPTURE

The great divide in modern French economic history falls between the Third and Fourth Republics; the watershed period is 1930–45. The Fourth and Fifth Republics distinguished themselves by their continuity. This periodization does not suggest a return to the simplistic contrast between the "Malthusian" Third Republic and the "modernizing" Fourth and Fifth Republics. We know too much about the economic revivals gathering momentum in the late Third Republic to retreat to this false dichotomy. What is certain, however, is that the post-1945 decades represent a major break with the past. If the post-war period marks a rupture in modern French economic development, then what is the nature of this break? One could argue that there was more change during this 30-year period of prosperity than in the previous half-century. Indeed, between 1950 and 1974 the French economy assumed its familiar contemporary profile.

Economic growth was unprecedented. The gross domestic product (GDP) grew annually at a rate of 5.2% – close to that of West Germany and Italy, and well ahead of the United States and Britain. This growth was faster and lasted longer than any previous period of prosperity, even 1906-13 or 1922-29. Moreover, the rate of expansion accelerated in the 1960s. (Growth, of course, was not continuous and the period 1950-74 included several recessions.) Labor productivity, another key measure of growth, rose at an average annual rate of over 5% and accelerated at the end of this period. This index was double pre-war levels and above average for Organization for European Cooperation and Development (OECD) countries in the 1960s. Investment, a third measure, was also exceptional. Previous levels of investment (as part of GDP) were 14.9% between 1896 and 1913, and 16.1% between 1922 and 1938. In 1949 this figure reached 19.7%; it fluctuated in the 1950s, and then accelerated to 25% in the 1960s, putting France ahead of most industrialized countries in this respect. The post-war boom represented the longest period of sustained, rapid growth in modern French history.

More important than economic performance were France's structural changes. Of these the most significant by far was the opening of the national economy to the outside world. (There was also a domestic opening to competitive forces that will be dealt with later.) Protectionism characterized French external relations from at least the early nineteenth century through the 1950s. The enduring sense of inferiority that fed this protectionist appetite surfaced as late as the parliamentary debate over entry into the Common Market, and was voiced by so prominent a modernizer as Pierre Mendès France. But, a century or more of protectionism came to an end in the later 1950s when the Common Market introduced France to the world trading system.

In the broadest terms, the French economy exchanged a protected, colonial market for Europe. Exports to the Franc area, for example, fell from 42% in 1952 to 10% in 1970, while exports to the European Economic Community (EEC) rose from 15% to 50%. The volume of exports between 1959 and 1972 expanded at an annual rate of 12.2%.[3] In addition to changes in geography and volume, French trade changed in character.

France gradually "advanced" its place in the international division of labor. In comparison with other EEC countries, French exports in 1960 were relatively specialized in agricultural products and traditional consumer goods such as clothing, and relatively weak in equipment. By 1971 agricultural specialization continued, but exports of consumer goods decreased markedly and equipment exports reached average EEC levels.[4] Finally, the enormous expansion of foreign investment in France in the 1960s, first American then European, testifies to the internationalization of the economy. The entry of France into the global economy must rank as the most dramatic and fundamental shift in the nation's recent economic history.

The redistribution of the work force was almost as important as the opening of the economy. Long before World War II, the population was already slowly leaving the land, but it was only during the post-war boom that the problem of "the vanishing peasant" emerged. Between 1949 and 1968 the proportion of farmers in the active population fell from 29% to 14.6%, and the rate of migration from rural settings increased from an annual 0.5% in the decade before 1949 to 43.3% in the two subsequent decades.[5] Nevertheless, total farm output and productivity also increased; France remained the major food exporter in the European Community.

Agriculture ceased being a separate way of life and was transformed into a sector producing foodstuffs. In 1939 agriculture still evoked the image of a traditional world, and the depression and war caused a certain regression. In the 1950s and 1960s, however, working conditions changed and the peasant became the farmer.

While the primary sector shrank, other sectors grew to reach parity in the 1960s. At this juncture, however, the growth of the active population employed in industry leveled off, and the growth of the service sector accelerated. Between 1949 and 1968 industry progressed slowly from 34.5% to 38.9% of the work force, while the tertiary sector jumped from 36.5% to 46.5%. If this sectoral shift is measured by value added rather than active population, the post-war rupture is even more evident. Whereas agriculture's contribution scarcely changed between 1913 and 1938, and industry's share even receded in the 1930s, industry produced the massive increases in value added during the post-war period.[6] France, while keeping a significant part of its economic potential on the land, had staked its future on industry.

A closer look at the industrial base reveals sectoral shifts that altered the pre-war profile – one drawn during the nineteenth century. The 30-year boom accelerated the long-term decline (measured by employees) of traditional consumer goods: between 1913 and 1969 workers employed in textiles, clothing and leather goods diminished from 42.4% to 13% of the industrial work force. A new, dramatic trend also began in the 1950s in the form of a decline in mining and then metallurgy. Between 1949 and 1968 some 760,000 workers abandoned the mining, metal, textile, clothing and leather industries, while some 2 million employees joined industrial branches.[7] The poles of attraction were energy, building and public works as well as what statisticians call the intermediate goods and equipment industries. Measuring change by value added, these four branches grew vigorously between 1952 and 1972, raising their share of total industry from 32.6% to 43.3%. Consumption industries lost ground (10.5% to 8.8%) while agro-food industries diminished sharply (19.6% to 12.6%).[8] The leading sectors with respect to most indices of growth were not only intermediate goods (for example, iron and steel, nonferrous metals, chemicals, construction materials, rubber, glass), but especially the equipment industries (for example, electrical manufactures and electronics, aviation, automobiles, household appliances, shipbuilding, armaments).

It would be simplistic to dismiss a shrinking industry such as textiles as "declining", when in fact it was being transformed by heavy investment, wider markets and new processes.[9] By the late 1960s the redistribution of employees among the various branches of industry made France closely resemble a composite of EEC countries.[10] The industrial base of the French economy had finally lost its nineteenth-century look.

Industrial enterprise in France also changed its scale during the post-war period. Measuring levels of concentration on a national, much less a comparative, basis is treacherous terrain for generalization. Nevertheless, data indicate that an industrial plant notorious for its small size improved its position during the 1960s. The merger movement affected all industrial sectors, but it was a case of the big getting bigger. Where technology required large-scale production units (such as automobiles, oil, steel, aviation, glass and shipbuilding), already heavily concentrated branches emerged as oligopolies in which the four largest firms controlled 40% to 60% of turnover.[11] Other branches like consumer products widened their scale, but not at nearly the same pace.

There is no denying that French industry continued to be dominated by small firms and, in this respect, was still lagging behind its international competitors in 1974. French manufacturers in technologies such as aviation and computers also had great difficulty – even with state aid – in competing with multinationals. Yet French business compensated by forming more diffuse industrial "groups" (units which tend to escape the statisticians calculating levels of concentration). Moreover, optimal firm size certainly depends on many factors. Big is not always best. If one measures average firm size by first excluding the large number of tiny firms (those with fewer than 50 employees), the size of French firms in the 1960s was not very different from the size of West German or American firms.[12] Without doubt, the merger movement of the 1960s made up ground between France and the most advanced industrialized nations.

One can also discern qualitative changes within the firm. Here too, generalization is risky, but evidence points to new management strategies.[13] In an economy known for its conservative business practice, the 1960s seem like a watershed. At the level of industrial organization this decade witnessed the arrival of American management techniques, for example decentralized decision-making, human relations, and staff and line organization. In business practice, French managers adopted a riskier investment strategy which relied less on realized profits and more on market opportunities. They resorted more to external financing, accepted greater indebtedness and diversified product lines outside their original specialities. Bankers paralleled industrial managers by adopting more aggressive behavior. The managers reading *L'Expansion* in the 1960s represented a major section of the business community while there were only a handful of "Americanized" readers in the 1920s.

Changes in business practice also found a counterpart in French households' pattern of consumption, which was conforming more to American ways. Between 1950 and 1973, French households spent increasing portions of income on health, housing, transport and leisure, whereas spending on food, drink and clothing diminished. The revolution in consumer durable goods arrived in the form of the private automobile, television and other appliances. Household income, moreover, grew at an annual average rate of 11.4% and 10.9% for 1949–59 and 1959–73 respectively, whereas consumer prices rose only 6.5% and 4.4%.[14] Changes in consumption patterns, as well as rising incomes, help account for the strong pull of demand in the post-war period.

Closely related to these advances in performance and structure was a shift in public economic policy. Again there was more continuity between the Fourth and Fifth Republics, between the 1950s and 1960s, than between the Third Republic and its successors. My own recent study locates the turning point in public policy in the early post-war years.[15] The basic choices for a neo-liberal order, mixed economy, rapid economic growth and a more open market were made at the outset of the post-war boom. The major institutional innovations, i.e., an expanded public sector and indicative planning, as well as the mechanisms for monitoring the economy and regulating the business cycle through countercyclical policies were in place by 1950. France had also entered the EEC before the decade was over. All these institutional and policy changes stand in contrast to the liberal order of the pre-war era which featured minimal intervention on behalf of the status quo. Economic policy therefore, also became "contemporary". In short, during the post-war boom France experienced a *rendez-vous* with industrialization. The meeting was belated and not entirely cordial, but it marked a sharp break with past events.

PATTERNS OF CAUSATION

Up to this point, my concern has been the description of the dimensions of post-war growth from a broad historical perspective. What is missing from this analysis is the dynamic dimension of growth, that is, an explanation of how the various features of growth relate to one another and form a pattern of causation.

There are, among economic historians, two general approaches – "soft" and "hard" – to explaining the post-war boom. On the one hand there are those analysts who stress the human, sociopsychological and institutional factors of change. Charles Kindleberger for example, in one of the earliest studies (written, in fact, even before the real takeoff of the 1960s), argued that the basic cause was "one of people and attitudes".[16] In a study written 20 years later, Christian Sautter writes in the same vein when he stresses expansionist public policy and the optimistic expectations of entrepreneurs.[17] On the other hand, there are observers who emphasize the physical determinants of growth such as capital formation, market size, relative costs and the size and quality of the work force. Their analyses are usually more quantitative and statistical. The work of François Caron, or the classic study on post-war growth by Edmond Malinvaud, are typical of this approach.[18] In the final analysis, differences between the two schools are only a matter of emphasis. For even Malinvaud gives high marks to public policy and planning, and leaves a large part of post-war growth unexplained in any quantitative way by his notion of a residue.[19] Similarly, Caron includes managerial strategy and public policy in his explanatory apparatus. The two perspectives on causality share a large common ground.

Before one enters these controversial waters it is useful to enumerate the certainties. What is striking about the 1950–74 period is the high rates of productivity (measured by output per man-hour) and investment (especially in the form of machinery). In the latter instance, starting in the early 1950s private sources replaced public ones in supplying investment. The French investment level in the 1960s and early 1970s (as per cent of GDP) equalled EEC averages and was ahead of that of the United States and Britain.[20] Malinvaud estimated that "productive capital" increased 90% between 1949 and 1966.[21] Capital formation, moreover, was directed at the most dynamic branches.

It is equally certain that foreign trade (growing at twice the rate of output) and high levels of aggregate demand (rising real incomes) were expanding rapidly. In contrast, at least until the mid-1960s, there was no large input from labor; labor's contribution to growth came more from sectoral shifts in employment and qualitative improvements than from increases in volume of the work force. But how do these variables relate?

Since there is no consensus about this problem, one can only offer an individual interpretation. What were the independent variables, the ultimate "causes" of post-war growth? (I exclude the early 1945–50 period which was more a matter of reconstruction.) My preference is for a modified demand model which stresses the momentum generated by both domestic and international circumstances, as well as human and institutional elements and assigns the push of supply an important, yet lesser, role. In essence, production responded to strong opportunities afforded by rising purchasing power and changing consumer demand, by a buoyant international market and low raw-material prices, and by expansionist government policies. The latter included an effective use of countercyclical policy; several "offensive" devaluations such as the one in 1969; the promotion of sectoral restructuring; and the reform of fiscal, lending and other policies.

Underlying this dynamic was an expansionist consensus that assumed everyone would benefit from growth, that growth was self-sustaining and continuous and that adaptation and inflation were acceptable costs. This interpretation leaves the supply side in a reactive role. It in turn conforms, approximately, to the econometric analysis advanced by Malinvaud that ascribes about half of post-war growth to factor inputs of capital and labor.[22] Alternatively, Sautter sees the relationship as the supply side playing a "permissive role": it allowed growth.[23] There is no doubt that heavy capital formation was an important input which, among other benefits, brought a more productive labor force. Since profit margins held up well right up to 1972, this helps explain the high level of investment.[24] With respect to labor inputs, there is no question that the shift away from rural work raised farm productivity. The effect of this displacement on industrial productivity is, however, dubious. The rural exodus swelled the tertiary sector rather than industry. Increases in industrial productivity came from intensified capital investment and improvement in the quality and use of labor.

Fortunately for France the normal constraints on growth did not play a major role in these years. Inflation, trade and budget deficits and strained capacity were minor obstacles. Thus, is it fair to ask to what degree the post-war boom rested on temporarily favourable circumstances for France? The 1950–74 period was one of low costs for raw materials, energy, transport, perhaps even labor, and it was a time without strong competition from the Third World. In so far as the boom rested on these fortuitous circumstances as well as on an optimistic yet volatile domestic consensus about the future, continued growth was uncertain. To the degree growth also concealed serious problems, it was precarious. By 1969–73 there was evidence that the boom was reaching its apogee.

CHRONIC PROBLEMS

This rather laudatory account of post-war growth must be balanced by considering certain enduring economic problems. The post-war rupture failed to remove, though in most cases it did alleviate, chronic weaknesses in the economy. What follows then is a presentation of the other, more somber, side of the *trente glorieuses*.

For the historian, the notion of modernization functions as a continuous commentary on those economic weaknesses associated with relative backwardness. According to some critics, France was already behind the times in 1890, and by the end of World

War I ministries were designing plans for a national economic overhaul which included government-sponsored cartels as a way of improving French competitiveness in international markets. By the 1920s the fashionable term was rationalization, which meant everything from product standardization to the scientific organization of work. If the 1930s represented a kind of regression in economic discourse, with a return to protectionism of all sorts, the Vichy regime left a more ambiguous legacy.

It was only in the early post-war period that modernization first appeared as the formulation of renewal. The term appeared in the formal title of the Monnet Plan *Plan de modernisation et d'équipement* and signified the following: the reconstruction and expansion of basic industries like energy which had been bottlenecks to development; a leap forward in the level of capital formation; a rapid rise in the standard of living; the overhaul of agriculture and an end to financial dependence on the United States. Modernization not only entered common parlance in the 1950s, but it also assumed a familiar contemporary meaning. It now referred to preparing industry for global competition; raising productivity; eliminating internal "rigidities"; promoting industrial reconversion; retraining labor and reforming the fiscal system.

The fifties anticipated the eighties; the current debate in Paris about modernization is not new to historians. What is most important about this historical review of the modernization theme, however, is the continuity of certain issues over nearly a century. Whether critics spoke of the need for rationalization or productivity, a common set of problems was raised. It is this nucleus of perennial economic problems of the *trente glorieuses* that I want to examine.

Industrial concentration is a problem that antedates even World War I. From early in this century critics rightly observed that French production units were relatively small compared to those of their principal British or German competitors. In the most dynamic industrial sectors, France lagged behind and the gap spurred a continuous flow of reforms. Whether it was a plea from the government for producer "self-discipline" in 1919, or a program to promote "national champions" in the 1960s, the intent was the same: overcome excessive market fragmentation and permit French firms to compete internationally. Despite the gains registered in industrial concentration after 1950, the lag persisted. The nation's largest firms in 1969 (those with over 500 workers) employed the same share of the work force as Italy, the Netherlands and Japan. France, however, was considerably behind West Germany and the United States.[25] More important, in an early 1960 sector-by-sector comparison of the scale of production units, France, like Italy, only ranked in the middle of a sample of advanced industrial nations.[26] Or, using the kind of comparisons made famous by *Fortune*, France in 1972, as in 1959, accounted for only 15 of the world's largest 304 firms (according to turnover), although the 15 had moved up in scale from the lowest to the middle group since 1959.[27] Even chemicals, a highly concentrated sector relative to other industries, fell short of its international rivals. In addition, many of the chemical industry mergers did not represent real integration of production units.[28] Finally, a swarm of small firms survived, and craftspeople still formed some 16% of the work force in 1970.[29]

A second theme for modernizers has been market sclerosis. France has historically suffered from a chronic case of low competitive pressure. Market forces were never very lively in the modern economy and virtually disappeared in the 1930s and 1940s under the weight of controls and corporatist privilege. The market meekly performed its functions of allocating resources and forcing out marginal producers. There was little need to be efficient: prices did not reflect costs, the big sheltered the small and the state protected producers from outsiders. The symbol of sclerosis was the power of the existing interests, those privileged interests which made twentieth-century republics resemble the *ancien régime*.

Thus, modern French economic history has featured a continuous attack against market "rigidities". There have been two villains of rigidity, the state which overregulates, and private interests which hide behind barbed-wire entanglements. Campaigns to free the economy from state influence are hardly new; the one led by Poincaré after World War I had little success. Campaigns to upend the *situations acquises* also made little headway – at least until the 1950s. The Armand–Rueff report (1959) catalogued the various sclerotic dimensions, for example cartels, tax fraud, closed professions. Nevertheless, both the Fourth and Fifth Republics worked to reduce these corporatist obstacles. By the mid-1950s the effort reached the point of rousing small-town France to mass protest in the form of Poujadism. The Poujadists rallied against the loss of fiscal protection under the guise of saving the French way of life from Paris, the technocrats and Coca-Cola. In the language of the time, "static" France was at war with "dynamic" France.

Like the problem of industrial concentration, French entrepreneurship and industrial organization were also at issue, even before 1914. The volume and tone of criticism grew until the 1950s when the epithet "Malthusian" came into usage to describe the typical French entrepreneur, who supposedly preferred security to risk-taking; demanded protected markets; chose to take profits rather than investing or innovating and in general lacked the dynamic, destructive spirit of Schumpeter's ideal entrepreneur. This critique of Malthusian directorship reached a peak in the 1950s with foreign observers, especially American social scientists, leading the attack. In France, Alfred Sauvy championed the cause, and those French business leaders and officials who were members of the Productivity Missions made negative comparisons between French and American business practice.[30]

In the 1960s the Malthusian reputation began to fade thanks not only to the economy's heady performance, for which entrepreneurs received due credit, but also because French management became self-consciously Americanized.[31] Once again a chronic problem receded without disappearing. During the 1960s Americanized French managers still denounced their hidebound peers for their authoritarian style, paternalism, narrow horizons and secretiveness. At the time, the head of Saint-Gobain-Pont-à-Mousson acknowledged the deficiencies of divine-right management style.[32] In short, entrepreneurial conservatism was another perennial problem which began to be faced only in the post-war years.

Yet another constant component of the modernization-versus-backwardness debate had been the size and composition of the nation's industrial base. A report by the Institut National de la Statistique et des Etudes Economiques (INSEE) showed that West Germany had 50.3% of its active population employed in industry in 1970, while France employed only 38.8%. Since Britain (46%), Belgium (44.7%) and Italy

(43.7%) also surpassed France in this respect, the country continued to have a relatively small industrial base. This comparison prompted the report to ask if France appears as more of an underdeveloped country. Why has France, in its recent history, seemed to avoid massive industrialization? In fact, the percentage of the total labor force in industrial work was the lowest in 1970 as well as in 1963.[33] In other terms, 13.4 million West Germans worked in industry compared to 7.9 million French. This relatively narrow industrial base did not, however, prevent the massive gains in output registered in the 1950s and 1960s. Here, growth came more from intensification of activity and more efficient use of production factors than from expansion.

Other persistent elements of industrial weakness which attracted the attention of modernizers have been the lag in exports, the slowness in sectoral adjustments and the dependence on foreign sources of energy. Only during the boom was the large gap in the composition, volume and geographical distribution of French exports narrowed. The drag of declining sectors like coal and steel was recognized belatedly and only met slowly and painfully. This was due in part to the Fifth Republic's penchant for helping "lame ducks".[34] Dependence on energy imports began in the nineteenth century and the economy's vulnerability to foreign oil supplies appeared as early as World War I. Remedies were sought but not found, and the latter weakness was to be the precipitating factor in the crisis that ended the post-war boom in 1974.

A final aspect of modernization centers on the problem of inflation. Can the history of the recent past answer the question of whether or not French growth has a strong inflationary bias? The evidence for the period 1948–73 is inconclusive. While French inflation rates, relative to average OECD rates, were very high from 1948 to 1952 and remained above average for the years 1952–61, they were just about average from 1961 to 1973, the years of most rapid expansion.[35] France did run ahead of the pack on this index between 1948 and 1973, but not by much. Economic growth was inflationary throughout the West in this period, and French performance in this respect was not distinctive. Whether or not the economy contained, nevertheless, some latent structural bias toward inflation, a tendency which had begun to surface well before 1974, is an open question.

LIBERALIZING THE FRENCH ECONOMY

While this list of problems raised by French modernizers over the course of the twentieth century is hardly comprehensive, it does serve to place the accomplishments of the post-war boom against lingering weaknesses. There is one additional issue that merits more extensive treatment – this is the question of "liberalizing" or opening the French economy to competition. At this point there is an intersection of historical trends and current concerns.

In the course of modern economic history, France moved toward a mixed economy comprised of its own peculiar amalgam of state interventionism and private enterprise. During the early post-war period the role of the state and market forces underwent a basic realignment, and the new order that emerged in the early 1950s has endured ever since. It is important to note that whatever changes have occurred in the relative roles of public and private actors, they have taken place within the context of the flexible, yet durable, mixed economy that appeared after World War II.

During the post-war boom, however, the balance within this mixed order has shifted from a closed to a more open, or liberal, economy. That is, there has been a move away from market rigidities, protectionism and state planning. The closed character of the economy was due to the defensive reflex of producers and to the *dirigiste* inclinations of officials. It took the form of internal rigidities and external protectionism. The nadir of protectionism cum *dirigisme* occurred between 1930 and 1950. Since then there has been a trend toward liberalization. It is impossible in this chapter to do anything more than sketch the contours of this trend.

The struggle of the post-war Republics against internal rigidities has already been mentioned. It included efforts to oust notorious *situations acquises*; remove the stranglehold of cartels; check fiscal fraud and lower barriers to entry. Needless to say such efforts were only partially successful.[36] Above all there was the historic end to external protectionism when the nation discovered Europe. France under the Fourth and Fifth Republics turned to heightened competition as the way to economic advancement.

A key element of this process was the disengagement of the state. While there are disputes about the merits and demerits of peculiar forms and instances of state intervention, the general consensus is that the role of the state has been excessive. And there is little question that since the early 1950s state planning has receded or, more precisely, changed form. It is virtually impossible to measure the magnitude of statism in France in its various manifestations, i.e. banker, manager and entrepreneur, much less compare it with other countries.[37] Whatever its comparative "weight", the French state relaxed the heavy-handed *dirigisme* of the late 1940s. Over the next two decades credit controls partially ceded to market mechanisms; the tax burden on private enterprise was lightened; relations with nationalized enterprise shifted from the *tutelle* to the contract; and even price controls were, at times, relaxed.[38] There was also a certain *débudgétisation* of public expenses, for example public enterprises were directed toward the financial market for funds and private investors assumed a larger part of capital formation.

Disengagement was less a matter of reducing the magnitude of state activity than an alteration of its form and spirit. As an illustration, one might note how the Treasury ceded its investment responsibilities to parapublic organs like the Caisse des Dépôts. The trend was to move from constraint to promotion, from direct to indirect supervision. In short, state intervention was made to conform more to the logic of the market. Taxes, credit, prices, public enterprise and even planning followed the dictates of the market more closely. Jean Bouvier and François Caron write of state intervention becoming more diffuse and evenly distributed in the 1950s and 1960s rather than shrinking quantitatively.[39] These historians also suggest that economic planning from the perspective of the 1980s looks less like a "third way" between *dirigisme* and liberalism, and more like a means of facilitating the transition from a closed to an open economy. What was possible for Monnet in the closed circumstance of the 1940s was impossible in the open conditions of the later decades. Accordingly, planning in the 1960s and 1970s became less ambitious and more flexible. In the meantime, planning helped both public policy-makers and private managers gain expertise and confidence about forecasting and planning the economic environment. In so doing, planners had readied the economy for liberalization.

FROM GROWTH TO CRISIS

Looking at post-war expansion from the long historical perspective of 1890–1974, trends and ruptures have been identified. However, a final, more short-term contemporary perspective, which views the period from the vantage point of the decade that followed 1974, suggests linkages between post-war growth and the economic crisis that followed it.

Seen in retrospect, there were warnings of imminent danger, especially during the feverish growth of the years 1969–73. These trouble signs represented internal problems as opposed to exogenous circumstances. Trouble was growing from within a prosperous economy. Unemployment, which had virtually disappeared in the early 1960s, began a systematic climb upwards after 1964. By 1973 there were 300,000 unemployed. Joblessness was being generated by an influx of young workers and women and by changes in the industrial base. The commercial balance had also begun to erode, especially after 1970. Starting in 1969, inflation accelerated as well. Some of the features of the stagflation to come were visible as the economy approached a new conjuncture. One counterfactual model of the crisis of the 1970s suggests that without external pressures, such as the increase in oil prices, France in the 1970s would have suffered from growing inflation and unemployment as well as slackening output.[40] Whatever the base, it is important to recognize the domestic features of the crisis.

The danger signs of the years 1969–73 announced fundamental problems.[41] On the one hand, many of what I have termed the perennial problems of French modernization lingered on during the years 1950–74. Weakness in foreign trade, internal rigidities and sectoral decline were some of these enduring issues. On the other hand, striving for openness and competition made the economy more vulnerable. A major consequence of post-war growth was the French economy's increasing dependence on outside forces.

This new, or heightened, vulnerability took different forms. Its most obvious manifestation was energy dependence. Energy had paradoxically outperformed all other industrial sectors in most respects during the boom. Energy consumption jumped 250%, yet growth created problems. Oil virtually replaced coal as the major source of energy in this period, meeting some two-thirds of the nation's primary energy needs. Energy dependence rose as a consequence. Whereas France imported 49.6% of its primary energy in 1963, a decade later it imported 76.3%. Neither West Germany (50%) nor Britain (47%) imported nearly this amount.[42] The implications of this dependence were masked by low petroleum prices until 1973.

Foreign trade and investment were a second area of deepening vulnerability. By 1976 imports and exports together represented one-fifth of the GDP.[43] Yet according to one INSEE report, despite strong efforts to raise exports in the 1960s, France remained "somewhat behind the world competition" in 1972.[44] At this time the most technologically advanced industries such as electronics exported only a modest part of their output. Also, the distribution of exports still did not measure up to that of industrial leaders. Perhaps the most striking evidence of fragility is that France ran a commercial deficit in manufactured products with all industrialized countries (except the Netherlands).[45] The opening of the Common Market had brought on a flood of imported manufactured products. Similarly, France had deficits in what may be called technological exchange (exchange of patents and licenses) with every industrialized country in leading sectors like pharmaceuticals and electronics.[46] Geographically, moreover, French exports may be becoming too concentrated on Western Europe at the expense of other global markets.

The data on foreign investment corroborates the weakness in foreign trade. The great expansion of foreign investment in France, led by the United States, came after 1959. EEC countries followed. The extent and direction of this flow of capital which seemed to threaten a takeover of vital industries became a political issue in the early 1960s. *Le Défi américain* became a best-seller. Outside investors focused on the most modern sectors of French industry, those, for example, which showed the strongest gains in productivity such as electrical manufacturers, electronics, automobiles, farm machinery and petroleum.[47] By 1971 some 56 of France's 200 largest companies were under foreign control (of which 22 were American multinationals).[48] American foreign investment in the 1960s only served to strengthen a deepening economic Atlantic link for France – one that had been forged by Bretton Woods and the Marshall Plan. What is particularly revealing is that the corresponding effort by French investors was feeble during the 1960s. French investors and firms were extremely reluctant to enter the toughest competitive markets like those of the United States and West Germany.[49] In the end, France held a negative balance in foreign investment during this decade.

A final aspect of the foreign-trade dilemma was the rising pressure from outside competition for further adaptation of the internal industrial structure. Competition was especially keen both for troubled sectors like steel and textiles as well as for more prosperous branches in the "exposed" equipment sector. The automobile industry, for example, was exporting 44 per cent of its output by 1972. French industry had entered an increasingly competitive international market which required continuous and rapid industrial redeployment.

The crisis of the seventies was thus prepared in the prosperity of the sixties. Once the buoyant external circumstances (such as low energy and raw-material prices) disappeared, a vulnerable economy burdened with serious internal problems faced a rather durable crisis.

COMMITMENT TO MODERNIZATION

No account of post-war growth should confine itself solely to an analysis of variables like markets, capital, labor, public policy, or entrepreneurship at the expense of the sociopsychological dimension. For perhaps the most enduring change that marks what I have called the rupture of the post-war period was a shift in national priorities. Jean

Monnet correctly observed in the days of the first economic plan that modernization, in the final analysis, was a state of mind. What is striking in reviewing French economic history over the course of the twentieth century is the acceptance in the post-war years of the priority of growth and the toleration of its attendant economic and social sacrifices. The pain of modernization, which had been unacceptable in 1900, was tolerable to most by 1970 because it was necessary. Over the *longue durée* the virtues of the balanced economy, the intrinsic value of maintaining a substantial rural populace, the advantages of small, independent enterprises and the closed domestic market all faded like an old tintype. At the level of collective attitudes, French economic priorities had shifted by the 1950s and 1960s. The days of missionary work in the name of modernization led by Monnet and the Productivity Teams were over. It was accepted that the nation must strive to stay abreast of the most advanced industrial societies and face the costs of continuous change. President Mitterrand was preaching to the converted when he announced in 1984 that modernization and global competitiveness were national goals. The contest for people's minds on these issues had been won decades earlier. The problem was more a matter of finding ways to attain these goals and easing the accompanying pain.

NOTES

1 The principal sources of statistical data for this chapter are: Institut National de la Statistique et des Etudes Economiques, *Fresque historique du système productif* (Paris, INSEE, 1974), Les Collections de l'INSEE, série E, 27; Bernard Guibert et al., *La Mutation industrielle de la France: du traité de Rome à la crise pétrolière* (Paris, INSEE, 1975), Les Collections de l'INSEE, série E, 31-32; the essays by François Caron, Jean Bouvier, René Girault and Pierre Barral in *Histoire économique et sociale de la France*, eds Fernand Braudel and Ernest Labrousse (Paris, Presses Universitaires de France, 1970-82), tome IV, vol. 3 (henceforth cited as HESF); Edmond Malinvaud et al., *La Croissance française: un essai d'analyse économique causale de l'après-guerre* (Paris, Editions du Seuil, 1972); François Caron, *An Economic History of Modern France* (New York, Columbia University Press, 1979); and Edward F. Denison, *Why Growth Rates Differ* (Washington D. C., Brookings Institution, 1967).

2 For slightly varying estimates of the growth of production and productivity see: Malinvaud et al., *Croissance*, pp. 31-2, 109-10; INSEE, *Fresque historique*, p. 62; Caron, *Economic History*, pp. 180-3, 192-3; HESF, pp. 1011-13. With respect to investment data see: Malinvaud et al., *Croissance*, pp. 156, 159; Guibert et al., *Mutation industrielle*, II, pp. 65-7; Caron, *Economic History*, pp. 194-7.

3 Guibert et al., *Mutation industrielle*, I, p. 47; Caron, *Economic History*, p. 218.

4 Guibert et al., *Mutation industrielle*, II, p. 216.

5 Malinvaud et al., *Croissance*, pp. 126, 214. For international comparisons of the distribution of working populations see Guibert et al., *Mutation industrielle*, I, p. 25.

6 Caron, *Economic History*, pp. 207-8.

7 Ibid., pp. 230-1.

8 INSEE, *Fresque historique*, p. 16.

9 HESF, pp. 1294-309.

10 Guibert et al., *Mutation industrielle*, I, p. 36.

11 Ibid., II, p. 209.

12 Ibid., I, p. 111-12.

13 HESF, pp. 1167-75, 1177-221. Also see Luc Boltanski, "America, America . . . Le Plan Marshall et l'importation du management", in *Actes de la recherche en sciences sociales*, 38 (May 1981), pp. 19-41.

14 HESF, pp. 1062-3. Caron and Bouvier observe a rise in the share of wages and social charges as a part of GDP between 1954 and 1973 though this share may not have grown in the 1960s (HESF, p. 1058).
15 Richard F. Kuisel, *Capitalism and the State in Modern France* (Cambridge and New York, Cambridge University Press, 1981).
16 Charles Kindleberger, "The Postwar Resurgence of the French Economy", in *In Search of France*, eds Hoffman, Pitts & Wiley (Cambridge, MA., Harvard University Press, 1963), p. 157.
17 Christian Sautter, "France", in *The European Economy: Growth and Crisis*, ed. Andrea Boltho (New York, Oxford University Press, 1982), pp. 449-71.
18 See the citations in note 1.
19 Analyzing the components of the 5% annual growth of production between 1951 and 1969 Malinvaud et al. (*Croissance*, p. 275) argue that about 1% is attributable to an improvement in the quality and occupational distribution of the work force; another 1.5% derives from the expansion and renewal of productive capital. This leaves a *résidu* of causality of 2.5% which cannot be quantified and was due to improvements in production techniques and management, public policy and intensified competition. An earlier quantitative analysis by Denison, *Why Growth Rates Differ*, did not credit the renewal of capital as much as Malinvaud and Denison and also awarded higher shares to the mobility of the work force, changing patterns of consumption, and economies of scale.
20 Guibert et al., *Mutation industrielle*, II, p. 65.
21 Malinvaud et al., *Croissance*, p. 198.
22 Cf. note 19.
23 Sautter, "France", p. 459.
24 HESF, p. 1143. Cf. HESF, pp. 1059-62 for an analysis of two other series of income distribution.
25 Guibert et al., *Mutation industrielle*, I, p. 114.
26 Ibid., I, pp. 117-18.
27 Ibid., I, p. 147.
28 HESF, pp. 1267-69.
29 Guibert et al., *Mutation industrielle*, I, p. 134.
30 An example of a French assessment of American productivity genius is Pierre Badin, *Aux Sources de la productivité américaine: premier bilan des missions françaises* (Paris, SADEP, 1953).
31 See note 13. Scholars like Maurice Lévy-Léboyer also contributed by reassessing the historical validity of the Malthusian stereotype in his article "Le Patronat français, a-t-il été malthusien?", *Le Mouvement social*, 88 (July-Sept. 1974), pp. 3-49.
32 Roger Martin, *Patron de droit divin* (Paris, Gallimard, 1984). Also see the testimony of managers like Jean Riboud of Schlumberger, in Roger Priouret, *La France et le management* (Paris, Denoel, 1968).
33 Guibert et al., *Mutation industrielle*, I, p. 21; II, p. 254.
34 Suzanne Berger, "Lame Ducks and National Champions: Industrial Policy in the Fifth Republic", in *The Fifth Republic at Twenty*, eds William G. Andrews and Stanley Hoffmann (Albany, SUNY Press, 1981), pp. 292-310.
35 Christopher Allsopp, "Inflation", in Boltho (ed.) *The European Economy*, p. 79. Comparing French rates of inflation with those of average OECD rates respectively for the four periods 1948-52, 1952-61, 1961-69 and 1969-73, Allsopp's data are (in %): 14.1 to 5.1; 3.3 to 2.3; 4.0 to 3.7; and 6.2 to 6.4.
36 For example the Commission des Ententes in 1969 declared that the economy due to restrictions like price cartels remained controlé (cited in HESF, p. 1132).
37 An INSEE report (Guibert et al., *Mutation industrielle*, II, pp. 133-69), nevertheless tried this comparison. It argues that the weight of the French state in the 1960s was not unusually heavy compared with other industrial nations with respect to its portion of capital formation and total consumption. And "tax pressure" (as a percentage of GDP) in the decade was relatively light though the nation's reliance on indirect taxes fell heavily on industry.
38 For these changes in state policy see HESF, pp. 1069-108 and Malinvaud et al., *Croissance*, pp. 521-65.
39 HESF, p. 1320 and Caron, *Economic History*, p. 351.
40 This econometric model created by Patrick Artus and Pierre Morin is summarized in HESF, p. 1622.
41 Contrast the broad historical interpretion of Robert Boyer who argues for the originality of the capitalist "structural crisis" of the 1970s by stressing how *blocages* in a monopolistic system of regulation prevented the recovery of depressed profit margins: "La Crise actuelle: une mise en perspective historique", *Critiques de l'économie politique*, 7-8 (April-Sept. 1979), 5-113.

42 HESF, p. 1250.

43 Ibid., p. 1619.

44 Guibert et al., *Mutation industrielle*, I, p. 67.

45 Ibid., I, pp. 46-8, 67.

46 Ibid., II, p. 20.

47 Ibid., I, 71-87; II, p. 217. Also: Michel Delapierre and Charles-Albert Michalet, *Les Implantations étrangères en France* (Paris, Calmann-Lévy, 1976); Guilles Y. Bertin, *L'Investissement des firmes étrangères en France, 1945-1964* (Paris, Presses Universitaires de France, 1963).

48 HESF, p. 1167.

49 Hervé Couffin, *Les Entreprises françaises sur le marché américain* (Paris, Economica, 1977).

2

The Current Economic Crisis

Its Dynamics and its Implications for France

ROBERT BOYER

During the golden years of growth for most OECD countries, France seemed but a part of the process. Within each country, of course, social analysts and politicians stressed national particularities. Paradoxically, however, the Italian miracle echoed the French, the West German, the Austrian and so on. With the exception of Britain and, to a lesser extent the United States, economic achievements were rather similar in most advanced countries. Now, more than a decade after economic strains appeared for the first time, country distinctions have become clearer. In an uneven, unpredictable world context, economic and social differences point to previously unnoticed, or at least downplayed, national specificities. In this respect, if not disconnected from world system trends, changes in France appear largely original.

Here, we suggest conclusions from both international and national-specific points of view. The first section relates social and economic evolution from 1968 to 1985 back to post-World War II growth. The second section presents a chronology of the major changes and downturns and discusses the factors and causes of the progressive economic slowdown in France. The third section looks at internal processes of capital formation and their link with income distribution and internal demand. The fourth section deals with the influence of the breakdown of the world financial and economic system upon France as a medium-sized, second-rank economy. France's external imbalance, thus documented, points to some key productive and socioeconomic organizational weaknesses. The fifth section asks where these unfavorable developments can be attributed to inadequate economic policies. The conclusion raises a paradox: has not the Left been a prisoner of the post-war social compromise, and the very success of the Keynesian strategies out of the 1929 crisis?

THE GOLDEN YEARS AND THEIR LASTING INFLUENCE

The French economy did not fare well during the inter-war period. Instead of a strong recovery in the 1930s, there was mass unemployment plus major social and economic barriers to modernization. By contrast, the period from the early 1950s until 1973 saw unprecedented growth, quasi-full employment, the diffusion of scientific management and a French variant of the American way of life.[1] After 1945, France, along with most European countries and Japan, caught up with American standards. Industries severely hurt by the crisis of the thirties and the war launched new processes and products which required restructuring and modernization.[2] The existence of such a technological gap was not in itself a factor of faster growth – Britain did not succeed in following this economic path, nor did most underdeveloped countries. Conversely, the Japanese case showed that a brilliant follower could overtake the leading country with respect to economic efficiency and mass consumption at low prices. Viewing this context in retrospect, it is possible that France could have failed at modernization after 1945.

France's relative success must be explained by internal and external structural changes. Here, following previous analyses,[3] we will review three major factors. First, a kind of social compromise between unions and employers was implicitly struck. Wage earners accepted rapid modernization in exchange for higher living standards. As a result, the mass production begun during World War I started anew after World War II, along with new mass consumption for wage earners in particular. Simultaneously, new middle classes emerged and transformed social and ideological life.[4] The next factor, a change in attitude about the state plus a complete renewal of political elites helped promote both social compromise and more general public intervention congruent with the new "Keynesian and Fordist" mode of development. The implementation of an extensive Welfare State, a modern tax system and significant subsidies to basic industries were parts of this.[5] Finally, the adoption of countercyclical fiscal and monetary policies dampened short-term fluctuations. The third factor of success, the construction of a coherent international system under American hegemony, which established built-in stabilizers and spurred OECD growth, created a complement between the American evolution and that of the rest of the world.[6] Europe, and especially France, benefitted from this drastic move away from a very unstable inter-war world system.[7] France could increase world market shares in manufactured goods, reduce import penetration, and more generally adjust her external balance through periodic devaluations of the franc and transitory austerity policies (as in 1958 and 1969, for example).

A new growth pattern progressively emerged from this transformation during the 1950s, and was based on new economic regularities, some of them at odds with the traditional dynamics of competitive capitalism. From an economic point of view, this post-war mode of development had some very appealing features.[8] During its heyday, conflicts about income distribution took place within a positive and increasing sum game. For example, wage increases benefitted both workers and firms as long as productive capacities were underemployed. Under Keynesian full employment, wages and profits, consumption and investment were mainly complementary. Of course, variations in the inflation rate were a common way to absorb macroeconomic disequilibria given the easy monetary policies which were followed.[9] But adjustments in exchange rates were sufficient to check any related deterioration in external competitiveness. Lastly, within the unemployment/inflation trade-off, France could choose a higher growth rate at the expense of more inflation than other countries. This was true even if the current, external constraints did not severely limit "national structural preferences".[10]

As economic success became more certain, public opinion and politicians changed their views. Social progress and economic efficiency were no longer perceived as competitors.[11] The parties of the Left attributed most economic imbalances to excessive inequality or insufficient democratic rights. But Center and Right politicians also agreed with the socialization program launched by de Gaulle in 1945. Simultaneously, and contrary to what prevailed in the United States, for example, state intervention was not seen as detrimental to efficient economic functioning. On the contrary, the concept of a "mixed economy" - widely accepted by firms, unions and public opinion - called for the better integration of competitive mechanisms and state regulation.[12] One last characteristic was important: every social group had grown accustomed to a steady and significant improvement in living standards.[13] Rapid growth had even allowed financial compensation for declining activities, thus helping prevent strong opposition from peasants, miners, small shopkeepers and other threatened groups.

FROM GROWTH TO CRISIS: INITIAL CHRONOLOGY (1965-85)

French political opinion lagged in taking the new crisis into account. The 1974-75 oil shock initially prompted a serious, but mainly sectoral, reaction.[14] After 1976 the first Barre plan admittedly reversed purely Keynesian views about counter-cyclical management, and combined a price and wage freeze with supply-side as well as monetary intervention. However, the long-term expectations and everyday behavior of most firms, unions and workers barely changed, despite the deep underlying transformations occurring in both the national and international economies. Public opinion was upset by the continuous rise in unemployment despite the promises of politicians in power;[15] this distinction provided one explanation for the electoral move towards the Left in May 1981. Yet, during the 1981-82 "state of grace", there was continuing optimism about the possibilities of combining a vast program of social reforms and Keynesian reflation in one country, however unfavorable the international situation was. After March 1983, a different diagnosis and therapy prevailed which acknowledged the structural character and depth of the world crisis together with France's major weaknesses. But part of public opinion still seemed convinced that a return to the global sixties was possible, if only state intervention was sufficiently strong and the expansion of social benefits and rights continued according to previous trends.

Of course, political changes must be related to economic evolution. As in the 1930s,[16] the crisis of the 1970s was initially milder in France relative to the United States, West Germany and most other countries. Main macroeconomic indicators nonetheless showed the approach of the crisis in three periods. During the first phase, the May-June 1968 political crisis preceded an economic boom which was launched by wage increases and sustained by favorable world markets. Thus, from 1968 to 1973 growth followed previous trends with the rapid increase of GDP, household consumption and investment. At most, there was a slight decline in the rate of industrial investment in the early seventies. Import shares in the domestic market climbed, but at a moderate and steady rate, while the share of exports in production also grew.

Of course, the inflation rate increased moderately; it did not cause a huge external deficit, however, despite a necessary devaluation in 1969.

From 1974 to 1979 there were significant changes, however. After a rather sharp recession in industry (milder for the economy as a whole), GDP growth underwent a notable slowdown, along with an important decline in household investment and to a lesser extent in industrial equipment. Consumption showed striking continuity, however. Rising oil import prices were partially offset by a boom in manufacturing exports, but they also triggered an inflationary spiral (directly via intermediate products, indirectly via consumer prices, wages, production costs and back again through final products). Most OECD countries experienced a similar process, but it turned out to be more significant in France. If the 1974–75 recession (and the subsequent reflation) were rather easy to explain (either by a lack of effective demand or by the shock on supply via relative price effects) it was trickier to interpret the decline in medium-term growth.

After 1980, earlier changes reinforced themselves until they triggered a near exhaustion of GDP growth, stagnation in productive investment and a strong decline in household investment. After 1982, even consumption slowed, and the French economy began to face a very new situation with respect to post World War II patterns. While other OECD economies entered a disinflationary process, France first kept her inflation under control, and after 1982–83 reduced it, but at a slower pace. To a large extent, the reduction of internal demand, combined with external rate adjustment, reduced the deficit on current external accounts. Thus, for the first time in two decades, France's growth rate was slower than her main competitors' exactly when world trends were far from optimistic.

All things considered, then, France has entered a crisis period, even if it is not a repetition of the inter-war years.[16] Before trying to point out some of the roots of this crisis, let us characterize it more completely. Virtually all the usual macroeconomic indicators have showed a clear decline since the end of the 1970s. The exhaustion of growth reduced the total number of hours worked, moderately at first, but significantly after 1980, since average productivity still grew. Of course, the number of hours worked on a weekly and annual basis have been reduced, but not enough to prevent global employment from declining continuously from 1979 to 1985. Next, activity rates and population evolution became less sensitive to short-term economic fluctuations. Surging unemployment has been the direct consequence of the diverging trends between the labor force and job opportunities. Unfilled vacancies are now 20 per cent of what they were in 1974, while the registered unemployed had multiplied five times by 1984. Unemployment has undoubtedly become the major concern of public opinion, because it is changing expectations as well as collective and individual behavior. Finally, external and public deficits are no longer endogenously leveled off either through the usual built-in stabilizers or by discretionary policies. Inflation differentials between France and the rest of the world have hardly been offset by devaluations of the franc, and in consequence, medium-term growth rates decline. Similarly, the state has acquired a large deficit whether in recession or expansion, no matter what it did to control public spending.

WHAT WENT WRONG WITH THE "FRENCH MIRACLE?"

We have a puzzle to solve. Why did investment not recover if consumer demand grew – at least until the early eighties? After all, this worked in the sixties.[17] Now, for the first time, in fact, the post-war social compromise and its institutional manifestations face widespread and lasting unemployment in a very unstable world economy. There seem to be two sides to the dialectical situation which has come to exist. On one side, collective agreements and welfare regulations imply ongoing real wage increases, and hence rising consumption. On the other, the related shift in income distribution shrinks profits and hence investment – which depresses production and employment levels.

Proposition 1: The old social compromise
stabilizes consumption but shifts income distribution

The 1973 surge in oil prices led to a relative increase in consumer prices compared to value added. Even if the law forbade it, the practice of indexing wages to consumer prices was widespread. Thus, real wages more or less followed past trends of growth despite signs of crisis. Similarly, employment levels did not completely adapt to the 1974–75 recession, since unemployment was perceived as temporary, rather than as an aspect of a new economic stage. In an interesting manifestation of this the law limiting layoffs was strengthened. That firms were obliged to bear most of the oil-shock burden was not surprising, therefore. All this amounted to a *de facto* income shift which, in turn, influenced firm decisions about production, employment and investment.[18] Managers first tried to limit further real wage increases by various means; in autumn 1976 a price and wage freeze was implemented. A slow decline in wage growth thus did occur during the seventies. Job reductions also occurred in industries – for example intermediate goods, nondurable goods and construction – which were more severely hit by the crisis. However, inertia in traditional services and the development of new services initially offset the decline in industrial jobs. Nevertheless, the divergence between labor-force size and employment which began in the mid-sixties widened from 1973 to 1979, even though there was continued growth in total employment.

Unemployment also took on a different form which was associated with its new structural character – the increased severity and frequency of unemployment spells for immigrants, young workers and women in particular. By the end of the seventies longer-term unemployment had clearly challenged the traditional French right to work.[19] Many unskilled jobs were phased out and not replaced. Urgent new concerns arose about training and retraining workers. The quasi-disappearance of unfilled vacancies and the surge of registered unemployment clearly demonstrated the secondary role of frictional unemployment in the mid-eighties.

Because of such changes, the Welfare State faced unprecedented problems in managing and financing a full-fledged social insurance system during massive and lasting unemployment.[20] The mere enforcement of existing laws and regulations led to a socialization of income larger than ever before, with the share of social benefits rising from one-fifth to one-third of household incomes between 1970 and 1985. These transfer payments had to be financed by both employees and employers. Because the Welfare State is not financed by personal income taxes in France, such a socialization of income led to an increase in the share of wages in total value added. This shift has been the key factor in both the evolution of consumption and the strong decline in the propensity to save. New incentives followed for French production – it had to be competitive with foreign goods. The same was true for investment – even it had to be financed by loans. If these two conditions could not be met simultaneously, France faced a vicious circle. This was precisely what happened.

Proposition 2: Investment decline and financial
instability undercut production and employment

Paradoxically, the same factors that stabilized short-term fluctuations also inhibited the medium-term strength and dynamism of the French productive system. Firms experienced a clear decline in income and retained profits, a mirror image of the position of wage earners. Consequently, the rate of return to capital, which leveled off in the early seventies, fell significantly during the last decade through 1982 (figure 2.1). The capital growth rate also declined, even if firms went into debt to prevent this.[21] In the long run, however, profit and investment go hand in hand. This may be the deeper root of the decline. The financial position of firms deteriorated until 1977, with an increase in debt-capital ratio (though less rapid than in the United States).[22] Afterwards, however, more restrictive monetary policies and rising global real interest rates compelled firms to reduce their indebtedness (figure 2.2). Initially, the collapse of profitability was partially offset by negative or low real interest rates supplying an important leverage effect for industrial profits. But after 1982, return on financial assets – in real terms – became higher than the rate of profit (figure 2.3).

This scissors effect, not seen since the thirties, had far-reaching consequences for business strategies. First, firms preferred to reimburse loans rather than expand production capacities. Financial investment became both more profitable, and to some extent less risky, than industrial investment. As real interest rates climbed, interest payments grew larger and their share in business income grew rapidly. The solvency ratio of business deteriorated, a second factor to add to the previous one, with failures climbing along with insolvency (figure 2.4). Plant closures connected with these developments aggravated the unemployment problem. Thirdly, and more fundamentally, the roots of growth were destroyed when the economic rate of return fell lower than the real interest rate, a theoretical conclusion confirmed by both macroeconomic analysis and financial management wisdom. From a practical point of view, French growth declined commensurately with the rate of profit, at least in the medium term (figure 2.5). Nevertheless, in the short term, the link was looser: in 1979–80, retained profits were partially restored, but growth and investment were not.

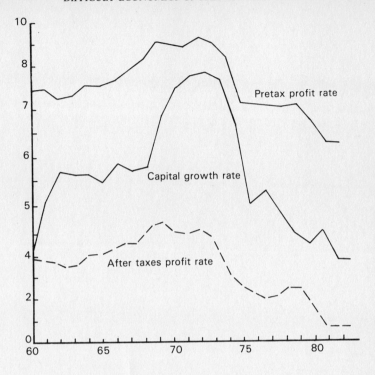

Figure 2.1 The investment slowdown at the core of the crisis: the profit rate falls after 1973

Source: V. Lévy-Garboua and G. Maarek *La Dette, le boom, la crise* (Paris, Economica 1985)

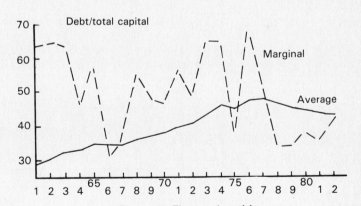

Figure 2.2 Firms go into debt

Source: V. Lévy-Garboua and G. Maarek *La Dette, le boom, la crise* (Paris, Economica 1985)

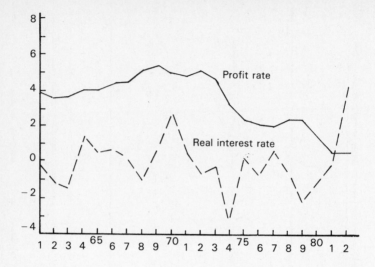

Figure 2.3 Firms benefit from a leverage effect which turned negative after 1981
Source: V. Lévy-Garboua and G. Maarek *La Dette, le boom, la crise* (Paris, Economica 1985)

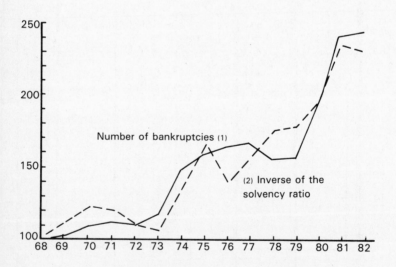

Figure 2.4 Hence failures increase with insolvency
Source: V. Lévy-Garboua and G. Maarek *La Dette, le boom, la crise* (Paris, Economica 1985)

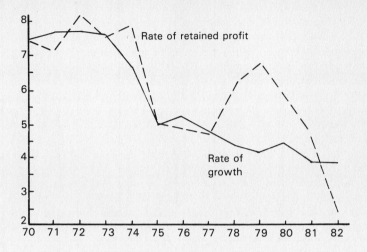

Figure 2.5 Less profit, lower growth

Source: V. Lévy-Garboua and G. Maarek *La Dette, le boom, la crise* (Paris, Economica 1985).

INTERNATIONAL CRISIS: THE VILLAIN - AND/OR MULTIPLIER - OF NATIONAL PROBLEMS?

The capital–labor compromise and state intervention consecrated by the post-war boom posed serious difficulties during the crisis. But what about the third pillar of post-war growth – the stability of the world system? This system has also undergone drastic changes toward greater instability, more uncertainty and less dynamism, as is well known. For some, the breakdown of the Bretton Woods system has been the sole, or at least the major, root of the crisis. If a new coherent system could be constructed, then almost all disequilibria and problems would vanish. In this view, France has had no responsibility for the deterioration of her economic position. In contrast, others point out that Japan, South Korea, and the United States are out of the crisis and are prospering within an international mess. Consequently, national problems must be due primarily to bad management, inadequate industrial and social organization and the like. The truth may lie between these opposing views. Let us therefore try to disentangle international and national factors for the French case.

France hit by sharp changes in the world economy

After 1971 the international financial system functioned with new and chaotic unevenness. Inflation, starting in the United States, accelerated and spread to the rest of the world. In reaction, oil prices soared and destabilized financial markets. The implementation of imperfectly floating exchange rates, far from granting more autonomy to national policies, fostered massive speculation without promoting any new stability in the world system. The Third World debt problem, caused mainly by American monetary policies from 1979 to 1982, consequently worsened. Moreover, exchange rates drifted so far from real purchasing power parities that creeping protectionism or dumping became common features in international trade. Obviously, France was affected directly and indirectly by all these events.

At least four mechanisms contributed to reducing French growth. The high volatility of exchange rates and their discrepancy with respect to the value of current account balances affected the French economy adversely. After 1979, the rise of the dollar's strength increased import costs (raw materials, oil) rather than spurring French exports, since American market shares were far lower than those of the EEC for France. Furthermore, the huge upturn in American real interest rates after 1982 spread to France, with French interest rates overshooting to offset inflation differentials with other important European countries, especially West Germany. Admittedly, the European Monetary System (EMS) limited instability within Europe, but it did not prevent the rise in real interest rates. Hence, there was a major increase in interest payments for foreign debt, the public deficit and firms' financial accounts. In turn, internal growth had to be limited, some public expenditures cut and financial consolidation chosen over productive investment.

When interest rates rise above rates of profit and growth, the world economy feels severe deflationary pressure. Unfortunately, at the key moment (1981–82), France could hardly reduce her traditional inflation differential. The French strategy of reflation was thus at odds with the evolution in OECD countries, newly industrialized economies and oil-producing countries. Total world exports at current prices was roughly constant from 1979 to 1984, in line with the medium-term trend towards stagnation. Moreover, most OECD countries adopted restrictive monetary policies and curbed nominal and real wages. In France, however, previous mechanisms of price and wage formation remained unchanged until 1982–83, despite earlier difficulties in 1976–78. The increase of the inflation differential was then easily explainable: France's main competitors succeeded in promoting more flexible wages and prices, while the highly institutionalized and centralized French system changed little and slowly.[23]

In addition, growth in world markets for manufactured goods slowed after 1979. The spread of austerity policies reduced internal demand and hence imports for OECD economies, highly indebted countries (Mexico, Brazil), Third World and even Oil-Producing and Exporting Countries (OPEC). Since France was traditionally linked closely to these last three markets, world demand for her goods slowed down. The maximum French growth rate compatible with the external equilibrium was thus divided by two, declining from 7.6 per cent in 1970–74 to 3.6 per cent in 1979–85.[24] The situation appeared even worse when the loss of export shares and import penetration were taken into account. The purely mechanical effect of the world trade crisis on France cannot be underestimated.

Finally, such changes sharpened competition between industrialized economies. The struggle for market share is now a quasi-zero-sum game. Open or disguised import controls, important subsidies to exporters, dumping and competitive strategies for exchange rates have become the various means for trying to sustain national economic activity at the expense of others – a new form of beggar-thy-neighbor policies. France has not been very successful at playing this tough game. Since 1979, French export shares have been declining, quite in line with Britain. As import shares increase, the maximum growth rate compatible with external balance is reduced to a level even lower than during the seventies. Of course, losses by some are gains for others. From the early eighties on, Japan has increased her export shares from 9 per cent to 14 per cent, while West Germany stabilized her losses. One can find no better examples of the sharpening of national specificities within the crisis. Hence, it would be erroneous to attribute the French crisis exclusively to world disorder. *La crise c'est les autres*! cannot be the whole explanation. Why did France not fare as well as Japan or, West Germany? The specific strengths and weaknesses of the French economy need investigation to answer this.[25]

A weakening of structural competitiveness, long unnoticed

Slow growth in France is also the consequence of a medium-term process which reduced the previous comparative advantage of France in some key exporting industries. Unlike West Germany, Japan, the United States (and even Italy and Britain),[26] France traditionally had very few industries with a steady and large surplus in international trade (the short list included motor vehicles and transportation equipment, weapons, and more recently food and agricultural commodities). During the last decade some of these industries faced problems, without being replaced by new export industries. After an outstanding performance during the early seventies, the car industry ran into trouble, while nondurable goods continued their long-term loss of competitiveness and the investment goods industry ceased to provide a lasting external surplus after 1979.[27] The problems became all the more severe since many analysts had relied on these industries to produce a large trade surplus.[28]

Few other industries were able to offset these losses by an improvement of their trade balances. The good performance in food and kindred products is worth noting: France finally learned to exploit her traditional comparative advantage in agriculture and food processing.[29] Similarly, a huge effort in nuclear power plants stabilized the energy deficit, in spite of a very strong dollar. But substitution of electricity for other energies has had its limits, such that the dependency ratio of France declined, but only slowly. Finally, in the engineering sector, large public works and tourism provided significant and positive contributions. These successes only partially substituted for the needed surplus in dynamic new high-technology areas, however. Whether the aircraft, aerospace and telecommunications industries may be such leaders in the future is an open question.

The crisis activated another traditional feature of France's international specialization. With respect to international trade theory, France appeared as an intermediate country mainly exporting average-skilled, medium-tech and rather standardized industrial goods to less-developed countries. Symmetrically, France imported sophisticated and more advanced industrial goods such as business equipment and machinery from leading OECD countries (United States, Japan, West Germany). Such trade was especially advantageous in the mid-seventies when some of the oil-producing countries launched ambitious industrial plans, requiring the type of industrial goods competitively produced by France. But later on, when these countries ran from external surplus to deficit, this became a drawback since France then had to struggle in OECD markets where competition was more acute and depended on different factors (quality, marketing, maintenance). In this respect, the geographical distribution of French surplus and deficit is illuminating (table 2.1). In the sixties, small deficits with the United States and West Germany were offset by a surplus with other countries. But after 1974, the external deficit with West Germany and most EEC countries rose steadily. In 1984 the related deficit was double that of oil-producing countries. If in the 1970s France underwent an oil shock, then in the 1980s she faced an industrial shock.

Why did France emerge as one of the weakest OECD economies? These adverse trade developments must be related to the internal process of accumulation and its crisis (analyzed in section three of this chapter). The shrinkage of firm mark-ups and ratio of retained profits caused a quasi-stagnation of productive investment for over a decade. Thus, the distribution of different "vintages" of productive goods flattened, in contrast to the triangular distribution observed during the sixties. The change was dramatic for intermediate and consumption goods, but did not occur for equipment goods.[30] Accordingly, firms were probably renewing products less frequently and may have lost their competitive edge through lagging product differentiation and quality improvement.[31] But, in markets where price competition is acute, French industry suffered from another handicap: from 1970 to 1984 French production costs grew faster than those of its competitors. Some of these divergences were in turn offset by a reduction of mark-ups on external marketing, a very dubious method for developing international networks and a long-term marketing strategy. These partial adjustments were not sufficient to compensate inflation differentials. The government

Table 2.1 France's loss of competitive position: France's deficit with OECD countries

France's External balance with	1959	1971	1974	1979	1984
Germany	0	−2.0	−11.0	−11.1	−28.0
Netherlands	−0.2	−1.0	− 2.6	− 5.2	−16.4
United Kingdom	+0.3	−0.8	− 0.3	+ 6.4	− 8.5
Italy	+0.4	+0.4	+ 6.5	+ 1.5	− 0.6
ECC*	+0.8	−2.6	− 4.1	− 8.7	−57.0
USA	+0.1	−7.8	− 8.9	−14.0	− 3.7
Japan				− 4.8	−14.8
Oil countries			−34.9	−38.8	−25.6
Other countries	+3.7	+3.8	14.2	19.0	+10.1
Total	+3.8	−4.0	−34.4	−42.4	−90.0

Note: * According to the boundary of the year considered.
Sources: Various issues of National Accounts.

thus had to devalue repetitively. Indeed, devaluation became the principle means for keeping French export prices in line with the rest of the world.

LEADER OR FOLLOWER - WHAT ROLE FOR ECONOMIC POLICY?

Discussing the precise effects of economic policy is largely beyond our scope. Let us limit ourselves to seven relevant points, without elaborate discussion.

Exchange rates

The choice of exchange rate policy may indeed be the most powerful tool for affecting external competitiveness. The point is obvious for the short term, but the implementation of an exchange rate regime shapes national specialization and industrial structures in the long term as well. During the seventies, a form of overvaluation of the franc seems to have prevailed, especially when one takes production costs into account, a characterization which is confirmed when real purchasing power parity is computed and compared with the actual exchange rate. In the sixties, the exchange rate was varied according to inflation differentials and after 1974 the franc was continuously overvalued, up to 16 per cent in 1980. These six years of discrepancy had, no doubt, some influence upon industrial health: the decline in intermediate and consumption-goods sectors accelerated, and the pressure towards rationalizing investment and productivity increased, probably at the expense of faster deindustrialization (industrial job reduction). Most of the macroeconomic studies conclude that this actually happened at the end of the seventies.[32] Thus, a strong currency may have had some disinflationary effects, but it also worked to the detriment of the cohesion and level of industrial employment.

Research and development

The decline in research and development (R & D) expenditures has often been blamed for the structural deterioration of French competitiveness.[33] Nevertheless, it is hard to find any clear and mechanical relation between this type of investment and economic achievements. Moreover, a substantial lag - a decade or more - usually occurs between innovation and the mass production of related goods.[34] Furthermore, Japan fared far better than France, with an equivalent R & D/GNP ratio. It is also difficult to assess the consequences of the absence of any clear and ambitious industrial policy in the seventies. The opposition between a niche strategy (*politique de créneaux*) and one of vertical integration (*stratégie de filières*) appears clearer on intellectual grounds than in the everyday management of firms - or even in the Ministry of Industry.

Monetary policy

After 1976, monetary policy was aimed at controlling exchange rates (mainly within the EMS) and checking inflation. With respect to the first goal, the Banque de France broadly followed the evolution of short-term interest rates in international markets. As mentioned earlier, the open American market seems to have been the key factor in setting French real interest rates. The second goal constituted the continuous adaptation of regulations and targets by public authorities, with two important turning points. From 1977 to 1980 official targets for monetary supply evolution were fixed. After 1980, many institutional decisions were made to foster financial markets and broaden access to the money market.

It is not easy to assess the outcome of these changes. The nominal money supply has grown more and more slowly, despite large short-term fluctuations; the rate of inflation has declined simultaneously. The issue is the direction of causality: it is far from obvious that rather cautious monetary targets had, by themselves, a strong impact on inflation. In fact, attempts at incomes policies seem to have helped in reducing inflationary pressures (witness the decline after 1976 and 1982). And credit control (which is the traditional French tool) seems to have been used more moderately in the eighties than in the seventies for both households and firms. This change is probably attributable to soaring interest rates which limited the need for quantitative and selective controls.

Taxation and redistribution

Tax policy and welfare management significantly affected income distribution between industries and households and, more generally, shifted the share of transfers in total disposable incomes. The continuity in social benefits was a rather surprising outcome: from 1973 to 1985 social benefits replaced self-employed income as the second largest component in total household resources. Until now, slowdowns in their growth (1976, 1983) have been mainly transitory. Direct taxes, roughly constant before, did climb after 1975. The evolution regarding firms has been far different. From 1965 to 1974, the share of taxes linked to production clearly declined, reducing inflationary pressures associated with struggles over income distribution.[35] After 1975, this ratio climbed again, reversing previous trends. The total fiscal burden on business fluctuated a great deal in the early stages of the crisis, rose from 1978 to 1982 and finally declined. Hence, the existing tax system and new decisions seem to have worsened the profit squeeze at first and alleviated it later.

When all these components are combined, a sharp contrast between pre- and post-crisis periods is evident. From 1965 to 1973, the total tax/GDP ratio was roughly constant, but it rose almost continuously after that. The shift, around 10 per cent of GDP, was not at all marginal. The interpretation and the likely effects are much more controversial, however. First, only 3 per cent can be attributed to tax increases, strictly defined. The rest of the shift is due to financial contributions to welfare programs. Second, by nature these are only transfers and not a net tax on income. Many statistical studies have shown that the effective compulsory tax level, transfers excluded and public accounts consolidated, has been roughly constant or even declined in the 1980s.[36]

More fundamentally, most of the related increases in social benefits involved the simple implementation of existing programs as affected by demographics, not the result of new decisions. Unemployment benefits have climbed with mass unemployment, whereas other social transfers (such as health and pensions) varied with demographic trends and relative prices of each component. Let us emphasize again that this is the first crisis faced by France as a fully developed Welfare State. The surge of related expenditures is therefore not necessarily evidence of tremendous mismanagement or a lax extension of social rights, but mainly the consequence of a conflict between past "institutionalized compromises"[37] and adverse economic trends.

Incomes policies

As the post-1973 "profit squeeze" is central to the unfolding of the crisis, the role of incomes policy has to be mentioned briefly.[38] Public authorities have traditionally interfered with direct income formation in France. Since 1945 existing regulations have allowed the state to control price formation more or less tightly and influence wages (via the minimum wage, general rules about indexing and so on). During the crisis period governments have been very active, if not always successful, in changing the rules of the price and wage game. As was pointed out earlier, the first decline in nominal wage rates, in 1976, was obtained through a temporary freeze, whereas a constant aim has been the promotion of a long-term liberalization of prices via the strengthening of competition. Both the price and wage restraint after June 1982 and the subsequent guidelines about deindexing wages followed the same line of reasoning. The short-term effects seem to have been significant, but the long-term results are still open to discussion. Nevertheless, these shifts did correct previous imbalances since they focused on restoring profits and investment. The danger for this effort concerns the subtle balance between wage restraint and a sufficiently dynamic internal demand.[39]

Public expenditures

Public expenditures are the fifth component of economic policy to be reviewed here. On average, their share of GDP seems to have been roughly constant over a long period. Nevertheless, the crisis has shifted various public outlays (table 2.2). The share

Table 2.2 Budget outlays by main function

	1961	1973	1979	1984
Capital spending	24.6%	19.6%	14.7%	15.5%
Investment and subsidies	(13.9%)	(12.2%)	(8.4%)	(8.4%)
War reparations	(2.3%)	(0)	(0)	(0)
Defense	(8.4%)	(7.4%)	(6.3%)	(7.1%)
Public debt	4.7%	2.5%	5.1%	7.4%
Functioning	42.6%	44.5%	45.0%	43.1%
Salaries	(29.1%)	(29.4%)	(30.3%)	(26.9)
Pensions	(6.8%)	(8.8%)	(9.1%)	(8.4)
Consumptions	(6.7%)	(6.3%)	(5.6%)	(7.8%)
Subsidies	28.1%	33.4%	35.2%	38.3%

Source: Tendances de la conjoncture, (Aug. 1985); M. Basle, Le Budget de l'état (Paris, La Découverte, 1985), p. 101; Comptes de la nation, 1983, 1984.

Table 2.3 The volume of investment (index)

	1973	1974	1975	1976	1977	1978	1979	1980	1981	1982	1983	1984
Whole economy	100.0	100.6	97.9	101.3	100.0	100.7	103.2	108.1	105.0	104.1	99.9	97.4
Large nationalized firms	100.0	105.0	128.7	132.6	147.3	165.4	180.3	188.6	179.2	174.7	171.5	159.9

Source: *Tendances de la conjoncture*, (Aug. 1985); M. Basle, *Le Budget de l'état* (Paris, La Découverte, 1985), p. 101; *Comptes de la nation*, 1983, 1984.

of functioning expenditures first increased and then stabilized. An implicit policy choice seems to have been made for subsidies and transfers (going from 33.4 per cent to 38.3 per cent of the total budget during the last decade), to the detriment of public investments. Within this category, civilian investments were affected more than defense. Perhaps under pressures of insistent short-term disequilibria and social demands, public authorities favored macroeconomic stabilization over long-term choices.

This tentative perspective has to be corrected by opposing tendencies in investment in large nationalized firms (table 2.3). Whereas investment in the whole economy was almost constant from 1973 to 1979, investment of the nationalized sector increased by 80 per cent. This was due largely to the nuclear program and telecommunications equipment. After 1980, there was a clear downturn when these programs either came to an end or were revised according to expected trends in energy demand. Thus, rather contradictory forces have transformed public outlays: priority was given to macroeconomic stabilization, the management of past social compromises and some long-term investment programs.

The budget

The net impact of the public budget summarizes most of the previous effects. By and large, the size of the deficit with respect to GDP has been kept in line with the average of OECD countries. But the French time frame was different from those of Japan, Britain and West Germany, countries in which this deficit was slowly reduced from 1978 to 1984. France was similar only to the United States, but conditions for financing the American deficit are far different. French deficits resulted partly from built-in stabilizers, and not necessarily from discretionary policies. However tricky, the split between automatic and voluntary deficits leads to an interesting picture. With the exception of 1975 and 1981, reflationary policies were very cautious, and countercyclical measures were frequent. Since 1982, the government's target of a public deficit not to exceed 3 per cent of GDP has led to quasi-neutral budgets.

To discuss possible crowding-out effects is beyond the scope of this chapter and would necessitate a full-fledged model. One main, probably more important, concern is external debt. Since 1979, according to available estimates, the debt trebled (table 2.4). Such trends, if extrapolated, are striking, but half of the related increase was due to the franc's floating exchange rates with respect to the European Currency Unit (ECU), and to the dollar vis-à-vis the ECU. Furthermore, foreign assets have to be taken into account. France's net position is less worrisome there, but the trends are still present. The latest figures suggest a significant slowdown in external debt growth. More fundamentally, the impact of this debt cannot be isolated from the use of related financial resources. The foregoing analyses suggest that economic policies have followed – more than caused – French economic problems. Continuities are rather striking, but some inflections or breakdowns may be underway.

Table 2.4 External position of France (billions francs)

	1979	1980	1981	1982	1983
Liabilities					
Sums of annual flow of	95.7	113.7	147.3	225.4	314.5
borrowing	− 1.9	+ 9.2	+ 40.4	+ 70.0	+ 136.5
Effects of floating exchange rates	93.8	122.9	187.7	295.4	451.0
Assets					
Loans to exports	104.7	119.7	139.7	168.7	196.2
Public loans to foreign	19.1	24.3	32.7	42.5	55.9
	123.8	144.0	172.4	211.2	252.1
Net position	+ 30.0	+ 21.1	− 15.3	− 84.2	− 198.9

Sources: Conseil National du Crédit, *Rapport annual 1984* (Paris, Banque de France, 1985), p. 124. André Ch. and Delorme R., *L'Etat et l'économie* (Paris, 1984), p. 108. *OCDE Perspectives économiques*, (July 1984), p. 47.

THE LEFT IN POWER, OR HOW TO BE A PRISONER OF HISTORY!

The French post-war compromise

After World War II, France implemented a specific variant of the growth pattern which all OECD countries more or less shared. The high degree of centralization and institutionalization of French social and economic life gave a special national flavor to the Fordist-Keynesian mode of development, based on an implicit tripartite compromise between French firms, unions and the state.

The persistence of compromise despite symptoms of crisis

These features may explain the particular unfolding of the French crisis. In contrast to sharp fluctuations observed elsewhere, France's entry into the crisis was rather gradual, lasting until the end of the seventies. During this period, a large consensus favoring high growth, even at the cost of inflation, persisted. Accommodating policies were thus followed, and only partially called into question after 1976.

Residues of the French compromise made response difficult

The very factors which initially cushioned the world crisis for France later came to inhibit long-term dynamics in investment, production and international specialization. The general change in economic trends did not bring equivalent transformations in the expectations, strategies and behavior of firms, workers, unions and governments. The "safety net" provided by the existing Welfare State and numerous types of public regulations appeared better than a painful search for new institutions and compromises.

Cul-de-sac

The depth, duration and bumpy evolution of the international crisis did not allow continuation along this path. When the slowdown in world markets and surge of real interest rates put severe constraints upon French national growth, the limits of the previous strategy appeared clearly. The French crisis therefore combined international roots with specific national causes. The weakening of French industry and its loss of dynamism are good examples of this intertwining of both sets of factors.

Stages of crisis in France

Three different stages have to be distinguished. From 1968 to 1973 there was a rapid boom with some unnoticed strains. Then there was a progressive slowdown after the first oil shock. Finally, after 1979, there was a new phase in which virtually all economic trends became adverse, a feature which contributed to the political change in May 1981. Public opinion had apparently been convinced by then that something new had to be done.

The Left responds – correct ideas for the wrong crisis

The very formation of Left economic thought dated from the New Deal, which had allowed a way out of the inter-war crisis. If the Left recognized the structural character of the new troubles that French society was facing in the seventies, its economic program was much more a variant of past Fordist – Keynesian management than anything new. Of course, some innovation could be found (industrial democracy, decentralization and so on), but it played only small roles in short-term economic evolution.

This general legacy was undoubtedly an obstacle during the first phase of the Left in power. But it may well help in finding a French variant out of the crisis – provided that something new emerges out of the present international quagmire.

NOTES

1 In the long run, the rate of growth climbs from 2.5% per year to 5%. See J. J. Carre et al., *La Croissance française: un essai d'analyse causale* (Paris, Seuil, 1972).

2 This interpretation has been worked out by S. Gomulka, *Inventive Activity, Diffusion and the Stages of Economic Growth* (Aarhus, University Press 1971).

3 See for example (for the United States) M. Aglietta, *Croissance et régulation aux USA* (Paris, Calmann-Lévy, 1976); *Régulation et crise du capitalisme. L'Expérience des Etats Unis*, 2nd edn (Paris, Calmann-Lévy, 1982). For France see CEPREMAP-CORDES, *Approches de l'inflation: l'example français* (research report, 1982).

4 Read the provocative and well-documented book by L. Boltanski, *Les Cadres. La formation d'un groupe social* (Paris, Editions de Minuit, 1982).

5 See Ch. André and R. Delorme, *L'Etat et l'économie* (Paris, Seuil, 1982), which provides a secular analysis of state interventions in France.

6 The links between the national dynamics and the international system after World War II are studied

along these lines by J. Mistral, "La diffusion internationale inégale de l'accumulation intensive et ses crises", in *Economie et finance internationales*, ed. L. Bourguinat (Paris, Economica, 1982); and *125 Ans de contrainte extérieure: l'expérience française* (Paris, CEPREMAP, forthcoming), no. 8505.

7 The approach adopted there is that by C. P. Kindleberger, *The World in Depression* (Berkeley, University of California Press, 1973).

8 For a complete statistical analysis and modelling of this system see H. Bertrand, "Une Nouvelle approche de la croissance française de l'après-guerre: l'analyse en sections productives", *Statistiques et études financières*, série orange, 35, (1978); and "Accumulation, régulation, crise: un modèle sectionnel théorique et appliqué", Revue Economique, vol. 34, no. 2, (March 1983).

9 Read J. P. Bénassy et al., "Régulation des économies capitalistes et inflation", *Revue économique*, 30, 3 (May 1979), pp. 397–441.

10 According to the word coined by Weiller. An evidence of the quasi-independence of OECD countries' growth with respect to their openness to world trade is shown by R. Boyer and P. Ralle, *Croissances nationales et contraintes extérieures* Economie et Sociétés, p. 29, (January 1986).

11 For more details read R. Boyer and J. Mistral, *The Present Crisis From an Historical Interpretation to a Prospective Outlook* (Paris, CEPREMAP, Feb. 1984), mimeo.

12 Most social scientists agree overwhelmingly on the topic. Among others see F. Fourquet, *Les Comptes de la puissance* (Paris, Editions Recherches, 1980); A. Shonfield, *Le Capitalisme d'anjourd'hui* (Paris, Gallimard, 1967); R. Kuisel, *Capitalism and the State in Modern France* (New York, Cambridge University Press, 1981).

13 Since the outbreak of the crisis this behavior has been blamed, largely in such best-sellers as F. de Closets, *Toujours plus* (Paris, Grasset, 1982). The title also serves as a leitmotiv.

14 More details of the author's view may be found in R. Boyer and J. Mistral, *Accumulation, inflation, crises*, 2nd edn (Paris, Presses Universitaires de France, 1983), ch. VII; or in R. Boyer, *The French Economic Policy since 1981: A Crucial Test for a Left-wing Variant of Keynesianism*, mimeo, presented at the Hofstra University conference "The Influence of Keynes on French Economic Policy", September 1983.

15 During this period, the Gallup polls show a correlation between the government's decline in popularity and the feeling of a deterioration in living standards – see M. Forse and L. Lebart, "Chronique des opinions et aspirations des Français 1983: un réalisme morose," *Observations et diagnostiques économiques, revue de l'OFCE*, 8 (July 1984), p. 69.

16 For a comparison of the two crises see Boyer and Mistral, *Accumulation*, ch. 6.

17 The comparison of 1973–79 with the post-May 1968 boom is enlightening. At that time, the firms' income and investments benefitted from wage hikes.

18 The argument will be developed in the following subsection.

19 The unemployment rate of young men, therefore, climbed from 6.7% in 1975 to 22.1% in 1984; from 10.1% to 30.2% for young women. Average length of unemployment grew from 6.7 to 12.8 months for men, while for people over 50 it went from 58.9 to 71.5 months: INSEE, *Données sociales* (Paris, INSEE, 1985).

20 During the thirties, various programs of the Welfare State were launched, but on a very minor scale. At most, social benefits represented 5% of the incomes of wage earners. For a closer comparison, read R. Boyer, "Les Transformations du rapport salarial dans la crise", *Critiques de l'économie politique*, 15–16 (April–May 1981).

21 The subsequent analysis follows closely the study by V. Lévy-Garboua and G. Maarek, *La Dette, le boom, la crise* (Paris, Economica, 1985), ch. 3, pp. 39–73.

22 From the early seventies to the eighties, the debt/capital ratio rose from 20% to 30% in the United States, from 38% to 45% in France. See Lévy-Garboua and Maarek, *La Dette*, pp. 59–60.

23 For international comparisons of price and wage formations, read for example J. D. Sachs, "Real Wages and Unemployment in the OECD Countries", *Brookings Papers on Economic Activity*, 1 (1983); P. Artus, "Formation des prix et des salaires dans cinq grands pays industriels," *Annales de l'INSEE*, (1983); and numerous OECD studies such as that by D. Coe and F. Gagliardi, "Détermination des salaires nominaux dans dix économies de l'OCDE", *Documents de travail OCDE*, 19 (June 1985).

24 This is the result of a very simple model, see Y. Barou and B. Keizer, *Les Grandes économies* (Paris, Seuil, 1984); or more complete models, see R. Boyer and P. Petit, *Le Progrès technique dans la crise: ses déterminants, son impact sur l'emploi* (Paris, CEPREMAP note, July 1981), mimeo; and "Politiques industrielles et impact sur l'emploi: les pays européens face à la contrainte extérieure", *Revue d'économie industrielle*, 27 (Jan. 1984).

25 This was precisely the title of the report F. Bloch-Lainé was commissioned to do after May 1981: F. Bloch-Lairé et al., *Rapport de la Commission du Bilan* (Paris, La Documentation Française, 1982).

26 This feature has been pointed out by many CEPII comparative studies, especially "La Concurrence industrielle à l'échelle mondiale", *Economie et prospective internationale*, (June 1979); and *L'Economie mondiale 1970-1990, la troisième révolution industrielle* (Paris, Economica, 1982).

27 This argument relies upon the evolutions of the export/import ratios (in volume).

28 Rather surprisingly, French experts of this industry, as well as Civil Servants, seem to have been slow in perceiving this deterioration. See for example the related chapter, in Commission du Bilan, *La France en mai 1981. Les grands équilibres économiques* (Paris, La Documentation Française, 1982).

29 During some years of the eighties, the trade surplus for agricultural commodities and foods and manufactured goods was the same size.

30 See, OECD, *Etudes économiques: France*, Paris, OECD, 1984), pp. 50-4.

31 Competition about quality becomes more important when the consumer goods markets are mainly for replacement rather than for initial purchase. According to this criterion, French industry seems to be lagging behind most foreign competitors, see M. Aglietta and R. Boyer, "Une Industrie compétitive en France et dans le monde", in *Une Politique industrielle pour la France*, ed. Jean-Pierre Chevènement, (Paris, La Documentation Française, 1982).

32 A central argument can be found in M. Aglietta et al., "L'Industrie française face aux contraintes de change", *Economie et statistique*, 119 (Feb. 1980), pp. 35-65. A permanent overevaluation of 5% would reduce unemployment by 1.2 million after 9 years. More generally, Aglietta et al. show that external rate policy has to be consistent with the existing industrial structures.

33 The ratio R & D/GNP declines from around 2.15% in 1967 to 1.75% in 1979, see OECD, *Indicateurs de la sciences et de la technologie. Ressources consacrées à la R-D* (Paris, OECD, 1984), p. 30.

34 For more details see Boyer and Petit, *Le Progrès technique*.

35 This point has been shown by a very simple macroeconomic model, see Boyer and Mistral, *Accumulation*, ch. 3.

36 The figures for this ratio were: 14.5% for 1980, 13.2% for 1981, 12.6% for 1982 and 1983, 13% for 1984, see *Comptes de la nation 1984* (Paris, La Documentation Française, 1984), p. 175.

37 This notion, coined by André and Delorme, allows a very stimulating study of the long-term trends in state and social expenditures.

38 The author's views about French incomes policy are to be found in R. Boyer, *Income Policies in France. What Lessons for the Eighties?*, mimeo, presented at the conference on incomes policies in Europe and America, University of Gröningen, May 1984.

39 This strategy has been pointed out by E. Malinvaud, "Nouveaux développements de la théorie macroéconomique du chômage", *Revue économique*, (Jan. 1978), and is now discussed by many other economists.

3

The Evolution of Economic Policy under Mitterrand

PETER A. HALL

This history of economic policy-making under the 1981–86 government is a story of the long learning-curve of the French Left. The Socialist economic experiment began during June 1981 in an atmosphere of jubilation, and it ended during March 1986 in a spirit of resignation. Over the intervening five years, the government learned a great deal about the constraints facing those who manage a mixed economy in a setting of international interdependence. It may be some years before a response to this period is fully integrated into the philosophy of the French Left; however, it is not too early to draw up a balance sheet of the economic accomplishments of the 1981–86 period. We can begin by characterizing the Socialist macroeconomic policies in terms of three stages: redistribution, *rigueur*, *relance*.

THE FIRST STAGE: REDISTRIBUTIVE REFLATION

The Socialists inherited a difficult economic situation. Partly because unit labor costs in France were substantially higher than those of her major trading partners, the profitability and long-run competitiveness of French industry had been deteriorating for almost ten years. In the wake of the oil price increases of 1973–74 and 1979–80, levels of investment and growth continued to stagnate while unemployment, inflation and the trade deficit rose. Widespread discontent with economic performance played a major role in the Socialist victory of 1981.

Accordingly, the Mitterrand government embarked on a series of reflationary measures in 1981–82. Foremost in the minds of its leaders seems to have been a concern to fulfill their electoral pledge to secure rising levels of growth and employment. However, they felt justified in ignoring the adverse effects of such a reflation on the trade deficit because most forecasters were predicting an upturn in world economic activity for 1982, which after a brief deterioration was expected to improve the balance of payments deficit.[1]

There are different kinds of reflation. Some rely on tax cuts, others on spending increases, to stimulate demand. Some target investment directly; others depend on the general expansion in consumer spending to inspire investment. Some leave the broad distribution of income intact; others seek to redistribute it. In the similar circumstances of 1975-76, for instance, Prime Minister Jacques Chirac expanded the economy primarily through corporate tax reductions, interest rate subsidies, fiscal incentives for private investment and massive infrastructure projects, such as the renovation of the telephone system, worth in total about 2.8 per cent of GDP. His reflation was targetted on industrial investment and designed to redistribute income toward the corporate sector.

In 1981-82, however, the Socialists reflated primarily through measures designed to increase public employment and the spending power of less-affluent households. In this respect, it was redistributive Keynesianism. The purchasing power of the minimum wage – or the Salaire Minimum Interindustriel de Croissance (SMIC) to which many other wages in the economy were tied – was increased by 10.6% in 1981-82, compared with only 3.3% in 1979-80. The basic housing subsidy and family allowances for those with two children grew by 50% over these two years and the minimum old-age pension was raised by 62%. In total, these measures were worth about 2% of GDP.[2]

In order to finance this reflation, the Socialist government increased the public sector deficit to 2.6 per cent of GDP in 1982 and increased taxes on employers and upper incomes by about 28.2 billion francs in 1981-82. In short, its policy relied heavily on the augmentation of demand to generate growth. Increases in public spending rather than reductions in taxation were employed to effect the necessary stimulation, and the measures tended to redistribute income away from private corporations toward the lower-income levels of the household sector.

The government knew that the wage and tax increases associated with these measures would put pressure on corporate balance sheets and threaten industrial investment. However, it proposed to stimulate investment directly by channelling tax revenues to a massive series of investment projects, primarily in the nationalized industries. In 1981-82, almost 26 billion francs was spent to increase the capital base of public enterprises in the competitive sector including those newly national-ized, and another 43.9 billion francs went to the nationalized enterprises in noncompetitive sectors, notably to Charbonnages de France and the railways (SNCF). Through the old Fonds de Developpement Economique et Social and later the new Fonds Industriel de Modernisation, loans worth 86.9 billion francs were made in 1982-83.[3]

THE SECOND STAGE: SOCIALIST *RIGUEUR*

There was a small chance that the 1981-82 reflation might have been sustainable, but that depended on favorable international conditions that did not emerge. Instead of international economic recovery, 1982 brought continuing global recession, marked by a sustained increase in the value of the (US) dollar and unprecedented increases in interest rates around the world. As a consequence, downward pressure on the already overvalued franc became too intense to resist. The French lost a major portion of

their foreign reserves and were forced to devalue the franc within the European
Monetary System (EMS) on three occasions – 4 October 1981, 12 June 1982 and
21 March 1983 – before a stable parity was attained.

Although the 1981–82 reflation itself increased the French trade deficit by 27 billion
francs, rising interest and exchange rates in the United States accounted for another
57.4 billion franc deterioration in the French trade balance (largely because it raised
the price of oil imports denominated in dollars), and reduced the French rate of growth
by about 1 per cent of GDP.[4] French efforts to persuade the United States to lower
her interest and exchange rates failed and foreign creditors forced the nation to accept
some deflation as a condition for continuing to support the franc. French policy-makers
themselves realized that deflation would be necessary to reduce the growing trade deficit
and restore the level of foreign exchange reserves.

The redistributive Keynesianism of 1981–82 ultimately foundered on France's
vulnerability to developments in the international economy. After almost two decades
in the European Economic Community (EEC), France now had a relatively open
economy. Her imports and exports were each worth about 20 per cent of GDP; and
as a result of reflation, higher levels of consumer spending had increased the volume
of imports, while a depressed world economy proved unwilling to buy higher volumes
of French exports. The latter were already relatively expensive and increasing rates
of domestic inflation threatened to make them totally uncompetitive.

Devaluation of the franc became inevitable, but the government still faced a series
of difficult choices. On the one hand, it could take deflationary measures to reduce
spending on imports and lower the domestic rate of inflation so as to render exports
more competitive. On the other hand, it could withdraw to some degree from
international economic arrangements. If it left the European Monetary System,
devaluation could be used more freely to correct for domestic inflation. If it imposed
a temporary system of mandatory financial deposits on imports, as Britain and Italy
had once done, it could reduce imports without such a drastic deflation while still
remaining within the EEC. Finally, France could go all the way toward withdrawal
from the European community to maintain domestic reflation behind high tariff barriers.

President Mitterrand pondered his options in June 1982 and again in March 1983.[5]
Some close advisors, such as Jean Riboud the industrialist, and Pierre Bérégovoy, urged
him to withdraw from the European Monetary System in order to permit a more
radical devaluation and to introduce a scheme of mandatory deposits on imports so
as to restrict their inflow. The Communist Party was interested in a complete
withdrawal from the EEC. Others, like Prime Minister Pierre Mauroy and Finance
Minister Jacques Delors saw deflation as the best option.

In the end, Mitterrand opted for deflation and continuing openness to the international
economy. Several factors seem to have played a role in the decision. First, devaluation
of the franc was inevitable regardless of the route chosen. Second, even limited moves
to withdraw from these international arrangements might well have intensified pressure
against the franc, eliminated several sources of foreign exchange support and necessitated
an even greater austerity. Third, the move to complete autarchy behind high tariff
barriers represented a radical step away from the pan-European strategy on which
France's economic success since World War II had been based, toward a policy that

seemed to fly in the face of international sentiment and long-term global trends toward economic openness. The dangers of retaliation posed a severe threat to French exports. Finally, Elysée studies indicated that deflation would have had to accompany any of these strategies if domestic inflation and massive import shortages were to be avoided.

Therefore, it is not surprising that President Mitterrand opted to remain within the EMS and the EEC rather than embark on an unknown economic path with some perceptible dangers and few short-term rewards. To do otherwise would have entailed adopting a radical and long-term strategy of the sort that governments can rarely develop in the midst of an economic crisis.[6] Instead, he turned to a series of deflationary measures in the hope that the need for them would prove to be temporary.

In June 1982, the government froze wages and prices until the end of October and agreed to limit the public sector deficit to 3 per cent of GDP. To accomplish that, public spending was cut by 20 billion francs in 1982. In addition, a series of measures were taken to improve the competitive position of French business. The level of employers' social security contributions was frozen for a year; company tax was reduced by 10 per cent; a portion of the cost of family allowances was transferred from employers to employees; accelerated depreciation allowances were introduced and value added tax was removed from tools for three years. In total, these measures meant that the wage and benefits bill facing French industry in 1982-83 would grow at only half the rate of the preceding year.[7]

When these measures failed to stem the tide of speculation against the franc, deflationary measures were intensified in March 1983, as the franc was again devalued against the deutschmark. Public spending was cut by another 24 billion francs in 1983 and taxes were raised by 40 billion francs. Out of 22 million taxpayers, 15 million were to pay a new 1% surcharge on their taxable income and 8 million were to make a compulsory loan to the government of 10% of their taxes repayable in three years. Along with increases in expenditure taxes, an 8% limit was imposed on wage and price increases for the following year to be followed by decelerating indexation. In addition, severe exchange controls were imposed on outflows of francs, including those that French tourists could spend abroad.[8]

The principal objects of this policy were to reduce the rate of domestic inflation and the trade deficit by curbing consumer spending. Pierre Mauroy was explicit about the objectives: "I want to change the habits of this nation. If the French resign themselves to living with an inflation of 12%, then they should know that because of our economic interdependence with Germany, we will be led into a situation of imbalance. France must rid herself of this inflationary disease."[9]

At the same time, this austerity plan had another focus. It was designed to restore the profitability of industry. In 1981-82, the costs of reflation had been imposed primarily on French business. Most firms had increased their indebtedness in the face of rising wages and taxes. As a result, their investment plans had not picked up in line with the increase in consumer demand during those years. Mindful of this experience, the government deliberately manipulated the costs of austerity in 1982-84 so that they would be imposed on workers and consumers rather than the corporate sector. Business was to benefit from an increasing range of tax breaks. With this step, the French Socialists recognized explicitly not only international economic constraints but also the domestic constraints of the mixed economy. If business was not to be nationalized entirely, it had to be persuaded to invest and such investment depended on the maintenance of a satisfactory rate of profit.

THE THIRD STAGE: NEO-LIBERAL *RELANCE*

The third stage of Socialist policy is less distinct than the others but nonetheless important. As the 1986 elections approached, a change in the governing team was to be expected, and President Mitterrand faced a choice. He could return to an emphasis on "socialism as social justice" associated with Pierre Mauroy, Lionel Jospin and the Party's first two years in power or he could stress the image of "socialism as scientific efficiency" represented more fully by Laurent Fabius and Pierre Bérégovoy. He chose the latter, appointing Fabius as Prime Minister and Bérégovoy as Minister of Finance in June 1984. The decision reflected Mitterrand's long-term belief that the Socialists' electoral future would be more secure if it were seen as a party open to a broad center coalition based as much on the republican tradition as on classic socialism; and, not surprisingly, the Communists withdrew from the governing coalition.

In keeping with his reputation and the President's own wishes, Prime Minister Fabius embarked on a reflation designed to raise the purchasing power of the electorate prior to the next elections. However, that *relance* took a specific form. If the reflation of 1981–82 had been based on increases in public spending, the expansion of 1985–86 was to be based on reductions in taxation. Where the earlier reflation had redistributed resources to the least affluent, this one was to show more concern for the *cadres* and the corporate balance sheet. Such policies had been foreshadowed in 1982–83, notably by the corporate tax measures of March 1983 and the reductions in social security benefits that Bérégovoy negotiated in November 1982 and 1983, but they were reaffirmed in 1984–85. The rollbacks in public spending and redistributive programs that were to follow could be anticipated in Prime Minister Fabius' 1984 observation that "The state had encountered its outer limits; it should not move beyond them."[10]

The 1985 budget cut the tax burden by about 40 billion francs or 1 per cent of GDP. The *cadres*, in particular, benefitted from reductions in surtax and social security charges and corporate taxes were cut by 10 billion francs, following a similar reduction in 1984. However, indirect telephone and gasoline taxes, whose incidence is far more regressive, were increased by 9 billion francs. To maintain the budget deficit at 3 per cent of GDP, 5000 posts were to be cut from the Civil Service and subsidies to the nationalized industries reduced.

The 1986 budget followed suit. With the exceptions of research and development, the police, culture, justice and technical training, departmental budgets were reduced by 5 to 10% in order to make room for a 3% reduction in the basic rate of income tax and a 5% reduction in corporate taxes. In addition, those who had paid the 10% tax surcharge in 1983–84 were to be reimbursed with interest only three months before the March 1986 elections. The government's object was to increase real disposable income and French levels of investment again before the next election without seeming to forsake *rigueur* altogether. As the popularity of the Communists fell and that of the Rassemblement pour la République (RPR) rose, President Mitterrand was clearly more clearly more concerned about being outflanked on the Right than on the Left.

INDUSTRIAL POLICY

Over the 1981–86 period, the evolution of industrial policy paralleled developments on the macroeconomic front. The Socialist era opened with a radical decision to nationalize 36 private banks, two finance companies and 11 industrial conglomerates. Rather than purchase a controlling interest, as Michel Rocard and others suggested, President Mitterrand opted to buy 100% of their shares at a cost of 25 billion francs over the next four years. Building on its previous holdings, the state was now responsible for 24% of the employees, 32% of the sales, 30% of the exports and 60% of the annual investment in the industrial and energy sectors of the French economy.[11]

However, it took the government quite some time to decide how to utilize its new acquisitions and industrial policy more generally. President Mitterrand ran through five industry ministers in as many years. They began with the notion that public policy could be used to escape many of the constraints traditionally associated with a capitalist economy. With infusions of public capital, the nationalized industries were to maintain levels of investment, even though the failure of business confidence depressed investment in the private sector. Similarly, through ANVAR and the new FIM, the state would encourage the development of high-technology industries in the absence of venture capitalists willing to take the risk.[12] With this in mind, it was announced that 140 billion francs would be spent over five years on the electronics sector. And public aid tied to ambitious reorganization programs would prevent layoffs in threatened sectors like steel and coal, where the government's initial objectives were to produce 26 million tons of steel in 1986 (compared with 21 million tons in 1981) and 30 million tons of coal by 1990 (compared with 18 million tons in 1981), despite a massive decline in the production of each sector since 1970.

The approach was symbolized by the Socialists' initial attachment to the notion of building *filières* or vertical lines of production in each sector that would obviate the need to forsake some products in order to concentrate on the specialized niches or *créneaux* that the Giscardians had favored. They rejected the very distinction between rising and declining sectors in favor of the notion that new technology could save virtually everyone's job. Pierre Dreyfus, an early Minister of Industry, was fond of saying: "There are no condemned sectors; there are only outmoded technologies."[13]

In the first two years of the government's term, then, the nationalized industries were told to maintain employment levels and vast sums were deployed to prevent layoffs in the private sector. By 1983, however, the newly appointed heads of the nationalized industries were complaining that such demands from the Ministry of Industry would force them to run continuing losses; and the government realized that even industrial aid would have to be reduced if the budget deficit were to be held at 3 per cent of GDP. In the face of a fiscal squeeze, the state could not afford to remain the principal source of industrial investment. Hence, a liberalization of industrial policy followed naturally from the imposition of *rigueur*. It began when Jean Pierre Chevènement was replaced by Laurent Fabius as Minister of Industry in February 1983.

Fabius continued to privilege the promotion of high technology. He created a new savings bond (the CODEVI) designed to draw private savings into the modernization fund administered by the FIM. Along with a growing number of his colleagues, however, he realized that French industry would have to be competitive in world markets if it was to grow, and to that end layoffs would have to be accepted in the nationalized industries, as elsewhere. Over the ensuing three years, those industries were gradually given greater operating freedom and, in line with the tightening fiscal exigencies of the state, their principal mission was to be, not the creation of jobs, but the achievement of profitability.

Funding for both the nationalized sector and industrial subsidies was cut back progressively in the budgets of 1984 and 1985. New plans for the coal and steel sectors, promulgated in March 1984, sought 25,000 layoffs in each and reduced the production targets to 11 million tons of coal and 18 million tons of steel in the coming years. At the same time, 5,000 jobs were declared redundant in shipbuilding. In September of that year, a plan calling for the elimination of 16,000 jobs at the former *vedette* of the nationalized sector, Régie Renault, was negotiated with the unions, and 6,000 more layoffs were declared necessary in 1985. The loss of jobs in declining sectors was not as surprising as the Socialists' new willingness to agree to them.

Effective management became the watchword of the government, as the chief executive of Régie Renault was replaced in the face of continuing losses and the old steel firm of Creusot Loire was allowed to go bankrupt when its directors refused to accede to government instructions in return for state aid. The state's strategy for increasing investment began to shift. Where it had relied originally on the nationalized sector and public subsidies to inspire investment, the government now hoped that reductions in corporate taxes and social security contributions would combine with continuing wage restraint to improve the profitability and investment plans of the private sector. As in the macroeconomic sphere, the Socialists' industrial policy had come full circle.

MACROECONOMIC PERFORMANCE

How well has the French economy performed under this set of policies? In May 1981, the Socialists promised a resurgence of growth and their opponents predicted disaster. The outcome has been neither as rosy nor as dire as the two sides anticipated. We might best gauge the Socialists' performance in comparison with that of the French economy in the preceding five years under President Valéry Giscard d'Estaing and Prime Minister Raymond Barre (see table 3.1). On average the French economy did not perform as well in 1981-85 as it did in 1976-80. Levels of growth and unemployment were particularly disappointing. However, it should be noted that the Socialists inherited an especially difficult economic situation. In 1980, the rate of inflation stood at 12.2 per cent, two oil price shocks and a chronically overvalued franc had put the trade balance heavily into deficit and the rate of unemployment had

Table 3.1 French economic performance under the socialists

Annual % change*	Average 1976-80	1981	1982	1983	1984	1985	Average 1981-85
Gross domestic product	3.3	0.5	1.8	0.7	1.6	1.3	1.2
Unemployment*	5.2	7.6	8.6	8.6	9.3	10.5	8.9
GDP price deflator	10.1	11.8	12.6	9.5	7.1	5.0	9.2
Investment* (GFCF % GDP)	21.7	21.5	21.2	20.6	19.8	20.0	20.6
Exports (volume)	7.1	5.1	- 1.7	3.4	6.9	4.3	3.6
Imports (volume)	9.3	1.8	5.8	- 1.5	2.3	3.1	2.3
Productivity (GDP/emplt.)	3.0	1.5	1.9	1.1	2.4	3.0	2.0
Current balance* (b.$US)	0.5	- 1.7	- 12.1	- 4.4	- 0.1	0	- 3.7
Budget deficit* (% GDP)	0.7	2.6	2.9	3.1	3.2	3.0	3.0
Real disposable income	2.6	2.9	2.7	- 0.3	- 0.7	1.1	1.1

Note:
* Indicates level rather than percentage change
Sources: OECD *Economic Survey: France* (July 1985); *L'Expansion* (8 March 1985); *Le Monde: bilan économique et social 1985*.

Table 3.2 The ratio of French economic performance to EEC averages[1]

Period	GDP growth	Level of unemployment	Average rate of inflation	Capital formation as percent of GDP
Giscard (1976-80)	1.09	.97	1.09	1.05
Mitterrand (1981-85)	1.0	.91	.97	1.06

Note:
[1]The figures in the table are the average French performance figures expressed as a ratio of (i.e. divided by) average performance figures for the European Economic Community nations over the period.

increased for six years in a row to 6.3 per cent. Levels of profit, investment, growth and employment had been in secular decline since 1975 and 1981-85 levels were barely below trend.

By contrast, the Socialists left the economy in relatively good shape in 1986. The annual rate of inflation was down to 5 per cent, the external account was heading toward surplus and both growth and investment were picking up after several stagnant years. Paradoxically, we can attribute these results to the peculiar effectiveness with which the Socialists had been able to impose economic austerity on the French populace. Despite Barre's reputation as an economic strongman, he had not been able to reduce transfer payments or disposable income to the extent the Socialists did. From the point of view of the Left it may be a dubious distinction, but Mitterrand was finally able to tackle a number of long-standing economic problems that had eluded the Right so as to limit the dangerous increase in imports, eliminate continuing imbalances in the budget for social security and revive the French stock market.

To allow for the impact of international trends, it would be more fair to judge the Socialists in terms of their performance relative to other EEC economies. For this purpose, table 3.2 reports the average French performance figures for 1976-80 and

and 1981-85 expressed as a ratio of the average performance figures for the EEC nations over these periods. The results are quite striking: French performance under Mitterrand was not significantly worse than under Giscard. In each period, the French results were quite close to the European average. On a year-to-year basis, the performance of the French economy did not correspond exactly to the European average since the macroeconomic stance of France in 1976-80 paralleled those of her European neighbors whereas the 1981-82 expansion and 1983-85 retrenchment put France out of step with the neighboring economies. In effect, the French Socialists behaved as several British Labour governments had before them. They used up most of the economic increment available to them in an early burst of expansion only to spend the rest of their term in office clawing back the transfer payments and income gains that various groups of workers had initially secured.

Some argue that the Socialists squandered the nation's patrimony in a fruitless dash for growth. According to this view, the devaluation of the French franc, growing public-sector deficit and rising external debt represent costs that will be imposed on future administrations. However, most of these fears seem to be groundless. When Mitterrand took office, the French franc was seriously overvalued on all conventional measures; thus, the Socialists' devaluations should be seen as a necessary corrective emulated shortly thereafter by an incoming Gaullist administration. The foreign debt did grow by about 27 million dollars (US) in 1980-84, but it had grown by almost exactly the same amount in 1974-80 and the French credit rating on international markets remained strong. Similarly, the French budget deficit grew from 1.6% of GDP in 1980 to 3.3% in 1985; but this was a period in which the average budget deficit in the EEC also grew from 3.8% to 6.5%.[14] Although interest payments on the public debt grew to 86 billion francs (8% of GDP) in 1985, enough to constrain budgetary policy quite considerably, a contemporary trend toward declining interest rates was likely to alleviate the problem in a short space of time.

More serious perhaps are the charges that the economic performance of France would have been significantly better if the government had adopted quite different policies. In general, three main alternatives have been proposed: an earlier devaluation in 1981 or more drastic devaluation in 1982; continuing domestic reflation behind protectionist trade barriers; and a different fiscal or monetary stance in 1981-82 or 1983-85. The issues are rather hypothetical, but some observations can be made about them.

Since the franc was overvalued and French unit labor costs were uncompetitive in 1981, President Mitterrand probably should have devalued immediately upon taking office, as new socialist governments did in Sweden and Spain about a year later. French reserves of foreign exchange were rather high in 1981 and might not have been eroded to the same degree over the ensuing two years. Moreover, the measure would probably not have been as politically unpopular as Mitterrand seems to have imagined it.[15] However, devaluation was no panacea for French problems, as the next five years were to demonstrate. Since world markets for French goods were relatively depressed in 1981-82, the immediate export advantages were likely to be small. Most important, although it is often regarded as a substitute to deflation, devaluation almost always requires an accompanying deflation in order to limit its inflationary effects (via higher import prices) and potential pressure on the trade balance (as more expensive imports are sucked into the economy before compensating improvements appear in exports). That would certainly have interfered with the Socialists' plans to reflate the economy.

Perhaps those very plans should have been scaled down: less reflation in 1981–82 might have rendered the need for austerity in 1983–85 less intense. A more cautious macroeconomic stance in 1981–82 now seems to have been desirable. However, economic management would not be so difficult if such judgements could always be made with the benefit of hindsight. On the basis of widespread forecasts of world recovery in 1982, it was not unreasonable for President Mitterrand to reflate that year.[16] He could expect growing international demand to diminish France's balance of payments deficit. At worst we can say that Mitterrand gambled boldly and lost.

In so doing, he provided a perfect refutation of many political business-cycle theories. Those theories suggest that it is most rational for a government to impose austerity early on in its term so that the electorate will forget it later when room has been made for reflation closer to the next election. This is usually seen as economically inefficient but politically optimal.[17] The economic policies of the French Socialists were neither as cautious nor as strategically planned as this model would lead us to expect. Here as elsewhere socialist policy was composed in a rather *ad hoc* fashion, responding incrementally to events of the day.[18] In contrast to the long-standing view that left-wing governments are less flexible and more oriented toward long-term reform, in the 1980s it was conservative governments that came to office with more rigid ideologies and more strategic plans than their socialist counterparts.

Finally, it can be argued that the Socialists should have taken protectionist measures in order to reflate behind a set of tariff barriers.[19] Given the current openness of the French economy, there is no doubt that sustained reflation would have been possible only if such barriers were present to limit the degree to which the spending power injected into the economy was spent on imports. However, it is not at all certain that sustained reflation would be possible even in these circumstances. In a context where imports are very expensive or limited in quantity, an expansion of demand is likely to be highly inflationary, as the prices of complementary goods are bid up and shortages appear before French sources of production can be generated. Hence, protection might well have to be accompanied by deflation and/or rationing. In a nation that currently imports a fifth of its purchases, living standards are likely to be lowered by any measure that raised the price or limited the availability of such commodities. Moreover, any retaliation from the purchasers of French exports would likely lead to layoffs and plant closures in that fifth of the French economy that depends on export sales.

The economic case for a siege economy was weak. At the very least, it would have entailed a complete reorientation away from the strategy on which 30 years of French growth had been based, toward an unknown endstate. The short-term adjustment costs would have been considerable and the long-term return highly uncertain. Such a move would also have had serious political ramifications. It implied rejection of the European Economic Community on which the peace of the continent and France's independent foreign policy stance had been based. It is not surprising that President Mitterrand shied away from such a strategy.

In short, while some variation in the timing and intensity of devaluation and the macroeconomic stance might have improved the overall level of France's economic performance in 1981–85, the room for maneuver was probably not great. French levels of growth, unemployment and inflation were close to the European averages, and there are few grounds for thinking that macroeconomic policy could have been substantially different given prevailing international economic and domestic constraints.

MICROECONOMIC PERFORMANCE

Any hope for a serious break with the past probably rested in the sphere of industrial policy. After two decades of phenomenal growth, France's economic industrial performance relative to those of her principal competitors began a secular decline after 1974; and that decline seems most closely associated with the eroding competitiveness of French industry at the microeconomic level. After growing steadily for 30 years, the French share of world exports began to decline, and European competitors in particular began to take an increasing share of the French markets for consumer durables and industrial goods, just as French products lost market share elsewhere on the continent. A long-standing pattern of dependence on "diplomatic" exports to the developing world (turnkey plants, arms, aircraft and nuclear equipment) finally took its toll on France's ability to compete for European markets. As Robert Boyer has argued, the long-term prospects for growth seemed to depend more on industrial restructuring than on macroeconomic management.[20]

How effective was the Socialists' industrial policy? This is difficult to measure partly because the long-term results are not yet visible; however, here too the verdict must be mixed. The annual increase in productivity under the Socialists, especially in industry, was slightly better than under Barre; but levels of investment continued to stagnate. The total volume of industrial investment fell by 7% in 1982 and 4% in 1983 before recovering in 1984 (10%) and in 1985. These figures contain a subtle commentary on the Socialists' policies. Their 1981–82 strategy, designed to increase industrial investment through reflation and massive infusions of capital into the nationalized industries, failed.[21] Investment picked up only in 1984–85 when the government shifted to a policy of reducing the tax burden on private enterprise and squeezing wages so that the corporate self-financing ratio and share of profits in value added would increase.[22] Once again, the structural constraints of a capitalist economy, in which investment depends on the rate of profit, had serious implications for the effectiveness of various Socialist policies.

The most prominent aspect of Mitterrand's platform, of course, was the nationalization program undertaken in 1982. Despite many dire predictions, the newly nationalized industries (Bull, CGE, CGCT, Péchiney, Saint-Gobain, Rhône-Poulenc and Thomson) were effectively restructured. If only one of these firms made a profit in 1982, only one was still in the red in 1985.[23] After some initial hesitation, the government gave its appointees at the heads of these industries considerable autonomy to undertake offshore investments, joint ventures with foreign firms and layoffs where appropriate. Nationalization facilitated the rationalization of many of these enterprises around more specialized corporate groups, especially in chemicals, steel and electronics.[24]

However, those on the Left who hoped that nationalization would also inspire new forms of work organization, marked by various systems of workers' control, were disappointed, as were those who thought that nationalization might somehow permit rationalization without layoffs. The Socialists proved to be effective managers of nationalized enterprise, but their very success at emulating the ruthlessness of private management raised some questions about the rationale for nationalization in the first place.[25]

In other spheres, Socialist industrial policy seems to have followed the broad lines established by preceding regimes. Ambitious restructuring programs were implemented in the electronics, machine-tools and textile sectors with some favorable results.[26] Notwithstanding a growing number of layoffs and plant closures after 1983, many of the declining sectors continued to receive large state subsidies. In 1981–84, for instance, the shipbuilding sector received subsidies totalling about 400,000 francs a year for each of the remaining 15,000 employees there.[27] Despite the elimination of deficits in the public enterprises responsible for coal (CdF), electricity (EdF) and gas (GdF), the steel (Usinor and Sacilor), railway (SNCF) and maritime (CGM) corporations remained black holes into which state funds were poured seemingly without end; and Régie Renault, once the model public enterprise, lost 12.5 billion francs in 1984 and 11 billion francs again in 1985.[28]

The most striking development in this sphere was the active manpower policy initiated by the Socialists. From 1981 a variety of innovative schemes were devised to deal with rising levels of unemployment, including the creation of public-sector jobs (135,000), early retirement programs (244,000), a reduction in the workweek to 39 hours (40,000), youth training (10,000) and negotiated industry or region-specific programs (179,000).[29] A system of part-time public employment for youth took another 140,000 off the unemployment rolls in 1984–85. Partly as a result, France lost only 436,000 jobs in 1981–84, compared with 1.3 million in Britain and 1.1 million in West Germany over the same period.[30]

In assessing these programs, we should distinguish between those that were designed to create jobs, those that provided training or limited work experience and those that simply reduced the active labor force or rates of participation in it. Very rough estimates suggest that, in total, the first type of program contributed to the creation of about 300,000 jobs; the second inspired about 570,000 people to withdraw from the labor force and the third provided another 571,000 with temporary employment or training programs lasting six months or more each year.[31] Obviously the value of each kind of program varies. For instance, the immensely popular system of early retirement did not creat any new jobs: it simply transferred existing positions from one group (the new retirees) to another (those who replaced them). But for these groups it made unemployment a voluntary act rather than an enforced idleness, transferring jobs from those who least wanted them to those who wanted them the most, and on conventional criteria, the welfare of both groups should thereby be increased. Similarly, where new jobs were created, their social value varied according to the extent to which they became permanent positions and contributed to the net productive capacity of the nation. The apprenticeship programs and internships for young people also made a contribution to the nations's human capital that varied according to the degree to which the training or work experience actually contributed to the participants' ability to find permanent employment.

In aggregate, these programs constituted something less than the long-standing systems of manpower planning found in nations like Sweden.[32] Their training component was not nearly as substantial as the portion designed to subsidize employment. They were also quite costly (3.4 per cent of GDP in 1983). Hence, most of these programs could serve only as temporary measures to relieve a conjunctural crisis. The early retirement scheme was terminated in 1984 when its 44 billion franc cost began to exceed that of unemployment insurance itself. Nevertheless, these programs were an important step away from reliance on macroeconomic management toward the use of direct measures against unemployment.

THE DISTRIBUTIVE EFFECTS OF SOCIALIST GOVERNMENT

We cannot judge the performance of a regime simply in aggregate terms. Most economic policies also redistribute resources away from some groups and toward others. This aspect of Mitterrand's policies was especially important. The government came to office with an explicitly redistributive project, which it began to implement in 1981-82. However, the austerity measures taken in 1983-85 entailed a shift in the distributive component of the government's strategy as well as in its macroeconomic stance. In this case there are two axes along which income distribution can be considered. The first concerns the distribution of resources between the household and corporate sectors. The second concerns the distribution of resources within the household sector.

In the 1981-82 period, resources were distributed away from private corporations toward households, notably by adding a fifth week of paid vacation and reducing the workweek to 39 hours; and within the household sector, resources were shifted from upper to lower-income earners by disproportionate increases in transfer payments and the SMIC. In 1983-85, the new concern with industrial competitiveness and investment inspired a deliberate effort to return resources to private corporations at the expense of households; and the new emphasis on tax reductions rather than spending increases brought relief to higher-income earners while transfer payments to the least affluent were being cut back. As a result, income redistribution under the Mitterrand government followed a U-shaped course over time along both axes.

One good indicator for the distribution of income between the corporate and household sectors of the economy is the share of value added devoted to wages. From 57.4% in 1980, that share rose to a peak of 58.5% in 1981. It was stabilized at 58% in 1982 and 1983 only to fall to 55.6% in 1985 and 53.9% in 1986.[33] This was one of the less-publicized objects and principal successes of the incomes policy operated by the government during the last three years of its term. Largely as a consequence, corporate profitability, which had been depressed in 1981, rose steadily over the rest of the period, and, somewhat ironically, share values on the Paris stock exchange reached unprecedented heights under a Socialist administration.

Within the household sector, the 1981-82 period saw a redistribution of income toward the less affluent. For instance, the ratio of the average hourly salary to the minimum wage fell from 1.33 in 1980 to 1.26 in 1983, as millions of low-paid workers benefitted from statutory increases in the SMIC. Similarly, the purchasing power of old-age pensioners entitled to only the minimum pension increased by 18 per cent between 1981 and 1983, while the pensions of more affluent *cadres* and non-*cadres* remained relatively flat. Millions of other workers gained from a fifth week of paid vacation per year and a reduction in the workweek to 39 hours without a corresponding drop in salary. In general, the economic measures of 1981–82 enhanced the purchasing power of the working class as a whole while privileging lower-paid workers and those supported by state expenditures.

The austerity measures of 1983–85, however, tended to reduce the purchasing power of virtually every social group. After rising by 2.9% in 1981 and 2.7% in 1982, real disposable income fell on average by 0.3% in 1983 and 0.7% in 1984 before recovering to grow by 1.1% in 1985. As table 3.3 indicates, skilled and white-collar workers were hit as heavily by these measures as the upper-income groups. Because the redistributive measures of 1981–82 provided many lower-income earners with a cushion, however, they did not see their purchasing power drop as radically over the entire 1981–85 period as did that of many upper-income earners (see table 3.4). On balance, therefore, the Socialists could legitimately claim to have reduced income inequality by the time they left office; but, after three years of austerity, most workers were more likely to recall their recent loss of purchasing power rather than their long-term gain in relative income.[34]

The distributive impact of austerity was also intensified by reductions in social spending. In order to limit the budget deficit in the midst of recession, the government ultimately had to cut back the very same transfer programs that it had expanded in

Table 3.3 Average change in real disposable income in France 1981–84

Social group	1981–82	1982–83	1983–84
Higher Managers	− 1.6	− 2.4	− 0.5
Middle Managers	− 1.0	− 1.2	− 1.4
Clerical Employees	0.9	− 0.5	− 1.8
Technicians	2.0	− 0.3	− 1.8
Skilled workers	3.0	0.1	− 1.6
Laborers	2.1	− 0.1	− 1.3

Source: Centre des Etudes des Revenus et Coûts.

Table 3.4 Variations in real disposable income per household, 1980–85 (% change)

	Inactive	Workers	Farm workers	Clerical employees	Farmers	Middle managers	Self-employed	Higher managers
1980–82	+ 5	+ 2	+ 4	+ 1	+ 6	0	0	− 1
1982–85	+ 2	− 3	− 6	− 4	− 10	− 5	− 7	− 6

Source: *Le Nouvel economiste*, 529 (21 February 1986).

1981–82. As a result, even the minimum old-age pension and family allowances were reduced in real terms during 1983–84. The average level of unemployment benefits was also cut by about 10 per cent during 1984–85 so as to reduce the growing deficit of the social security system. In distributional terms, the unemployment benefits of those who once held higher-paying jobs fell substantially less during 1984–85 than did the benefits of those who had less-than-average earnings or a more uncertain employment situation.[35] That tended to intensify the existing discrepancies of income and security associated with different positions in the labor market. Moreover, almost 40 per cent of the registered unemployed remained uncovered by these schemes in 1985. A substantial portion of these were young workers, single mothers and unemployed individuals with large families. They had to live on a varying mixture of family allowances and welfare payments that often left them in abject poverty. The growing numbers of people who could neither find work nor qualify for unemployment benefits contributed to a growing perception after 1982 of *la nouvelle pauvreté* in Socialist France.[36]

CONCLUSION

In order to understand the economic fate of the Mitterrand government, it may be useful to think of its task as one of achieving appropriate demand-side and supply-side conditions for growth. For the growing demand that inspires firms to invest, the government could look to international expansion in the economies of its trading partners or to domestic consumption that might be stimulated by higher levels of wages and government spending. However, rising demand generates sustained growth only in the presence of appropriate supply-side conditions. In a mixed economy, the latter include: competitive unit labor costs (which allow French firms to sell more cheaply than their competitors), liquid corporate balance sheets (which enable firms to raise funds for investment) and favorable interest rates (which render productive investment feasible and more attractive than financial speculation). Although this schema is oversimplified, it allows us to understand why the Mitterrand government encountered economic problems.

In 1981, the government concentrated almost exclusively on the demand side of this equation. It expected an imminent expansion of international demand and reflated the domestic economy in the interim. However, the government does not seem to have given enough consideration to the adverse supply-side conditions left over from the preceding regime. Rising unit labor costs in 1980–81 rendered French industry uncompetitive in European markets. The self-financing rate of French firms – a good indicator of corporate liquidity – had fallen dramatically in 1980–81 to its lowest level in 20 years. Under American influence, real interest rates were climbing to a post-war peak in 1981. Therefore, French firms were not in the best position to take advantage of demand expansion in 1981. The new industrial policies of the Socialists were all oriented to the longer term; in the short term their effects on business confidence were likely to be negative. To make matters worse, the international expansion expected in 1982 did not materialize. As a result, the investment plans of French industry failed to respond to the increase in domestic demand, which led instead to an influx of imports.

As it grappled with the growing trade deficit in 1982-83, the government eventually realized that supply-side conditions in the private sector also needed attention. Accordingly, it devalued the franc, imposed an incomes policy to limit French wage increases and reduced corporate taxes. Over the next two years, these measures improved the state of French industry to a considerable extent. The ratio of the unit labor costs of France's main trading partners to French labor costs rose from 91 in 1981 to 98 in 1984. The rate of corporate self-financing rose from 49.4 per cent in 1982 to 71.2 per cent in 1984. And international interest rates fell sufficiently to render industrial investment a more attractive proposition in France. In 1983-85, therefore, supply-side conditions in France were again more favorable to growth and investment.

However, these supply-side measures, in turn, reduced the level of domestic demand in France. As real disposable income fell in 1983 and 1984, under the impact of rising taxes and a wage squeeze, consumer spending in France also fell. At long last, the international economy had expanded sufficiently to increase the volume of French exports by an annual average of 4.6 per cent in 1983-85, but that was not enough. In the absence of growing domestic demand, levels of investment and production in France continued to stagnate. They began to pick up again only in the last 12 months of the government's term in office, as the trade deficit improved sufficiently to permit another mild reflation just before the 1986 elections. After the dashed hopes of 1981-82 and three years of austerity, however, this last-minute improvement in performance was hardly adequate to restore the electorate's faith in the economic management of the Socialists. A newly elected conservative government was to benefit from the improved supply-side conditions that the Socialists left it.

In short, Mitterrand encountered some bad luck on the international front. Global expansion did not materialize as expected in 1982. International interest rates, the (US) dollar and world oil prices remained high to reduce the rate of growth of French GDP by about 2 per cent in 1982-83.[37] Otherwise, his reflationary gamble of 1981-82 might have succeeded. Similarly, he inherited a particularly difficult economic situation. The preceding regime had not taken effective measures to stem rising unit labor costs, a growing trade deficit, climbing levels of unemployment and falling levels of corporate liquidity. The supply-side conditions of French industry were particularly adverse in 1981. At a more fundamental level, however, the economic timing of the Socialists was off. Caution would have dictated a policy that corrected supply-side conditions before embarking on a major expansion of domestic demand so that French producers might be in a favorable position to take advantage of rising demand. In fact, the sequence of French policy was reversed.

Hence, the story of Mitterrand's economic policies yields several lessons for socialist governments. It suggests that the economic and political fates of a regime are intertwined at numerous levels. The Socialists lost the 1986 legislative elections partly because their economic performance did not match the high expectations they had raised during several decades of opposition. Although they performed about as well as other administrations facing comparable economic challenges, their rhetoric had prepared the electorate for adventure rather than austerity. Moreover, like the British Labour government of 1974-79, the French Socialists spent the increment of public resources most readily available to a new administration in the first 18 months of their term in office, leaving little room for economic stimulus or innovative social spending in the later years of the regime. Any voters inclined to ask "What have you done for me lately?" found only negative answers during the run-up to the 1986 elections. In periods of international economic retrenchment at least, Socialist politicians would do well to temper the optimism of their promises in favor of a rhetoric of crisis and conscience that the Right has recently appropriated from them. The Mitterrand government turned in this direction too late to avoid dashed expectations and an impression of *volte-face* in the face of mismanaged circumstances.

The turn toward austerity itself might have been less abrupt if the Socialists had developed a more complete appreciation of the degree to which their policies would have to mesh with the existing institutional structures of a mixed domestic economy and an increasingly interdependent world economy. Many influential members of the Socialist Party were not fully reconciled to the mixed economy.[38] At best they saw the private sector as an element of the economy to be tolerated rather than cultivated. Many hoped that the new nationalized industries would become the real motor behind French economic performance.

Even after the extensive nationalizations of 1981–82, however, over half of French production and employment remained under the control of private capital; and continuing membership in the EEC meant that French firms, whether public or private, would still have to compete with foreign business in domestic and world markets. Hence, the nationalized industries alone could not stem rising levels of imports or unemployment; and the matrix of incentives facing private capital had to be structured quite carefully if overall levels of production and investment were to remain buoyant. The initial increases in business taxation, ancillary costs per employee, and corporate regulation associated with the social programs of 1981–82, while far from devastating, tended to discourage a response in investment commensurate with the fiscal stimulus of those years.[39] It remains to be seen whether the principal objectives of a socialist program can accommodate a concern for market incentives and resource flexibility in the remaining private sectors of a mixed economy. Nevertheless, the attractive distributional fruits of coincident growth in the public and private sectors render that a goal worth pursuing.

If a consideration of the constraints implicit in capitalism sharpens our critique of the French Socialists, however, it also partially exonerates them. As we have seen, the preceding government did only slightly better at the cost of borrowing on Socialist time. The task of achieving a balance between supply-side and demand-side conditions that will generate growth is not easy. Many of the conventional measures used to correct one side of the equation worsen conditions on the other side; and there is much to be said for the *regulation* school view that the institutional preconditions underpinning an earlier balance have broken down.[40] No one has been quite sure what to put in their place, and the complete range of tasks associated with economic rejuvenation may well be beyond the immediate capacities of any government.

In short, the 1981–86 period of Socialist rule is best viewed as another stage in the long learning-curve of both the French Left and the French electorate. In future, the Socialists are likely to be less sanguine about the virtues of unrestricted Keynesianism even if a coherent alternative on the Left has yet to be developed. Similarly, the French voters are less likely to view another Socialist government as a transformative force worthy of euphoria or despair. Although the Socialists failed to forge a lasting coalition between workers and professionals that was capable of keeping them in power, they emerged from the 1981-86 years with an enhanced reputation for fiscal responsibility, and current public opinion polls suggest that substantial electoral support remains for socialism, participation and social spending in France.[41] Another Socialist government would not be quite as intimidating a prospect as it was for many in 1981. At the same time, however, the Socialists are faced with the daunting task of reforging their program in such a way as to give more realistic importance to the constraints of a mixed economy without sacrificing the transformative vision that has always been at the heart of French socialism. That is not an easy problem; but in economic terms at least, the Mitterrand years do not seem to mark the end of an era in French socialism so much as an intellectual and electoral step forward.

NOTES

1 See the interview with President Mitterrand in *Le Témoinage chrétien*, (11-17 July 1983), p. 17; and Thierry Pfister, *La Vie quotidienne à Matignon au temps de l'union de la gauche* (Paris, Hachette, 1985), ch. 5.

2 See Alain Fonteneau and Alain Gubian, "Comparaison des relances économiques de 1975 et 1981-82", *Problèmes économiques*, 1956 (8 Jan. 1986), pp. 3-11.

3 See Fontenau and Gubian, "Comparaison des relances", p. 8.

4 See *Le Monde*, (24 March 1983).

5 This account is based on Pfister, *La Vie quotidienne*, and Philippe Bauchard, *La Guerre des deux roses* (Paris, Grasset, 1986), chs. 2, 3.

6 British Labour governments had been equally unwilling to embrace a radical economic strategy in the midst of the exchange rate crises of 1967 and 1976 despite far less attachment to the European Economic Community.

7 *L'Express*, (25 June 1982); *Le Monde*, (1 Jan. 1983).

8 *Le Monde*, (26-7 March 1983).

9 *L'Express*, (8 April 1983), pp. 38-9.

10 Cited in the excellent introduction by Howard Machin and Vincent Wright to their edited collection *Economic Policy and Policy-making under the Mitterrand Presidency 1981-1984* (London, Frances Pinter, 1985), p. 3.

11 See André Delion and Michel Durupty, *Les Nationalisations 1983* (Paris, Economica, 1982); *Revue économique*, (May 1983): Christian Stoffaës, "The Nationalizations 1981-1984: An Initial Assessment", in Machin and Wright (eds), *Economic Policy and Policy-making Under the Mitterrand Presidency 1981-1984* (London, Frances Pinter, 1985), pp. 144-68; and Peter A. Hall, "Socialism in One Country: Mitterrand and the Struggle to Define a New Economic Policy for France", in *Socialism, the State and Public Policy in France*, eds Philip Cerny and Martin Schain, (New York, Methuen, 1985).

12 ANVAR or the Agence Nationale pour la Valorisation de la Recherche was established in 1968 but revitalized by the Socialists for the purpose of improving the technological level of French industry. FIM or the Fonds Industriel de Modernisation was created by Industry Minister Laurent Fabius in April 1983 as a state investment bank to channel 8 billion francs over 1983-84 in low-interest loans to firms seeking to modernize. See Diana Green, "Administered Industrialisation: Managing Industrial Crisis in France", in *Managing Industrial Crisis*, eds Kenneth Dyson and Stephen Wilks (London, Martin Robertson, 1984); André de Lattre, M. Pebereau and Christian Stoffaës, *La Politique economique de la France* (Paris, Institut de'Etudes Politiques, 1983); and Béla Belassa, "La Politique industrielle socialiste", *Commentaire*, 8, 30 (Summer 1985), pp. 579-89.

13 *Le Monde*, (24 March 1983), p. 16; cf. *L'Express*, (19 Nov. 1982), p. 44.

14 Vito Tanzi, "Public Expenditure and Public Debt", *Administration*, 34 (1986), pp. 16-37.

15 See Bauchard, *La Guerre des deux roses*, ch. 1.

16 See Alain Fonteneau, "Les Erreurs des prévisions économiques pour 1982", *Observations et diagnostics économiques*, (4 June 1983).

17 See James Alt and Alec Chrystal, *Political Economics* (Berkeley, University of California Press, 1984), for a broad introduction to this literature.

18 This is the impression conveyed by most accounts of policy-making inside the government. See Pfister, *La Vie quotidienne*; Bauchard, *La Guerre des deux roses*; and Gabriel Milesi, *Jacques Delors* (Paris, Belfond, 1985).

19 See Alain Lipietz, *L'Audace ou l'enlisement* (Paris, SYROS, 1982).

20 Robert Boyer, "From Growth to Crisis: The Changing Linkages Between Industrial and Macroeconomic Policies". Paper presented to a conference on industrial policy in France at the Brookings Institution, Washington, D.C., September 1984.

21 The Socialists put about 21 billion francs a year into the nationalized industries in 1982-84.

22 For a complementary, but slightly different, argument see Jeffrey Sachs and Charles Wyplosz, "Mitterrand's Economic Policies", *Economic Policy*, (April 1986), pp. 261-305.

23 See Jean Gloaguen, "Nationalisées: la vérité des chiffres", *Le Nouvel economiste*, 527 (7 Feb. 1986), pp. 54-58; and Henri Rouilleault, "Groupes publics et politique industrielle", *Problèmes economiques*, 1963 (26 Feb. 1986), pp. 5-15.

24 See Stoffaës, "The Nationalizations 1981-1984".

25 See the introduction to Machin and Wright (eds), *Economic Policy and Policy-making*, for a more extensive discussion of this issue.

26 See Hall, "Socialism in One Country" and de Lattre et al., *La Politique économique*.

27 *Le Monde*, (16 March 1986), p. 17.

28 *Le Monde*, (30 March 1986), p. 13.

29 The figures in parentheses indicate the approximate number of persons removed from the unemployment rolls by each program. See Jean-François Colin, Michel Elbaum and Alain Fonteneau, "Chômage et politique de l'emploi: 1981-83", *Observations et diagnostics économiques: revue de l'OFCE*, (7 April 1984).

30 Bela Belassa, "Five Years of Socialist Economic Policy in France: A Balance Sheet", *Commentaire*, 33 (Spring 1986), pp. 62-71; *Le Monde*, (25 March 1986), p. 44.

31 These are very rough estimates compiled from the detailed discussion in Alain Fonteneau and Pierre-Alain Muet, (eds) *La Gauche face à la crise* (Paris, Fondation Nationale des Sciences Politiques, 1985). ch. 5. As such, they must be treated with caution. In particular, we do not know precisely how long the jobs whose creation was directly associated with the Socialist programs lasted nor how many of these might have been created even in the absence of these programs.

32 See Jonas Pontusson, "Comparative Political Economy of Advanced Capitalist States", *Kapitalistate*, (1984), pp. 43-73.

33 "Situation de l'économie Française", *Problèmes économiques*, 1959 (29 Jan. 1986), p. 28.

34 Cf. Christine Mital, "Les Largesses du Souverain", *L'Expansion*, (22 June 1984), p. 69.

35 See Centre d'Etude des Revenus et des Couts, *Constat de l'evolution récente des revenus en France (1981-1984)* (Paris, La Documentation Française, 1985), pp. 104-7; *Le Monde*, (18 Nov. 1985), p. 34; and (15 April 1986), p. 37. In 1984 almost half of the unemployed received no benefits; one third received about 30% of the SMIC; and another third received about 80% of the SMIC.

36 See Elisabeth Pascaud and Bernard Simonin, "La Pauvreté et le précarité, diversité des recours a l'aide sociale", *Consommation et modes de vie*, 9 (March 1986); and *Le Monde*, (9 April 1986), p. 37.

37 See Pierre-Alain Muet, "Economic Management and the International Environment, 1981-83", in Machin and Wright (eds), *Economic Policy and Policy-making* p. 82.

38 This statement applies even more fully to the Socialists' coalition partner, the French Communist Party.

39 See Jeffrey Sachs and Charles Wyplosz, "The Economic Consequences of President Mitterrand", *Economic Policy*, 2 (April 1986).

40 See Robert Boyer and Jacques Mistral, *Accumulation, inflation, crises* (Paris, Presses Universitaires de France, 1983); Alain Lipietz, *La Crise* (Paris, Serios, 1983).

41 See *Le Point*, 649 (25 February 1985), p. 37.

III
The Left in Power and the Evolution of French Political Life

Introduction

The Left's victories in May and June 1981 were viewed as a great turning-point. Speakers for the Left, in particular, concluded that at last the institutional facts of French politics had caught up with its sociology. The *France de gauche* that had voted for the Right in 1978 (to paraphrase the title of an important study of the 1978 election) had finally voted Left.[1] Many felt that the events of 1981 would inaugurate a period of Left power comparable to the 23 years that the Right had enjoyed after 1958. Such feelings were premature, however. By 1983 the Left was in rapid electoral decline after its initial reforms had angered many and pleased few, having suffered a merciless buffeting by the disastrous, if somewhat hidden, economic situation of France, compounded by its own "state of grace" policies. These events, plus the government's dramatic policy changes, accentuated disunity and accelerated ideological change on the Left itself, while dividing and demobilizing the social forces upon which the Left counted most. The Parti Communiste Français (PCF) had returned to sectarian leftist opposition by 1984, while the Parti Socialiste (PS) rapidly moved to the Center. Buoyed by its sudden good fortune and carried by the tide of liberalism that swept Paris under the Left, the Right rather vocally regained its confidence and embraced a new, neo-liberal, outlook.

In the following chapters, Alain and Marie-Thérèse Lancelot carefully sift the evidence about electoral behavior, first emphasizing the relative narrowness of the Left's 1981 victories and then exploring the structures of the Left's subsequent decline. Steven Lewis and Serenella Sferza then examine the internal contradictions of a socialist party which had been carefully structured to win power but which turned out to be ill-prepared to cope with the task of being a party of government. Georges Lavau next reviews the Left's *crise de conscience* and processes of self-change as it lived through the difficulties of government. The remarkable trajectories of the Right from despondency to triumph and from Gaullist statism to liberalism are then recounted by René Rémond.

One of the great uncertainties of 1981 was, of course, how the Constitution of the Fifth Republic – designed by the Right for the Right and theretofore used only by the Right – would stand up under the strains of the first *alternance*. Olivier Duhamel's chapter provides answers to such questions. Finally, John Keeler and Alec Stone discuss the only real constitutional surprise of the post-1981 period, the emergence of the previously inoffensive *Conseil Constitutionnel* as a serious critic of and obstacle to certain Left government policies.

NOTES

1 See Jacques Capdevielle et al., *France de qauche, vote à droite* (Paris, Fondation Nationale des Sciences Politiques, 1981).

4

The Evolution of the
French Electorate: 1981–86

ALAIN and MARIE-THÉRÈSE LANCELOT

If opinion surveys have been accurate, the French electorate swung from one pole to the other between the parliamentary elections of 1981 and 1986. In June 1981, Right/Left distribution was the most favorable to the Left since 1946. By 1986, however, the relationship had become more favorable for the Right than at any time since 1968. Did this shift reflect a cultural transformation of the French electorate? Such a question demands careful reflection. It is impossible to deny formidable change, but it is also necessary to investigate the factors which produced the Socialist tidal wave in 1981 and those which led to the liberal victories of 1986. In both instances, phenomena which seemed at the time to indicate unprecedented strength may have merely represented circumstantial fluctuations – inclinations to punish incumbents just as much as inclinations to support their prospective successors. The simplest procedure to deepen our understanding is a consecutive examination of the Left's 1981 victories, its recurrent subsequent setbacks and lastly, voters' preferences, represented by opinion surveys prior to the decisive moment in 1986.

1981: AN AUTOPSY OF THE SOCIALIST VICTORY –
MITTERRAND'S VICTORY AND THE "10 MAY COALITION"

It is important to remember the extent to which the first ballot in the 1981 presidential election was generally unfavorable to the Left. In relation to the first round of the 1974 election, there was but a slight advance (47.25% of the ballots, in comparison with 46.08% seven years earlier). More importantly, Right/Left distribution on 26 April 1981 was more favorable for the Right than during the first round in the 1978 parliamentary elections (when the Left obtained a 50.2% majority) or during the 1979 elections for the European Parliament (47.46% for the Left as a whole).

Detailed electoral surveys make it possible to proceed beyond this elementary observation.[1] Relatively realistic estimates of vote flows between the Right and the Left from the first round of the 1978 parliamentary elections until the first round of the 1981 presidential election show that Left-to-Right shifts outweighed Right-to-Left: 1,300,000 votes in contrast to approximately 700,000. If scrutiny is limited to the non-Communist Left, whose irresistible expansion has been proclaimed repeatedly, there would still seem to be an unfavorable exchange of votes with the Right between 1978 and 1981. Whereas the non-Communist Left did indeed gain 700,000 votes from the Right, it lost another 800,000 votes to the Right.

Even though the first round of the 1981 presidential election was relatively unfavorable for the Left, the second round was, in contrast, exceptionally favorable. François Mitterrand actually obtained a larger victory than Valéry Giscard d'Estaing had in 1974. Within metropolitan France, the margin between the two candidates consisted of 1,322,854 votes, in comparison with 344,399 seven years earlier. The Socialist candidate received more than twice as many ballots as he had during the first round.

Mitterrand received an extremely high level of support from voters who had cast ballots for other Left candidates during the first round, to begin with. On 26 April 1981, Georges Marchais, Arlette Laguiller, Michel Crépeau and Huguette Bouchardeau received 6,031,125 votes. Of these, approximately 5,600,000 were transferred to Mitterrand on 10 May. This extensive transfer was accompanied by mobilization of leftist abstentionists from the first round. From one round to the next, the number of ballots cast grew by 1,256,321 and this increase in voter turnout was somewhat more advantageous for the winner than for Giscard. Mitterrand's net gain among voters who did not participate in the first round may have been approximately 750,000 votes, whereas the outgoing president obtained only 500,000. To this wave of new votes, one must add a sizable bloc of Ecology voters, who had cast 1,118,232 ballots during the first round. By combining the results of surveys and the results of ecological analysis of aggregate data, one gets approximately 650,000 additional votes. Thus, we have successively added 5,600,000 leftist votes, 750,000 former nonvoters,[2] and 650,000 Ecology votes to the 7,400,000 votes which Mitterrand retained from one round to the next. The total figure is 14,400,000, whereas Mitterrand actually received 15,541,905 votes on 10 May. The difference – consisting of approximately 1,150,000 votes – was attributable to the shifting loyalties of voters who had supported the Right on the first ballot.

Two principal factors account for this transfer of votes which ultimately elected a Socialist president. First of all, the Left seemed less threatening than in 1974. Secondly, the Right seemed less attractive. The first factor was essentially connected to the decline of Georges Marchais. In 1973, the most recent point of reference for the 1974 presidential election, the Communist Party still outstripped the Socialist Party, even when one included the *radicaux de gauche* and other Leftists. The Communist Party received 21.41% of the ballots, in contrast to 19.10% for the Socialist Party and 21.23% for the entire moderate Left. After 1978, the balance of power within the Left shifted, intensifying in 1981, with catastrophic results for the Communists. With only 15.48% of the votes, Marchais became a *force d'appoint*. Now it was the Communist Party's turn to occupy the role of hostage within the Union of the Left. With this turn of events, many moderate voters could reexamine their instinctive hostility to Mitterrand's strategy.

Simultaneously, Giscard d'Estaing appeared far less appealing than in 1974. At that time, the "middle-of-the-road" candidate had actually succeeded in attracting some of those with aspirations for change. By 1981, however, he was defending his record when the nation was in the throes of crisis. Moreover, he had to do this while enduring extremely harsh criticism from the RPR whose relation to the Barre government after 1979 had been "participation without support". A portion of the electorate which had voted for the Right (Chirac, Debré, or Garaud) during the first round of the presidential election had strong reservations about Giscard. Some were unwilling to trust him for another seven years, and others probably decided to punish the Giscard-Barre duo for its inability to overcome rising unemployment and inflation. To these voters, a Mitterrand apparently exonerated from debts to the Communists and who would necessarily focus the winds of change on a situation which needed change may have represented an acceptable second choice. Thus the exceptional surprise of 10 May emerged. Mitterrand's victory was not entirely logical given the Left's poor performance on 26 April. Nor was his victory entirely illogical when the disarray of the Right was taken into account. It was a felicitous combination of chance and necessity.

THE SOCIALIST TIDE IN THE PARLIAMENTARY ELECTIONS

There was no shortage of metaphors to characterize the "Socialist wave", or the "pink tide" which welled up during the June 1981 parliamentary elections and led to the election of an absolute Socialist majority in the National Assembly. In terms of numbers of votes, however, this tidal wave was only relative, because the Left as a whole received a few less votes than during the 1978 parliamentary elections, when it had been defeated. Indeed, the Left received only a few more votes than it had obtained during the less-than-favorable first round of the presidential election. This discrepancy between the image of a dramatic victory - suggested by the results expressed as percentages (55.64 per cent for the entire Left, 36.05 per cent for the Socialist party), and the relatively modest nature of the Socialists' performance in terms of numbers of votes, is associated with the high level of nonparticipation.

Many commentators concluded from this that the Left only won by default in June 1981. This viewpoint, despite its attractiveness when scrutiny of electoral results is limited to a national or departmental level, does not withstand analysis of statistics for the smallest units (boroughs or districts). Indeed, when a more precise level of analysis is adopted it becomes obvious that the Left's supporters were practically as vulnerable to nonparticipation as the Right's. The most reasonable estimates give 55 per cent of the increase in abstention to the Right, 45 per cent to the Left and the Ecology movement. Of the 3,680,000 abstentions and additional blank ballots tallied for 14 June in comparison with 26 April 2,030,000 could be attributed to the Right, and 1,650,000 originated from the Left and from Brice Lalonde's voters (1,520,000 for the Left and 130,000 for the Ecology movement).

The undeniable existence of significant nonparticipation on the Left allows the Left's gains to be viewed from an entirely different angle. In comparison with the first round of the presidential election, votes for the Left rose from 13,468,000 to 13,811,000, a gain of approximately 350,000 votes. Nevertheless, because the Left had lost 1,520,000 votes as a result of blank ballots and abstention, it was clearly aided by an inflow of 1,870,00 votes (1,520,000 plus 350,000), originating from the Ecology movement and from the Right. Because it is impossible for votes transferred from the Ecology movement to have exceeded 650,000, at least 1,220,000 votes had come from the Right in comparison with the first round of the presidential election.

In general terms, this transfer had the same breadth as the trend observed between the two rounds of the presidential election. This general equivalency should not deceive us, however, because in this instance, the votes which the Right lost came not only from Giscard d'Estaing's former electoral base, but also from Chirac's, a point demonstrated by geographic analysis at the borough or district level. The difference in origins among voters who swung to the Left on 10 May or on 14 June undoubtedly reflects differing motives. On 10 May the flow of votes to the Left represented discontent with the incumbent president, "punishment ballots" whose negative origins may have outweighed positive content. On 14 June the transfer of votes to the Left was undoubtedly less dependent upon negative motivation. In other words, with a change in the nature of the threat, many voters who had not remained loyal to the Right may have been preoccupied with new dangers, such as the institutional crisis which could follow election of a rightist legislature immediately after election of a Socialist president, or a recovery of strength by the Communist Party which could possibly be averted by giving the Socialists the means to hold their ground. As we have said, there were many voters whose loyalties changed. Yet it is obvious that all of them were not disloyal voters. The support which emerged for the Left during the parliamentary elections undoubtedly included a significant share of "goodwill". From this perspective, trends anticipated the "state of grace" which existed during the first months of the Left's power.

The overall meaning of voting patterns during 1981 was therefore relatively complex. It would clearly be erroneous to regard the second round of the presidential election as a "realignment". Mitterrand's victory arose more from dissatisfaction than from strong loyalties. Nevertheless, this election set in motion the process which produced the Socialist sweep in the parliamentary elections, as if voters, even without knowing it themselves, had travelled too far to be able to shift backward. One of the strongest pluralities which a government had obtained since 1958 therefore rested upon a fragile foundation. Nonetheless, the Left could hardly avoid being distracted by success. Instead of taking stock of the relatively fortuitous nature of its triumph, it saw the situation as the culmination of a long process, or as the starting point for a far-reaching transformation. These erroneous appraisals quickly led to profound disappointment. After the Left's decisive 1981 victories, it consistently lost all intervening elections between 1982 and 1985.

RETURNING TO THE STARTING POST: 1982–85, RECURRENT SETBACKS FOR THE LEFT IN MID-TERM ELECTIONS

The parliamentary by-elections of January 1982, on one hand, and the March 1982 cantonal elections, on the other, gave some measure of the quickly changing situation. Because of invalidation of the 1981 parliamentary elections in four districts (Paris-2,

Paris-12, Seine-et-Marne-4 and Marne-3), by-elections were held on 17 January 1982. These four districts had been strongholds of the Right, and the outcome of the second round of the 1981 parliamentary elections had been extremely close (the Socialist Party had won in three and the RPR in one district). Nevertheless, the Socialists hoped to derive advantages from a continuing "state of grace". In January 1982, 60 per cent of those surveyed expressed confidence in Pierre Mauroy's ability to solve the problems facing France.[3] It was also possible to hope for advantages from the unification of the majority, seen in the presence of a single Socialist candidate for the first round and by active campaign participation of Communist ministers. The reality of the 17 January elections imposed another perspective: the opposition swept the four districts, beginning with the first round.

For those four districts as a whole, percentage changes in voting patterns since the first round of the 1981 presidential election were as shown in Tables 4.1 and 4.2: The gains which the Left had foreseen since May 1981 had evaporated, while the Right reestablished a strong majority in each of the four districts. In terms of percentages of registered voters, a slightly different trend emerges because of decreased voter participation during the June 1981 parliamentary elections and, to an even greater extent, during the January 1982 by-elections.[5]

On 26 April 1981, the Right had a 4.58% lead in terms of registered voters, a margin which had risen to 8.04% by 17 January 1982. From the first round of the 1981 parliamentary elections until the by-elections of January 1982, the Right's share of registered voters rose by 0.92%, whereas the Left's declined by 10.28%. Here, too, it is necessary to refrain from attributing increased nonparticipation solely to the Left's supporters. Undoubtedly, a certain section of the traditional right-wing electorate did not participate in the by-elections, and the stability of increased support for the

Table 4.1 Voting in 1981 and 1982 by-elections: % of votes cast

| | 1981 presidential election | | 1981 parliamentary elections | | 1982 by-elections |
	1st round	2nd round	1st round	2nd round	1st round
Left	45.08	50.60	52.03	50.12	41.99
Right	50.90	49.39	47.48	49.87	55.04
Other*	4.01		0.4		2.96

Note:
* For details of "other" candidates, see note[4].

Table 4.2 Voting in 1981 and 1982 by-elections: % of registered voters

| | 1982 presidential election | | 1981 parliamentary elections | | 1982 by-elections |
	1st round	2nd round	1st round	2nd round	1st round
Left	35.55	41.61	36.16	37.37	25.88
Right	40.13	40.61	33.00	37.18	33.92
Other	3.16		0.03		1.82

opposition certainly reflects a return to the fold by voters whom the Left had attracted during recent years. Nevertheless, in proportional terms, the Left was undoubtedly more severely affected than the Right by decreased voter participation, especially in areas where the Communist Party retained strength. Was this the first sign of discontent or, at least, disillusionment among Communist voters? Perhaps. Nevertheless, it is also possible to conclude that a low turnout among this sector of the electorate was due to the absence of Communist candidates. If the Left had "cast its nets further", it might have obtained electoral support more effectively.

In any event, the 17 January by-elections – whose symbolic effect was reinforced by the reelection of Alain Peyrefitte to the National Assembly – were an extremely harsh surprise for the Left. Louis Mermaz, of course, stated that "this is a warning, but not a defeat". Bernard Delanoë, a Socialist Party spokesperson, was more realistic in referring to it as a "cold shower".

THE 14 MARCH AND 21 MARCH 1982 CANTONAL ELECTIONS

The local elections of spring 1982 provided an even more interesting indication of trends among voters, inasmuch as 18,660,000 registered voters, or nearly half of the French electorate, participated.[6] Because of extremely active campaigning of the kind usually focused upon national political events, there was record participation for this type of election (68.3%, as opposed to 65.3% in 1976 and 1979, 53.3% in 1973). Increased participation was not advantageous for the governing majority. Whereas the Left (in the broadest sense, with inclusion of "other Left" candidates) had traditionally maintained a majority in cantonal elections since the earliest years of the Fifth Republic, its performance fell below the 50% mark for the first time, while the Right narrowly missed reaching this level (see table 4.3). It is impossible to differentiate the outcome of the cantonal elections from the results of earlier nationwide elections (see table 4.4).

The Right had thus achieved its most successful results in four years, whereas the Left, deprived of the additional second-round votes from the presidential and parliamentary elections of 1981, was driven back to its point of departure at the end of Giscard d'Estaing's seven-year term.

A detailed scrutiny of the cantonal elections permits a more precise analysis. In the first instance, the Communist Party, with 15.92% of the ballots, had not recovered from its 1981 decline. Some observers have introduced the theory of the "effective

Table 4.3 Cantonal elections: first-round results

| | % of votes cast | | | |
	1973	1976	1979	1982
Left	54	56.5	55.4	49.7
Right	46	43.5	44.15	49.9
Pro-Ecology	—	—	0.5	0.4

Table 4.4 First-round results: elections 1978–82

	1978 parliamentary elections	1981 presidential elections	1981 parliamentary elections	1982 cantonal elections
Left	50.2	47.2	55.7	49.7
Right	47.5	48.8	43.2	49.9
Other	2.3	3.9	1.1	0.4

Note:
* See note[7].

ballot" to explain the Communist Party's decline in 1981, but this theory does not stand up to the previously cited data. In turn, the Center–Left (Socialist Party, *radicaux de gauche* and other Left candidates) obtained a 33.2% share of the electorate (with 29.9% for the Socialist Party), in contrast to 32% six years earlier, only gaining an additional 1.2% of the ballots, (whereas the Communist Party had declined by 6.6%). Therefore, the relative strength of the Center–Left was not sufficient to offset the misfortunes of its Communist partner.

The cantonal elections constituted a considerably more significant warning for the government than the four by-elections in January. Even though the government was still able to claim a certain degree of support, its popularity had begun to deteriorate. In February 1982, 59% of the persons interviewed by SOFRES continued to express confidence in Mauroy, against 35% negative. By April, the proportions had shifted to 51% and 40%. The belated and poorly explained transition to the first austerity plan in June 1982 transformed the decline into a reversal: by September those with confidence in Mauroy were a minority (46% versus 47%).

THE MUNICIPAL ELECTIONS OF 6 MARCH AND
13 MARCH 1983: 10 MAY IN REVERSE

The March 1983 municipal elections were the first elections after 1981 in which the entire electorate participated. They took place in an atmosphere which was extremely unfavorable for the Left. Only 39% of the persons polled expressed trust in Mauroy in March (53% did not), while Mitterrand himself was stuck in the polls: in January 1983, 48% of the persons polled expressed confidence in him, 47% did not. By March, the proportions were 48% and 46%. Inevitably, the Left would also suffer from comparison with the 1977 municipal elections, which had represented its best performance in a decade.

The results demonstrated effectively that the Left was "at low tide".[8] Nationwide, the Left did not obtain 40% with the Right at nearly 51% (the remainder having been cast for "other candidates") These results were even more significant considering the extremely high turnout (78.4%). Would the argument of distinctive nonparticipation on the Left fall apart? Overall data is hardly relevant for municipal elections because of the high number of small towns where the political content of the electoral process

Table 4.5 1983 municipal elections: results by size of town

	Inhabitants					Total participation (%)
	Less than 9,000	9-30,000	30-50,000	50-100,000	More than 100,000	
Voter participation (%)	84.2	74.7	←——————— 69.9 ———————→			78.4
Left	34.8	47.3	51.2	47.8	39.4	39.7
Right	49.2	51.3	47.3	50.4	58.0	50.9
Others	15.9	1.4	1.5	1.8	2.6	9.4

Table 4.6 Election results 1977-83: % of votes cast

	1977 municipal elections	1978 parliamentary elections	1981 presidential elections		1981 parliamentary elections	1983 municipal elections
			1st round	2nd round		
Left	50.8	50.6	48.3	53.0	56.9	44.2
Right	46.3	45.7	47.5	47.0	41.6	53.6
Others	2.9	3.7	4.2	—	1.5	2.2

varies greatly. It is more interesting to examine the results in relation to the size of these towns (see table 4.5).

From table 4.5, one observes that to a surprising extent the Right dominated urban France in 1983. The Left was ahead only for the group of towns of 30,000 to 50,000 persons. In extremely large cities, the Left was practically reduced to its poor results in the smallest municipalities. The three largest cities in France – Paris, Lyon and Marseilles –were no exception. When the municipal elections were properly situated within the electoral history of the preceding six years, they marked a strong leap forward by the Right. If examination is limited to towns of more than 30,000, the results shown in table 4.6 emerge.

It was true that the second round of the municipal elections offered a slightly different image in towns with more than 30,000 inhabitants, inasmuch as the Left obtained a 48.5 per cent of the vote, in contrast to 50.9 per cent for the Right. Nevertheless, the apparent gain by the Left can be reduced to more reliable proportions by comparing the second-round results with first-round results for municipalities where a decisive plurality did not emerge (see table 4.7). Unequal distribution of the Ecology electorate between Left and Right would suffice to explain the Left's gains. "Reactivation" of voters who had abstained from the first round – in larger cities, this category was especially large – would not appear to have brought large-scale benefits to the Left, at least as a general rule.

As a whole, if one attempts to evaluate the relative strength of the Right and the Left in France subsequent to the municipal elections, combining the results from both rounds reveals an incontestable 53/43 ratio between Right and Left. Two years after 10 May 1981, the balance of electoral power had been reversed.

Table 4.7 Municipalities with more than 30,000 inhabitants where no party won on the first round

	(%)	
	1st round	2nd round
% of votes cast	67.9	72.2
Left	46.5	48.5
Right	49.9	50.9
Others	3.5	0.5

1984–85: EARTHQUAKE ON THE FRINGES

In spite of Mauroy's promises, the municipal elections were followed by a more severe austerity plan, with Mauroy called upon to oversee its implementation. Mitterrand thus did not use his opportunity to change the atmosphere by replacing his Prime Minister and paid the price. After June 1983, the President ceased to have a favorable standing: 46% of the public expressed trust in him, 51% had lost confidence. Mauroy's decline also accelerated: although 37% of the persons surveyed trusted him, 57% did not. The municipal elections had clearly ended the state of grace.

Moreover, the impact of the municipal elections continued after March 1983. Between the autumn of 1983 and the spring of 1984, a series of municipal by-elections accentuated the rout of the Left. In towns with more than 30,000 inhabitants, seven by-elections took place between September 1983 and May 1984 and the Left lost all of them. (The PS losing one and the Communist Party six). The by-elections also introduced a new phenomenon; the rebirth of the far Right. In March 1983 the National Front obtained an average of only 0.3% in towns of more than 30,000 inhabitants. In certain by-elections, however, National Front candidates registered dramatic inroads: 16.7% in Dreux, 9.3% in Aulnay and 4.1% in La Seyne.

The deteriorating economic situation was clearly radicalizing the political climate. The government and the Socialist Party at its Bourg-en-Bresse congress, obviously misunderstanding the dissatisfaction around them, called for a new political offensive in which educational and press reform would be the leading themes. This quest for ideological firmness produced a formidable countercurrent in support of liberalism exemplified in the many demonstrations in favor of private education in 1984.

THE TREMOR OF THE 17 JUNE 1984
ELECTIONS FOR THE EUROPEAN PARLIAMENT

The so-called European elections – "European" only in name, because they were dominated by domestic political considerations – represented a decisive point in the electoral "stations of the Cross" travelled by the Left since it had come to power. The sharp expansion of the gap between Left and Right was clear. The two dominant coalitions were separated by more than 18 percentage points, with the Left dropping below 40 per cent for the first time since 1969 and the Right almost duplicating its June 1968 successes (see table 4.8). How far events had travelled since the 1981 parliamentary elections! The high (43.3 per cent) abstention rate certainly detracted from the value of the comparison. But the experience of the European elections of 1979 showed that built-in low participation had little effect on the political representativeness of the results. It is thus very likely that a new opening up of the French electorate occurred in June 1984.

The second significant characteristic of the European elections was the further decline of the Communist Party. Communist votes, which had climbed to 20.6% in the European elections of 1979, had leveled off at 15–16% in 1981–82 (15.5% in the presidential election of April 1981, 16.1% in the legislative elections of June 1981 and 15.9% in the 1982 cantonal elections). They fell to 11.2% in June 1984. The Communist party seemed to be reliving its history in reverse. Its 1981 showing was close to that of 1936 while its 1984 results recalled the low-water mark of 1924–28. A process of marginalization – almost completed in certain departments – seemed to be underway.

The third and final factor in the political upheavel of the European election was the spectacular rise of the extreme Right. With 11.1%, the Le Pen slate trailed the Marchais slate by only 17,500 votes in Paris. In 1979, a Tixier – Vignancour slate had obtained 1.3% of the votes (vs the Marchais slate's 20.6%!). This growth of the extreme Right had certainly been foreshadowed in several by-elections: municipal elections, like those in Dreux and Aulnay mentioned above, and the December 1983 legislative election in the second Morbihan district in which Le Pen, a native, obtained 12%. But a national surge on this scale altered the French electoral landscape. The electoral success of the extreme Right was quite regionalized. Were it to score fewer than five percentage points in but three departments (as compared with eight for the Communist party), it would only exceed 10% in an area east of an imaginary line connecting Le Havre, Nevers and Carcassonne (the region where the number of immigrants is highest).[9] In placing a liberal personality like Simone Veil at the top of its list, the opposition left space open to its Right into which the National Front leaped eagerly. But it broke through only when immigration allowed it to.

Table 4.8 1984 European elections vs 1981, 1982 results: % of votes cast in 1st round

%	1981 parliamentary elections	1982 cantonal elections	1984 European Parliament elections
Left	55.6	49.7	39.1
Right	43.2	49.9	57.4
Difference	+ 12.4	– 0.2	– 18.3

THE MARCH 1985 CANTONAL ELECTIONS: STABILIZATION OF DISEQUILIBRIUM

The March 1985 cantonals were the last important elections before March 1986. The situation was very different from that of June 1984. The Left's school-reform plans had been dropped and, above all, the page of Union of the Left had been turned: Fabius had replaced Mauroy and the Communists had left the government. From the rhetoric of "change followed by rigor to allow us to profit from change" there had been a turn to the more cautious and measured discourse of modernization and *rassemblement*. The President won little from this change – 39% had confidence in him (59% against) in February 1985 and 40% (56% against) in July 1984. The new Prime Minister, in contrast, did much better than his predecessor. The last confidence rating for Mauroy was alarming (25% for, 68% against). Fabius' rating in February 1985 was 50% for, 40% against.

Would this governmental recentering be enough to minimize the President's lack of popularity? Apparently not, judging by the results of the 1985 cantonal elections, which echoed closely the relative strengths in the European elections (with an abstention rate lower by nearly 10%); 57.9% for the Right versus 41.3% for the Left in March 1985 as opposed to 57.4% versus 39.1% in June 1984.

If we compare the three most recent cantonal elections, the decline of the Left and the ascent of the Right and the extreme Right are striking (see table 4.9).

In comparison with the European elections we get an impression of consolidation, with, in addition, a slight shift away from the extremes to moderates. The extreme Right lost 2.3 per cent of the votes and the extreme left 1.7 per cent (see table 4.10). This decline is in part attributable to the nature of the polling and the method of analysis.

Relative to the European elections, the extreme Left lost 3.2% (0.6% from 3.8%) of which the Communist Party only regained half (12.5% from 11.2%), in spite of approximately 200 officials running. Despite its changed position with respect to the government, then, the Communist Party thus remained marginalized. As for the extreme Right, it participated in only three-quarters of the districts (1521 out of 1954 in the capital). In extrapolating its continuous success to the nation as a whole – a calculation that works exaggeratedly in its favor – we find 11.9% vs the 11.1% of the European elections. Even taking into account the special difficulties encountered in these sorts of calculations with respect to the extreme Right, its staying power on the whole was very good.

Table 4.9 Cantonal elections 1979–85: % of votes cast

	1979	1982	1985
Extreme Left (including Communist Party)	23.4	16.5	13.2
Moderate Left	32.0	33.2	28.1
Total Left	55.4	49.7	41.3
Ecology Party	0.5	0.4	0.8
Moderate Right	44.1	49.7	49.1
Extreme Right	—	0.2	8.8
Total Right	44.1	49.9	57.9

Table 4.10 1985 cantonal vs 1984 European elections: % of votes cast

	1984 European elections	1985 Cantonal elections
Extreme Left	14.9	13.2
Moderate Left	24.2	28.1
Total Left	39.1	41.3
Ecology Party	3.4	0.8
Moderate Right	46.3	49.1
Extreme Right	11.1	8.8
Total Right	57.4	57.9

Table 4.11 Results of the two rounds of cantonal elections in March 1985 in the only districts voting

	1st round	2nd round
Left	45.0	46.1
Ecology Party	0.8	—
Right	54.2	53.9

As far as the moderate Left and the moderate Right were concerned, gains were apparently more marked in the Socialist camp (+3.9%) than in the liberal camp (+2.8%). But when one takes into account the disappearance of the ecologist electorate, which leaned predominantly to the Left, the "tremor" in favor of the government party appeared weaker than the growth of the parliamentary opposition, which by itself was close to attaining an absolute majority. The second round of the March 1985 cantonal elections also yielded valuable indications of the reality of rifts in the electorate. In the first place, it shows a very great consistency in relative strengths in those districts voting (see table 4.11). This consistency had one surprising implication: Right/Left bipolarization had sustained a sharp blow through the transformation of the Communists into a *de facto* opposition following their exit from the government and through the ascent of an extreme Right ready to lump the other parties into the famous "Gang of Four". But what is true at the party level was not reproduced – not on a large scale in any case – at the level of voters. The parliamentary Right, which had obtained 55.2% of the seats in the decisive round, obtained 66.9% of the seats, whereas the Left only obtained 32.9% (versus 42% of the votes). The existing majority electoral law exaggerated the victory but did not create it. In addition, it had the advantage of taking into account the disaffection suffered by the extremes in the second round (the Communist Party only had 7.1% of the seats versus 12.5% of the votes in the first round, and the National Front with 8.8% of the votes and very few seats did even worse).

The profile of change: changes in right-left balance
in the different categories of the electorate

Table 4.12 allows us to understand the evolution of Right–Left balances from the first round of the presidential election of 1981 to the European elections of 1984 in groups of the electorate defined by sex, age and occupation (with attention of course to the differences in participation, which prohibit us from carrying the comparison too far).

The first impression one gets from table 4.12 is that the change represents more a broadening of the traditional power bases of the right than a need to call into question the underlying structure of the French electorate. Behind the change in magnitude – in favor of the Right – this traditional structure is still visible. Upon closer examination, however, the shift to the Right was far from uniform. It was especially marked in groups that were the most favorable to the Left in 1981: workers (among whom the Left's lead dropped from 40 to four percentage points in three years); those under 25 (the Left led by 19 points in 1981 and trailed by 16 points in 1984);[10] middle managers and clerks and even male voters. After an even more detailed comparison of the votes cast by different social groups in the 1978 legislative elections and in the 1984 European elections Elisabeth Dupoirier[11] noted that:

> in 1984, the independent middle classes returned in large numbers to the fold of the Right . . . On the other hand, the erosion of the Left's position among the salaried middle classes is not any more detectable in the aggregate than its decline among the rest of the population . . . and the Socialist Party still had some of its best successes there . . . However, upon closer examination, the success of the Socialist Party is far from generalizable even here . . . The Socialist Party's vote only exceeded the national average in those categories that had long been rooted in the Left . . . Are these salaried middle classes in the process of losing their political homogeneity, and is the Socialist Party losing one of its chief electoral bases?

Communist losses and losses on the Left as a whole

The Communist decline does not come near to accounting for the total decline of the Left. The Communist Party lost 5% from 1981 to 1984, while the entire Left lost 8%. But a comparison of Communist decline and that of the Left in various categories of the electorate does yield a wealth of information (see table 4.13). The most striking phenomenon is the significant change in the breakdown of the Communist vote in different age categories. In 1981 the Communist vote was strongest among the youngest categories and dropped regularly with age. In 1984, the Communist vote was no longer linked to age, as shown by the fact that its level was lowest among the young! From 1981 to 1984, the power of the Communist Party decreased greatly among those under 35 and shrunk consistently all the way through age 50. However, above that age it gained most notably among those over 65. As far as occupation is concerned, the huge decline in Communist strength among workers only accounts for two-thirds of the decline of the entire Left in this group, and its decline among white-collar employees only accounts for half of the Left's total losses.

Table 4.12 Left and Right in the different categories of the electorate in 1981 and 1984

	1981 Presidential (1st round)		1984 European		Difference	
	Left	Right	Left	Right	Left	Right
Total	47	49	39	58	− 8	+ 9
Sex:						
Male	51	45	41	56	− 10	+ 11
Female	43	53	36	60	− 7	+ 7
Age:						
18–24 years	54	35	39	55	− 15	+ 20
25–34 years	58	36	47	47	− 11	+ 11
35–49 years	47	51	38	59	− 9	+ 8
50–64 years	42	56	35	63	− 7	+ 7
65 and over	37	62	37	62	—	—
Voter occupation:						
Farmers	27	72	27	70	—	− 2
Small business, craftspeople	27	66	18	80	− 9	+ 14
Upper mangement, liberal professions	30	66	31	65	+ 1	− 1
Middle management, clerks	56	38	42	54	− 14	+ 16
Workers	68	28	50	46	− 18	+ 18
Religion:						
Practising Catholics						
Regularly	16	81	13	84	− 3	+ 3
Occasionally	36	62	26	71	− 10	+ 9
Nonpractising Catholics	55	41	43	54	− 12	+ 13
No religion	76	16	74	21	− 2	+ 5

Source: SOFRES polls (postelectoral in 1981, election-day in 1984).

THE RIGHT'S GAINS AND THE RISE OF THE NATIONAL FRONT

Did the gains of the Right correspond essentially to the rise of the National Front? Table 4.13 shows the limits of this correlation. Where the relative strength of the Right has gained the most (among those under 25, workers, white-collar employees and middle management), the surge of the National Front by no means accounts for the size of the gains. In those groups in which the Right's influence gained little or declined (those over 50, farmers, upper management and liberal professions), the National Front's rise, by contrast, was much greater than the gains of the opposition and must therefore have occurred at the expense of the moderate Right. The only groups in which the two shifts seem truly linked is small business and craftspeople,

Table 4.13 Electoral shifts from the 1st round of the 1981 presidential election to the 1984 European elections in %.

	Losses on the Left	1981 Communist Party	1984 Communist Party	Losses Communist Party	Gains on the Right	National Front votes
Total	– 8	16	11	– 5	+ 9	11
Sex:						
Male	– 10	17	12	– 5	+11	13
Female	– 7	14	10	– 4	+ 7	9
Age:						
18-24 years	– 15	24	8	– 16	+20	11
25-34 years	– 11	23	12	– 11	+11	9
35-49 years	– 9	15	10	– 5	+ 8	10
50-64 years	– 7	11	12	+ 1	+ 7	13
65 or over	—	7	12	+ 5	—	10
Voter occupation:						
Farmers	—	2	7	+ 5	– 2	9
Small business, craftspeople	– 9	9	5	– 4	+14	17
Upper management, liberal professions	+ 1	7	5	– 2	– 1	14
Middle management, clerks	– 14	18	12	– 6	+16	10
Workers	– 18	30	18	– 12	+18	10

Source: SOFRES polls.

although here the gains of the extreme Right exceed by three points those of the Right as a whole.

GREATER ELECTORAL HOMOGENEITY

The fact that the Left declined more in those groups which had shown the most support for it implies a certain homogenization of the electorate. In table 4.13 the maximum difference introduced by each criterion shrunk between 1981 and 1984. The decline was slight for religion, the maximum difference shrinking from 65 to 63%, but it was much more perceptible for occupation (from 44 to 34%), age (from 27 to 16%) and even – in relative value – for sex (from 8 to 5%).[12] This homogenization, which confirms the nationalization of French elections, emphasized time and again over fifteen years,[13] is certainly one of the strong trends in French political sociology. It corresponds to a shift noted for a long time in consumers, whose behavior is "explained" less and less by social/occupational groupings. Events seem to indicate that the reasons for political and social behavior can no longer be found in the objective situation in any group but rather in the possession of certain sociocultural values and in choice of a "strategy". In this respect, France is experiencing the same changes as most Western nations, where "gambling" is on the increase.[14] This development is, of course, coupled with greater mobility. In behaving as if it could rely upon the natural voting habits of a "people of the Left" whom it would suffice merely to mobilize, the Left could not have avoided bitter disappointment.

FROM RESULTS TO OUTLOOKS:
INFORMATION ON VOTER INTENTIONS

The results of polls on the March 1986 elections were quite uniform, as we may judge from table 4.14. Given separate party lists, intentions in favor of the Right wavered between 55% and 59% in October 1985 with those in favor of the Left stable at 38%. A united Right slate did not affect the Right/Left relationship – one extra point for the Right according to IFOP, no change according to SOFRES. Voter intentions for the legislative elections therefore suggested a Left/Right relationship very close to that observed in the 1984 European elections and in the 1985 cantonals. This parity

Table 4.14 Voters' intentions for 1986 legislative elections (October 1985) in %

	SOFRES 3–8 Oct.	BVA 12–18 Oct.	IFOP 14–19 Oct.
1st hypothesis: separate votes			
PSU – Extreme Left	2	2	2
Communist Party	10	9	10
Socialist Party	23	23	24
MRG	3	4	2
Total Left	38	38	38
Ecology Party	3	4	7
UDF	20	17	18
RPR	25	24	30
Miscellaneous opposition	5.5	8	
National Front	8.5	8	7
Total Right	59	58	55
2nd hypothesis: united slate			
PSU-Extreme Left	2		2
Communist Party	10.5		10
Socialist Party	22.5		24
MRG	3		
Total Left	38		36
Ecology Party	3		8
UDF-RPR	42.5		49
Miscellaneous opposition	7.5		
National Front	9		7
Total Right	59	58	56

was also duplicated at the level of parties: on the Left, the best reference point was the European elections, while on the Right - especially for the National Front - it was the cantonal elections.

Resemblance between by-election results and voters' intentions - inherently hypothetical - for the 1986 legislative elections clearly strengthens our confidence in judging these intentions. This confidence is also reinforced because this measurement has been made regularly since 1981; current results fit perfectly with the continuation of a trend whose import is clear, as it can be gleaned from the graph in figure 4.1, prepared by BVA based on monthly results. Everything from June 1981 to October 1985 thus points to a transformation from a relationship of 56/43 per cent in favor of the Left to a similar one in favor of the Right. Such a strong shift in only four years is indeed striking.

FROM MOBILITY TO VOLATILITY: INTRODUCTION OF
THE PRESIDENTIAL HYPOTHESIS - VOTER INTENTIONS IN
THE FIRST ROUND OF A PRESIDENTIAL ELECTION

The introduction of the hypothesis of a presidential election allows us to view the attitudes of the French electorate differently, revealing very great voter sensitivity to the candidates. More specifically, it shows that two personalities who are slightly marginal to the party game, Raymond Barre and Michel Rocard, had in October 1985 considerable potential constituencies at their disposal. When Barre was present and Rocard absent, the Right rose above 65%, according to the IFOP October 1985 preelectoral poll. When they were both present, the gap narrowed - a little bit according to IFOP, much more according to BVA (see table 4.15).

The BVA poll, which gave the Left 46% of voters' intentions in the presidential first round, also contained six different candidacy hypotheses for the runoff (see table 4.16). The results confirmed the appeal of Barre and Rocard, which cancelled itself out when the two men were head-to-head (50/50). But it allowed Barre to win over all other candidates on the Left and Rocard to defeat Chirac, who tied with Fabius but beat Mitterrand. The Right therefore swung from a maximum of 60% to a minimum of 46% based on the nature of candidacies! It is very tempting, then, to speak of electoral volatility.

Could the Barre and Rocard effects have changed the outcome of legislative elections if each had agreed to sponsor independent slates? This question smacks a bit of political fiction, but it is raised naturally by the foregoing. We are unable to answer as far as Raymond Barre is concerned - despite rumors circulating that the RPR suffered greatly, even in Paris, from the competition of the Barre slate - and the question is perhaps less interesting because it really concerns the balance of strength within the Right more than the relative strengths of Right and Left. On the other hand, a BVA poll for L'Evénement du Jeudi[15] allows consideration of the effects that introducing Rocard slates alongside the official Socialist slates would have had (see table 4.17). The results were striking: the Left/Right gap was certainly not reversed, but it was considerably narrowed, and the Rocard slates outstripped those of the Socialist Party.

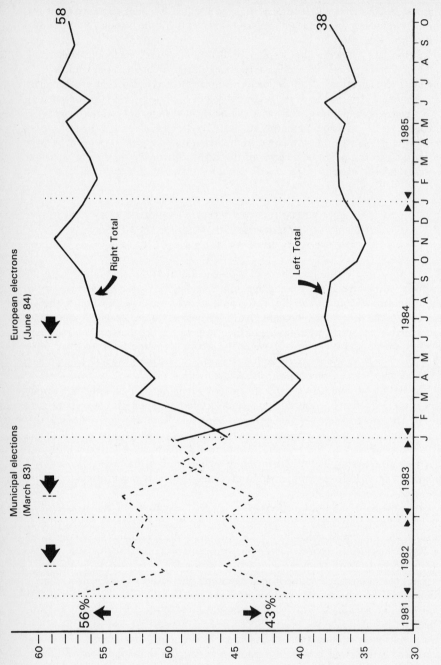

Figure 4.1 Left vs Right, voting intentions (Parliamentary) 1981–85

Table 4.15 Voter intentions for a presidential election (1st round) in October 1985

IFOP (14–19 Oct. 1985)						
1st form of candidates			2nd form of candidates			
G. Marchais	7	} 33%	G. Marchais	6	} 39%	
F. Mitterrand	26		L. Fabius	10		
			M. Rocard	23		
R. Barre	29	} 67%	R. Barre	26	} 61%	
J. Chirac	22		J. Chirac	22		
V. Giscard d'Estaing	11		V. Giscard d'Estaing	9		
J-M. Le Pen	5		J-M. Le Pen	4		
BVA 11–13 Oct. 1985)						
1st form of candidates			2nd form of candidates			
G. Marchais	7	} 46%	G. Marchais	8	} 46%	
F. Mitterrand	11.5		L. Fabius	11.5		
M. Rocard	27.5		M. Rocard	26.5		
R. Barre	26.5	} 54%	R. Barre	26.5	} 54%	
J. Chirac	20.5		J. Chirac	19.5		
J-M. Le Pen	7		J-M. Le Pen	8		

Sources: Le Point, (28 Nov. 1985); *Paris-Match,* (8 Oct. 1985).

Table 4.16 Voter intentions for a presidential runoff (2nd round) in October 1985)

Candidates	%
F. Mitterrand	40
R. Barre	60
L. Fabius	42
R. Barre	58
M. Rocard	50
R. Barre	50
F. Mitterrand	46
J. Chirac	54
L. Fabius	50
J. Chirac	50
M. Rocard	54
J. Chirac	46

Table 4.17 Voter intentions in legislative elections with and without Rocard slate

	Candidature hypothesis			
	Without Rocard slate		With Rocard slate	
PSU and Extreme Left	1.5		1	
Communist Party	10.5		10	
Socialist Party and MRG	21.5	37%	14	43%
Rocard slates	—		16	
Other Left slates	3.5		2	
Ecology Party	5.5		6	
UDF	18		18	
RPR	24.5	57.5%	20	51%
Other Right slates	7		5	
National Front	8		8	

Table 4.18 PS, UDF, RPR in April 1981, October 1985

	April 1981			Oct. 1985		
	PS	UDF	RPR	PS	UDF	RPR
Favorable opinions	60	38	39	41	40	41
Unfavorable opinions	30	46	47	47	39	42
Difference	+ 30	– 8	– 8	– 6	+ 1	– 1

Source: SOFRES barometer, Figaro Magazine.

THE RETURN OF THE "SANCTION-VOTE"

It is no accident that today's most popular political figures – Raymond Barre and Michel Rocard – each occupy a special position in their camps. Adept at "speaking the truth", these two favorites have for the most part escaped the double discredit that has fallen, inequitably but undeniably, upon the two majorities which tried to resolve the crisis before and since 1981.

Disappointed by the Right in power under Giscard, French electors had set their hopes on the renewal which socialism would bring. Alone among all the French parties, the Socialist Party benefitted from largely positive ratings from 1974 to 1982. Since then, it has suffered from the rise of the "deçus of socialism". Its rating remained positive on average in 1983, though by very little. It became negative in 1984 and 1985.[16] But this disaffection from the Socialist Party was not accompanied by a comparable resurgence of popularity for the RPR or the UDF. For example, we can examine the ratings of the three parties in April 1981, on the eve of the presidential election, and in October 1985 (see table 4.18). The reestablishment of the Right parties – limited because the UDF's rating was "in the red" six times and that of the RPR eight times in the first nine months of 1985 – was thus far from absorbing Socialist losses and did not at all represent the Right's overwhelming electoral dominance.

Another sign of this double disaffection with the Right and the Left, revealed by the poll conducted by SOFRES for Le Monde at the end of 1983, was that the French did not feel that their concerns were taken into account by political figures (see table 4.19). The situation was greatly worse in this respect in 1983 than it was at the time of the rise to power of the Socialist Party and the Union of the Left.[17]

SKEPTICISM CONCERNING THE ABILITY
AND PROGRAM OF THE OPPOSITION

The French expected miracles from the Socialist Party. Its failure has cured them somewhat. We can observe this by comparing the answers to the same questions posed by SOFRES in March 1979 and September 1985 (see table 4.20).[18] Similar questions

Table 4.19 In your opinion, on the whole, do political figures care about what people like you think?

	September 1977	December 1983
A great deal	15 ⎱ 53%	10 ⎱ 45%
A little bit	38 ⎰	35 ⎰
Very little	28 ⎱ 42%	29 ⎱ 52%
Practically not at all	14 ⎰	22 ⎰
No opinion	5	4

Table 4.20 Of the following political parties, which seem to you most capable of:

	% of poll sample	
	March 1979	September 1985
Fighting unemployment		
Communist Party	15 ⎱ 48	7
Socialist Party	33 ⎰	22
UDF	16	12 ⎱ 29
RPR	8	17 ⎰
National Front	—	3
No opinion	28	39
Making the changes and reforms the French desire		
Communist Party	13 ⎱ 48	5
Socialist Party	35 ⎰	27
UDF	17	13 ⎱ 31
RPR	9	18 ⎰
National Front	—	3
No opinion	26	34

posed by IFOP confirm that "neither the majority nor the opposition can claim to be the repository of hope, be it with regard to inflation and unemployment or with regard to purchasing power".[19]

Our study of the transformation of the French electorate over the last five years leads us to view the scope of the 1981 Socialist and 1983 liberal "double cultural revolution" from a relative perspective. In both cases, "sanction voting" clearly won out over confidence voting. Obviously this sanction was the product of greater illusions in 1981 than in 1985. Between May and June of 1981, the French "acted as if" they truly had confidence in the new government. The latter disappointed them, and they did not hesitate to make that clear at election time.

The recurrence of negative votes, inspired by the electorate's judgements of government politics, seemed to indicate that "circumstance" is becoming increasingly important compared with "structure" in the electoral sociology of the Fifth Republic.[20] But it is also important not to neglect factors pointing to very profound changes in French political culture. The cultural forces that carried socialism forward in the dual traditions of the worker's movement and the republican state is in the process of being overtaken by an individualist liberalism which may be becoming the dominant new ideology. None of the existing political forces truly represent this new trend. Out of this disparity between what is being offered and what is being sought may come new surprises. It seems to us that the French electorate will, for a long time to come, continue to be asked to live under the sign of change. Nothing in the results of 16 March 1986 belies this conclusion. Returned to power with little enthusiasm and facing the simultaneous complexities of cohabitation, volatility on the extremes and an impending presidential election, the new moderate Right majority will itself have hard work discerning a new path.

NOTES

1 François Platone, Jean Ranger, "L'Echec électoral du Parti Communiste", in Les Élections de l'alternance, ed. A. Lancelot (Paris, Fondation Nationale des Sciences Politiques, 1981).

2 The calculations would be slightly more complicated if we were to distinguish between abstentions and null votes. Here we are speaking of unused votes.

3 SOFRES "barometer", Figaro Magazine.

4 The "miscellaneous" are the Ecology candidates and those who stood in the name of "independent radio" in 1982.

5 We are counting in these four constituencies 78.8% of votes used on 26 April, 1981; 82.2% on 10 May; 69.5% on 14 June; 75.6% on 21 June; and 61.6% on 17 January 1982.

6 This pertains to the renewed series of 1976. We must recall that Paris did not have district elections.

7 This refers to the Ecology candidates. The "miscellaneous leftists" were included with the Left.

8 Cf. Alain Lancelot, "Vue sur la gauche à marée basse. Les élections municipales des 6 et 13 mars", Projet, (May 1983), pp. 437–53.

9 Maps taken from an excellent article by Pascal Perrineau, "Le Front National: un électorat autoritaire", Revue politique et parlementaire, (July–Aug. 1985), pp. 24–31; maps p. 28.

10 Regarding "the swing to the Right of young voters" from the 1983 municipal elections to the 1985 district elections, cf. Jean-Luc Parodi, "La Répétition des européennes", Revue politique et parlementaire; (July–Aug. 1985), pp. 5–18.

11 Elisabeth Dupoirier, "L'Électorat français, le 17 juin 1984", in Opinion publique 1985, SOFRES (Paris, Gallimard, 1985), pp. 207–30.

12 On the male-female breakdown, cf. Parodi, "La Répétition".

13 Cf. Alain Lancelot, *Les Élections sous la Cinquième République* (Paris, Presses Universitaires de France, 1983), pp. 101-2.

14 Cf. especially the discussion of "The Changing American Voter".

15 *L'Evenement du Jeudi*, (3-9 Oct. 1985), p. 33.

16 Cf. Jérôme Jaffré, "La Chute et les espoirs", *Le Monde*, (11 Oct. 1985), p. 8.

17 Cf. "Les Français jugent la politique", in SOFRES, *Opinion publique 1985*, pp. 18-29.

18 Cf. Jaffré, "La Chute", p. 8.

19 Denis Jeambar, "RPR-UDF: l'aise!", *Le Point*, (2 Sept. 1985), p. 42.

20 Cf. Alain Lancelot, "1978-1981: les rendez-vous manqués de la structure et de la conjoncture", in Lancelot (ed.) *Les Élections de l'alternance*.

5

French Socialists between State and Society

From Party-building to Power

STEVEN C. LEWIS and SERENELLA SFERZA

The France of François Mitterrand – if it ever existed – never became the France of the Parti Socialiste (PS) and of Lionel Jospin. The PS, perhaps the most ideological European socialist party, has turned out to be one of the weakest. This might appear a somewhat contradictory statement concerning a party which – after 25 years of absence from power and five years of managing an economic crisis – was still the largest political formation in the country after the 1986 elections, had succeeded in replacing the Communist Party as the largest party of the Left and has given the Left governmental respectability.

If one considers the PS's performance outside the electoral arena, however, the balance sheet is much less positive. The party has largely squandered the rich heritage of militant energies that grew out of the wave of left-wing mobilization of the early 1970s. It has failed to create durable or effective links to the social groups whose support has been a critical factor in the success of North European social democracies. At the same time, the PS has neglected to cultivate less traditional movements and interests – the new social movements – whose effervescence over the last decade signaled new fissures in the old system of interest representation. In short, the Party has failed to fill, either directly or by encouraging more autonomous initiatives, the gap between the state and individuals or existing interest groups.

As a result, the Left's substantial, if belated, contribution to economic modernization must be compared to the PS's inability to transform itself into an instrument of political modernization. Certainly, the concept itself is slippery, its use and the theories behind it are often ideological. In contemporary France, however, there seems to be a near consensus on identifying political modernization with a limitation of state intervention to a more arbitral role on the one hand, and an expansion of civil society beyond the boundaries defined by the narrow interests of its components on the other. Some observers see political parties as obstacles to such a development; their weakening is thus welcomed as a precondition for further modernization. Yet, parties have never been strong in France. Moreover, if they have been weakened further in recent years, has this really been accompanied by a strengthening of alternative bridges between individuals and the state, whose power in France remains far from negligible? Did we in fact witness a rise of stable and strong interest groups – necessary ingredients

100

in a modern polity – or have new and old interests become so enmeshed that existing institutions of representation have been undermined without new ones having been created? Changes in modes of participation are, especially in France, unimaginable without a profound transformation of political culture. Indeed, it was in large measure the expectation that the PS might facilitate these changes that made the Party so attractive.

The failure of the PS in this respect is hardly surprising for most observers. In one view, the PS's recent history might be seen as simply another episode in the ineluctable decline of political parties – a decline helped along, in France, by the overwhelming presence of the state and the institutions of the Fifth Republic. For others, the PS's inability to serve as a permanent bridge between civil society and the state – cultivating new modes of political participation in which general and specific interests might be mediated without leading to an irreconcilable confrontation of particular demands and the general will – is consistent with what Lavau has termed the French tradition of "parties of abstraction".[1]

And yet, the PS was, and still is, far more than a *décor* for a presidential candidate. During the 1970s, the Party underwent a far-reaching renewal of its organization and ideology, attracting the support of many groups previously estranged from party politics. New recruitment channels, drawing heavily on reservoirs of nontraditional militants, were constructed, while the grip of old-style *notables* on the party apparatus was effectively loosened. These, and other less spectacular changes, provided the PS with a unique opportunity to overturn entrenched patterns of political and civic behavior and to develop a more participatory political culture on the Left. Even in its stewardship of the state after 1981, the Socialists not only supplied a new group of leaders – more *boursiers*, less *héritiers* – but also a novel style of governmental behavior that reflected their past Party experience and militancy.[2]

Why, after such a promising beginning, did the PS shrink to what it is today – hardly a replica of the old Section Française de l'Internationale Ouvrière (SFIO), but a far cry from the robust mass party many observers and supporters had expected it might become? The PS originally displayed a healthy capacity for attracting groups in civil society. Why did the initial enthusiasm the PS inspired give way to disillusionment among these would-be allies?

These questions also address a larger paradox of recent French politics: the resurgence of Jacobinism within the PS after 1981 occurred when this vision had lost its appeal within French society. In the view of many, this outcome was an inevitable result of the functioning of the French state and the deep roots of Jacobinism in the traditional Left's political culture. Yet, while such an interpretation might seem to fit the events *post hoc*, it is in fact a highly misleading guide to the actual politics and behavior of the PS over roughly the last decade and a half. We hope to show that the resurrection of an apparently declining political vision was caused by the weakness of the Socialist Party itself and not by the inherent vitality of Jacobinism or its efficiency as a method of government.

PARTY-BUILDING: THE GOLDEN YEARS

The new PS was born in 1971 to a heterogenous coalition united by a common rejection of the available models of socialism. The closest negative model, of course, was the SFIO itself. Discredited by Mollet's performance during the Algerian War, divided over de Gaulle's comeback, the SFIO had lost its militant potential by the late 1960s and its wider socialist ambitions were no longer credible. In electoral terms the SFIO had shrunk to a regional phenomenon with a few traditional strongholds dominating party functioning. The three largest federations represented 43 per cent of total membership, for example, and 33 others less than 10 per cent. The number of seats contested by the Party in national elections had declined since the war as well. In short, the SFIO combined the worst of a party of ideological abstraction with the traits of a party of *notables*.[3]

The new PS's first years, therefore, saw sweeping changes in leadership, organization, patterns of militancy, ideology and alliance strategy all designed to reestablish the Party's credibility by distancing it from the legacy of the SFIO. The first task was to reaffirm the Socialists' national ambitions and presence. The PS made its internal functioning more democratic and transparent in order to attract new members. Whereas the SFIO had been dominated by a restricted group of leaders – most of whom were cautious managers of their own fiefs with little interest in party debate and no stature in national politics – new PS militants had to learn, as the CERES put it, to view their Party as an instrument for socialism and not vice versa.[4] The most important departures from the SFIO's internal stalemate and ideological monolithism were the formal recognition of organized tendencies or currents and the adoption of proportional representation of such groups at all levels of party governance.

Both measures were critical for the PS's expansion, since they transformed the Party's ideological diversity, which might have been seen as opacity and incoherence, into an asset for recruitment. The transparency and coherence lacking at the global level were asserted within each current, while the existence of multiple sensibilities allowed the Party to broaden its appeal. Through their militancy in a current's network, newcomers were thus able to subscribe to those aspects of the Party they found most attractive while disavowing those with which they disagreed. Furthermore, the tendencies provided multiple channels of contact between the national and the local leaders, as well as between the more experienced and the more recent members, thus acting as important agents of integration and participation. Finally, they lessened tensions between competing groups by giving political dignity and legitimacy to the personal conflicts which the building of a new party necessarily produced.

The network of associations inherited from the SFIO was a very poor basis for the expansion of the Socialist party. The SFIO's mass organizations had either disappeared altogether or existed only on paper.[5] In the universities, among youth, and, most important, among workers, the PS had to begin from scratch. The Party took steps to establish its presence in the workplace by reviving the network of factory-level organizations – the *sections* and *groupes d'entreprise* – that the SFIO had abandoned in the 1950s, while simultaneously renewing its relationship with the CGT and CFDT.[6] The Assises du Socialisme, a convocation of socialist groups held in Paris at the end of 1974, completed the incorporation of most Socialists within the PS. By bringing into the Party a highly visible group of activists from the CFDT, PSU and Left Catholic groups characterized by a rich militant experience and a high concern for participation and *autogestion*, the Assises stressed the distinctiveness of the PS's identity, strengthened its most innovative components, thickened its militant ranks and broadened its overall appeal.

Even the SFIO's impressive legacy of elected officials – survivors of the Party's electoral stagnation thanks to an opportunistic system of local alliances – was as much an embarrassment as an asset for the PS. This local, loosely partisan network rooted in clientelism, sociability and family tradition was not receptive to the Party's new emphasis on activism, or the strategy of allying with the PCF. Thus, the loss of many of these old notables, either through electoral defeat or outright defection, was a blessing in disguise for the Party, increasing the PS's appeal to militants estranged from party politics and to groups which had earlier rejected the SFIO. To militants whose distaste for the *"politique politicienne"* had been nurtured by unions, *gauchisme*, the GAMS (Groupes d'Action Municipale) or other associations, or finally, by the Catholic subculture, the Party's weakness at local level was actually an advantage, for it reduced the risks of organizational opaqueness and rigidity they so sharply resented. At the same time, the prominence of the national PS leadership, and particularly Mitterrand's performance in the 1965 and 1974 presidential elections, provided a guarantee of effectiveness which smaller organizations such as the PSU could not match.

In doctrinal terms, it is easier to say what the PS did not advocate than what it did, since the Party's ideological makeup was composed of overlapping layers of unity and disunion. If the Party was unanimous in rejecting the SFIO's narrow anti-Communism and *laïcité* combined with abstract Marxism, it was divided on the question of what to put in its place. One group, represented by leaders such as Chevènement, Poperen and Joxe, wanted to conserve the Left's statist tradition, and viewed the Socialist Party as its jealous and uncompromising guardian. Others, like Michel Rocard, but also more traditional leaders who had been formed in the SFIO such as Pierre Mauroy, were more sensitive to the limits of state-led change and the virtues of decentralization and participation.

This basic conflict between statists and decentralizers, however, was complicated by the common determination of both groups to avoid being identified with either Leninism or social democracy, which they perceived, although for different reasons, as discredited models for socialism. Marxists and statists repudiated social democracy for not being daring enough, while participationists condemned it for being too bureaucratic. Similarly, *autogestion* as a meeting ground only gave an appearance of consensus since it meant different things for different groups. In the 1970s, however, such confusion was itself a source of strength for the party, for it enabled the currents to cast their separate political nets much wider than would have been possible in a monolithic party.

The PS's alliance with the PCF was the final break with the legacy of the SFIO. While there was unanimity in rejecting "Third Forcism" as inadequate to the Party's electoral and political ambitions, the Socialists were nevertheless divided over the meaning of the PS–PCF alliance. Some supported the Union of the Left for purely electoral reasons, an alliance of convenience imposed by the majoritarian ballot. For others, it was a more aggressive policy aimed at contesting the PCF's electoral and militant hegemony and reequilibrating the Left to the PS's advantage. For a third group, the Union was an integral part of a wider restructuring of the Left aimed at a more unified labor movement.

Despite this multiplicity of motives, however, the alliance with the PCF favored the strengthening of the PS as a party. In order for the strategy to be credible, the Socialists needed to convince potential supporters, as well as their own members, that the Party could stand up to the Communists. As even those Socialists who saw the alliance in purely electoral terms recognized, this entailed reinforcing the Party's own organizational and ideological resources. The popularity of the Programme Commun, furthermore, offered the Party additional opportunities to profit from mobilization to increase its own membership and improve its militant image. Finally, the Union of the Left provided the standard for measuring the PS's capacity to respect its commitments. In this sense, it functioned as a sort of *rite de passage* from *Mollètisme* to the new PS.

By the mid-1970s, the PS did indeed look different from the SFIO. Many once-stagnant federations had become promising melting-pots bringing together activists from a variety of cultural and ideological backgrounds. Party congresses were no longer controlled by a few bosses; by 1982, in fact, the three strongest federations controlled only 25.6 per cent of total mandates. New members brought a valuable militant capital from union and associational movements which could be used to extend Party influence among previously hostile or indifferent groups such as Catholic workers or peasants in Western and Eastern France. Total membership increased by roughly 12,000 in 1972, initiating a process of growth which continued, with the exception of 1979, until 1982, when the PS claimed 213,000 members.[7] In ten years, the Socialists more than doubled their membership: only in 1936-38 and in 1945-48 had they done better.

The PS' membership acquired a much younger and, to a lesser extent more female profile: by 1980 only a third of the members had joined before 1974, 23% of Party members were women and 25% were under 35.[8] Opening the Party to Catholics had paid off, as attested by their share of delegates at Party congresses: 37% and 40%, respectively, in 1973 and 1977.[9] Local elites had also been substantially renewed. Of the 165 Socialist mayors elected in towns with more than 15,000 inhabitants in 1977, 18.3% had been elected for the first time in 1971 and 60.4% in 1977.[10] By the municipal election of 1977 the PS had bypassed the PCF and by the national election of 1978 it had become the largest French party. The PS proved more successful in attracting those middle strata of working-class origins owing their social mobility mainly to the acquisition of cultural capital, than in attracting blue-collar workers. In 1980, in fact, blue- and white-collar workers accounted for but 25% of Party membership, and their presence shrunk as one moved from simple membership to higher levels of responsibility.[11] The Socialists did, however, enjoy strong credibility among unionized workers. In a 1977 poll, 77% of the CFDT and 76% of the CGT respondents expressed confidence in the PS, compared with 42% and 71% respectively for the PCF. By 1981 more workers voted for the PS than for the PCF.[12]

PARTY-BUILDING PHASE TWO: WORMS IN THE APPLE

The new PS, then, represented a marked departure from the SFIO in organization, personnel, ambitions and choice of allies. Some of these changes are indeed irreversible – a return, for example, to the old ban on organized tendencies is unimaginable; others, such as the displacement of *notables*, democratization of party life and the development of stronger roots in civil society have, however, been more superficial. Indeed, the most striking feature of the "new" Socialist Party has been the rapidity with which many of these new practices and structures have given rise to a logic of internal stalemate and hermeticism reminiscent of its predecessor.

This retrenchment, paradoxically, was to a large extent a product of the young party's early political successes. The openness of the PS in the years immediately following its creation – in terms of internal debate and willingness to seek outside support and participation – had been promoted and sustained by fierce competition among the various organized tendencies. In their scramble for influence, these tendencies actively recruited allies from the socialist diaspora: the myriad of associations and splinter groups of the Left, plus various fragments of the Catholic Left. As these reservoirs emptied and possibilities for significant new influxes diminished, however, the currents' attention shifted increasingly inwards toward the narrower and often Byzantine stakes of internal party alliances. This, in turn, encouraged the development of a Malthusian attitude toward party growth. The currents came to prefer stagnation to expansion that risked destabilizing the delicate balance of power that had been reached between various tendencies. Intercurrent rivalry, for example, undermined the development of the Party's nascent factory sections and stunted the Socialist youth and student movement (which were seen, not incorrectly, as vehicles for the CERES).

The sclerosis of the currents also weakened the Party's ability to respond to new issues. The PS' difficulty in adapting its program to the changing economic climate of the 1970s was perhaps the most notable product of this rigidification of internal debate. For example, the drafting of the *Project Socialiste*, rather than occasioning a *"grand débat d'idées"* was turned into an opportunity for the CERES to ostracize the followers of Michel Rocard.

Next, the Socialists' impressive electoral gains in the local elections of 1973 and 1977 turned out to be a mixed blessing. In a sense, the "long march" of the PS may well have been too short: these quick victories meant that many of the Party's most able leaders had to shift their priorities from party-building to the more pedestrian tasks of administering their new electoral *patrimoine*.[13] The subsequent "municipalization" of party life encouraged a pervasive attitude of complacency among lower and mid-level leadership and made the Party less eager to seek support and participation of local allies.[14]

The decline of the currents as agents of party growth and integration and the new preoccupation of Party leaders with problems of local government gave rise to a double self-fulfilling prophecy. First, the Party's declining will to maintain contacts with outside groups and weave networks of support created a vacuum which was filled by entrepreneurial leaders, who could thereby gain autonomy from the Party apparatus by exploiting their personal connections. To be sure, personal loyalty had always been an important element in PS politics but, whereas in the golden years of party-building such loyalty had been channelled mainly through the tendencies, and hence given a political basis, new patterns of recruitment were increasingly based solely on loyalty to individual leaders. In turn, the rise of what looked like a new class of *notables*, which the PS had itself encouraged through its lack of societal entrepreneurialism, only confirmed the Party apparatus' suspicions concerning the harmful effects of external contacts and pressures on internal politics, and reinforced its determination to tighten control over potential *notables*. Both responses were in a sense justified, for the political entrepreneurs could hardly afford to refuse the support of groups still within the Party's reach, while many leaders rightly detected in such practices "the risk of the Party's identity being diluted in a dim constellation of associations and unions".[15]

Second, this isolationism damaged the PS' image in the eyes of societal groups who had expected the Party to act as a moralizing force by introducing greater accountability and transparency. As their access to the Party diminished or was reduced to the level of personal relationships, many of these groups, with a low esteem for party politics from the outset, found their worst suspicions confirmed and confronted a choice of either withdrawing from party politics or short-circuiting the Party by collaborating exclusively with the municipality. For other groups, such as the CFDT, which placed a high value on participation, this was an unacceptable choice. Outside groups, notably those representing women, workers and ecologists, that refused to be merged into one of the Party's major currents, did not manage to obtain a real voice.[16] In the view of leaders like the CFDT's André Jeanson, the brief opening of the PS had been followed by a return to "politics as usual".[17]

As relations between the Party and other organizations deteriorated, many militants who had been co-opted into leadership positions in the Party came to feel more like hostages than representatives. Some, like Jeanson, resigned; others chose to remain but found that they had to cut their connections to the groups who had sponsored them. In the words of a Socialist deputy and former labor activist, "In order to succeed in the Party, to make myself heard, I finally had to stop behaving like a unionist".[18] The Party thus inherited a substantial reservoir of militants with strong roots in the associations and unions. It failed, however, in exploiting their potential for building lasting alliances between the Party and external groups.

The final area in which the Socialists' success had negative implications was in their dealings with the Parti Communiste Français (PCF). The Union of the Left had been perceived as a marked improvement over the opaque politics of the SFIO: Socialist ideology and Party strategy were finally reconciled. At the same time, the alliance worked to undermine this new transparency by imposing a heavy premium on internal discipline and stifling Party democracy. If the credibility of the Union as a governmental alliance was to be maintained, the PS had to contain its criticisms of the PC within relatively "fraternal" boundaries. The struggle for leadership over the United Left, moreover, increased the risks that internal dissent within the PS, whether on the part of the unitarian CERES or the more autonomist *Rocardiens*, would be exploited by the Communists to destabilize their partner. As relations with the PCF deteriorated, "foreign relations" came to eclipse "domestic politics" in the priorities of the party's leadership, often leading to repression of initiatives within the Socialists' ranks. This attitude proved particularly demobilizing after the Union of the Left was reduced to a purely electoral alliance in 1978. Some amount of damage to Socialist morale was probably inevitable, but the Party's response – the further tightening of internal discipline – amplified the problem by cutting off debate precisely when it was most needed to give militants a new political perspective.

At a deeper level, this strategy of ideological retrenchment transformed the PS into a conservator of the Programme Commun, even of those aspects that most belonged in a museum. Thus, for example, the Party continued to refuse a revision of its doctrines regarding the economic crisis. The drafting of the *Projet Socialiste* in 1979, which many leaders hoped would be an opportunity to renew internal debate, became instead an occasion for the Party's new majority to check the "revisionist" aims of Rocard. The *Project* became a bible, enshrining the Left's most outdated myths.

1981 AND AFTER: THE PS BETWEEN STATE AND SOCIETY

When the Left came to power in 1981, the PS was already a party suffering from a crippling disproportion between its ambitions and its means. On the means side, with 38 per cent of the vote and an absolute majority in the Assembly, the Party possessed an impressive mandate, which it used to push through an unprecedented amount of legislation. The PS's own popularity, which remained strong both before and after the elections, indicated that the victory itself was more than simply a presidential phenomenon. For the first time in the history of the Fifth Republic, moreover, the Prime Minister enjoyed a higher level of confidence than the President himself, further proof that the PS was more than a president-making machine.[19] If mass parties can be seen as banks of trust[20] between state and civil society, then the Party's credit rating appeared solid.

However, nationalizations, social legislation and other reforms, although integral parts of the Left's project, were only a prerequisite to fulfilling its wider promise to "change society and change life". As the fate of some of these reforms, such as decentralization and the Auroux Laws, showed, their successful implementation required a high degree of initiative and support from the constituencies they were designed to serve. Little of this was forthcoming, however, and the PS's poor performance as a connection between the state and civil society undermined a range of government policy initiatives where support from societal groups was needed. Nowhere was this more visible than in the rapid decay of relations between the government and unions. The organized labor movement was arguably the most fertile ground for developing new alliances. Not only had both the Party and the President stressed their commitment to increasing workers' rights, reducing class-based inequalities and creating a "new citizenship" within the factories, but the government of Pierre Mauroy moved rapidly to institute a series of reforms, ranging from the Auroux Laws to the establishment of local tripartite employment commissions – the Comités Locaux pour l'Emploi (CLE). Such reforms were intended to buttress the power of unions and provide them with an expanded role in decision-making. Finally, the government made clear its objective of involving the main union confederations in concertation at the national level. What went wrong?

From the very start, the government's actual behavior was confused and contradictory. In some cases, the government relied on the CGT–PCF transmission belt, with the PCF acting as the government's *de facto* "minister of labor". Despite the effectiveness of the PCF–CGT link, and the Communists' apparent willingness to sacrifice their militants for newly found governmental respectability, this strategy was doomed to fail. By excluding the other unions, in fact, it forced them to take an oppositional stance, even when they actually supported the policy in question.[21] On other occasions, the government tried to play on existing union divisions to weaken the CGT–PCF couple.[22] This strategy of *divide et impera*, by encouraging interunion rivalry, however, ran against Mauroy's stated intentions of "favoring the existence of a homogeneous union front which could become a partner for the state".[23] In short, the government neither made a clear choice in favor of concertation, nor, alternatively, did it press for the unions to work out their differences and present a united labor front.[24]

This oscillation in turn encouraged a politics of *"surenchère"* between government and unions, wherein labor leaders turned to the only form of voice left to them – public criticism of the government. Confronted with unpopular economic policies and deprived of a legitimate and institutionalized role in decision-making, the unions were nevertheless perceived as closely associated with the Left and hence blamed for the outcome. If the CGT was restrained from giving full vent to its disappointment as long as the PCF remained in the government, other unions were less inhibited.[25] Their complaints were meant to change the policy-making process via greater labor participation, not to sabotage the Left. This use of "voice", which was meant to prevent "exit", however, was interpreted by both the government and the PS as a breach of solidarity. When the government did finally substitute its statist approach to labor issues with more autonomous bargaining, as in the case of flexibility, its closest union allies had been so weakened by previous defeats that they were unable to ensure the compliance of their members. Consequently, the government was obliged to return to direct state intervention.[26]

In our view, the Socialists' difficulty in finding a *modus vivendi* with organized labor was aggravated by their inability to solve, whether in the government or in the Party, the problem of the division of political labor between the Party and unions. While the PS had paid lip service to union autonomy, in practice it had often tried to limit the actual scope of union competence or to trespass on what the unions perceived as their own territory (setting up factory sections or presenting its own slates at elections for worker representatives to the boards of the nationalized firms, for example). Even when the government did encourage the treatment of labor problems at a decentralized level, as in the case of the CLE, these initiatives fell victim to the deep mistrust which had built up between Socialists and unionists. The CLE, created in the fall of 1981, were designed to ease unemployment through the joint efforts of local elected officials, unions and employers. The success of this project required the Party and the unions each to sacrifice a measure of their respective jurisdiction and autonomy in favor of a more complementary relationship in which both sides stood to gain: the unions had to recognize the electoral concerns of the élus, the Socialists, the need of the unions to derive a portion of the credit for the CLE's achievements. The CFDT, although dependent on Socialist elected officials to secure the participation of employers, was eager to dismiss the interest of the *élus* in the CLE as illegitimate electoralism; the *élus*, in turn, saw the CFDT as a potential competitor and tried to appropriate leadership of the CLE or absorb them into preexisting institutions of local government under their direct control. The experiment ended with each side accusing the other of acting in its own exclusive interest, a common pattern in union–Party relationships.[27]

The failure of initiatives such as the CLE and the souring of government–union relations deepened the initial distrust between the PS and its would-be labor allies while strengthening the isolationist tendencies within the Party. Indeed, the two sets of developments went hand in hand: the more outspoken the unions became in criticizing the government, the more PS Jacobins felt vindicated in their view that the Party had to develop its own resources rather than relying on unworkable division of labor with outside groups. As Jean-Paul Bachy, National Secretary for Enterprises, explained, only the Party itself could guarantee government support in the working class.

> The unions themselves cannot offer any direct political support for the government. The couple CGT/PC is ambiguous, but the CGT is increasingly adopting a contestatory tone which the PC cannot do itself due to governmental solidarity. The CFDT . . . still suffers the temptation to want to take our place in bringing the message of democratic socialism to the workers. There is therefore, in fact, frequently a competition between the Party's political activities in the factories and those of the CFDT. Force Ouvrière, divided into contradictory factions, alternates between blowing hot and cold. Under these conditions, the government has no choice, it can only count on a single force to relay its politics in the factories: that of the militants of the Socialist Party. And they can only count on themselves.[28]

However, Party militants alone were unable to accomplish very much. When the Socialists and Communists organized a national campaign to publicize the Auroux reforms in 1984, for example, the initiative fell flat amid accusations that it had been sabotaged by union apathy.[29] In fact, the PS's isolationism, by deepening the gap between the "political" and "union" Lefts, deprived the government of a potential ally in presenting austerity measures in a more favorable light. By 1985, the government's image was so blurred that, when asked whether they believed it was "conducting a policy of the Left or the Right", a full 43 per cent of the workers were unable even to locate the government on the Left–Right spectrum.[30]

The fate of decentralization provides another example of how the Left's ability to realize its project suffered from a lack of coordinated societal support. This reform, which was optimistically termed the *"affaire du septennat"*, has in fact proved to be one of the Left's least popular achievements, rating only slightly higher than nationalization.[31] The lack of public enthusiasm is hardly surprising: while the reform has brought about major changes in local political life, these have been characterized by a redistribution of power and competence within the class of elected officials, not by the widely expected move toward greater participation and *autogestion*.[32]

The reasons for the Socialists' failure to strengthen participation via decentralization do not lie, as many critics would have it, in the government's Jacobin intentions. For, the Socialists, fearing that local groups might be too fragmented or vulnerable to municipal control to take full advantage of the reform, did plan to offset the increased powers of elected officials by granting associations new rights. Both the government and the associations, however, abandoned this project when they realized that it required a distinction between eligible and ineligible recipients for which no unambiguous criteria could be found.[33] Nor can the poverty of local participation be blamed on the ill will of Socialist elected officials. In keeping with the Party's Municipal Program of 1977, most Socialist mayors did, in fact, introduce innovations aimed at encouraging participation.[34] Their initiatives, however, were often thwarted by the entrenched system of local power centered on the primacy of the mayor and mayoral complicity with the administration, which, by depoliticizing issues, delegitimized activism in parties and associations alike. As a result, in most cases – Grenoble being perhaps the most outstanding example – the participationist attitude of the *mairie* ironically produced a further "municipalization" of associations as well as a virtual identification of the PS with the local administration.[35]

The Socialists' failure to strengthen civil society by providing alternatives to the *élus* as the only legitimate links between state and citizens, brings us back to the shortcomings of party-building and its relationship to political modernization. A more visible Party presence at the local level might have served as a catalyst for debate and as coordinator of local interest groups, thus offering a barrier against municipalization. The Socialists never consistently pursued such an objective, however. Neither the Jacobins nor the *autogestionnaires* were sufficiently concerned with party-building at the local level. The Jacobins feared that too great an involvement in local matters would distract militants from the national level where the true stakes of politics lay. As one leader put it, too great an emphasis on local matters would "encourage our members to take their town clock as the natural horizon of politics".[36] The *autogestionnaires*, on the other hand, were too confident in the vitality of civil society and wary of the tendency of political parties to anesthetize participation, to take much of an interest in the day-to-day management of Party affairs. Both attitudes paradoxically strengthened the position of *notables* in the Party and thus encouraged the predominance of the very elected officials who now stand between decentralization and an extension of local participation.

The Socialists' lack of concern for building up the Party's own ranks persisted after the Left's victory. Membership increased only slightly in 1981, mostly prior to the presidential election and stagnated afterwards.[37] At the local level, many sections and federations questioned the motives of potential recruits, whom they suspected of seeking patronage, while at the national level the congress of Valence too closely resembled an *affaire de famille* to attract outsiders (indeed, it even repelled many insiders!). Even more damaging was the PS's inability to choose among conflicting views of its role: to what extent could it identify with governmental policies, without losing its own autonomy? How much should it be an extragovernmental forum for debate – but how to prevent such debate from weakening the government? How could it serve as a tool for consolidating the Left's social base – but with what means? The PS debated at length to find a formula for resolving these ambiguities of its status as a majority party in the Fifth Republic. It was agreed that the PS would be neither *le parti au gouvernement* nor *du gouvernement*, but rather *le parti de gouvernement*, a definition that recognized its autonomy while respecting the primacy of the executive.

Despite its linguistic brilliance, however, this "solution" worked only on paper. In practice, the PS went underground and when it did reemerge periodically, this was either to confirm positions already adopted by the government, or, less frequently, to contest what it perceived as governmental intrusions on its own terrain.

The Party's isolationism and its overall weakness in society were partly to blame for this failure to create a more positive role. When the wave of spontaneous mobilization that many Socialists had expected would follow the Left's electoral victory failed to appear, the Party proved incapable of organizing support for its programs. In short, the Socialist shoe was not thick enough to be a good *godillot*. The freezing of internal party politics along lines of cleavage set in place during the early years of party-building was a further obstacle to the Party's ability to serve as a laboratory for new ideas when it became clear that Mitterrand's electoral program would not be a sufficient guideline for success. These divisions did begin to thaw, but far too slowly and out of phase with the pace of external developments to provide an adequate framework for recasting the Left's wider project. The truncated and abstract debates at the PS's post-1981 congresses and conventions reflected this partial stalemate. As a result, the Party was never at the forefront of the ideological changes signaled by shifts in governmental policy. For example, the PS only became concerned with modernization well after this was already the government's central theme, and even then it failed to add much programmatic depth to the notion.

In one area – jurisdiction over electoral campaigns – the PS did successfully avoid being a *parti du gouvernement*, but only at the price of becoming the *parti du président*. When a dispute erupted between Prime Minister Laurent Fabius and PS General Secretary Lionel Jospin, over who should lead the legislative campaign in 1986, the conflict was resolved by Mitterrand assuming the leading role himself. Some have seen this as a further example of the presidentialization of French parties. It was the unique role played by Mitterrand in building the new PS, and his lasting authority within the Party, however, that made this arrangement possible; it is doubtful whether any future Socialist president would be able to gain such control over his party.

Despite the Socialists' contradictory, and often self-defeating, responses to their governmental role, the PS did show important signs of adaptation, and these changes have accelerated now that the Party is out of power. The PS has, albeit reluctantly, embraced the cause of modernization, in the process trading its economic dogmas for realism, accepted a more complex as well as more conflictual view of society, shown a wider interest in other varieties of socialism and, finally, recognized the need for a greater opening to the outside. The crisis of the PCF, which not only killed the Union of the Left as a viable electoral, as well as political, perspective but also cured the Socialists' ideological and organizational complex *vis-à-vis* their Communist allies, has encouraged this mutation. Even the most hard-line Socialist ideologues, men like Jean Poperen and Didier Motchane, for example, are now calling into question concepts which, like the "Front de classe", were once viewed as sacrosanct pillars of the Socialists' ideological arsenal against the PCF.[38] Perhaps the most dramatic illustration of the political trajectory covered by the PS in the new legitimacy of social democracy as a positive model in party debates.[39]

Has the experience of power, together with the weakening of the PCF, then, signaled what many observers have termed the long-overdue Bad-Godesberg of French Socialism?[40] Indeed, some of the changes described above may point in such a direction. The PS's stated goal of attracting 40 per cent of the electorate, furthermore, would seem to imply its transformation into a centrist catch-all party. And yet, neither the notion of catch-allism nor the reference to Bad-Godesberg capture the dilemmas facing the PS. The sociological composition of a party's support is only one measure of catch-allism, and does not necessarily dictate its political identity. A party might well be sociologically diversified and yet contain several partly integrated, partly discrete ideological traditions, a combination that would place it somewhere between a catch-all and a classical mass party. This is precisely the case of the PS. The CERES, for example, with its swing from the "rupture with capitalism" to the "modern Republic", is the component of the Party that has undergone the most profound transformation in a seemingly catch-all direction. The Republican idea, however, may well prove too divisive to serve as a value issue and as a rallying flag across political borders. Even within the Left, republicanism continues to nourish sharply conflicting views of socialism. Finally, Bad-Godesberg itself has little to offer French Socialists. On the one hand, no less than the Programme Commun, it assumed rates of economic growth and levels of social spending that are now out of reach. On the other hand, the institutional setting for social democracy, a strong link between the Party and a unified labor movement, is now less present in France than ever.

CONCLUSIONS

According to one image, mass parties are bridges that link state and society. In our view, an appropriate reading of the PS would have to conclude that these turned out to be "drawbridges" which the Socialists raised too soon, leaving its actual and potential allies with little choice between besieging the fortress or retreating. Is this a sign that Socialism has lost its appeal as a political project backed by a party? Or, alternatively, does it vindicate theories which posit a seesaw relationship between social/associational movements and political parties?

Both interpretations would be broadly consistent with the notion that French politics have lost their national specificity. Contrary to the seesaw theory, however, French social movements and associations have not suffered from the PS's ability to coopt them, but from its failure to do so. Because of this lack of symbiosis based on reciprocal challenge and support, social movements never managed to make more than symbolic inroads into the political system, while parties remained identified with the state more than with civil society.

Have the Socialists presided over the "banalization" of French politics? Yes and no. For, if the demand for more societal autonomy is genuine, the rejection of Jacobin visions of socialism more firm, the ability of French society to organize itself is still abysmally low. If French society continues to resemble a desert, with nothing to buffer the violent winds that occasionally sweep it, the weakening of parties may signal a further deterioration of the *flora* rather than a first step toward a more temperate landscape. Indeed, French parties might themselves be the victims of insufficient political modernization, their weakness having been – even before the advent of the Fifth Republic – the main cause of their tendency to vanish into the state. In our view, a greater emancipation of civil society may thus be served better by a strengthening of political parties, than by their further weakening.

What of socialism itself? The electoral resilience of the Socialist Party – its performance in the 1986 legislative elections was its best after the second *tour* of 1981 – indicates that the Party still occupies an important space in French politics. As for the questions of what socialism, and with what means, the future is less clear. Whether or not a new project can be constructed from the existing fragments depends largely on the lessons the Party and its allies (both past and future) will draw from the recent past. Our own analyses of this experience, however, suggest that whatever socialism might come to mean in France, its realization will demand a stronger party than the present one, rather than, as some would have it, its withering away. It is not the least of the PS's legacies that the prospects for such a strengthening appear dim.

NOTES

1 Georges Lavau, "Parties of Interests and of Abstractions", in *European Politics: A Reader*, eds Mattei Dogan and R. Rose (London, Macmillan, 1971).

2 See Brigitte Gaiti, "Politique d'abord: le chemin de la réussite ministérielle dans la France contemporaine", in *Les Elites socialistes au pouvoir, 1981-1985*, ed. Pierre Birnbaum (Paris, Presses Universitaires de France, 1985).

3 Pierre Guidoni, *Histoire du nouveau Parti Socialiste* (Paris, Tema Editions, 1973); Jacques Kergoat, *Le Parti Socialiste de la Commune à nos jours* (Paris, Le Sycomore, 1983); Harvey G. Simmons, *French Socialists in Search of a Role* (Ithaca, Cornell University Press, 1969).

4 Quoted in C. Marjolin, *Une Fédération du nouveau Parti Socialiste*, unpublished dissertation, Université de Paris I, 1973.

5 Cf. Simmons, *French Socialists*, ch. 11.

6 On the *sections d'entreprise*, see Roland Cayrol, "Le Parti Socialiste à l'entreprise", in *Revue Française de science politique*, 6 (Dec. 1978).

7 Kergoat, *Le Parti Socialiste*, p. 367, *et passim*.

8 Information reported in *Le Poing et la rose* (new series, 42 (1980).

9 Roland Cayrol, "Les Militants du Parti Socialiste", in *Projet*, 88 (Sept.–Oct. 1974); and IFOP survey in *Le Point*, 249 (27 June 1977).

10 Philippe Garraud, "Le Renouvellement des élites politiques locales socialistes: les mairies de plus de 15,000 habitants", unpublished paper, Association Française de Science Politique, Paris (1978).

11 *Le Poing et la Rose*, 42 (1980).

12 Louis Harris Poll, *Le Matin*, (27, 28 Oct. 1977), quoted in *The Left in France*, N. Nugent and D. Lowe, (New York, St Martin's Press, 1982), p. 230.

13 Referring to the federation of Belfort, for example, Jean Pierre Chevènement complained that the 250 new Socialists elected in the department during the 1970s represented the "fine flower of the militants recruited between 1972 and 1973", in *Nouvelle revue socialiste*, 37 (Feb. 1979), p. 22.

14 See Patrick Hardouin, "Les Militants", *Intervention*, 5-6 (Aug.–Oct. 1983); Stéphan Dion, *La Politisation des administrations publiques: l'exemple de l'administration communale française*, unpublished dissertation, Fondation Nationale des Sciences Politiques, Paris 1984.

15 *Nouvelle Revue socialiste*, 38 (March 1979), p. 12.

16 See Wayne Northcutt and J. Flaitz "Women, Politics and the French Socialist Government", *West European Politics*, 8 (Oct. 1985); Helène Hatzfeld "Municipalities socialistes et associations: Roubaix", *Revue Française de Science Politique* 3 (June 1986).

17 *Faire*, (Jan. 1980), pp. 41-2.

18 Interview with Michel Coffineau, Paris, 4 April 1984.

19 Data from the series, "Chronique de l'opinion publique, profile de l'année politique", *Pouvoirs*, esp. 23 (1982) and 31 (1984).

20 The term is borrowed from Alessandro Pizzorno, "Interests and Parties in Pluralism", in *Organizing Interest in Western Europe*, ed. S. Berger (New York, Cambridge University Press, 1982).

21 Nowhere was this more evident than in the case of Talbot, where the CFDT, after arguing publicly for a tough policy on industrial restructuring, had to reassert its own legitimacy and right to be consulted, and could do so only by sabotaging the deal worked out between the CGT and the government. And, although many observers have argued that the CGT did receive concessions from the government in return for its cooperation, the legitimacy of this agreement in the eyes of many unionists was further eroded by its secrecy. In the end, even the CGT felt compelled to retract its initial consent. For a summary of the Talbot *"affaire"*, see *Libération*, (11 Jan. 1984).

22 Thus, for example, the government and the PS encouraged the CFDT to press its own opposition to union-sponsored lists in the election of worker delegates to the boards of the nationalized firms. If the CFDT was reluctant to become directly involved in management, the Socialists were mainly concerned with limiting the CGT's inroads in the nationalized firms – transcript of a meeting between the CFDT's Bank Federation and Alain Rannou, Secrétaire d'Etat rattaché au Premier Ministre, Paris, 27 July 1981, (private source). After the Talbot fiasco, the government tried once again to play the CFDT and FO against the CGT, see "Une Stratégie pour marginaliser la CGT?" *Libération*, (6 April 1984).

23 Pierre Mauroy, *C'est ici le chemin* (Paris, Flammarion, 1982), p. 60.

24 See, "La Tentation de se substituer aux partenaires sociaux", *Le Monde*, (14 Feb. 1984).

25 The CFDT's general secretary, for example, became notorious for his *"coups de gueule"*, such as his announcement of the second austerity plan from the steps of the Elysée ahead of the government and before the impending municipal elections of 1983. For this episode as well as the reaction it provoked in the PS, see "Le PS pour une code de conduite entre gouvernement et syndicats", *Le Monde*, (22–23 May 1984).

26 On the breakup of the negotiations on "flexibility", see "Flexibilité de l'emploi: l'enterrement d'un accord", *Libération*, (28 Dec. 1984).

27 By January 1983, over 300 CLE had been created, although the vast majority of these were little more than paper organizations owing to the withdrawal of either the unions or the Socialist officials. See Steven C. Lewis, "The Political Limits of Autonomy: Reforming the Union–Party Relationship in France", paper presented to the American Political Science Association, annual meeting, August 1985.

28 Minutes of the Comité Directeur, in *Le Poing et la rose*, (edition responsables), 27 (Nov. 1982).

29 For a description of the campaign and a summary of the PS's reactions to its failure, see, "La Campagne du PS et du PCF sur les Lois Auroux", *Le Monde*, (25–26 March 1984).

30 SOFRES-*Libération* poll, *Libération*, (28 Jan. 1985).

31 Ibid.

32 See Yves Mény, "La Politique de décentralisation, réforme de société ou réforme pour les élites?" *Révue Française d'administration publique*, 26 (April–June 1983).

33 This was one of the conclusions of a meeting between leaders of the PS and associational leaders participating in the Forum des Associations held on 9 December 1984, in Paris; as Jean-Michel Bélorgey, put it, referring to the importance of associations, "without sufficient counterweight, local life is the coffin and not the cradle of democracy". (Private source.)

34 See the survey in Jacques Rollet, *Le Parti Socialiste et l'autogestion*, unpublished dissertation, Institut d'Etudes Politiques de Paris, 1982, p. 392 ff.

35 On Grenoble, which was supposed to have been the showcase for the new municipal socialism, see the series of articles analyzing the defeat of the Left, in *Libération*, (11, 20 March 1983).

36 Jean Pierre Chevènement in *Nouvelle revue socialiste*, 37 (Jan. 1979), p. 23.

37 See Jacques Kergoat, *Le Parti Socialiste*; also *Libération*, (25 April 1986).

38 See Paul Bacot, "Le Front de classe", *Revue Française de science politique*, 2 (April 1978).

39 See the interview with Lionel Jospin, *Libération*, (5–6 Oct. 1985); one Socialist leader's view of what the social democratization of French socialism might look like is spelled out in Jean Poperen, *Le Contrat Socialiste* (Paris, Editions Ramsay, 1985).

40 See Maurice Duverger, "L'Heure de Bad-Godesberg", *Le Monde*, (8 Oct. 1985); and the interview with Jacques Delors, *Le Monde*, (15 Oct. 1985). Moderate Socialists like Delors have previously expressed such views in private, but it is only since the Congress of Toulouse in October 1985, that the Party has tolerated public discussions of this theme by its leaders.

6

The Left and Power

GEORGES LAVAU

HOW SOLID A VICTORY?

The Left won an almost complete victory in June 1981. Barring unforeseen circumstances, nothing could have impeded its control of almost all central power positions for at least five years. The old Radical Party, even at its zenith, never achieved such triumph. Moreover, when the Radicals had been the dominant party, they had had to work within a constitutional framework which did not include the Fifth Republic's advantages for the majority party. In 1936 Léon Blum could be held in check by the defection of either the Communist Party or the Radicals. From 1981 on, however, Mitterrand and his Prime Ministers needed steady support from the Socialist Party (PS) alone, and there was no reason to fear a weakening of this support. The Socialists' charismatic leader held the presidency and clearly kept the Party's control in his hands. In addition, practically the complete leadership of the PS held key positions within the government and the National Assembly. And within a few short months, most key positions in the high Civil Service had been conferred on men regarded as loyal to the new government.

From what or where might serious threats arise against this hegemonic Socialist Party? A libertarian social explosion in the mode of May 1968 did not seem a likely prospect. Whether such an explosion was even conceivable in a time of economic depression and unemployment was questionable, of course. In any event, such a burst seemed even less likely against a government of the Left than against de Gaulle and Pompidou. Furthermore, it could not have endangered the Socialist government unless it was relayed by large unions which energetically mobilized their followers for confrontations – an even less likely prospect. The Fédération de l'Education Nationale (FEN) had such tight links with the PS that it would not protest even under the greatest stress. Only the Confédération Générale du Travail (CGT) might have moved to open conflict with the government (but certainly not during the first years). Even the CGT would probably have contented itself with leading sporadic and local guerilla actions as long as the Communist Party (PCF) did not declare open war on Mitterrand. Moreover, CGT and PCF leaders were aware that CGT influence had been declining since 1979, and that, in addition, during the preceding decade there had been a decrease in the number and duration of strikes, the number of strikers and in the number of companies hit by strike movements.

In fact, as of October 1981 only two types of threats to the Socialist Party seemed conceivable. The first was the possibility of rapid economic collapse and bankruptcy.

The choice of Jacques Delors as Minister of Finance and Economy made this possibility unlikely. Still possible were politically compromising weak results in economic policies, and lasting deterioration, which would result in a slow undermining of Socialist authority. The second threat, during these five long years of Socialist reign, was a possible defection of a significant fraction of the voters who had – to some extent accidentally – given the PS complete control of the state apparatus. The election agenda in this period contained no fewer than four major elections in 1982, 1983, 1984, 1985, not to mention by-elections and ceaseless opinion polls. The threat posed by this calendar was all the more worrisome because the good electoral health of the PS was anything but guaranteed.

Since 1976, for the electorate as a whole, the PS had received many more favorable than unfavorable evaluations in the polls. Still, the support it enjoyed, while distributed across a wide spectrum, was rather shallow even among its voters. Thus, depending on the moment, 11% to 18% of Socialist supporters had reservations about the Party's alliance with the PCF, 15% (even if generally sympathetic to the PS) hoped for the final victory of the Right, while more than one-third (on the eve of the 1978 election) were in favor of a majority coalition composed of the PS and the UDF. The existence of such superficial support permitted the prediction after 1981 that the PS – depending on the economic situation and the government's performance – would either draw additional new voters or fall flat. The result, as is widely known, was that all the elections between 1982 and 1985 were unfavorable to the PS. By 1983, the balance between positive and negative polling opinions about the PS had become negative, with the decline especially impressive among salaried white-collar workers (17 points lower than in the 1977 polls).

One of the most important consequences of the PS's total victory in 1981 was unseen at the outset, but became increasingly obvious in 1982 and beyond. This was the fact that the dismantling of Socialist hegemony could not be accomplished completely as long as Mitterrand or another Socialist candidate continued to occupy the presidency. Consequently, all mid-term elections became preparatory rounds for the 1988 presidential elections. The 1986 legislative elections, in particular, were conducted as the first round of the 1988 election. One of the anticipated consequences of the new system of proportional representation devised for these elections was that this electoral system would dilute the presidential significance of the legislative election.

HOPES, ILLUSIONS, FACTS: WHAT IS TO BE DONE WITH POWER?

Aside from the clear victory of the Socialist Party in 1981, many other things remained unclear. How would the winners understand the practical meaning and consequences of a prolonged period of unshared power? What guidelines would they follow while in power? The old doctrinal distinctions made by Léon Blum in the 1930s were useless in answering these questions. The numerous programmatic statements of the modern period, from the 1972 Common Program to the 110 Proposals of 1981, provided no definitive answers either. Unlike Britain and West Germany, France had no previous experience of what a socialist party in power might be. Would it be a party using the same language as before but acting differently? Would it be aware of its inexperience and ready, if necessary, to change and renew its beliefs in explicit ways? Would the Party compel its comrade president and ministers to implement the entire Socialist program?

To answer these questions and to propose some suggestive analyses we must, first of all, consider the explicit and unexpressed ideologies of the Party, its rhetoric and its usual modes of conciliating ideology with action. Next we must review the Party's assets in governmental experience, economic knowledge and expertise. Finally, there are the various obstacles and constraints the Party leaders encountered. Let us now turn to some brief comments about these three sets of factors.

Ideologies

Once in power, it is rather easy for a party to forget certain limited and precise proposals if they become embarrassing and useless. The French Socialists easily forgot some of their previous proposals: for example, the reduction of the President's mandate to five years (instead of seven), the abolition of Article 16 of the Constitution, restrictions on the *vote bloqué* in the legislative process, and a freeze on developing new nuclear power stations. It is less easy, however, to renounce from one day to the next ideological themes with deep roots in the Party's history. This is not only because they may be useful as long-lasting electoral resources, but also because they often provide a tested course of action in coping with upsetting and unforeseen circumstances.

The catchword in the Metz congress in 1979 was "breaking with capitalism". The preamble of the Socialist Party's Constitution states that, "because Socialists are consistent democrats, they believe no genuine democracy can exist in a capitalist society. In that sense, the PS is a revolutionary party." In part, such flamboyant statements were nothing but rhetoric and tribal idiom. Much more important are less articulate cognitive schemes which derive from the great principles and which usually shape the understanding and reasoning of Party members and leaders. This is quite clear in the field of economics.

Although the Socialists toned down their radical rhetoric, especially after 1983, they were not yet prepared to acknowledge objective economic constraints. I do not accuse them of being alone in misunderstanding the real economic environment: many leaders of the Right behaved the same way. What characterized the Socialists was a general denial that economic constraints actually existed. In their view, so-called economic constraints were nothing but a capitalist plot. It followed that it was a sign of submissiveness and renunciation for a Socialist government to bend to economic constraints generated by the world capitalist system. Instead, the cry of the Socialist Left was to resist and overcome them.[1] Hence, especially during the two first years after 1981, one saw the predominance of political will over prudent and gradual action, and the wager that rapid and inflexible implementation of the whole Socialist program, without break, would be the safest path to success. In addition to such ideological commitments and cognitive schemes, there were also moral feelings. The average Socialist activist approached the challenge of power with an obsession about the perennial nonachievements of Socialism in France, impatient to blot out memories like Guy Mollet and Robert Lacoste's reversal on the Algerian issue. These obsessions did not completely disappear even after mid-1983 when the Party was obliged to accept a cure of economic rigor.

Another moral incentive for the Socialists was the belief that what was given to less well-off people – retirement pensions at 60, increases in the minimum wage, old-age allowances, shop councils in factories – could not be considered wasteful. Rather, such actions were simple justice. Socialists believed that such redistributive social policies could never have devastating consequences on the economy, on the financial equilibrium of the state and businesses, on labor costs, or on the international competitiveness of French production. On the contrary, they thought such policies would certainly invigorate and energize economic mechanisms. The French economy was a sleeping beauty. Socialist government, bearing social justice, would be the prince to awaken her.

After 1982, this whole set of ideological commitments, preconceptions, obsessions and moral feelings did not withstand challenge from the facts. Sometimes gradually, sometimes suddenly, the Socialist government changed its policy approach in many sensitive domains, for example industrial policies, labor regulations, taxation, social insurance, foreign investments. I will limit my discussion here to the ways in which the Party and, more generally the Left, accepted and adhered to these changes.

The answer is clear only for the Communist Party. With the lone exception of the four Communist ministers (in the government until July 1984), the PCF leadership protested more and more bluntly against this reversal of policies. "We are not opposed to economic rigor," stated Georges Marchais, "but rigor cannot mean austerity for workers and gifts for employers." One may characterize the situation on the PS side in the following way: from the end of 1982 the Party itself grew more and more cautious, sparse with words and general statements, while retreating to the defensive and devoting itself to beating back the attacks by the Right and the Communists. At the same time the President, his ministers and the leaders of the Socialist group in the National Assembly were in charge of expounding, explaining and justifying the new course of action. Among Socialist militants and officials some probably thought about the challenge of facts and gradually changed their ways of thinking. Others, while more or less silent, probably remained adamant in their beliefs.

Still we cannot thrust aside the assumption that the most common attitude within the PS was simply the coexistence of both ways of thinking, without any pressing need to choose between them and achieve consistency. The more opinion polls were unfavorable and 1986 approached, the more these floating Socialists (along with prominent leaders) sensed that dual self-perception and language might be the most attractive electoral platform. This is why it was possible for the PS, after 1986, to return to its old oppositional syndrome. The last Socialist congress at Toulouse (October 1985) showed some signs of this return; Michel Rocard himself felt obliged to state: "Now that we have removed the dust from our flag, we are ready to brandish it unfurled in the coming battles." Whether or not the dust was removed is debatable.

The assets of experience and expertise, and the capacity to learn

I begin with the Communist Party because its case is by far the simplest. Its capital in previous governmental experience was nonexistent. Its experience in city management was hardly transferable to the state level and furthermore, Communist mayors were not usually the kind of men in whom the PCF placed complete trust. The PCF had few and sparse relationships with high Civil Servants and experts. Instead it trusted its own Party experts, many of whom were clever but were accustomed mainly to providing the leadership with arguments to hit the Party's political targets. The enormous, and sometimes sophisticated, knowledge accumulated by the Communists was oriented not to the exercise of state power but to agitprop, mobilization, breeding class-consciousness and training Communist officials. For more than six decades, the PCF worked to persuade its militants to resist bourgeois knowledge and to adopt the Party's spirit. This line was unlikely to change at a moment when the PCF was declining and when it bitterly perceived itself to be held hostage by Mitterrand. Thus, not only was the Communist Party unprepared to learn much from the government's risky experience, but it also used considerable resources to persuade its officials to resist any temptation to learn and thereby postponed the battle.

The case of the Socialist Party was different.[2] Although without direct government experience since 1959 – only Jacques Delors and Michel Jobert (in the first Mauroy cabinet) had served on Gaullist governmental staffs – Mitterrand and Pierre Mauroy could rely on the competence and dedication of many high Civil Servants, experts, managers and even some entrepreneurs sympathetic to the PS. It could have been expected that their influence over people would radiate outwards and therefore secure the loyalty of the whole state establishment. The only uncertainty was whether these people could accommodate themselves to the oppositional syndrome which dominated the Party's approach to political action. It clearly became the joint responsibility of Mitterrand, the Prime Minister and Lionel Jospin to see to this matter without too much delay. It was obviously not done at the Valence Congress in 1981. My own opinion is that, despite real improvements over time, a sound balance was never achieved, partly because any potential equilibrium was disturbed by rivalries between internal Socialist currents, Mitterrandists and Rocardians in particular.

Although the domestic political knowledge and expertise of Socialist leaders and officials were very high, particularly in reference to electoral processes and parliamentary procedure, they remained almost uncultivated in day-to-day governmental operations. More or less spontaneously, a *modus vivendi* was reached whereby Party activists and politicians continued to be inspired by their professors' culture, but accepted the experts' guidance in day-to-day matters. Above all, their expertise in international matters was – and remained – rudimentary. They were not knowledgeable about the actual balance of forces in the world which, when combined with their preconceptions about economic constraints, could have had serious consequences. They were largely unaware of the rapidly increasing international integration of big oligopolies, and had a poor idea of international competition as well as the interdependence between national economies. Obviously, the Socialist leaders could learn (preferably, not too late), and some were willing to learn. Nevertheless, most of them, when obliged after 1982 to confront the real state of the world, complied out of necessity but retained bitter feelings that their beliefs and commitments had been restrained and that, in the future, circumstances would be more propitious.

One final remark about this. No party, no president, no prime minister can rely only on personal forces, friends and sympathizers. It is often very helpful to enlarge the range of available support and advice. For example, de Gaulle after 1958 succeeded in rallying many individuals and groups who were not ready to join any Gaullist party. Obviously, Mitterrand could not hope to attract more than a half-dozen second-rank politicians from the Right, but overtures might have been made toward the CFDT and various other associations. Occasional independent support could have been sought from some influential journalists, intellectuals, and entrepreneurs, on the condition that the Party would not be too suspicious about criticism and complaints. Such endeavors were not wholly neglected, to be sure, and some results were attained, even if they were uneven. Nevertheless, it soon appeared that new recruitment did not extend much beyond a circle of friends and complacent followers. Then, with poor election and opinion results, the PS became increasingly touchy, finding CFDT leader Edmond Maire's unpredictable criticisms exasperating, for example. Also, André Fontaine's *Le Monde* was no longer the Socialist government's voice. In the heat of the summer of 1983, Max Gallo launched (in *Le Monde*) a large inquiry asking intellectuals why they were so "silent", which was to be understood as a request for an explanation of their refusal to applaud. Replies were scarce, but those who did reply wrote splendidly stupid and arrogant pieces. It appeared that what the PS sought was not truth, advice and warnings, but love. The most irritating thing was that this love was not really denied, but was being offered to Michel Rocard rather than to Mitterrand, Fabius, Jospin, or to Socialism.

Internal and external constraints

The Socialists did not face insuperable institutional and political constraints. François Mitterrand was right when he said that the 1958 Constitution, although not tailored for him, fitted him perfectly. With a disciplined Party under his control, an absolute majority of seats in the National Assembly, his major lieutenants (representatives of the Party's various currents) in key positions and the security of a long-term mandate, Mitterrand had no obstacles to fear. Only the Senate and the Constitutional Council could delay, but not block, his action. Furthermore, like his predecessors, he was quite free to replace his prime ministers. In addition, according to a perennial French tradition, the majority party in the Assembly could pass a law imposing a new electoral system to ensure it the best possible returns. For five years, there were no constitutional constraints. The difficulties and uncertainties were to come when the Right parties won the 1986 elections and if maneuverings around *cohabitation* resulted in a failure or stalemate. That, however, is another story, one in which perhaps Mitterrand's destiny and the PS's will diverge.

Political constraints were also minimal, except for the duty to follow the electoral agenda in 1982, 1983, 1984 and 1985. As shown before, the hegemonic PS had little to fear. No real danger could come from its political alliance system. The CGT, CFDT, FEN and other groups could grumble but not coalesce into any unified protest movement. In any case, the Socialist Party and government did not depend on them as long as there was no great problem of public discontent. The Communist Party, deeply weakened by its defeat in 1981, needed to recover and hesitated about the best strategy for doing so. It expected some help through its participation in government, but could not renounce its identity or abandon its position of urging the Socialists to move ahead more vigorously. The PCF never considered itself to be completely committed to the success of the Socialist experiment. Its main concern – unchanged since its Twenty-First Congress in October 1974 – was to pull free from the PS's hegemony of the Left and to recover the political space which the PS had taken away. Its open move into studied opposition after July 1984 did not weaken the Socialist position either. The failure of the protest rallies, strikes and demonstrations launched by the PCF in 1985 demonstrated the Party's weakness, if not the PS's strength. To be sure, a Communist Party openly at war with the PS and thoroughly mobilized against it could have harmed the Socialists if the previous electoral system had been maintained. Under the 1985 proportional representation system, however, the PS protected itself against this risk.

From the very beginning the Socialists were quite aware that their two most serious constraints would be economic and external. Nevertheless, they did not accurately understand and evaluate the way in which these constraints might interfere with their plans. They had imagined economic constraints as the obstinate resistance of employers trying to torpedo reforms, refusing to invest, hiding their capital in Swiss banks, etc. They had also imagined that international banks and the International Monetary Fund (IMF) would put stringent conditions on loans. In order to preempt such threats, the Socialists planned large-scale nationalizations, strict economic controls and solemn warnings combined with good behavior. In short, there was a carrot-and-stick approach of incentive and appeasement policies. The difficulties surfaced elsewhere, however. The Socialists had greatly underestimated the structural frailties of the French economy, the longer-run consequences of the second increase in oil prices after 1979 (whose peak of $32 a barrel was reached in 1982) which resulted in a transfer of a 3 per cent of French GDP to oil-producing countries and a massive tax upon French consumption and investment capacities.[3] They were not fully aware of the fact that by this time (contrary to what had occurred in 1975–76), France was not alone in its pain; almost all European countries were in trouble. Consequently, it was unwise to rely on an anticipated international recovery from which France could benefit. Although they had been warned by some of their better experts that, with the increasing flexibility and mobility of international oligopolies in their location strategies, there were no longer any real nationally closed markets, the Socialists chose as their central strategic target "reconquering the independence of internal markets". In consequence, they made some ambitious and very expensive plans, especially in industrial policies.

Above all, the PS shared with other political parties, the PCF and RPR in particular, the belief that the decisive causes of economic success and failure were political. Therefore they strove to enlarge the powers of state economic agencies and to draw very intricate coordination plans between these agencies and leading firms.[4] That is why they also chose the formula of state-owned companies instead of simply purchasing a majority of shares. The same reasons partly inspired their decision – despite skepticism about the results – to increase coal production and stimulate shipbuilding and steel industries.[5]

With regard to external constraints, the Socialists thought that their firmness toward the Soviet Union, their unambiguous stance on issues of Western defense and finally, their commitment to EEC institutions, would dispel prejudices and suspicions from abroad. They gradually discovered, with the persisting economic crisis, the declining attractiveness of common European policies and regulations. The PS also learned that alignments in international trade, world economic strategies and tariff negotiations did not always follow the same patterns as in diplomatic and military affairs (with these latter becoming more flexible themselves).

Between mid-1982 and 1985, the Socialists revised many of their preconceptions about economic and external constraints. In many economic domains, the reversal was drastic, especially in the summers of 1983 and 1984. Rigor, severe anti-inflationary policies, modernization, the control of excess manpower, flexibility in labor regulations, cuts in public expenditures, incentives to firms – such were the catchwords. Mitterrand and the government praised such policies for providing the unique means to get out of the crisis and lower unemployment. Laurent Fabius solemnly declared that he would not, even under electoral pressures, abandon these heroic remedies.

STRATEGIES

Whether because these reversals were disappointing or for other reasons, François Mitterrand, Laurent Fabius and the Socialist Party accumulated bad results in public opinion polls. Amazingly, Michel Rocard – who, apparently, did not disagree with the general line of the government's new economic policies – constantly received high marks in the polls. This asymmetry has existed since 1978. When the Left seems to be at bay (March 1978, 1984–85), Mitterrand's popularity goes down and Rocard's goes up. It is as if there were still reserves of nostalgic confidence in the PS for which Rocard was the standard-bearer.[6] An interpretation complementary to this is also possible. Rocard's popularity, like Simone Veil's and even Raymond Barre's, might express a wide, although latent, stream of opinion which is unhappy with rigid partisan alignments and frustrated by the present structure of electoral conflict. These individuals are in search of an unknown liberal – socialist party which would marginalize the Union of the Left and talk of "breaks with capitalism", and commit itself ideologically to the people of the Left-Center.[7] If this interpretation is accurate, Michel Rocard's popularity is not to be credited to the Socialist Party, but to Rocard alone as a presidential candidate.

This is the crux of the matter. The Socialist Party's leaders are aware that the cases of Michel Rocard and Raymond Barre are different. Barre might have a chance of being elected even if he were not officially sponsored by a large party. Rocard will have to be annointed by the PS as its candidate. Rocard needs the Party's support for 1988 just as the PS needed Rocard's popularity in 1986. At the last Party congress (Toulouse, October 1985) each camp did its best to improve its own position. The final compromise was that the Rocardians obtained a larger share in Party leadership while Lionel Jospin obtained a clearer commitment from Rocard concerning his involvement in the 1986 Socialist campaign.

Officially, Mitterrand has not been personally involved in such maneuvers. In actuality, of course, he has never ceased overseeing and controlling all strategies. He knew that proportional representation – although it might prevent the RPR and UDF from jointly winning an absolute majority of seats in 1986, and although it might preserve a rather comfortable number of deputies for the PS – would not be enough to allow him to avoid appointing a prime minister from the Right. He also knew that the transitory strategy of *cohabitation* after 1986 would appear as acceptable and manageable if he shaped, well in advance, an image of himself as a *rassembleur* detached from Socialist Party politics. If he succeeded in doing this and if, at the same time, the Right refused to cooperate with him, the government could be painted as overly partisan and ignoring political consensus. Nobody, to my knowledge, can yet answer the question whether or not Mitterrand, during the last year of his term, will be ready to reduce the role of Fifth Republic President to a conciliator's role, somewhat in the manner of the Fourth Republic. The fact remains that beginning at the end of 1983, Mitterrand tried to present himself as a *rassembleur*, free of prejudices and responsible for policies that could conceivably rally consent from a large majority of opinion. The choice of Laurent Fabius as Prime Minister was designed to embody this idea in a concrete human form: polished (but not always polite), soft-spoken, nonideological, and pragmatic.

Whether this consensus-oriented strategy will be successful, or simply protective, nobody knows. However, its major inconvenience was that it did not take into account the passions and interests of the Socialist Party as a party. The PS kept itself under tight control for almost three years – although it must be said that it did not encourage any independent strategy and was therefore obliged to follow Mitterrand and the government – but it did not disappear. With the coming of March 1986, the PS was less and less likely to disappear. Thus it was unthinkable for the Party to let Laurent Fabius lead the electoral campaign alone; his policies were far too unattractive. To mobilize the Left, to prevent it from abstaining or voting for the PCF or extreme Left in despair, the Socialists themselves, and in particular Lionel Jospin, had to carry the flag. Consequently, the Socialist campaign in 1986 differed from its 1981 strategy. The tone was less aggressive, more defensive; many Socialists learned from the past five years. Finally, of course, they were constrained by the concern not to destroy the chances of the Left's candidate in 1988.

A BALANCE SHEET – WHAT LEFT, WHAT FUTURE?

Although the Left complained excessively about the "disastrous legacy" it inherited from Giscard d'Estaing and Raymond Barre, it may be true that it found a difficult economic and external situation. How then did the Left use the opportunity it had sought since 1959? Curiously, the final results were not the most disappointing in the domains where the obstacles were the greatest and in which the Socialist Party's inexperience and preconceptions aroused concerns. However reluctantly, many Socialist leaders quickly recognized that many obvious mistakes had been made prior to the spring of 1982. Incorrect economic policy paths had been followed whose results would take long to undo. Many would also concede that, even after the Socialist government reversed its economic policy, further mistakes were made which could have been avoided.[8]

Notwithstanding, on the whole I am ready to agree with Alain Fonteneau and Pierre-Alain Muet when they claim that the Socialist government, through its post-1982 economic policies, has quietly worked out a French version of Bad-Godesberg revisionism.[9] Although it is difficult to balance the respective weights of, on the one hand, a fourfold increase in the external debt and slowly rising unemployment against, on the other hand, an inflation rate limited to 5 per cent (much lower than in 1980), the efficiency of a price and wage freeze, a limited but stable growth rate and the stabilization of GDP, the result is by no means disastrous. Compared with other European countries, all without exception severely shaken by the crisis (and none prepared to regenerate economic expansion), France did not perform the worst. When reading harsher evaluations than those of Fonteneau and Muet – Alain Cotta, for example, or Eli Cohen and Michel Bauer – one is struck by the fact that many mistakes made by the Socialists had their sources in errors similar to those of their predecessors and in the same deep-rooted "national" economic culture. Here one finds protectionist temptations, lack of awareness of international economics and excessive fondness for state economic steering and big "national champions". The same errors – perhaps with less arrogance and sometimes with less ambition – inspired Charles de Gaulle, Georges Pompidou, Jacques Chirac and Giscard d'Estaing, with no better results.[10]

It is more difficult to determine whether the low rate of strikes and comparative weakness of social protest are the consequences of a climate of social anesthesia, anxiety over unemployment, fatalism and the collapse of the hopes put in the Left. Or did these weaknesses instead express a process of learning and maturing on the part of the people who expected uninterrupted redistributive policies from the Left? Perhaps the two arguments ought to be combined.

In his press conference of November 1985, Mitterrand mentioned some positive changes about which everybody might agree: retirement at 60, increased minimum wages, etc. There were other actions of the Left which deserved to be praised. One may understand – but not approve – the reason why Mitterrand said nothing about Robert Badinter's distinguished record, for example. It is astounding, however, that he did not mention the creation of the Haute Autorité for radio and television. In these two areas, the Left government was not only faithful to its commitments, but also took actions which had no strong partisan character and which had been implemented long ago in other countries not ruled by Socialist leaders.

In other areas there were mistakes which could have been avoided. Many people were irritated by the atmosphere of a royal court surrounding the President, by rash utterances, by the smugness and aggressiveness of some leaders and by many absurd postures which persisted long beyond their utility. All of these, in the long run, depleted Socialist credibility. In addition, the government wasted its resources when – either because of interest-group pressure or because it was simply too certain of the rectitude of its own cause – it persisted in pushing forward with certain questionable policies which were really not urgent. Here the list is impressive: the Higher Education Reform

Act, the Savary project on private schools and colleges, the Press Act (designed to shake down newspaper mogul Robert Hersant's empire), but one ought not to forget some dubious international actions such as Chad and the *Greenpeace* affair.

Will the Left learn from its partial failure? My personal guess is that it will, precisely because it is not a complete failure (which the Left would have attributed to evil manipulation). One conclusion seems beyond doubt: the challenge of exercising power in difficult circumstances has, in the short run, resulted in an electoral defeat. In the long run it may be salutory, however, because it has provided the only path to adjustment, responsibility and learning. It has permitted the Left to construct a new and different future.

But what Left? A definitive answer to this question must await the results of the highly complex period of *cohabitation* which has just begun. One aspect of it is clear, however. It is no longer true that the phenomenon once labelled "the Left" can be built around possible agreement, at least electorally, between Socialist and Communist Parties of more or less equal strength. The dramatic and continuous decline of the PCF since 1981 has changed all this. The PCF fell to the level of its 1928 electoral power - 11.28% - in the elections to the European Assembly in June 1984, a trajectory which was accentuated in the March 1986 legislative elections (9.8%). In seven years (1979-86) its electoral influence has been cut in half, most notably in its traditional fiefs in the Paris region. The PCF has done only marginally better in declining industrial regions and the Mediterranean *Midi* (see table 6.1). Just as important, according to polling data from 1984, the PCF has lost nearly half of its support from young voters,

Table 6.1 Evolution of the Communist vote from 1979 to 1984 according to level of influence in 1979 (base 100)

Départements where the PC received votes in 1979 (%)	No. of départements	1981/79	1984/81	1984/79
less than 10%	(6)	78	54	42
10%-14.9%	(19)	75	65	48
15%-19.9%	(29)	74	68	51
20%-24.9%	(22)	76	71	54
25% and more	(20)	78	77	60
Total (urban)	(96)	76	72	54

Source: Jean Ranger, "Le Déclin du PCF," *Revue Française de Science Politique*, 36, 1 (Feb. 1986)

Table 6.2 Communist vote according to age group in 1978 and 1984

Age group	% of PCF vote in 1978	% of PCF vote in 1984
18-34	21.4	11.5
35-49	19.9	11.0
50-64	16.2	10.7
65 and older	11.5	11.8

Source: Enquêtes IFOP

formerly one of its great areas of strength. They have moved away from the Party even more than other demographic groups (see table 6.2). PCF decline is also evident in the evaporation of new Party memberships, the attenuation of voluntary militant activism and persistent internal Party problems. Moreover, in both the 1981 and 1986 legislatures the Party had such a small number of deputies (44 after 1981, 35 after 1986) that it could not, by itself, move to censure a government.

After leaving government in July 1984, the PCF returned to the strategy that it had adopted – with such catastrophic results – between 1977 and 1981. It wanted – at any cost, it seemed – to convince working-class voters of the Left not to vote Socialist. Its deep concern was to avoid being completely marginalized by the PS. To do this, its priority had to be the struggle against the notion of the "useful vote" for the PS, which had become second nature to many of its former supporters. This led it to an aggressive campaign, with the feeble help of the also-declining CGT, against the PS itself. Despite all this, however, opinion polls continued to show that the bulk of remaining loyal PCF voters had become even more convinced that defeating the Right was more important than ensuring PCF revenge against the Socialists. This was why, as 16 March 1986 came closer, PCF leaders tried to blend two incompatible discourses, the first calling electors to block a Right victory, the second not to count on the PS to stand up to the Right; consequently, a vote for the PCF was necessary.

It may seem paradoxical that after five years in power, during which the Left's achievements were varied but clearly positive in a number of areas, it ended up weaker and more divided than before. The paradox is superficial, however. In fact, the 1981 victory ought not to mislead. The total number of Left candidates after round one of the 1981 presidential elections won barely 47% of the vote. As for Left disunity, it was as profound on 26 April 1981 as it is today. The 1981 victory was, to an important degree, an artifact of presidentialism rather than an index of a Left breakthrough. The PS, with its 32% in 1986, seems to be slowly gaining strength. The collapse of the PCF makes the Left a distinct minority, however. What Left and what future for the Left will remain the essential questions, therefore.

NOTES

1 "The so-called economic laws that the Right feigns to consider as eternal are in fact the principles of management ruling the capitalist economy", Final Resolution, Congrès de Metz, 1983. A few weeks before the Bourg-en-Bresse Congress in 1983, Jean Poperen uttered sinister prophecies: "A government of the Left will certainly fail if it sacrifices its political commitments to economic constraints", quoted by Pascal Perrineau, "Adolescence et maturité précoce du PS", *Intervention*, 5-6 (Aug.-Sept. 1983), p. 33.

2 In the Fifth Republic's system, the situation of a party that was in opposition for 20 years is dramatic. The unbalanced concentration of powers in the hands of the Executive, the Parliament's weak means for investigation and control, the uncertain boundaries of president's *domaine réservé*, separates this party from information about governmental operations; it has no access to the most important dossiers.

3 See for instance Alain Cotta, *Les Cinq erreurs* (Paris, Olivier Orban, 1985), pp. 38-55. An excellent and balanced evaluation is to be found in Alain Fonteneau and Pierre-Alain Muet, *La Gauche face à la crise* (Paris, Fondation Nationale des Sciences Politiques, 1985).

4 See Cotta, *Les Cinq erreurs*, chs 4 and 7; many striking examples may be found in Elie Cohen and Michel Bauer, *Les Grandes manoeuvres industrielles* (Paris, Belfond, 1985).

5 About the heavy cost of subsidizing these industries, see Cotta, *Les Cinq erreurs*, pp. 134–35.

6 See Jean-Luc Parodi and Pascal Perrineau, "Les Leaders socialistes devant l'opinion, F. Mitterrand et M. Rocard", *Projet*, 134 (April 1979); Jean-Luc Parodi et al., "François Mitterrand et Michel Rocard: deux ans de concurrence devant l'opinion", *Pouvoirs*, 13 (1980).

7 See Anne Sa'adah, "The New Center: Illusion or Reality?" unpublished paper, Dartmouth College, May 1985.

8 Cf. especially Fonteneau and Muet, *La Gauche face à la crise*, chs 2 and 3.

9 Ibid., p. 368.

10 A lot of evidence in Cotta, *Les Cinq erreurs*; Cohen and Bauer, *Les Grandes Manoeuvres*. For a comparison of Chirac's *relance* in 1976 with Mitterrand's *relance* in 1981–84, see Fonteneau and Muet, *La Gauche face à la crise*, pp. 130–39.

11 See the excellent article by Jean Ranger, "Le Déclin du PCF", *Revue française de science politique*, 36 (Feb. 1986).

7

The Right as Opposition and Future Majority

RENÉ RÉMOND·

The title of this chapter, which brings together two distinct concepts, suggests duality. The first concept, the Right in the role of opposition, describes the obvious state of affairs between 1981 and 1986. The other expresses a possibility that the Right could acquire a plurality again. Until 16 March 1986, however, this was only a probability and nothing more. Obviously, past a certain point during the Left years the possibility of the Right becoming a majority was highly credible. In anticipation, it exercised an increasingly decisive influence over political protagonists as the vital date approached. Analytically, it is prudent to refrain from mingling the two levels of interpretation.

TASTING OPPOSITION

The spring of 1981 shall continue to be an important moment in the recent history of the Right in France. Two consecutive elections led to loss of the authority which it had held from the origins of the Fifth Republic. On 10 May, François Mitterrand, the candidate of Union de la Gauche, defeated the incumbent, Valéry Giscard d'Estaing, who had been elected by a unified Right in 1974. There was only a slight gap between the winner and the defeated candidate – less than 3 per cent – and it would have been sufficient for only 650,000 voters to have voted differently for Giscard to have won. Moreover, the Right had indirectly contributed to this turn of events as a result of its own lack of unity, as Alain Lancelot's chapter in this volume shows clearly. Nevertheless, the Right lost the presidency of the Republic and this was an exceedingly harsh blow.

Such an unexpected reversal exacerbated divisions among leaders. Giscard d'Estaing cursed those who had betrayed him. In turn, legislators facing the prospect of dissolution sought to take their distance from the outgoing President, hastily lining up behind Jacques Chirac. Chirac, who had not suffered a loss of authority despite his unfavorable first-round showing, aspired to lead the Right. As a result the Right regrouped under the label "Union pour une Nouvelle Majorité" (UNM).

Parliamentary elections on 14 June and 21 June produced a new disaster. The gap between Left and Right had been less than 4% in the presidential election. It increased to 12%, 56% for the Left and 44% for the Right, in June. This was an exceptionally large difference for France. The automatic multiplication of votes into legislative seats built into the electoral system gave the Socialist Party by itself an absolute majority. The various *courants* of the Right ended up with only 155 deputies while the Left won twice as many.

Such unending adversity left the Right weak and speechless. Only a few months before the presidential election there had hardly been any doubt about Giscard's reelection. After 23 years, the Right had become so accustomed to exercising power that everything seemed to unfold spontaneously. Only a few years earlier, Alain Peyrefitte, one of the most astute interpreters of French politics and a former Secretary-General of the UDR (Union Pour la Défense de la République), had noted that "We shall be in power for thirty years if we don't do anything foolish". In other words, these were hopes of ruling until the end of this century. What "foolish" errors had the Right committed to undercut this optimistic prognosis?

As one is inclined to do in such circumstances, the Right thought in terms of analogies with recent precedents. Recognizing that the Right had governed without interruption for more than a quarter of a century, many leaders were inclined to believe that they would henceforth be in opposition for as long as the Left had been. This belief molded their behavior and explained their avoidance of the limelight during the initial months. Nothing was more significant in this sense than the silence and absence of the Right leadership during the important parliamentary debates of summer 1981. Young and virtually unknown, deputies were obliged to carry the entire burden of combatting the Socialists' proposals. Michel Noir, Philippe Seguin and certain others waged a series of hopeless skirmishes against nationalizations and decentralization. They were thus able to test their skills and later reaped benefits from their stance. Nevertheless, the disappearance of the leadership fully reflected the general disarray and discouragement of the Right.

The reversal of roles did not have exactly the same meaning for each segment of the Right. One group on the Right, in fact, had spent a longer period in opposition than in power. Jean Lecanuet and his followers did not join the majority until 1974, after having opposed it for more than 12 years. Similarly, the Gaullists had been in an intermediate position for several years under Giscard, excluded from vital responsibilities and opposed to Giscardian hegemony. Both groups had also accommodated leftist currents which included more figures who had held key positions between 1958 and 1981 (Jacques Delors, for example, who had served as an advisor to Jacques Chaban-Delmas from 1969 until 1972, and Edgard Pisani, who had been a cabinet member under de Gaulle).

Between its electoral defeat in June and the end of 1981 the Right lived in a "state of disgrace" which was the mirror image of the atmosphere surrounding the new majority. This had an especially harsh effect upon political parties. Public opinion considered them responsible for the disaster, and their leaders tried to slip into oblivion. Whatever confidence remained on the Right was redirected toward other institutions, clubs in particular. A similar phenomenon had already been observed on the Left after 1958; at that point, clubs had appropriated the role of discredited and powerless parties. The clubs worked to explore the reasons for the defeat, to prepare for reconstruction and to promote contemplation of the future. Although certain clubs were tied to the principal parties, most were not, and their members' origins were diverse. The press played an important role at the same time, partly filling the vacuum formerly occupied by the parties. Certain Paris dailies waged unsparing battle against the new majority: Robert Hersant's *Le Figaro*, for example (along with *Figaro Magazine*, which argued an even stronger line), *Le Quotidien de Paris*, whose circulation doubled during the summer of 1981 and others such as the *Nouveau Magazine*.

On New Year's Day 1982, the wind began to shift. Four by-elections during January provided an indication. Although their outcome did not have the slightest effect upon the balance of power, their symbolic impact was great. In each of the four by-elections the Right's candidate gained an easy first-round victory, together with a significant increase in votes. The uniformity of the results and the eloquence of the numbers created a sense of astonishment which, to a degree, countered the effects of June 1981 on the Right. After having been thunderstruck by the extent of its rout, the Right suddenly renewed hope and began to foresee a return to power sooner than the end of the century.

These events also tended to confirm an interpretation which François Goguel had presented in *Le Monde*. Comparing voting statistics for 1978 and 1981, Goguel had argued that the Left had not grown at all. Rather, its victory had come because of the defection of 25% of the Right's voters. These voters, either discouraged by Mitterrand's victory or granting such a high degree of legitimacy to the presidential election that they could not enthusiastically contemplate a majority in opposition to the Head of State, had abstained. Goguel concluded that the electorate had attempted to express a desire for change, but without granting the Left a mandate for transforming society. In a book with the somewhat hucksterish title of *Quand la Rose se fanera*, Alain Peyrefitte developed similar themes.[1] To Peyrefitte, June 1981 was the result of a misunderstanding. The Left believed that the outcome confirmed its conviction of representing the innermost wishes of the French people, which had finally regained its sovereignty. The seizure of power by the Right in 1958 had introduced a hiatus. In contrast, Peyrefitte argued that although the electorate had voted for the Socialists, it had not voted for socialism.

The questions raised by Goguel and Peyrefitte transcended the 1981 elections. If the misunderstanding thesis was correct, it meant that it was the Left's victory, rather than the long occupation of power by the Right, which was the anomaly. This called into question a number of related ideas. It followed, for example, that in Fifth Republic France to a certain extent the Right had become a standing majority in contrast to the conditions which had existed prior to the World War II (and which had long been regarded as reality by the Left). The axiom whereby the Left, because it had a "social" majority, would sooner or later emerge as a political majority – an axiom which François Mitterrand had reiterated so often – would also be exposed as a myth. Casting doubt upon this would have even harsher effects considering that, according to the axiom, the rapid transformation of France in recent decades ought to have given the Left unshakeable electoral superiority because of the massive expansion of its sociological base. Had not the proportion of wage earners, the Left's base among the adult population, risen from 62 per cent to 82 per cent in 20 years? If the Goguel/Peyrefitte contentions were correct there would be irrefutable evidence that political choices and voting patterns were not determined by social and occupational conditions and that any explanation of voting behavior according to infrastructural data ought henceforth to be suspect.

RENEWING HOPE

Whereas the Right concluded that the four by-elections of January 1982 allowed new challenges to the legitimacy of the Left's majority, the Left replied to the effect that "one swallow doth not a springtime make". It also suggested that the Constitutional Council, whose majority was suspected of hostility to the Left, had been playing politics in calling these elections in the first place. This confident and defiant mood did not last, however. After January 1982, nearly all elections taught the same lesson: the Right had become a majority again. Jérôme Jaffré and Jean-Luc Parodi, eminent interpreters of elections and polls, published a series of analyses to this effect. The Right continued to win to a point so that it was ahead by nearly 20 per cent before the gap stabilized for a number of months. At the beginning of 1985, the Socialist party claimed to detect symptoms of a certain "tremor" indicative of a diminishing trend in the gap between the Right and Left. Three months prior to the March 1986 elections, however, this "tremor" had turned out to be minor indeed. The electoral campaign itself did narrow the gap a bit, but it still remained exceptional in the history of elections in France, where the difference between the two currents has rarely exceeded 10 percentage points.

Comforted by its long chain of victories, the Right renewed its hopes. Confident that it spoke for a majority, its sense of its own legitimacy was reinforced, while the legitimacy of the parliamentary majority fell under a dark cloud. The leaders of the Right no longer doubted that they would soon win back what they believed to have been lost by mistake. Under these conditions, there was no willingness to compromise with the Left, no matter how insignificant the issue. The Right rejected any idea of entente with those who only held power provisionally. The RPR initially refused to accept several chairs of legislative commissions, for example. And rejection of compromise extended to nearly all of the bills introduced by the Left, even when certain provisions were tolerable to the Right. Thus for nearly four years the Right pursued unconditional opposition to the ruling party, as the Left had done in the past. In this way, the Right made itself vulnerable to the same complaint that it had often registered about the Left, namely that it was behaving as a contrived opposition and failing to recognize the legitimacy of a government which had won power through universal suffrage.

Changes in vocabulary showed how the revitalized Right had regained confidence. In contrast to the concept of the "Left" which benefitted from favorable connotations, the notion of "Right" had long borne a negative and repelling charge. The Left proudly drew upon its past and freely stated its own identity. The Right, however, had been extremely reluctant to identify itself as such. Only the far Right had no qualms about adopting the label, a usage which intensified the impulse of others to flee from the term. Between 1958 and 1981, the parties which had constituted a governing majority constantly denied being "of the Right", instead seeking acceptance for the designation of "the majority", whose neutral content was far less compromising inasmuch as it referred solely to a numerical relationship. This obfuscation ceased working as soon as these parties lost their majority, of course. They quickly discovered the usefulness of an inverse expression, and began calling themselves the "National Opposition". At the same time, however, they also willingly consented to being referred to as the "Right", to the astonishment of the Left, which had hoped that this label would discredit its adversaries and diminish their support. Nothing of the sort occurred. This was a sign of a far more significant change than a mere electoral realignment or the loss of majority status. The resuscitation of the Right was spurred by a shift in public opinion which began prior to 1981, although the Left's victory had been a contributing factor. Liberal beliefs were gaining new strength.

In its constant battle against the government, the Right cleverly exploited the Left's tactical errors and misfortunes and successfully established itself as a defender of freedom from the allegedly antilibertarian aims of the Left. For three years, the Right took advantage of the presence of the Communist Party in the majority coalition, claiming that the Socialists were intentionally or unintentionally yielding to Communist pressures and underlining the PCF's alleged alignment with the USSR. The unpopularity of the Soviet Union thus adversely affected not only the Communists, but the Left as a whole. The most rabid of right-wing pamphleteers did not hesitate to depict the Gulag as the probable outcome of the Left's policies.

The Right also benefitted from the imprudent proposals and exaggerated language of Socialist leaders during the initial months of power, at the Special Conference during the summer of 1981, or at the Socialist Party's October 1981 congress in Valence, only a few months after the triumph of the Left. André Laignel's barb, "You are legally incorrect because you are a political minority" hurled at the Right gave credence to the notion that the majority would quash the rights of opposition and jeopardize a government founded upon law. In turn, when Paul Quilès, the Socialists' third-in-command, urged the government to lop off some administrative heads, if only metaphorically, his words earned him a persistent reputation for sectarianism and the nickname of "Robespaul". As a result, fears about a spoils system increased in the uppermost layers of the civil service, and the Right emerged as their protector.

After principled battles around nationalizations and decentralization, the opposition launched several wars of attrition. It adopted the relatively unconventional tactic (in French politics) of systematically obstructing the majority's programs on higher education. The Left believed that it was necessary to repeal the statute which had been applied to France's universities since 1968, and the Minister of Education presented a new statute whose content was discussed in the National Assembly during the spring of 1983. Encouraged by student elements which had never accepted some of the consequences of 1968 (members of the syndicat autonome and UNI), the parliamentary opposition launched a seemingly endless struggle, submitting more than 2,000 amendments, many of which were repetitious. Debate went on for several weeks, paralyzing Parliament. Demonstrations by rightist students receiving open encouragement from faculty members were echoed by parliamentary debates. Right-wing newspapers rhapsodized about a "1968 in reverse" even if the number of demonstrators never approached 1968 levels. Subsequently, inasmuch as the opposition did not lay down its new weapons, some universities declined to adopt the new charters which the statute required them to draft.

The second bill pertained to the press. The primary target of this bill was the so-called "Hersant empire", the conglomerate which the owner of *Le Figaro* built in violation of a 1944 statute prohibiting ownership of a chain of publications. When Pierre Mauroy announced at the Bourg-en-Bresse congress of the Socialist Party (October 1983) that draft legislation would be filed, he was throwing a bone to the militant wing of the PS to console them about *rigueur* and the abandonment of reform. Nevertheless, the Right seized the opportunity to denounce this bill as an electoral maneuver whose intent was to deprive the opposition of a means of expression (even though some of the law's provisions were eminently reasonable). Restrictions on owning multiple newspapers and the required disclosure of financial backing were intended to prevent monopoly control and to preserve freedom of the press. Despite this, the Socialist Party and the government enabled the Right to pose as defenders of freedom of the press against the alleged illiberal intentions of the Left. Interminable debate ensued, punctuated by incidents such as one which led to the suspension of three right-wing spokespeople. Nonetheless the Right, helped by the opposition in the Senate, finally obtained a watered-down version of the original bill.

The third battle, over the school question, was of an entirely different magnitude. As Antoine Prost shows in his chapter in this volume, politicians did not provide the original impetus. This skirmish over relationships between public and private education was one last vestige of a 200-year-old struggle between church and state, between Catholics and the Left. The Left's victory in 1981 reawakened the fears of those who sought to preserve freedom of choice in education. The 110 proposals advanced by Mitterrand as a candidate included establishment of a unified and secular public education system. On the other hand, Mitterrand had quickly promised that the transformation would occur on a voluntary basis, without coercion or plundering. For three long years, Alain Savary, the Minister of Education, attempted to remove pitfalls and find a solution acceptable to both sides. Both camps sought to activate their troops and influence the progress of negotiations. The bishops, who did not want new hostilities, obliged their hard-liners to behave politely. They hoped to prevent the issue from being captured by political parties, and almost succeeded. The church maintained its control over the large gatherings which took place in an impressive crescendo between January and March 1984, in Bordeaux, Lyon, Rennes and Lille, culminating with the massive rally in Versailles, with hundreds of thousands of participants. Legislators were present, but they were kept at arm's length and did not deliver speeches. Some of them even became irritated with the ecclesiastical hierarchy.

After a sudden shift in the tone of debate in May 1984, as a result of the intransigence of the secular wing of the Socialist Party, the entire opposition mobilized in a huge demonstration on 24 June attended by nearly 1.5 million demonstrators from every region of France, one of the largest gatherings in recent French history. Even though the Right had not inspired this event and even though its leaders did not play a highly visible role, the opposition was indirectly aided by its success, and the majority was harmed. The events of 24 June produced results which three years of political battles had failed to achieve. The government withdrew its bill, announced a referendum, the Minister of Education and the Prime Minister resigned, the government's composition changed and the Communist Party quit both the government and then the majority itself.

THE TRIUMPH OF LIBERALISM

Thus in three situations and in response to three government bills – higher education, the press and schooling – the Right acquired a semblance of credibility as a rampart of civil liberties blocking a government that was allegedly seeking to extinguish freedom. This was consistent with the renewed public favor which liberal ideas found and which was mentioned earlier. The phenomenon was not exclusively French and had begun before 1981, but the Left's victory had accelerated it. The inability of governments to predict or to overcome the economic crisis not only ruined the prestige of economists, but caused new doubts about the abilities of the government to organize economic activity. Inasmuch as the public sector no longer protected individuals' jobs and was no longer capable of regulating trade, there was less tolerance for the dislocations which accompanied government intervention. As long as the notion of the government-as-deity had remained a dogma which hardly anyone in France dared to challenge, liberals had preached in the wilderness. In the 1980s, however, "less government" became the watchword. Everyone, Left or Right, had formerly thought like Keynes. Now everyone on the Right and even some on the Left began to think like Hayek. After 1981, liberalism became the watchword, banner and supreme point of reference for the Right, from one end of the opposition to the other. Only liberalism could restore the flexibility, elasticity and vigor of the economy. Socialism had failed and threatened individual creativity and autonomy. The new buzzword thus proved particularly useful for the Right in gathering up the *déçus du socialisme*.

This newly unanimous invocation of liberalism was somewhat astonishing, because, deeper down, not all of the components of the opposition had always shared it. Thus far we have described the Right in the singular, as if it were completely homogeneous. That is hardly accurate, however, and the final phase of Giscard's term had already demonstrated dramatically that the Right was not only diverse, but divided in ways which had played a decisive role in the Right's 1981 defeats. In fact, liberalism had been a subject of particular disagreement, instead of facilitating Right unification. The term best suited that portion of the Right which supported Valéry Giscard d'Estaing, who had announced that he would practice a form of "advanced liberalism". Indeed, the measures which he had promoted at the beginning of his seven-year term reflected a liberal program in most domains, not only for private morality and behavior, but for the economy. This stance drew significant criticism, and a portion of Giscard's voters turned away from him as a result.

The other principal current within the pre-1981 majority, the supporters of Jacques Chirac, had evolved very differently. They invoked the heritage of General de Gaulle, of course, attempting to update an authoritarian tradition which challenged private interests and had confidence in the state's ability to provide arbitration. Had not the

RPR frequently criticized the President's liberalism and denounced the weakness of his government between 1976 and 1980, condemning it for not seeking a vigorous economic recovery through intervention? Could it be possible, therefore, that the adoption of liberal maxims by the Gaullist Right might have been a tactical maneuver arising from the need to reconquer sectors of public opinion which appeared to have been converted to liberal beliefs?

Strategic considerations have certainly been a factor in this transformation, but it should be kept in mind that Chirac and his followers had not waited for the watershed of 1981 to pursue their conversion. During his presidential campaign, Jacques Chirac had begun by departing from certain traditional Gaullist positions, by denouncing the so-called "rampant socialism" of Valéry Giscard d'Estaing and by adopting a clear position in favor of "less governement". Subsequently, the influence of Chirac's advisors, especially Alain Juppé, had intensified his movement toward liberal policies. A transformation of this kind abandoned certain of General de Gaulle's fundamental orientations and it raised a question of particular relevance across the entire political spectrum. What had become of Gaullism after the major ideological upheaval produced by the triumph of the Socialist Party and the vigorous regeneration of liberalism as doctrine? In particular, where was Gaullism situated as an alternative, given that the fundamental debate within France appeared to have been reduced to a struggle between liberalism and socialism? Gaullism seemed no longer congruent with the Right. The Left had even appropriated some of its themes in order to acquire another weapon against the Right.

The opposition did not have exceptional difficulty in maintaining unity in action in the face of defeat. On the contrary. The Union pour la Démocratie Française, or UDF (whose name derived from the title of Giscard's book[2] clearly indicated that this current was centered on the President) not only withstood but survived the rigors of defeat. It did not dissolve, and its various components retained their cohesion. For example, there was a unified parliamentary group led by Jean-Claude Gaudin. And the UDF usually nominated a single candidate or a combined list for elections. In addition, close ties between the two "families" of the Right were reestablished despite having been broken at the end of Giscard's incumbency. Giscard's injunction to "dump bitterness into the river" was followed and disputes were settled. It is reasonable to hypothesize here that pressure from the electorate helped reconciliation, that voters strongly favored unity and that they disapproved of internecine brawling.

Were these the same voters? Did the choice between the UDF and the RPR reflect two different categories of supporters, or were the two political tendencies drawing their water from the same well? Experts had different answers to these questions. At times, they have considered it possible to discern two clearly differentiated sectors of the electorate, but there is an increasing tendency to affirm that pronounced differences no longer exist among the supporters of one current or the other.

In response, leaders changed strategies, and on more than one occasion reversed roles. As elections for the European Parliament (June 1984) approached, for example, it was Chirac and the RPR who sought and obtained development of a combined UDF–RPR slate under the leadership of Simone Veil, who had insisted that unity was a precondition for her agreeing to be a candidate. In the 1986 legislative elections, however, the UDF preferred the highest possible number of unified slates. On the other hand, the RPR, which believed that its star was rising and hoped to acquire a higher number of parliamentary spokespeople in the new Assembly, was somewhat resistant to the UDF's requests and only partly acceded to them. Nevertheless, the opposition managed to preserve a relatively unified external appearance, and developed a joint program.

Certainly sectors of the opposition hoped to preserve a distinct identity and were not willing to forfeit their autonomy. Individual leaders' ambitions, or their aspirations for the presidency, were not the sole cause of disagreements. Deeper sensibilities, as well as susceptibilities and memories, contributed to the persistence of differences. Hence there were levels of liberal conviction and significantly different concepts of how a liberal program should be applied. The most liberal elements belong to the Parti Républicain, affiliated with the UDF. Influenced by certain thinkers and publicists and by the "new economists", they hoped to pursue liberalism's logic to its ultimate conclusions. Alain Madelin even endorsed denationalization of the educational system, for example. This *courant* believed exclusively in private initiative. Nevertheless, there was widespread uncertainty about the consequences of total deregulation. Many did not believe that public opinion, which was accustomed to social protection, would permit the dismantling of social security and that any onslaught against the social security system might well threaten to cause a social explosion. And those who remained loyal to Gaullist concepts did not want to renounce the essential prerogatives of the state. The Centre des Démocrates Sociaux, a successor to the Mouvement Républicain Populaire (MRP) and Social Catholicism, also had not outgrown its traditional distrust of liberalism, remaining firmly committed to legislation, regulation and forms of authority to ensure a minimum of social equality and protection.

SHADOWS OVER THE ONCE AND FUTURE MAJORITY

From 1983 on, two new phenomena added complexity to the horizon of the opposition, as well as introducing disagreements which might shatter the unity of the Right at some future point. One of these phenomena was the resurgence of the far Right, in the form of the National Front led by Jean-Marie Le Pen. This phenomenon did not arise until the autumn of 1983, originating during municipal elections in Dreux, where the National Front slate obtained 16% of the vote. Considerable astonishment ensued: the far Right had been practically absent for more than fifteen years. The last occasion when it had done well was in the December 1965 presidential election, when Jean-Louis Tixier-Vignancour received approximately 5%. Since that point, extreme Right candidates had never done better than 1%. Everyone was inclined to believe that the far Right had disappeared. The Dreux election dictated a reevaluation of that viewpoint.

The far Right was no longer isolated. The clever tactics of Jean-Marie Le Pen, who carefully selected the localities where National Front candidates would run, produced a series of successes which were crowned by the election for the European Parliament in 1984, where his slate obtained more than 11%, nearly matching the PCF result.

The time had therefore come for the National Front to enter the select group of major parties. The media facilitated this by giving considerable attention to the National Front's initial successes. The ruling party and the majority likewise played a part. It was strategically prudent for the Socialists, who were beset by difficulties, to embarrass the followers of Giscard or Chirac by portraying them as the National Front's allies or by insinuating that they supported it. Neither the level of publicity nor this short-term tactic sufficed to explain why the National Front's share of the electorate had risen from 1% to 11% or 12%, however.

The advances of the National Front, like any trend of similar magnitude, were the combined product of multiple factors. The foundation upon which Jean-Marie Le Pen had built his success was the persistence of a far Right which, despite appearances, had never totally disappeared. The prestige of General de Gaulle and the presence of the Right in power had reduced the far Right to silence, but did not cause its demise.

The far Right was the most intensely ideological sector of the National Front's following. It incorporated the heirs of Action Française, the admirers of Marshal Pétain and those who yearned for his "national revolution", as well as advocates of Algérie Française and veterans of the Organisation de l'Armée Secrète (OAS). It is also necessary to add (even though these were often the same persons) "integralist" Catholics who disapproved of changes in the Church, such as the followers of Monseigneur Lefebvre, for example, who endorsed the National Front. Indeed, the National Front's slate for the European elections included some of Lefebvre's followers in prominent positions. And for any other people remaining loyal to counterrevolutionary traditions, could there truly be anyone else who deserved their support, even if Jean-Marie Le Pen's program did not reflect these origins? Other groups of voters joined the initial nucleus for various reasons: specifically, anyone who was dismayed by changes in customs or by excessively rapid social progress, anyone who was displeased with insufficient strictness in education or with courts which did not punish criminals severely enough, and anyone who sought a restoration of traditional values in terms of order, discipline and authority.

Historians may be tempted to place the National Front on a continuum where various precedents exist, *Boulangisme*, the leagues which emerged prior to World War II, and, most recently, Poujadism. Indeed, the success of the National Front offered more than one similarity with earlier movements, but comparisons were not equivalencies. Poujadism originated in areas where economic progress had slowed, and it represented a sense of despair among social and occupational groups whose existence was threatened. The National Front has won more support in the cities than in rural areas, and it was more successful in industrial suburbs than in villages. The age distribution was extremely balanced. It sought members among the lower classes, especially in localities where the population included a high proportion of immigrants. This point permits us to identify the most distinctive aspect of the phenomenon and, perhaps, to explain its impact: the National Front centered its line of reasoning on the problem of immigration, and it exploited the fears arising from increasing crime rates. The National Front capitalized on the desire to preserve a national identity and the concerns which arose from the sense of a lack of safety felt by many city-dwellers. These themes naturally received a more favorable response in regions where the proportion of immigrants, especially from North Africa, was higher than the national average, and also in suburbs inhabited by large numbers of foreign workers. Hence, the National Front was most successful in the departments along the Mediterranean and in the big urban areas surrounding Paris, Lyon and Lille, where lower-income voters have a portion of its support.

Does the National Front have a future, or is it likely to dissolve abruptly, in the same way as comparable movements of the past? The question can be asked in another form. Can Jean-Marie Le Pen succeed at maintaining unity among the various groups of voters who have supported him thus far? The answer will depend to some extent upon the stance of the parties of the Right. Prior to March 1986, the rise of the National Front created an ethical and tactical problem for their leaders, who were divided with respect to this issue. Indeed, some repeatedly shifted positions. Certain leaders of the Right, such as Philippe Malaud, the chairman of the Centre National des Indépendants et Paysans, found no reason to treat the National Front as anything other than an equal partner. It was part of the national opposition, and keeping it at arm's length, at the risk of losing legislative seats, would foolishly play into the hands of the Left. On the other hand, leaders of the Centre des Démocrates Sociaux, notably Bernard Stasi and Jacques Barrot, affirmed that the opposition would be betraying its ideals and discrediting itself if it displayed tolerance for Le Pen's racist views. Raymond Barre initially responded in intermediate terms. Without indicating any acceptance of the ideas of the National Front, he agreed to meet with its leader and stated that he could not reject the voters who had voted for Le Pen. Later he clearly expressed his hope that no political force would exploit anti-immigrant themes for its advantage. As for Jacques Chirac, he adopted an extremely clear position in his debate with Laurent Fabius: he would never form a majority bloc with the National Front. Therefore, the principal tendencies within the Right had set themselves apart from the National Front three months before the 1986 elections. They did so not only for reasons of principle but because of their evaluation of the probable distribution of power, which allowed them to anticipate that, in the new Assembly, the "parliamentary Right" would possess an absolute majority and could therefore avoid the embarrassing situation of needing National Front votes in order to govern. This evaluation came very close to being wrong at national level. And on the regional level the parliamentary Right and the National Front were forced into agreement in several places.

Prior to March 1986, cohabitation created another obstacle to the cohesion of the opposition. Should the Right agree to share power with Mitterrand, or should it refuse as long as Mitterrand remained Head of State, sparing no effect to force his resignation? This debate encompassed disagreements about interpreting the Constitution, differences about strategy and different policy perspectives. What did the Constitution indicate? There were two opposite points of view emanating from the desire to maintain the dignity of the presidency. Jacques Chirac and Valéry Giscard d'Estaing proposed that the President, who was elected for a seven-year term, should remain in office until his term expired. If the President were to leave office because of the emergence of a different plurality from the one which had placed him in office, this would mean that presidential terms would constantly depend upon the results of the next legislative election. Legislative elections would thus, *ipso facto*, acquire equivalent importance to presidential elections. Chirac expressed himself in these terms partially because of his loyalty to the Gaullist origins of present-day institutions. In turn, Giscard d'Estaing remained loyal to the stance which he had adopted in January 1978, shortly before the March 1978 elections, where there had been the possibility of an outcome similar to that of March 1986.

Raymond Barre, however, adopted an opposing position: that the President should resign because it would not be appropriate for him to be a powerless witness to the implementation of policies which constituted a rejection of his own platform; such a situation would discredit the presidency. It is not impossible that more personal motives had a certain amount of influence upon these various viewpoints. Raymond Barre would obviously have benefitted if the presidential election were advanced from 1988 to 1986. On the other hand, he was also wary of the powerlessness which could affect a government for two years if the president and the Assembly were obliged to devote a major portion of their energy to neutralizing one another. The majority of the public which supported presidential legitimacy was opposed to weakening the presidency and appeared to prefer *cohabitation*.

Cohabitation, of course, occurred as a result of March 1986. In the process Raymond Barre's anti-*cohabitation* strategy came up short, causing considerable damage to Barre's public standing. The April 1985 electoral law worked as it had been designed to work, reducing the parliamentary Right's margin – minus the National Front – to a handful. The Right as opposition had succeeded in becoming the Right as majority again, but in circumstances which made the future very difficult to anticipate. How would presidential rivalries on the Right affect the already complex situation of *cohabitation*, and vice versa? What, if any, equilibrium could be reached in such a situation between the different currents of the parliamentary Right? How much of the Right's newly found liberalism would stand up to the demands of power? What would happen to the National Front in all this? How would *cohabitation* and the inevitable difficulties of governing affect the respective chances of rightist and Socialist candidates to the next presidential election? These were the questions raised, in the spring of 1986, by the narrow victory and the constitutional choices of the Right.

NOTES

1 Alain Peyrefitte, *Quand la Rose se fanera: du malentendu à l'espoir* (Paris, Plon, 1983).
2 Valéry Giscard d'Estaing, *Démocratie Française* (Paris, Fayard, 1976).

8

The Fifth Republic
under François Mitterrand
Evolution and Perspectives

OLIVIER DUHAMEL

Political analysts, if asked to give an account of a country's constitutional evolution, are inclined to stress what has changed. Talking about what has stayed the same can easily become boring, and may seem to indicate a lack of imagination on the part of the speaker. It is more fashionable to spot what is new. Moreover, history hardly ever repeats itself and few constitutional analysts see why they should leave the discovery of change entirely to other specialists.

The temptation to stress innovation is all the greater when the country being discussed is France under the Mitterrand presidency. Mitterrand's arrival to power represented the first real alternation France had seen under the Fifth Republic, after 23 years of rule by the various right-wing groups. It was only the second time in French history that a Socialist had become President of the Republic, the second time that Communists were included in the government (and their first time in a homogeneous left-wing coalition), the first time that a Socialist leader had been directly elected by the people and finally, the first time that a conjunction of constitutional structure and political events handed both presidential and parliamentary power – in short, the full power of the state – to the Left for a period of five years.

It is worth adding that the new President had voted against the new Constitution in 1958 and denounced its practice in a book entitled *Le Coup d'état permanent*.[1] Moreover, the coalition that brought him to power fed upon an antipresidential tradition in French politics that goes back more than a century. Even though the Left, slowly and unevenly, rallied to the Fifth Republic, it remained open to the charge that it had drawn back from the constitutional debate merely in order to win power, with the (same) ultimate objective of changing the nature of that power.

Lastly, in the closing years of Valéry Giscard d'Estaing's presidential term, several factors appeared to reopen the debate on the problem of excessive presidential power. Among these were the "aristocratic modernism" of the President himself, rumors about protocol at the Elysée, the positions enjoyed by the President's family and the gifts of African diamonds from Bokassa's Central-African Empire. These were weapons that the left-wing opposition, and above all its leader, François Mitterrand, preferred not to use directly to destabilize Giscard. They were, however, able to draw attention to these improprieties implicitly by criticizing the Republic's "monarchist drift". The *Créteil Manifesto*, adopted by the Socialist Party on 24 January 1981, which included Mitterrand's famous 110 Propositions, started with a denunciation of

> shifty schemes and cynical appetites . . . [which] give a clouded image of those who govern us. The degradation of the public spirit has gone hand in hand with that of our public institutions. The incumbent President monopolizes everything, concerns himself with everything, and turns the smallest matter into the instrument of his own power. We are witnessing a slow corruption of the principles of the Republic. Our democracy itself is at stake.

A little later in the *Manifesto*, the Socialists conclude "We are living in a sort of monarchy."[2]

In short, the Socialists set out to "change the way we live" (*changer la vie*), transform society and alter the nature of power. Did they succeed? As to the way the French live, or the societal impact, other studies will have to answer. In regard to the nature of power, relations between central and local government were clearly transformed by the vast process of decentralization, relations between the judiciary and its "client" were modified by the Badinter reforms, and those between the media and viewers and listeners were changed by the emergence of private radio and television stations. Again, other chapters will deal with these reforms. The author's purpose here is limited to recent developments and future perspectives at the top levels of the Fifth Republic. In other words, what has changed in relations between the President, Parliament and French citizens? A short answer would be, "nothing". But, this "nonchange" was by no means preordained. Indeed, it is still not clear to everyone, and therefore requires illustration (in the first part of this chapter). Furthermore, it has not prevented the occurrence of a few subtle changes and even some real new developments, as the second part will show.

THE CONTINUITY OF THE FIFTH REPUBLIC

The absence of major change in the way France is governed is visible, firstly, in juridical terms: the Constitution has not been revised. This is confirmed by the continued supremacy of the President, something François Mitterrand has ensured both structurally and in practice.

Constitutional revision: not an objective but a game

Constitutional change was on the program of the major political parties during the 1981 campaign. The project was perhaps modest and discreet – and certainly confused – in the presidential campaign, but it was definitely there. Among Mitterrand's 110 Propositions there appears to be only one, the 45th, which clearly involved a constitutional revision: "The presidential term will either be reduced to five years, renewable once only, or limited to seven years without possibility of renewal."[3]

Once on the threshold of power, the Socialists nuanced this position. From their 1972 program, *Changer la vie*,[4] to the *Projet socialiste pour la France aux années 80*,[5] the Socialists talked of reducing the presidential term to five years. Once his election became a possibility, Mitterrand preferred to leave open the choice between a five-year or a seven-year nonrenewable term. After his arrival at the Elysée, he again did nothing to adopt the reform. No major obstacles to change were in his way, even though a constitutional revision, as laid down in Article 89 of the Constitution, requires agreement of both assemblies and thus of the Senate, where the Left is in the minority. This substantial constitutional constraint, however, does not apply to the reduction of the presidential term, since President Pompidou managed to get both the National Assembly and Senate to vote for the five-year term in October 1973. He let the matter rest there, since he feared not obtaining a three-fifths majority if a vote of both assemblies in common session were called. In addition, he could not call for another referendum after his hollow victory of the 23 April 1972 referendum concerning the entry of Britain, Ireland and Denmark into the EEC. Mitterrand, on the other hand, could have legally resuscitated the project and submitted the five-year term directly to referendum.

De Gaulle established a precedent in his reform of the dates of parliamentary sessions. The bill was adopted by the National Assembly in 1960, but was then withdrawn from the agenda of a hostile Senate. Three years later, it found its way back onto the Senate's agenda (without passing the Assembly a second time) even though a general election had entirely renewed the National Assembly in the meantime. The French, moreover, approve of the five-year term;[6] therefore it is clear that Mitterrand's reticence on the issue was due to the fact that he himself did not wish to pursue it. There is also no doubt that he was keeping the project on hold for the day when he would need to regain the legitimacy that was tarnished by successive electoral defeats and record-low popularity ratings "I have not made any decision to move forward with such a project. I shall do so if it is clearly in France's interest and if it is desirable that the nation should be consulted."[7]

In saying this, Mitterrand was adopting Georges Pompidou's highly tactical conception of the referendum: "I have no plans to call a referendum. For a referendum you need the right occasion and a subject – a good question and a good subject."[8] This is one example among many of Mitterrand's "Pompidolianism", halfway between de Gaulle's Caesarian obsession with the referendum – as a means of securing direct popular approval – and Valéry Giscard d'Estaing's phobia of referenda. Giscard was always much happier with traditional elections that occurred at the appointed time.

For François Mitterrand, then, both the referendum and constitutional revision were trump cards, not necessities of principle, in the political game. Nothing illustrates this better than the episode in the summer of 1984 when he attempted to revise, by referendum, the constitutional provisions governing referenda, to allow a further public vote on the school issue.

The sequence of events went roughly as follows: first of all, the government's bill on private, essentially Catholic, education had aroused passionate opposition from the RPR, the UDF, the Catholic hierarchy, parents' associations and public opinion, culminating in a huge demonstration in Paris on 24 June. On 5 July the Senate adopted a proposal to submit the bill to referendum, by virtue of Article 11 of the Constitution, even though Article 11 limited the use of the referendum to bills concerning "the organization of public authorities". On 6 July the National Assembly rejected this motion, which was therefore not transmitted to the president. Next, Mitterrand appeared on national television on 12 July, announcing the withdrawal of the Savary Bill on private education, and, at the same time, agreeing that a referendum on matters such as the school issue was a good idea. Unfortunately, he added, the text of the Constitution did not allow it. He therefore proposed to change this through the provisions of Article 89, that is, by identical vote of the Senate and the National Assembly followed by a referendum. Only after this constitutional revision took effect would the way for a referendum on the school issue be open. Then, on 25 July, Alain Poher, President of the Senate, requested the submission of the bill widening the scope of referenda to include "public freedoms". He did not, however, propose that the issue be decided by popular referendum (as in the first option of Article 89) but rather, by joint session of the two assemblies in Congress (the second option of Article 89). In the last act, Mitterrand refused to be deprived of his first referendum. The Senate, in contrast, refused to have this first referendum imposed on it, and did not want to wait in uncertainty for the referendum on the school issue. In declining to debate the constitutional revision, the Senate effectively buried the whole project.

How much the French really understood of all this remains a mystery, but they probably understood what was most important: it was just one more distraction in the game between the left-wing government and the right-wing opposition. Just because Mitterrand's project was not accepted did not necessarily mean that he failed in his goal. It can be argued that the purpose of the whole episode was to cover the tracks of a retreat on the school issue, and that Mitterrand never believed that the Senate would vote for his constitutional revision plan.

The above accurately illustrates Mitterrand's relationship with the Constitution. He did not take the same kind of liberties with it that de Gaulle had – if the General had wanted a referendum on the school issue, he would not have been concerned with the niceties of Article 11; if he had wanted to broaden the field of application of Article 11, he would not have got bogged down in the parliamentary procedures of Article 89, but would have gone directly to the electorate.

Mitterrand did not reduce the Constitution to its traditional functions like Giscard did. (If faced with a similar problem, Giscard would have simply let Parliament water down the government's bill.) Without flaunting it, Mitterrand used the Constitution as a tool in the political game in order to put conflicts in a new context and to settle problems by complicating them. More than ever, the government conceived of the Constitution as an instrument which had kept the Left in power for five years. No constitutional revision with any chance of passing could have enabled the government to stay longer in office. The most that was possible was a limit on the reversal of the Left's fortunes by changing the electoral system. That, finally, was done (cf. below, in the second part of this chapter). In the meantime, the main thing was to retain full mastery of state power for a five-year period.

The preservation of presidential power

"France's institutions were not made for me, but they suit me well enough."[10] Mitterrand had hardly moved into the Elysée before announcing his ease there. The path he followed to power led him to accept not just the letter of the Constitution, but the institutions themselves, state power directed by the President. Up through March 1986, when the unique situation of *cohabitation* began, he adopted the pyramidal conception of the Fifth Republic, one in which the President dominates the government and the government, in turn, dominates Parliament: "The commitments I have made represent the charter of governmental action. I should add that, since the people have chosen a second time, these engagements represent the charter of your legislative action."[11]

Regarding the President's relations with his Prime Minister, Mitterrand reaffirmed the distinction made constantly by his predecessors at the Elysée, the Head of State makes major political choices, and the prime minister runs the day-to-day affairs. The President manages what de Gaulle called "France's destiny", Pompidou "the essentials", Giscard "the long-term problems" (*la durée*) and Mitterrand "the major defining options" (*les grandes orientations*); the Prime Minister is left to deal with "the action of the moment" (de Gaulle) or, still less grand, "the problems of daily life" (Mitterrand).[12] This continuity of relations was not, however, confined to speeches. All of Mitterrand's political activity was in the tradition that guarantees the structural permanence of presidential power, both *vis-à-vis* the Assembly and within the executive branch.

In relation to Parliament, presidential dominance was ensured by "dissolution for alternation" (*la dissolution d'alternance*). By dissolving the National Assembly the day after he took office, Mitterrand did more than simply get rid of a hostile majority before it had time to voice its opposition or experiment with *cohabitation*. He also ensured that he would get his majority in the Assembly. That of course meant a Socialist majority – 285 deputies including 20 *apparentées* (semi-independents voting with the Socialists), 39 more than an absolute majority. Above all, it meant a majority elected in the wake of the presidential election – on Mitterrand's initiative – in support of Mitterrand, and thus practically without legitimacy of its own.

In taking this bold step, which in retrospect seems an obvious one, the President was making use of a vital weapon to ensure his own power. De Gaulle used it as early as 1958 when he dissolved the Fourth Republic and, incidentally, the National Assembly. Pompidou used the weapon on 30 May 1968 – admittedly, via the General – but without letting a single UDR deputy elected the following month doubt that it had been he, Pompidou, who had pulled back from the disastrous referendum de Gaulle wanted and planned. Giscard alone never undertook a "dissolution for alternation". He thus never had his own majority in the National Assembly. And he lost the 1981 presidential election. Mitterrand did not repeat this mistake. Instead, after 1981 he returned to the Fifth Republic tradition established by de Gaulle and Pompidou, under which the majority in the National Assembly owes its election to the president, and is under his thumb.

This dissolution "at the source" also solved the main problem of presidential relations within the government, since no government could expect to win parliamentary support against a president to whom the parliamentary majority directly owes its allegiance. To consolidate and complete the subordination of the Prime Minister to the President, it is also useful for the President to have complete freedom of choice in appointing and dismissing the Prime Minister. Here, too, Mitterrand behaved like his predecessors, particularly the Gaullist ones. The first Prime Minister is not chosen during the electoral campaign. (The exception to this rule was Gaston Defferre, who ran in tandem with Pierre Mendès France all the way to a 5 per cent share of the vote in 1969.) The Prime Minister is, however, a politician who actively supports the President's conquest of power. With the passage of time, the Prime Minister is worn out, as minor disagreements with the President multiply, and the President "lets him go" with varying degrees of discretion and elegance. This occurs to some extent on the Prime Minister's own initiative, but always – except in the case of Chirac in 1976 – the final choice is the President's. The President then chooses a second Prime Minister, whose general profile, date of appointment, electoral "mission", and long-term ambitions have been strikingly similar throughout the Fifth Republic (see table 8.1). Here again we see the triumph of continuity.

Table 8.1 The choice of second Prime Ministers under the Fifth Republic

President:	De Gaulle	Pompidou	Giscard d'Estaing	Mitterrand
Moment: 3 years after presidential election	1962 1968	1972	1976 (one year early)	1984
Person: A "president's man" a technician	Pompidou Couve de Murville	Messmer	Barre	Fabius
Less political than the first Prime Minister	Debré 1959	Chaban 1969	Chirac 1974	Mauroy 1981
Less political than other possible candidates	(Chaban)	(Giscard)	(Chaban)	(Rocard)
Mission 1: lead the parliamentary campaign	Pompidou 1962, 1967	Messmer 1973	Barre 1978	Fabius 1986
Mission 2: successor to the President	Pompidou	exception	Barre?	Fabius?

Notes:
1 Parentheses indicate the most likely alternatives to the individual ultimately appointed.
2 ? indicates speculation on the likeliest candidate.

In order to secure power, the President brings his supporters into the government. We have little detailed information on the respective roles of President and Prime Minister in choosing Fifth Republic governments. It is worth noting, however, that despite the Left's parliamentary traditions, Mitterrand continued the practice (a "Gaullo-Giscardian" one this time) of appointing ministers from outside Parliament (table 8.2). Daniel Gaxie rightly observes that these individuals are often chosen "in exchange for services rendered to the President at some stage during his rise to power," (for example, Jacques Delors, Pierre Bérégovoy, Jack Lang, Yvette Roudy, Georgina Dufoix, Henri Nallet). He adds that "some of them only entered politics by becoming ministers, and were appointed because of their personal experience with questions relevant to their ministry – Claude Cheysson, Alain Bombard, Pierre Dreyfus, Hubert Curien, Alain Calmat, Haroun Tazieff and perhaps Robert Badinter." If Mitterrand followed the example of Giscard in this respect it was because, like his immediate predecessor (but unlike de Gaulle or Pompidou), he needed to broaden a diminished electoral base, as measured by percentage of votes cast on the first ballot of the

Table 8.2 Percentage of ministers chosen from outside parliament, 1959–84

De Gaulle Debré	De Gaulle Pompidou	De Gaulle Couve de Murville	Pompidou Chaban	Pompidou Messmer	Giscard Chirac	Giscard Barre	Mitterrand Mauroy	Mitterrand Fabius
37.5%	27.4%	3.2%	2.2%	6.1%	33.3%	29.2%	23.0%	31.1%

Source: Daniel Gaxie, "Immuables et changeants: les ministres de la Ve République," *Pouvoirs*, 36, Jan. 1986; *Le Ministre*, (Paris, Presses Universitaires de France, 1986).

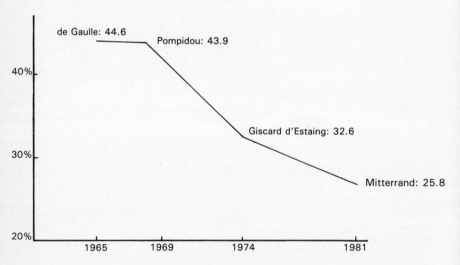

Figure 8.1 The weakening of the President's personal electorate; percentage of votes cast at first ballots of presidential elections

presidential election (see figure 8.1). This objective constraint helps, perhaps, to explain the permanence of presidentialism behind different tendencies and people. Whether or not this is always the case, it seems clear that the appointment of nonparliamentarians, or even nonpoliticians, reinforced the President's power. Mitterrand broke with Pompidou's practice in this respect – but in a stronger presidential direction.

With his power thus structurally established, the President was left to maintain it. Presidential preeminence in relation to the government does not mean the Elysée actually governs – if only because the absence of a presidential Civil Service prevents it from doing so. Mitterrand also put an end to Giscard's practice of personally laying out the government's work program in documents that were made public. Thierry Pfister reveals that this rather humiliating governmental procedure was abandoned at the request of Pierre Mauroy: "Was it not at least possible [Mauroy asked] to leave him to draw up his own work program, given that the President always made final decisions in cases of conflict, and the final version of any document was approved in full Council of Ministers?" Pfister adds, however, "From that moment, written presidential messages became fairly rare. But, in conformity with the most ancient traditions of the state, the sovereign's desires had the status of orders."

It should be noted that from Pfister's vantage point in the Mauroy cabinet, an innovation of the Fifth Republic was turned into an "ancient tradition of state". As for the rest, the division of power was not fundamentally modified. There were struggles for influence between Elysée and Matignon aides (the Prime Minister's office), but the publicity these conflicts received was probably the only new element here. The President defines the "inspiration" of policy, the Prime Minister leads the governmental activities – apart from any direct links individual ministers enjoy with the Elysée – and the President intervenes in any questions he feels concern him.

The battle over the school issue again provided a good example of the above. In spring 1984, Pierre Mauroy requested a presidential decision on the matter, but was told to "sort it out for yourself ".[14] The parliamentary amendments that followed on 23 May intensified the confrontation. In July, the Prime Minister learned – after Mitterrand's address to the nation had already been recorded and only one hour before it was aired – that the school bill had been withdrawn at the personal behest of the President, although there was nothing in the Constitution that granted him this power.[15]

The "unequal diarchy" founded in 1958 thus continued without interruption from 1981 to 1986. Pfister somewhat treacherously recounts how Mauroy asked the President to discontinue the protocol requiring the Prime Minister to appear beside the presidential airplane each time the Head of State leaves or returns to France, whatever the hour of day or night. "François Mitterrand. . .did not deem it necessary to take any action."[16] Aside from such symbols, there is probably less novelty in the role of Prime Minister than in the perception of that role by the French public. For a long time, the public was too dazzled by the rise of the presidential star to do anything other than underestimate the Prime Minister. Presidential supremacy vis-à-vis Parliament, and particularly the National Assembly, was maintained whenever necessary, and even when it was not.

Lawmaking remained a largely governmental preserve, despite the Socialists' absolute majority and announcement of the Créteil Manifesto's 46th proposition that "the constitutional rights of Parliament will be restored." The executive branch in fact initiated more laws than ever before. The parliamentary regime of 1958, like its predecessors, shared the prerogative of initiating legislation between the Prime Minister and the Parliament. Between 1981 and 1986, however, the proportion of laws initiated by Parliament diminished even further, making left-wing governments the least "parliamentary" of the Fifth Republic (see table 8.3).

Table 8.3 Evolution of the origin of laws 1959–October 1985

	No. of laws of parliamentary origin	Total no. of laws	Laws of parliamentary origin as % of total
De Gaulle 1959–1968	103	878	11.7
Pompidou 1969–1973	81	492	16.5
Giscard d'Estaing 1974–1981	95	756	12.6
Mitterrand 1981–30 Oct. 1985	44	486	9.1

This lawmaking phenomenon is confirmed by the government's recourse to ordinances, the procedure by which Parliament delegates a normative power to the government. Ordinances were issued at an unprecedented rate after 1981, concerning national as well as foreign policy questions. The unemployment benefit reform, the extension of pension rights to 60-year-olds and the shortening of the workweek were all put through by ordinance. Indeed, the 39-hour-week decision was not only not made by Parliament; its essential provisions were imposed by the President over the opposition of Pierre Mauroy and Jacques Delors, but with the insistent support of the Secretary-General of the Elysée as well as Force Ouvrière and the CGT. In particular, Mitterrand decided that the 39-hour week should be applied across the board and employees should be paid the same wages as under the 40-hour week. This was instead of linking the shortened workweek to wage sharing.

Where Parliament did discuss and adopt laws, it did so under strict majority rules. "What the Socialist deputies decide is law", as the President of the Socialists' National Assembly group stated crudely.[17] True, the opposition made abundant use of its right to table amendments, but only 7% of adopted amendments originate in the RPR, UDF or Communist Party,[18] with the right opposition responsible for 5%. This was no more than the Left total under Giscard. All other amendments came either from the government (22%) or, above all, from the relevant committee accompanied by governmental – i.e. Socialist – agreement.[19]

When Socialist solidarity was absent, the executive could bring out the constitutional "big guns", (see tables 8.4, 8.5) especially Article 49.3, which allows a "vote of confidence" to be called on any given bill. Such bills are considered passed unless there is a motion of censure by an absolute majority. Thus, forced to choose between accepting the government's bill or forcing its resignation, majority deputies have always chosen to toe the line – whether under de Gaulle, Giscard, or Mitterrand. A certain statistical continuity, however, conceals an evolution here. Article 49.3 can be used

Table 8.4 Use of the Executive's constitutional weapons against the National Assembly

		Constitutional Inventory	
	Article used		Bills
Dissolution	Art. 12	22 May 1981	
Ordinances	Art. 38	6 January 1982 – social measures	
		4 February 1982 – reforms in New Caledonia	
		22 April 1983 – austerity: financial measures	
		20 December 1983 – unemployment benefit reforms	
		23 April 1985 – further New Caledonia measures	
Making a bill a question of confidence in the government	Art. 49.3	26 January 1982 – nationalizations	
		25 June 1982 ⎫ 9 July 1982 ⎬ – wage and price freeze 13 July 1982 ⎭	
		23 November 1982 – careers of insubordinate generals (Algerian War)	
		22 May 1984 – Savary Bill (private education)	
		5 July 1984 ⎫ – bill on press 7 November 1984 ⎭	
		11 December 1985 – flexibility of work	

Table 8.5 Use of Executive's constitutional weapons against the National Assembly

	Evolution of number of times used by President				
Weapon	De Gaulle 1959-65	De Gaulle 1965-69	Pompidou 1969-74	Giscard 1974-81	Mitterrand 1981-85
Dissolution	1	1	0	0	1
Ordinance Art. 38 (of which on overseas)	4 (2)	4 (1)	1 –	6 (5)	5 (2)
Art. 49.3	3	1	–	5 (Barre)	6

not only to bring the majority into line, but also to break obstruction by the opposition (which was forthcoming on nationalization bills, private schools and the press). The executive did not hesitate to use Article 49.3, even though it had denounced it when in the opposition. Article 49.3 was even invoked on one occasion where no vital policy question was at stake, in order to affirm the ultimate power of the President to make the final decision on any question forcefully and symbolically. On 23 November 1982, the Socialist deputies were forced, again under the threat of seeing their government resign, to accept the reconstitution of the career rights of army officers who had participated in *putsches* during the Algerian War. One could continue quoting an abundance of examples. No change in constitutional practice furnished Parliament with new rights. No rules reform of the National Assembly gave new rights to the oppostion. This was in spite of some useful proposals by a working party which suggested first a weekly debate on topical questions with the agenda to be set alternately by the majority and opposition, and next an annually created opposition investigation and monitoring committee. Not only was this extension of monitoring power not granted to Parliament, the increase in the number of parliamentary monitoring committees (from 7 to 17 under Giscard) ceased.

Above all, the Socialist majority failed to keep an eye on the state that their Socialist partners in the executive ran. Most investigation and monitoring committees were set up by the Senate, and of the three created by the Assembly, two – one on the Service d'Action Civique, another on the "sniffer planes" affair – were aimed against pre-1981 governments. Thus, nearly all the indications concerning National Assembly activities paint a coherent picture. The exceptions concern the expansion of parliamentary work: extraordinary sessions, amendments and written questions in particular. This, however, was largely the result of governmental concern for reform, plus a few filibusters from the opposition. As for the rest, this type of parliamentary activism started before 1981, and corresponds to the autonomous logic of the parliamentary machine as it was perfected in the 1970s.

In general, the period from 1981 to 1986 prolonged earlier tendencies. If it had any distinction at all in the history of the Fifth Republic, it was due to its having the most "presidentialist" legislature. The reason for this apparent anomaly (given the parliamentarist traditions of the Left) is easily found. The Socialist Left had already become "aconstitutional" – lacking a clear constitutional project – in order to reach power. The Left became even more so to exercise its new power, using a purely instrumental reading of the Constitution. Michel Debré even congratulated himself on this in a rather ironic fashion: "What a fine array of resources this Constitution has given you! I can almost hear a new generation of professors teaching their pupils that I drew up a constitution especially for a Socialist government and majority."[21]

EPHEMERAL AND DEEP CHANGES

The way France was governed from 1981 to 1986 did not, then, change fundamentally. This central fact should not obscure, nor be obscured by, the relatively minor mutations that did take place. These changes pertain less to the five-year period during which the Socialists enjoyed the plentitude of power than the period of cohabitation which followed.

Inflections (1981-86)

Some of the inflections which ocurred may be explained by the prospect of the Right's return to power in 1986. In 1981, few believed that this would happen. A right-wing victory became plausible after the Left's setback in the March 1983 municipal elections; probable after the opposition's success in the June 1984 European elections; and increasingly certain as the parliamentary election day – 16 March 1986 – drew closer. This growing certainty explains two of the three evolutions in the practice of political power – the rise of "conflictual bicameralism" and a withdrawal of the President from the political limelight. The third change is more directly linked to the specificities of the Socialists and their leader, and has introduced a new variant into the conception and practice of majority power.

Majority power

Socialist supporters called majority power "contractual democracy", while their opponents termed it "partisan government". In either case, there is little doubt that the logic of majority power was fully assumed during the Socialists' five-year term, and this modifies the picture of strict continuity drawn above.

First, this fact is evident at the level of principles. Mitterrand's supremacy was justified neither by his own virtues, nor by any doctrinal attachment to executive power, but rather because his election was seen as an act of popular will. The "charter of governmental action" and the "charter of your legislative action" referred to by Mitterrand (see above) were presented not as a legitimation of the President's desires, but as a commitment by the presidential candidate ratified by the nation.

This contractual conception may perhaps modify our assessment of relations between the President and the Socialists. The 110 Propositions, which represented the contract's goals, were produced and passed by the Socialist Party. Thus, even if the President looked like the real legislator, preparing bills from an "upstream" position to an Assembly that merely ratified them, the Socialist Party itself occupied a position upstream of the President. It was the party that first took the initiative on nationalizations, on the reduction of the workweek, on the lowering of retirement age, the expansion of workers' rights on the shop floor, the abolition of the death penalty, the abolition of special courts and, last but not least, on decentralization.

This point is worth stressing since no presidential candidate has ever run on a platform as detailed as Mitterrand's. But the Socialist Party's upstream role does not contradict what has already been argued – for three reasons. First, the President and his government enjoyed almost total freedom in deciding when and how to undertake the reform programs. Secondly, they were equally free to drop any given proposal for varied reasons, be they financial (Proposition 32, which abolished the VAT on products of primary necessity; Proposition 82, which granted women retirement benefits at 55);

military (the reduction of military service); industrial (giving workers' plant committees' veto rights on hiring and firing); or political (imposing a freeze on the nuclear program pending a referendum, or granting immigrant workers the right to vote in municipal elections). Thirdly, the Socialist government policy could not be reduced to the 110 Propositions; later, policy substantially diverged from original propositions. The wage and price freeze of June 1982 and the drastic industrial redeployment plans of April 1984 are good examples of this.

For Mitterrand voters, the contract of 10 May 1981 certainly did not include the "'economic treatment' of unemployment, following a principle dear to Professor Barre".[22] The President himself probably changed, worrying less and less about yesterday's political contract, and more and more about tomorrow's historic image – about "the mark he would leave," as Jean-Marie Colombani put it: "That business should be rehabilitated in the public mind and politics devalued was not the least of the paradoxes in the rule of a man who carried the cult of the political so high."[23]

If the role of the Socialist Party was of limited importance, the same could be said of the famous Elysée breakfasts. True, the President did meet for breakfast with the Prime Minister, the First Secretary of the Socialist Party, the Secretary-General of the Elysée and his own special advisor, Jacques Attali. And the same group lunched with Gaston Defferre, Laurent Fabius, Louis Mermaz (President of the National Assembly) and Jean Poperen (the Socialist Party's second-in-command) after Wednesday's cabinet meetings. This customary presence of top Socialist leaders could be seen as contradicting the traditions of the Fifth Republic. However, to assume that the Party's unofficial and hidden power dominated the state would be to mistake informational meetings for decision-making bodies. This would indeed be a conspiratorial view of history. No supporter of the government-by-the-party thesis can cite a single instance when the Socialist Party leaders, or its parliamentary group, imposed a policy decision on the government. Examples to the contrary, whether large or small, abound. In a word, the Socialists' majority power remained "soldered", and in cases of conflict, the Party base always retreated from fighting decisions taken at the state summit.

Conflictual bicameralism

It was precisely the unity of the majority bloc that explained one of the rare clear institutional changes that took place, the proliferation of conflicts within the Senate, where the opposition had a majority throughout the period. This institutional evolution was both quantitative and qualitative.

Until 1981, 97% of all bills were passed, in identical form, by both chambers. From 1981 to March 1986, this proportion fell to 75%, including ratifications of international treaties and conventions. (During the seventh legislature – 1981–86 – 550 bills were passed, including 156 treaties and conventions. During the fifth legislature – 1973–78 – 638 bills were passed.) Major bills, in case of disagreement, went to a joint committee with equal representation of both chambers; this has occurred 202 times since 1981. Before 1981, this procedure led to agreement between the two chambers in 71% of the cases; since 1981, the figure had dropped to 30%. In summary, more than twice as many bills were passed without the Senate's agreement during the five years of Socialist government than during the previous 23 years (see table 8.6).[24]

Table 8.6 Laws passed by the National Assembly without Senate agreement 1959-86

		Presidency		
De Gaulle 1959-65	De Gaulle 1965-69	Pompidou 1969-74	Giscard 1974-81	Mitterrand 1981-30 Oct. 1985
23	15	17	6	140

Qualitatively speaking, two phases should be distinguished. In the first phase, the Senate, helped initially by the "state of grace", practiced no systematic opposition. It even voted for the abolition of the death penalty and the abolition of the State Security Court. It also voted the Quilliot Law reinforcing tenants' rights, despite vigorous opposition by landlords which only found acknowledgement in amendments. If the Senate rejected some bills it did not like, it left obstructive tactics to the Young Turks of the National Assembly, for example, over nationalization.

The year 1984, however, saw a radicalization of the opposition in the Senate which nearly led to an unprecedented constitutional crisis over the school issue. Led by Charles Pasqua, the President of the RPR group, the Senate discovered the delights of obstructionism. This was all the more exquisite because the government did not have the means of retaliation in the Senate that it had in the National Assembly. Since the Senate's confidence is not required, the government cannot enforce Article 49.3, and can only stop a filibuster by negotiating with the senators. If the Senate refuses to debate a bill, the government can only refer the text back to the National Assembly and interpret the Senate's silence as a defeat for the bill. Such an authoritarian act would create a crisis which could only be resolved by the Constitutional Council.

The conflict over the school issue ended with a Socialist retreat. On the press bill the Senators finally appealed to the Constitutional Council. The Council was even better equipped than the Senate to oppose the government. Events since 1981 have, as John Keeler notes, tended to intensify its activities and to widen their range, even though the Council has generally been consistent with its earlier jurisprudence. [25]

Presidential withdrawal

The third minor evolution in the exercise of power - a withdrawal on the part of the President - can also be explained by the approach of the 1986 elections. Mitterrand anticipated *cohabitation* by leaving the center of the political stage to his Prime Minister. Observers noted a return by the President to his "reserved domain".[26]

Two qualifications should be assigned to such an assertion. First, since both the Prime Minister and the government had some say on foreign policy and defense questions, it was a "privileged" domain rather than a "reserved" one. Secondly, as long as the President still had his parliamentary majority, he was free to define the extent of his "privileged domain" and to add the creation of a fifth television channel to it, as he did in November 1985, for example.

In his speeches, on the other hand, Mitterrand undeniably pushed the government to center stage. During his visit to Brittany on 7 and 8 October 1985, he underlined, on no fewer than eight occasions, that the problem he was talking about depended more on the government than on himself.[27]

That aside, the French felt after May 1981 that the government was playing a leading political role. They felt similarly under Georges Pompidou, but not under Valéry Giscard d'Estaing (figure 8.2). Other indicators may give substance – over and above what the President said or what the public thought – to the idea of a "governmentalization" of politics. Thus, interministerial councils, chaired by the President, became steadily rarer under Pierre Mauroy, and practically disappeared under Laurent Fabius. This left more room for interministerial committees (chaired at Matignon by the Prime Minister) to solve interdepartmental disputes. Little information is available on the question, however, since most of it is classified.

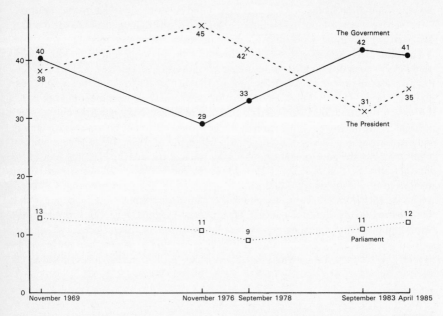

Figure 8.2 Which do you think plays the most important role in fixing the main directions of policy in France at present – Parliament, the President or the Government? (SOFRES)

Even if this is true, and although the first austerity package (June 1982) was put together at Mauroy's initiative, the second, more important one (April 1983) resulted from presidential action after a near crisis within the executive. Similarly, industrial redeployment at the expense of major redundancies was also approved at the Elysée in April 1984. No fundamental political decision after that can be attributed to Laurent Fabius. In so far as presidential withdrawal has occurred, it has been more appearance than reality. More important, it is quite minor relative to what will become necessary under *cohabitation*.

CHANGES IN DEPTH (1986–?)

A complete exposé of all possible changes after the 1986 elections is not feasible here. Changes prior to the elections are real "novelties," and are the results of the Left's tenure of power. It seems premature, however, to analyze them fully since they have not produced their full effects.

Very briefly, the Left wanted the first change – the adoption of proportional representation (PR) – although it turned out to be precarious; the second – *cohabitation* – was definitely not sought by the Left, but the President had to submit to it; the third – the progress of French democracy – applies to everybody but still seems fragile to many.

Semiproportional representation

The new electoral system, adopted in 1985 for the elections of 16 March 1986, was only semiproportional. The territorial basis, the *département*, was small, and there was a 5 per cent minimum required to win a seat in the larger *départements*. This meant that only major parties could elect deputies. The number of parties represented in the National Assembly after March 1986 increased from four (Communists, Socialists, the "liberal" UDF and the Gaullist RPR) to five, with the addition of the far-right Front National.

Why did Mitterrand wait so long to adopt this reform? The most likely reason is that for a long time he hoped that the Left could keep the majority in 1986. In addition, the semiproportional system would not have allowed the Socialists to win an absolute majority in June 1981 (table 8.7). The two-ballot majority voting system that had served the Socialists so well was abandoned for two reasons. Firstly, Union of the Left had broken down, with the Communists returning to their old "tribunal" opposition (to use Georges Lavau's term). The old system had placed a high premium

Table 8.7 Results of June 1981 parliamentary elections

		Majority system		If proportional system	
	% of vote	No. of seats	% seats – % votes	No. of seats	% seats – % votes
Communist	16.1	44	– 7	81	– 2
Socialist	37.8	285	+ 20	242	+ 4
UDF	19.2	62	– 7	118	+ 1
RPR	20.9	88	– 3	125	+ 1
		PS alone has majority of 39 in an Assembly of 491 seats		PS alone is 46 seats short of majority in an Assembly of 577 seats	

Source: SOFRES, retrosimulations for *L'Express*, (April 1985).

on electoral alliances within Right and Left. Secondly, the PS on its own seemed incapable of repeating the Gaullists' achievement of becoming the single dominant party. On the contrary, under the majority system, the Right had an excellent chance of winning a massive majority, and reducing the Left's representation in the Assembly to the low it reached in the rout of June 1968.

Mitterrand chose PR based on the *département* in the hope that the Right's electoral lead over the Left would narrow, and that the elections would not result in an overall majority, as would have been the case if PR had been used for the 1978 elections (table 8.8). The Right's lead did not narrow enough, however. The RPR and the UDF thus won an overall majority, even if it proved miniscule and depended on nonparty rightists. This, in turn, posed a major threat to the President's power.

Mitterrand, then, took the only measure capable of limiting the effects of a right-wing victory. No democratic electoral system, however, could have prevented the election of a parliamentary majority opposed to him.

Cohabitation

It is worth remembering that the French system has two electoral circuits, and that government is chosen by the man elected by the first circuit (the President), but is responsible to the deputies elected by the second circuit.

How constitutional power is exercised thus depends on the political structure of the Assembly; seven possible scenarios are outlined in table 8.9. The 1985 electoral reform excluded the two extreme cases in which one party has an absolute majority. Moreover, the period from 1986 to 1988 will be dominated by the preparation for the presidential election, to be held in spring 1988 at the latest. Mitterrand will be unable to exercise the kind of presidential leadership that he had until 1986, and will be obliged either to concede the reversal of some Socialist policies or resign. The Right

Table 8.8 1978 Parliamentary elections and simulation by PR

	% of vote	Majority system (491 seats)		Proportional system (577 seats)	
		No. seats	% seats–% votes	No. seats	% seats–% votes
Communist	20.6	86	– 3	129	+ 2
Socialist	25.0	113	– 2	147	+ 1.5
UDF	20.6	124	+ 5	127	+ 1.5
RPR	22.6	154	+ 9	153	+ 4
		UDF & RPR have 28-seat majority		UDF & RPR are 9 seats short of a majority ("other Right" has 11 seats)	

Source: SOFRES, retrosimulation for *L'Express*, (April 1985).

Table 8.9 Scenarios for relations between President and Parliament under the Fifth Republic

	Parliamentary majority against President			Parliamentary majority for President			
Political Situation	Absolute majority of one party	Majority of a united coalition	Heterogeneous majority against the President	Heterogeneous majority for the President	Majority of a coalition in which the presidential party is a minority party	Majority of a coalition dominated by the presidential party	Absolute majority of the presidential party
Example	—	1986?	1986?	1958–62	1974–78 1978–81	1962–67 1967–68	1968–73 1981–86
Constitutional consequences							
Presidential power	annihilated	reduced	constitutional	extended			
Government	impossible	parliamentary	mixed	presidential			
Presidential relations with Assembly	immediate crisis	deferred crisis		stability: submission of Parliament to President			

Note:
? indicates a hypothetical situation

is fairly united against the President, but less so concerning the rapidity at which they see him resigning. Raymond Barre's interest in an immediate presidential election led him to reject *cohabitation* out-of-hand prior to March 1986, despite the traditions of the UDF. His poor showing in the March 1986 elections, however, neutralized his claims. Jacques Chirac, however, had every reason to wait until he overtook Barre in the polls and to accept *cohabitation* in the meantime, despite the very firm traditions of the RPR. Whether or not the 1988 presidential election is followed by a dissolution of Parliament, harmony between executive and legislature and the presidential bias of the Fifth Republic will in all likelihood be restored, given the Right's electoral strength. Still unclear, however, is the extent to which the contradictory interests and complex games of *cohabitation* will change the nature of French democracy.

The final change under the Left's tenure of power has been the normalization of French democracy. After 23 years of government by the Right in various guises (itself preceded by a chaotic constitutional history and a parliamentary republic which prevented long mandates for any party) the French finally saw power alternate – the majority became the opposition and the opposition became the majority. The Left was finally perceived as being capable of governing France without turning it into a Communist country, or experiencing a *coup d'état*. Parties which were once excluded from power had to discover, at the risk of continued decline, the constraints and limitations of power. Those who grew accustomed to having power soon found that they could both lose it and win it back rapidly. As long as *cohabitation* does not destroy these realizations, the Fifth Republic under which the French Left was reborn will emerge more deeply rooted in the nation.

NOTES

1 François Mitterrand, *Le Coup d'état permanent* (Paris, Plon, 1964). After this book went out-of-print, the President's literary executors authorized its republication (Paris, Julliard, 1984).

2 *Manifeste de Créteil*, Extraordinary Congress of the Socialist Party, 24 January 1981, in *Le Poing et la rose*, supplement (Jan. 1981), p. 8.

3 *Idem*. It should be added, however, that the *Créteil Manifesto* preceding the 110 Propositions declared that "the constitutional modifications included in the Socialist program will be submitted to Parliament". That entailed the abrogation of Article 16 on full presidential powers and the revision of Articles 11 and 89 (to avoid any further constitutional revision that did not pass through Parliament); Article 34 (to extend the area of application of laws); Article 65 (on the higher council of the judiciary); and Article 72 (for decentralization).

4 *Changer la vie, programme de gouvernement du Parti Socialiste* (Paris, Flammarion, 1972), p. 98. The text proposed a five-year presidential term, the number of terms being limited to two.

5 *Projet socialiste, pour la France aux années 80* (Paris, Club Socialiste du Livre, 1980), p. 265. The five-year term is still there, but not the limit on the number of terms.

6 Sixty per cent for the five-year term, 35% for the seven-year term and 5% undecided in September 1983 – cf. SOFRES, *Opinion publique 1984*, (Paris, Gallimard, 1984), p. 109. The Communists were divided 49-49, the Socialists by 53 (for 5 years) to 43 (for 7), while opposition sympathizers showed a two-thirds

majority for reducing the term of the President to five years. (It is unclear whether they had the incumbent particularly in mind.)

7 François Mitterrand, interview, Antenne 2, 16 January reported in *Libération*, (17 Jan. 1985).

8 Georges Pompidou, New Year's message, 4 January 1972, *Le Monde*, (6 Jan. 1972).

9 Cf. SOFRES, *Opinion publique 1985* (Paris, Gallimard, 1985), pp. 50–1.

10 François Mitterrand, interview in *Le Monde*, 2 July 1981).

11 François Mitterrand, message to Parliament, 8 July 1981.

12 Charles de Gaulle, *Mémoires d'espoir* (Paris, Le Livre de Poche, 1971), p. 68; Georges Pompidou in *Le Monde*, (20 April, 1970); Valéry Giscard d'Estaing in *Le Monde*, (23 Nov. 1978); François Mitterrand, interview with the BBC, 8 September 1981, in *Le Monde*, (9 Sept. 1981).

13 Thierry Pfister, *La Vie quotidienne à Matignon au temps de l'union de la gauche* (Paris, Hachette, 1985), p. 146.

14 Ibid., p. 280.

15 Ibid., p. 339.

16 Ibid., p. 130.

17 Pierre Joxe, in *Le Monde*, (27 Oct. 1983).

18 Michel Couderc, *Sur Quelques tendances du travail legislatif*, paper presented before the colloquium on "L'Assemblée Nationale Aujourd'hui", Association Française des Sciences Politiques; and *Pouvoirs*, (21–22 Nov. 1985), p. 13.

19 Philippe Salomon, *Le Droit d'amendment*, paper presented before the colloquium on "L'Assemblée Nationale Aujourd'hui" (cf. note 18 above).

20 Cf. Raymond Forni, *La Non-réforme du règlement*, paper to colloquium on "L'Assemblée Nationale Aujourd'hui".

21 Michel Debré, speech to the National Assembly, 28 July 1982, *Le Monde*, (30 July, 1982).

22 Jean-Marie Colombani, *Portrait du Président* (Paris, Gallimard, 1985), p. 117.

23 Ibid., p. 208.

24 Couderc, *Surquelques tendences*, p. 6. The other figures in table 8.8 are based on Didier Maus, *Les Grandes textes de la pratique institutionelle de la Ve République*, 2nd edn (Paris, La Documentation Française, 1985), p. 140.

25 John Keeler, "Confrontations juridico-politiques: le Conseil suprème face au gouvernement Socialiste comparé à la Cour Suprème face au New Deal", *Pouvoirs*, 35 (1985), p. 133.

26 Colombani, *Portrait du Président*, p. 130.

27 "Little by little, Mr Mayor, you are making me leave my role of President of the Republic for that of Head of Government. I have always been against that, even if people have sometimes thought the contrary", (speech at Lannion, 7 October 1985). Among other remarks to this effect

On the *Greenpeace* affair: "I intervened publicly twice: the first time was to ask the government for an inquiry, the second was to ask it to act on its conclusions. Apart from that I have nothing to add to what the Prime Minister has said", (interview with *Ouest-France*, 7 October 1985).

"People have said to me, 'you take too much time over things'. As if I were the government . . . I suppose, and I think it is reasonable to suppose, that one can't stay buried in the text of the Constitution from dawn to dusk", (speech at Plessale Cultural Center, 7 October 1985).

"I shall not go right through the questions you have raised, Mr Mayor. In the first place they are not within my competence", (speech at Quimper Town Hall, 8 October 1985).

"A number of confusions have arisen on the role and the competence of the President of the Republic. They don't really bother me . . . but after all, the Constitution does exist. And as far as possible, it is my job to put it to work for you, to interpret it, in the full respect of proper checks and balances", (speech at Lorient, 8 October 1985).

"Thank you for providing me with a synopsis and a reminder of this question. I shall not fail to bring it to the attention of the government for its most careful consideration", (speech at Vannes, 8 October 1985).

"I am not the government. Sometimes people confuse me with it, I don't know why, but I am not the government. I have it in my power to bring certain matters to the attention of the government and if need be to give it advice", (speech at Brest, 8 October 1985).

"I would like to point out that since the beginning of this conversation, you have been trying to place me in a rather odd constitutional position. I can already hear what people will start saying after next March . . . 'the President of the Republic is trying to run everything!' I have never asked to run everything – it's you who are asking me these questions, who are trying to put me in that position", (interview with FR-3-Rennes, 7 October 1985).

9

Judicial-Political Confrontation in Mitterrand's France

The Emergence of the Constitutional Council as a Major Actor in the Policy-making Process

JOHN T. S. KEELER and ALEC STONE

As Olivier Duhamel argues quite cogently in chapter 8, virtually all the institutions of government in France manifested much more continuity than change during the Socialist era. The subject of this chapter, the Constitutional Council, stands as perhaps the major exception to that rule. Hailed by the opposition as "the last rampart against Socialism" and denounced by the Left as "dinosaurs of the Palais Royal" intent on substituting a "government of judges" for government of the people, the Constitutional Council played a role during these five pivotal years that was unprecedented, controversial and often irksome for the government. Many of the failures and frustrations of the Socialist experiment cannot be fully understood without an appreciation of the dynamics of an institution traditionally all but ignored in political science textbooks.

An attempt will be made here not only to assess the implications of the conflict between the Council and the Socialist governments of the Mitterrand era, but also to establish the status of this judicial - political confrontation as a major case worthy of attention by comparativists. A number of French public-law specialists – including the most prominent one, Louis Favoreu – have attempted to down the significance of this confrontation, arguing that the Council did not prevent "the realization of reforms" and that, in fact, "its action . . . served much more as a *garantie de l'alternance* than as an obstacle". While acknowledging that the Council did at times frustrate the government by moderating proposed laws, Favoreu contends that it manifested "very great prudence" and actually aided the government by giving its reforms a sort of "certificate of authenticity" such that, once promulgated, "it [was] no longer possible to contest them (at least in regard to their conformity to the Constitution)". It will be argued here that the Favoreu thesis is gravely flawed, especially in regard to the degree to which the Council functioned as an obstacle to reform. A comparison of the French case with the most celebrated of judicial - political confrontations, that of the United States during the New Deal era, will illustrate that the Constitutional Council was by some measures even more of a problem for the Socialists than the Supreme Court was for the Roosevelt administration.

THE EVOLUTION OF THE CONSTITUTIONAL COUNCIL 1958-81

The Constitutional Council was originally conceived by those who drafted the 1958 Constitution essentially as "a canon aimed at Parliament", the traditional powers of which were to be significantly curtailed under the Fifth Republic. What necessitated the creation of a body like the Council was the distinction made in the Gaullist Constitution between *the domain of law* (spelled out in article 34), within which Parliament was free to legislate, and *the domain of regulation* ("matters other than those which fall within the domain of law", according to Article 37), within which the executive could act through decree. The founders expected that the principal role of the Council would be to "police the frontier" between law and regulation, through Articles 41 and 37.2, so as to prevent encroachment by an assertive Parliament on the new prerogatives of the executive. This did indeed prove to be the Council's most important function through the 1960s and, as anticipated, the majority of its decisions favored the executive at the expense of parliament.[2]

Along with this procedural policing power and some less significant duties[3], the Fifth Republic's founders also accorded the Constitutional Council under *Article 61.2* what was potentially its most important role: the power to judge the constitutionality of (ordinary) laws referred to the Council, before promulgation, by the President of the Republic, the Prime Minister, the President of the National Assembly or the President of the Senate.[4] By all accounts, the founders neither hoped nor expected that Article 61.2 would elevate the Constitutional Council to the status of a major actor in the policy-making process. As Luchaire has written, the *raison d'etre* of this article was simply the same as that of the others related to the Council: "to block Parliament from transcending the (limited) powers allocated to it by the Constitution". Concerned though they were with constraining parliament, "they shared the traditional French dislike of judicial control of legislation" and had no intention to make the Council into an activist Supreme Court (as in the United States) or Constitutional Court (as in West Germany) that would frequently engage in substantive judicial review. It was anticipated that the Council's review role would remain limited as a result of both the restricted right of referral and the fact that the text of the Constitution listed very few "rights" or "liberties" of citizens which the Council might cite as the basis for overturning legislation. While the preamble to the 1958 Constitution ("The French people hereby solemnly proclaim their attachment to the Rights of Man . . . as defined by the Declaration of 1789, reaffirmed and complemented by the Preamble of the Constitution of 1946") referred to a host of such rights, a representative of the founders stated explicitly that it was "certainly not" to be considered as possessing binding constitutional force.[5]

From the establishment of the Fifth Republic through the end of the 1960s, the Constitutional Council seemed to go out of its way to avoid arousing fears of a "government to judges", discharging its duties in just the low-profile and pro-executive manner envisioned by the founders. Until 1971 the Council was convened under Article 61.2 on only five occasions, four times by the Prime Minister and once by the President of the Senate, and every time it ruled in favor of the Executive.[6] The most celebrated of these rulings, that regarding de Gaulle's successful effort of 1962 to amend the Constitution through Article 11 (with a referendum on the establishment of a directly elected president) rather than the obviously appropriate Article 89, did more than anything else to tarnish the image of the Council in the eyes of those who hoped it would develop into at least a mildly assertive, independent guardian of the Constitution. When the Council announced simply that it was not competent to rule on such a matter (a technically correct judgement in the opinion of many constitutional experts), Senate President Gaston Monnerville proclaimed that "the Constitutional Council has just committed suicide" and François Mitterrand averred that the Council had shown itself to be no more than a "Supreme Court from the *musée Grèvin*, the derisory cap of a derisory democracy".[6]

Self-restraint was manifest not only in the positions taken by the Council during the 1960s, but in its jurisprudence as well. While the preamble's "constitutional value" continued to be debated, the Council never invoked it and thus seemed to confirm the view that it would not – and perhaps should not – ever be used as the basis for rulings. Many analysts noted that the classic liberalism of the 1789 Declaration appeared all but impossible to reconcile with the socialist and interventionist principles enumerated in the 1946 preamble. If the Council were to claim that the 1958 preamble was of binding force, therefore, that would entail assuming a power of interpretation so large that it would risk transforming "the control of constitutionality" into a highly controversial "judgement of appropriateness".[7] It thus seemed likely that the Council would continue to exercise self-restraint and play no more than a minor role in the governmental system. Two events of the early 1970s, however, would soon necessitate a very different analysis. In June 1971 the Constitutional Council asserted its independence in an unprecedentedly bold fashion by ruling unconstitutional a government-sponsored law authorizing prefects to delay, until the completion of a judicial investigation, the granting of "full legal personality" to any association that "appeared to have an immoral or illicit purpose". This decision soon came to be viewed by most analysts as the functional equivalent of the American Supreme Court's famous *Marbury vs Madison* case. Not only did it mark the Council's first significant venture in substantive judicial review, but it also expanded the jurisprudential bases (the *bloc de constitutionnalité*) on which future decisions could rest, for it was predicated on the preamble to the Constitution. In the words of Jean Rivero, the 1971 decision constituted nothing less than "a revolution", as the effective Constitution was "doubled in volume solely by the will of the Constitutional Council". Although representatives of the Left applauded the 1971 ruling as a defeat for the government, some of them were quick to note that there were potential "dangers" for the Socialists and Communists in the expansion of the *bloc de constitutionnalité*, for a rigorous application of the 1789 Declaration would provide "sufficient means to paralyze [future] legislation of the Left" dealing with nationalization of industry and other matters.[8]

Given the strict limits that Article 61.2 set on rights to challenge the constitutionality of a law, the 1971 ruling alone hardly sufficed to make the Council a major actor in the governmental system. From the time of its establishment through May 1974, it was called upon to examine only 0.6 laws per year. In October 1974, however, newly elected President Valéry Giscard d'Estaing sponsored a constitutional amendment expanding Article 61.2 so as to allow *60 deputies or 60 senators* to petition the Council. This reform, which Giscard viewed as a means of appealing to moderate elements of the Left and a step toward *décrispation*, was important primarily because it gave a potentially significant new right to the parliamentary opposition. It should be noted, however, that the parties of the Left voted against the amendment. From their perspective, this *réformette* seemed "insignificant but also rather dangerous" as long as the composition of the "political and even partisan" Council was left unaltered. Its impact would be insignificant while the Left remained in opposition, they reasoned, for it seemed unlikely that a Council including no Left appointees would respond favorably to their referrals. On the other hand, it appeared that it could pose "a future danger for a government of the Left". Despite their opposition to Giscard's "mini-reform", the parties of the Left did not hesitate to make use of their new right of referral from 1974 to 1981. Whereas the Constitutional Council would have continued to review less than a law per year had Article 61.2 not been altered, it received 60 referrals from deputies and/or senators of the Left (as well as seven from "the minority of the majority") and rendered 6.7 decisions on constitutionality per year, 23 per cent of which resulted in at least partial annulment.[9]

None of the Constitutional Council's rulings during the 1974–81 period amounted to an earthshaking defeat for the government, but it is fair to say that the opposition parties achieved minor victories more frequently than they had expected given the political orientation of "the sages". Among the most noteworthy of these victories were the overturning of a law which gave police broad powers to search vehicles on public highways (1977), the annulment of certain provisions in a law limiting the right of radio-television employees to strike (1979) and the annulment of an article restricting the rights of defense attorneys in the "Security and Liberty Law" (1981). The 1974 reform thus did enhance the power of the parliamentary opposition to some degree, but as late as 1980 the Socialists were lamenting that even a few "swallows don't make a spring" and insisting that the Council could assume a truly important role as a guardian of civil liberties only with a change of its composition.[10] In an ironic twist, the failure to alter the mode of designating the *conseillers* was one factor which soon assured that the Council's power would increase – but at the expense of a government controlled by the ex-opposition.

JUDICIAL-POLITICAL CONFRONTATION IN MITTERRAND'S FRANCE

When President François Mitterrand and his leftist government began to push their ambitious reform program through Parliament in mid-1981, attention was focused as never before on the part that the Constitutional Council would play in the policy-making process. "The only constitutional weapon henceforth available to the opposition", noted the conservative *Le Figaro* during debates over the nationalization bill, "is referral to the Constitutional Council . . . its members were all named under the former government (a politically novel situation)". Newspapers hostile to the government commonly referred to the Council as "the last rampart" against the "Socialo-Communist government". Some Socialist leaders responded in disdainful terms. PS deputy André Laignel dismissed conservatives' allegations that aspects of the nationalization bill were unconstitutional with what became a celebrated line: "You are juridically wrong, because you are politically in the minority." Lionel Jospin, the First Secretary of the PS, fueled the fire by proclaiming that "never have great currents of reform been allowed to be stopped by a Supreme Court" and adding, in what was construed as a scarcely veiled threat to the Council: "I imagine that these men will be aware . . . that they must reason as magistrates of the Constitution . . . and not as possibly partisan men."[11]

Many observers, in a spirit of either hope or trepidation, compared the situation of 1981 in France to that of the 1930s in the United States, when Roosevelt's New Deal administration found itself confronted by a conservative Supreme Court. The analogy was apt, but it is important to note the ways in which the two settings for judicial-political confrontation differed. In the single most crucial respect, the situation of Roosevelt was more problematic: the American Supreme Court functioned with a power of judicial review that was both better established and more widely perceived as legitimate. However, in several other important respects, the French Socialists faced the more troubling prospect. First, *the French Council contained more members whose partisan or ideological orientations were likely to predispose them to view the government's reforms in an unfavorable light* than had the American Court. While the latter included in 1933 four "tenacious conservatives", it also featured three men "safely in the liberal camp" and two moderates. In contrast, as table 9.1 shows, seven of the nine members of the Council had been affiliated with parties of the former majority and not one was a Socialist or Communist.[12] Second, *the French Council would come into play earlier* than had the American Court. Whereas the American system of hearing cases on appeal from lower courts had prevented the Supreme Court from ruling on a major New Deal act until the administration was in its third year (1935), the French system of reviewing legislation before promulgation meant that the Council would be able to rule on laws well within the Socialist government's first year – appearing as a sort of interloper during the "honeymoon" period – and had the potential to nip reforms in the bud. Third, since the French system entailed decisions on laws challenged by parties of the opposition rather than cases appealed by private citizens, *the negative rulings of the Constitutional Council would appear to both politicians and the public as much more direct, partisan victories for the opposition*. In short, the setting of France in the 1980s seemed at the outset to feature a potential for the judicial obstruction of reform roughly comparable to that of the United States in the 1930s, and even more potential for the derailment of laws in a fashion which could rapidly frustrate the government and slow the momentum of reform.[13]

To what extent did the Constitutional Council actually prove to be an obstacle to reform during the Socialist era? Was its impact at all comparable to that of the American Supreme Court of the 1930s, the case that both French politicians and public lawyers have traditionally considered as the apotheosis of *gouvernement des juges*? The impact of the Council must be assessed in three different ways, through a statistical analysis of the Council's treatment of referred cases, a consideration of the importance of the principal decisions and an accounting of the effect of what has been termed *"autolimitation"*.

Table 9.1 The composition of the Constitutional Council 1981–86

	1981–83	1983–86	1986
Named by the President of the Republic	Roger Frey, President Gaullist deputy and minister 1959–1974	*Daniel Mayer*, President (appt. Feb 1983) SFIO minister in 1940s; member of PS from 1970 onward	Resigned presidency in Feb. 1986; term expires 1992.
	Georges Vedel Law Professor		Term expires in 1989
	André Segalat Conseiller d'Etat; Sec.-Gen. of government 1946–58		*Robert Badinter*, President; Socialist Minister of Justice 1981–86
Named by the President of the National Assembly	Louis Joxe Gaullist deputy and minister 1959–77		Term expires in 1989
	Achille Peretti Gaullist deputy 1958–1977; Pres. of NA 1969–73	*Paul Legatte* (appt. April 1983) Chargée de Mission for Mitterrand 1981–83; Con. d'Etat.	*Robert Fabre* Former Pres. of Mouvement des Rad. de Gauche
	René Brouillet Diplomat; member of de Gaulle's cabinet 1944–46	*Pierre Marcilhacy* (appt. Feb 1983) Senator non-inscrit 1962–83; close to Mitterrand in recent years	Term expires in 1992
Named by the President of the Senate	Gaston Monnerville Gauche Dem. senator 1946–74; Pres. of Senate	Léon Jozeau-Marigne (appt. Feb 1983) Repub.-Indep. Senator	Term expires in 1992
	Louis Gros Repub.-Indep. senator 1948–57	Maurice René Simonnet (appt. Oct 1984) MRP deputy; UDF deputy in European parliament	Reappointed in 1986; term expires 1995.
	Robert Lecourt MRP deputy and minister 1946–58		Term expires in 1989

A statistical analysis

From June 1981 through January 1986 the Council dealt with an unprecedented number of cases and overturned an unprecedented number of government-sponsored laws. Whereas the Council handled only 0.6 cases per year before May 1974, and only 6.7 cases per year from June 1974 to May 1981, it ruled on *14.7 cases per year* in the Socialist era. During that period the Council considered 66 laws, all referred by the opposition, and it declared *over half* 51.5% of them to be at least partially unconstitutional. In contrast, the Council struck down all or part of only 23.4% of the laws that it reviewed during the Giscard presidency. Not only did the Council of the Mitterrand era thus represent an unusually formidable obstacle by the standards of the Fifth Republic, it was even – by statistical measures – more of an obstruction to the Socialist government than the American Supreme Court was to the Roosevelt administration. Whereas the French Council overturned all or part of 34 laws from June 1981 to January 1986, the American Court struck down only 13 New Deal acts (12 in 1935–36).[14]

The Importance of principal decisions

A statistical analysis alone, of course, cannot gauge fully the importance of the Council as an obstacle to reform. Such an analysis must be complemented by a consideration of the importance of the negative rulings rendered by that body. How many of the Council's decisions actually frustrated the Socialist government's effort to achieve significant policy goals? In terms of the importance of the laws deemed unconstitutional, how did the judicial obstruction of the French Council compare to that of the American Court in the New Deal era? Before turning to the French case, let us examine what is considered to be the classic example of *gouvernement des juges*.

Over the past few decades, scholars have established that the Supreme Court served as far less of an impediment to the Roosevelt administration than the mythology surrounding the era would lead one to believe. There is no denying that many of the Court's decisions in 1935–36 shocked and outraged Roosevelt as well as much of the country. It was because FDR felt that the Court had "improperly set itself up as a third House of the Congress" and was thus thwarting the will of "the American people" that he launched his abortive Court-packing scheme in 1937. However, at

---

(Note to Table 9.1)

Note:
The President of the Republic and the Presidents of the two houses of Parliament each appoint three of the nine members of the Council. The terms of the Councillors are staggered so that, except in cases where a death or resignation requires an extraordinary appointment, each of the three Presidents appoints one member every three years. All of the Councillors serve nine-year terms that are non-renewable except when (as in the case of Simmonet) the Councillor was originally appointed to replace, because of death or resignation, a Councillor whose term expired in less than three years. The President of the Republic names the President of the Council. The Councillors whose names are underlined in the table were appointed by Socialist officials.

least in part as a result of the President's counterattack, the Court's "judicial arrogance" endured for only 17 months (January 1935 to May 1936). Its abrupt surrender was signaled by Justice Robert's famous "switch in time that saved nine" in March 1937 and, in subsequent years – as a flood of presidential appointments created a solid "Roosevelt Court" – it reversed many of its earlier decisions.[15]

Of the 13 New Deal acts that the Court overturned, the scholarly consensus is that only *seven* were important. All of these were measures related to the administration's economic recovery program; three dealt with industrial regulation, three involved regulation and debt relief for agriculture and one established pensions for railroad employees. The annulment of each of these acts entailed some costs for the government. However, it must be stressed that all of these acts were allowed to stand for periods of up to two years before being overturned, that at least some of them exhausted their usefulness during that time and that all of those deemed vital by the administration were rapidly replaced by new – often almost identical – programs whose constitutionality was upheld by the Court when tested from 1937 onward. "Whatever some of the eminent justices might have thought during their fleeting moments of glory," argues Robert Dahl, "they did not succeed in interposing a barrier to the achievement of the objectives of the legislation; and in a few years most of the constitutional interpretation on which the decisions rested had been unceremoniously swept under the rug." Ironically, the act whose annulment generated the greatest attention at the time, the National Industrial Recovery Act (which established the NRA), is now recognized by scholars to have been of little further use for the New Deal. Roosevelt had come to consider it an "awful headache" and many of his advisors were to some extent "relieved" by the Court's decision. The parts of it worth salvaging, on the other hand, were rapidly reinstituted through "piecemeal legislation" and its labor provisions were not only reenacted but strengthened by the Wagner Industrial Relations Act of 1935.[16]

Turning now to the French case, it must be acknowledged at the outset that, whereas more than 50 per cent of the Supreme Court's negative decisions during the New Deal era represented important (if temporary) defeats for the administration, a smaller percentage of the annulments delivered by the Constitutional Council from 1981 through 1985 were of major consequences for the Socialist government. Nearly half of the Council's partial annulments were based on procedural violations (most commonly, failure of Parliament to consult the assemblies of the overseas territories or inclusion of an inappropriate nonfinancial measure in an appropriations bill) and thus constituted no more than trivial concerns for the government; moreover, a few of the Council's other negative decisions related only to minor matters.[17] However, *at least seven* of the Council's negative rulings on Socialist legislation were important and controversial, and some of these – unlike the American Court's decisions – entailed a complete blockage of reform desired by the government. As one of the few former Council members sympathetic to the Left has commented, these decisions were generally based on "very solid juridical argumentation" and could thus hardly be categorized as "political" in the pejorative sense of the term. Nonetheless, they consistently manifested the conservative "political philosophy" of the Council majority and reflected an interpretation of the "control of constitutionality" sufficiently assertive to appear –

in the eyes of many observers – as an encroachment on Parliament's exclusive right
to exercise the "control of appropriateness". Given space limitations, the role of the
Council as a conservative obstacle to reform will be illustrated through an examination
of only four of the most controversial annulments that it delivered from 1981 through
1985.[18]

The most important Constitutional Council decision rendered during that period
was indubitably that of January 1982 concerning *the nationalization law*. This was "the
first time in the history of the Fifth Republic," as Jospin remarked, "that the
Constitutional Council ha[d] blocked the promulgation of a law . . . at the heart
of the program enacted by the President of the Republic and a legitimately elected
national assembly". Recognized as an embarrassing "defeat" for the government and
as a source of "jubilation" for the opposition, the nationalization ruling made the
Council the focus of front-page news in all French papers. Given the traditionally
low profile of "the nine sages," a *Le Monde* journalist commented that many Frenchmen
would no doubt first learn of the existence of the Council "as a result of the step
which it has just taken".[19] What exactly was that step, and how problematic was
it for the government?

The two most important aspects of the Council's 30-page decision, both predicated
largely on Article 17 of the Declaration of the Rights of Man ("Property being an
inviolable and sacred right, no one may be deprived thereof except in case of a *public
necessity* . . . and on condition of *just and prior compensation*" – emphasis added), were
as follows. On the one hand, the Council ruled, contrary to arguments of the opposition,
that the nationalizations were acceptable in principle, for there was no "manifest error"
in Parliament's contention that they were justified by "public necessity", i.e. by the
need "to give the *pouvoirs publics* the means to deal with the economic crisis". In this
regard, at least, the Council's judgment was less problematic for the Left than some
had anticipated at the time of the 1971 and 1974 debates. On the other hand, the
Council declared that the proposed compensation formula was not "just" and that,
as the articles containing this formula were "inseparable" from the whole, the law
could not be promulgated in its present form.[20]

Welcome though the decision on "public necessity" was, the negative rulings of
the Council were far more severe than the government had expected. In regard to
the crucial compensation provisions, even moderates such as Michel Rocard felt that
the Council had overstepped proper bounds; "instead of stating the law", he quipped,
the judges "are stating the price". Government speakers protested that the provisions
struck down by the Council had been approved by the Conseil d'Etat ("Constitutional
truth on one side of the Palais Royal, constitutional error on the other side of the
same palace" was the sardonic reaction of the Minister of Justice, Robert Badinter)
and were more generous than those in the nationalization law of the Liberation period,
while journalists reported that many financial experts had considered the government's
compensation plan to be sufficiently generous. A number of prominent public lawyers
defended the Council's ruling on compensation, noting that comparisons with the
Liberation case were legally irrelevant (as no body had been charged to rule on the
constitutionality of laws at that time) and that it seemed reasonable to require Parliament
to take into account the 14 per cent inflation rate of 1981. Even some of them, however,

acknowledged that judicial self-restraint on this complex matter would have been understandable and that the Council's decision was much less restrained than comparable judgements by the Italian Constitutional Court had been.[21]

The government's resentment over the negative ruling was compounded by the Council's failure to stipulate what would constitute "just" compensation, which meant that officials would be forced to grope toward a new, more expensive formula – that might in turn be declared unacceptable – while trying to mollify elements of the Left convinced that even the initial formula was excessive. Advocates of nationalization were also piqued by the ruling of "inseparability", for this meant that promulgation would be delayed for some time, leaving the enterprises on the nationalization list in a state of uncertainty and preventing a rapid launching of the recovery program. "In losing time", National Assembly President Louis Mermaz lamented, "we are going to lose money".[22]

As the government set to work reformulating the stricken provisions of the law, a minor constitutional crisis unfolded. The Communists denounced the "rearguard political operation by the defeated of 10 May", while many PS speakers engaged in what the opposition termed "a campaign of denigration" directed at Council President Roger Frey (or "Roger *Frein*", as *Le Canard enchaîné* called him) and the other "*messieurs veto*". Threats were issued on a daily basis against the nine men who were said to be intent on substituting "the government of judges for the government of the people". A *Le Monde* journalist portrayed the judicial–political confrontation in these dramatic terms:

> On one side, nine "sages" named by representatives of the former majority; on the other, the 15,714,598 Frenchmen who voted . . . in favor of M. François Mitterrand . . . Which of these two legitimacies is more legitimate? For the PCF, and PS and their deputies, the answer is clear: the Constitutional Council is wrong because it is blocking the change desired by the country.

Even the Prime Minister's office joined in the fray, as a counselor of Pierre Mauroy cautioned the Council against precipitating a "test of force": "one time yes, two times no, M. Mitterrand would not accept it".[23]

The "tempest" was eventually calmed, in the short run, by the Council's approval of a revised nationalization bill in February, but the economic and political costs for the government were quite significant. The recovery program was delayed, the bill for compensation was increased by an estimated 8 billion francs (nearly 30 per cent), a tax hike was necessitated, factions of the Left were forced to squabble over the proper means of handling the Council and the heretofore divided opposition was given both a morale boost and an issue around which to rally. After two Council members took the unusual step of speaking out against the "injurious and dishonest" attacks leveled against them by the PS, *Le Figaro* headlined an article "Defend the Republic" and Gaullist leader Jacques Chirac proclaimed that the country's political divisions were no longer between Left and Right, but rather between "Republicans" and "Marxists". The Council thus played, however inadvertently, a major role along with the Socialists themselves in bringing the government's "honeymoon period" to an end.[24]

In November 1982 the Council stirred passions on a different front by overturning a provision of the municipal elections reform law stating that no party list in communes of more than 3500 inhabitants could include "more than 75% candidates of the same sex". This measure was actually intended, of course, to institute *a 25% quota of women candidates*. Its curious wording was expressly designed to obviate problems of constitutionality. A prominent legal scholar appointed to the Council in 1980, Georges Vedel, had written an article in 1979 explaining that "a text which reserved a certain number of places for women . . . without doing the same for men . . . would be contrary to the principle of equality", but that a text in the form of the 1982 law should present no such problem. Vedel had also argued on that occasion that such a law would probably not be deemed an unconstitutional infringement on the liberty of either voters or potential candidates, given the fact that a variety of other restrictions had traditionally been accepted. In the face of such authoritative legal arguments and the considerable electoral weight of women, *all* parties in Parliament had voted for the quota by an overwhelming majority and even those individuals who had referred the law to the Council raised no objection to this measure.[25]

Many observers thus responded with indignation to the Council's annulment. Legal scholars repeated the arguments of Vedel and noted that, in examining the two texts on which the Council's argument rested (Article 3 of the Constitution and Article 6 of the 1789 Declaration) the first seemed entirely irrelevant to the case while the second – written at a time when women were denied even the vote – appeared applicable only if interpreted in an extremely conservative manner.[26] A female deputy observed that less than 9 per cent of municipal councillors were women and concluded that only an "antique reflex of misogyny" could have prevented the Council from recognizing that the quota system conformed to the spirit of the law. Given the bipartisan support for the provision in Parliament, a Socialist speaker was led to proclaim that there seemed "to be a new allocation of roles within the Right, the Constitutional Council daring to do that which the parliamentarians of the same ideology would not". Such a charge may have been unfair, especially since it was evident that even some Socialists had supported the quota with reluctance, but the fact remained that many within the Center-Right were troubled by a Council decision appearing to vindicate the Left's contention that "the sages" were out of tune with the will of the people. As a newspaper seldom sympathetic to the government noted, the Council could not develop a "backward" image "without losing a measure of its authority".[27]

Despite the fact that three councillors, including the President, were replaced by men sympathetic to the Left in 1983 (see figure 17.1), the Council remained dominated by appointees of the ex-majority and continued to loom as an obstacle for the government. This point is worth stressing, for it represents another way in which the judicial-political confrontation of France in the 1980s was more troublesome for the elected officials than was the American confrontation of the 1930s. In the latter case, the "nine old men" overturned federal acts during a period lasting only *17 months* (January 1935 to May 1936). The American Court's famous "switch in time that saved nine" had no counterpart in the French case, however. May 1983 marked the point 17 months after the Council's ruling on the nationalization law. Several important annulments were rendered after that date, the final one (to be discussed later) coming in August 1985 – *44 months* after the "black weekend" of 1982.

In October 1984 the Constitutional Council was called upon to review the most hotly debated piece of legislation referred to it since the nationalization law: the reform intended to *limit the concentration and assure the financial accountability and pluralism of press enterprises*. This press law had been presented by Prime Minister Pierre Mauroy as one of the government's most crucial reforms, a means of assuring liberty in the face of abuses committed, often under a cloak of secrecy, by wealthy individuals and groups. Although Mauroy and Mitterrand had generally discreetly avoided acknowledging the chief target of the law, many Socialists had openly stated the obvious: the principal *raison d'être* for the reform was to force dismantlement of the press empire (19 dailies, including *Le Figaro*, 7 weeklies and 11 periodicals) controlled by a notorious conservative, Robert Hersant. Hersant had often been charged with using questionable or even illegal tactics in operating his papers, and – quite like William Randolph Hearst, who had mobilized his American press empire to condemn what he termed FDR's "Raw Deal" – he had spearheaded attacks against the Socialist government's alleged campaign of *"liberticide"*.[28]

Throughout the 10-month-long legislative process that produced the press law of September 1984, the parliamentary opposition had vehemently condemned what it portrayed as nothing more than a partisan "settling of accounts" with Hersant and had used every tactic of obstruction possible: both the number of amendments proposed (2491 by the RPR and UDF alone) and the hours consumed in debate (more than 166) during the first reading had broken all records for the Fifth Republic; a motion of censure had been filed even before debate commenced, and the government had felt compelled to terminate the second reading debates by invoking Article 49.3, making the vote on the bill a vote of confidence in the government and thus triggering another censure motion. Once the law had finally been passed, it was proudly claimed by an opposition deputy that his party had actually achieved its principal goal: delaying passage of the law long enough to prevent its application to the Hersant group before the 1986 legislative elections.[29]

By the time the press law reached the Constitutional Council on referral by the opposition, the central political issue involved could not have been more apparent. For good measure, however, Hersant himself underscored it for the Council. Along with a lengthy lawyer's brief citing no less than 13 reasons why the law should be viewed as unconstitutional, Hersant sent the Council a personal note alleging: "For the first time in the history of five Republics, a law . . . prepared by a political party . . . has been directed against a single man."[30]

Despite the fact that the Council's decision of 11 October implicitly rejected many of the legal arguments of Hersant and the opposition, declaring constitutional virtually all provisions of the press law, a small section of the 34-page document constituted an enormous political defeat for the government. It was ruled by the judges that: (a) whereas Parliament was free to impose its proposed limits on the concentration of press ownership, such restrictions on a public liberty could apply to *"existing situations"* only if these situations "had been illegally acquired" or if subjecting them to the new limits "would really be necessary to assure the obtainment of the constitutional objective pursued", and (b) that no existing situation in this case met either requirement. In short, the Council blocked the government from forcing dismantlement of the Hersant group.[31] Just as in the nationalization decision of 1982, which had been drafted under the direction of the same *rapporteur* (Vedel), the Council thus upheld the government's legislation in principle but disallowed its implementation in the form desired. In the press law case, however, the government's "victory" in principle was even more hollow than before, as it was compelled to abandon completely the central objective that it had sought.

Predictably, the Council's decision provoked reactions of unusual fervor. Hersant and all of the opposition forces exulted in their triumph, with a Gaullist going so far as to demand the resignation of the minister responsible for the offensive law. At the same time, a Socialist speaker proclaimed that the Council's evolution in the direction of "a government of judges" had clearly reached a "dangerous" point. As always, the commentaries of public law specialists were mixed, but a good number argued with unprecedented vigor that the Council's exercise of judicial review in this case had gone beyond the "control of constitutionality" to the "control of appropriateness". The reputation of the Council had been tarnished, concluded one former Councillor of State, for it was beginning to "behave like a third legislative assembly, remaking laws . . . according to options more political than juridical".[32]

In August 1985 the Constitutional Council was convened to consider another law dealing with an extremely sensitive political issue: *reform of the electoral and governmental system in New Caledonia*, by far the most troublesome of France's overseas territories (TOM). The Fabius–Pisani Law had been designed to replace the existing system, in which the white (French-origin) majority monopolized territorial power and exercised it in such a way as to provoke violent protests and increasing demands for independence on the part of the sizeable Melanesian minority, with a new system that would assure a measure of power-sharing during a transitional period leading up to a referendum on "association–independence" in 1987. Under the proposed system, New Caledonia was to be divided into four new regions, each of which would elect a council whose members would serve together in a semiautonomous territorial congress. The boundaries were drawn in such a way as to assure that the indigenous Kanaks would enjoy a majority in two of the four regions, and the most heavily populated white-dominated region (Noumea) was accorded fewer councillors per caput than the other regions (1 per 4700 vs 1 per 2200-2600) so as to prevent the whites most staunchly opposed to any alteration of New Caledonia's traditional status from obtaining an absolute majority of seats within the congress.[33]

In the parliamentary debates, government representative Edgard Pisani had argued that these provisions would guarantee the rights of both the whites and the Kanaks while encouraging the two sides to abandon violence in favor of "a democratic political debate" on their future. On the other side of the aisle, the opposition had condemned the reform as "a sort of apartheid policy" that would simply encourage the separatists and "could lead in the long run to partition". To the Center–Right forces, the proposed electoral system had seemed especially objectionable on political grounds and also unconstitutional – a violation of the right to "equal suffrage" guaranteed by Article 3 of the Constitution. Pisani and other officials had dismissed such an interpretation, asserting that the Council should find their proposal acceptable in light of not only the special conditions in New Caledonia, but also well-established practices in metropolitan France; under the electoral system employed for every parliamentary election since the advent of the Fifth Republic, it had been noted, the number of deputies per caput varied from district to district by as much as a factor of 10.[34]

The decision rendered by the Council on 8 August rejected Pisani's reasoning. Whereas the judges confirmed the constitutionality of most aspects of the New Caledonia reform, they struck down the proposed electoral system, arguing that it "manifestly exceeded" the limited degree to which, within the terms of Article 3, the principle of equal representation could be compromised in favor of "other considerations of the general interest".

Once again the government thus received a "severe blow" from the Council. While the opposition was applauding what it termed "the condemnation of injustice", speakers for the Left harshly criticized "the growing and exorbitant role" played by "the government of judges" and complained that the Council's latest ruling – like that of 1982 on shareholder compensation – was perplexingly obscure. The Council had asserted that "representation need not necessarily be proportional to the population of each region", remarked a PS deputy, but had cast "no light" on the issue of how far proportionality could be sacrificed to accommodate "the general interest".[35]

The decision of "the sages" not only sent the government back to the electoral drawing board with little guidance, but also seemed to necessitate a lengthy delay – which would be politically problematic, with parliamentary elections in the offing – in holding the New Caledonian election. President Mitterrand avoided the expected delay (more than a month, for a new law would have required approval by the New Caledonian Assembly), to the surprise of many, through an unprecedented procedural move. Invoking Article 10, which had never before been used in the wake of a negative Council decision, Mitterrand ordered that the stricken article of the law be sent back to Parliament for another deliberation. Resorting to Article 10 was enough to upset the opposition, but this political transgression was compounded by the fact that the President opted to convene immediately a special session of Parliament, interrupting the sacrosanct summer vacations of deputies and senators. Through a stroke of bad luck, this move proved to be even more of a political problem than expected, for it meant that the opposition forces were assembled in Paris and eager to pounce when the first news of the *Greenpeace* scandal broke.

Despite the frustrations and negative political fallout that it engendered, the New Caledonia matter was ultimately resolved in a surprisingly satisfactory manner for the government. Ignoring opposition demands for a more profound reformulation of the stricken article, the Socialists gambled that the Council would approve a modest compromise through which Noumea would receive 21 of 46 rather than 18 of 43 congress seats. The Council, faced with an impatient, beleaguered government and widespread concern among public lawyers that a second annulment could undermine the legitimacy of the French system of constitutional control, approved on 23 August both the retouched electoral law and the contested procedure used to push it through Parliament.[36]

The auto-limitation effect

While declarations of unconstitutionality were indubitably the most dramatic means through which the Constitutional Council constrained the Socialist government, the power of "the sages" came into play in an indirect manner as well. A complete accounting of the Council's role as an obstacle to reform must consider what has been termed *autolimitation*: the government's exercise of legislative self-restraint resulting from anticipation of a referral to and an eventual negative decision by the Council.[37] It is often difficult to discern whether the watering-down of a bill should be attributed to autolimitation as defined here rather than simple *political prudence*, i.e., governmental concern over the potential political costs of pursuing a more radical reform. Confusion on this score has sometimes been caused intentionally by government officials, as they have found the (alleged) necessity of autolimitation to be a convenient pretext for abandoning radical measures once promised to party activists but now viewed with misgiving.[38] In most important cases, of course, the content of bills has been genuinely affected by *both* constitutional and political considerations. A few key examples will illustrate the extent to which autolimitation affected policy and the policy-making process during the era of Socialist government.

The first major reform launched by the Socialists, the *nationalization* law, was indirectly affected by the Constitutional Council months before "the sages" delivered their ruling of January 1982. It has been documented that concern about the Council compelled the government to abandon some problematic measures criticized during debates over the nationalization bill. Moreover, this concern forced the government to consider seriously the legal reservations expressed by the Council of State in regard to the *projet de loi*, which was thus moderated considerably even before reaching Parliament. At the suggestion of the Council of State, the vital compensation provisions were altered so as to increase shareholder payments by more than 20 per cent (the advice of the Council of State proved to be of little help in this instance, as the Constitutional Council struck down those provisions, forcing the government to revise the mode of calculating compensation and to increase payments by another 30 per cent). According to informed observers, this was a classic case in which both autolimitation and political caution came into play.[39]

The government's second major reform, *decentralization*, was even more profoundly affected by autolimitation. Those charged with formulating this bill were aware that some of the decentralization measures long advocated by the PS could be instituted only through an amendment to the Constitution. Such an amendment stood no chance of passing in 1981 or 1982, however, given the certain opposition of the Senate. As a result, the delicate task facing Interior Minister Gaston Defferre was to prepare legislation incorporating as much decentralization as the Constitutional Council would be likely to accept in the form of an ordinary law. Many of the new powers that the Socialists had pledged to grant to the communes, departments and regions thus had to be weakened and accompanied by caveats assuring respect for the traditional responsibilities of the state, the unity of the Republic and principles such as the equality of citizens before the law. It was only because the Socialists' original proposals were watered down in this manner that the Council's ruling on the decentralization law in 1982 constituted merely an uncontroversial partial annulment.[40]

The *press law* of 1984 is another example of Socialist legislation that was significantly affected by autolimitation. After the government had taken advantage of a pause in the legislative process during the winter of 1983–84 to revise 26 of the press bill's 42 articles, one analyst commented: "Rarely has the Constitutional Council's role as guardian of the fundamental law had such an effect through the simple fear of what its decisions might be." The two most important concessions reluctantly made by the government to the specter of the Council were a reduction of the powers of the inspectors who were to serve as the enforcement arm of the proposed press commission, and the elimination of a key passage granting that commission the power to engage in "preliminary authorization" of a proposed press acquisition; in light of the Council's 1971 decision regarding political associations, it was feared that any such "prior restraint" clause would be viewed as unconstitutional.[41]

The year 1984 also featured an unusual case of autolimitation: the government's decision in July to withdraw from Parliament the Savary Bill dealing with *reform of private (clerical) education*. There is no doubt that Mitterrand's abandonment of this project was due primarily to political prudence; the bill provoked impassioned resistance – including a massive protest demonstration in June 1984 – by supporters of private schools. However, in the eyes of public-law experts, another important factor in the decision was anticipation that, even if the bill were forced through Parliament at significant political cost, its central provisions would ultimately be overturned by the Constitutional Council as an infringement on the right of private schools to maintain their "distinctive character".[42] In a wide variety of contexts, therefore, autolimitation served as a subtle yet significant obstacle to Socialist reform.

CONCLUSION

Originally an obscure institution conceived to play a marginal role in the Fifth Republic, the Constitutional Council has gradually moved toward the center stage of French politics and acquired the status of a major actor in the policy-making system. Since its pivotal 1971 decision it has served with increasing frequency as a guardian of individual rights, and since passage of the 1974 amendment it has also become the chief instrument of *contre-pouvoir* available to the parliamentary opposition.[43] The period from 1981 to 1985 illustrated vividly just how potent that *contre-pouvoir* can be, given a reformist government facing a Council dominated by appointees of the ex-majority. A political situation structurally analogous to that of the United States in the 1930s produced effects on policy which, if different in detail, were strikingly similar.

Some public-law specialists have attempted to play down the significance of the judicial–political confrontation in Mitterrand's France, arguing that the Council acted in a self-restrained manner, did not pose a significant obstacle to reform and in fact benefitted the government by providing controversial reforms with a "certificate of authenticity". But such an argument suffers from several central flaws. First, it greatly understates the extent to which the Council acted as a brake on the Socialist's program of reform. It may be true, in a sense, that the Council generally behaved with considerable "prudence". It is plausible to assume that, in some cases, a desire to obviate political confrontation led it to render decisions less negative than the Constitution seemed to allow. The fact that the Council keeps its votes secret and publishes no dissenting opinions makes it virtually impossible to assess the body's political dynamics. Certainly it must be said that the Council stopped far short of creating a literal "government of judges". Nonetheless, it constrained the government's policy-making efforts to an extent unparalleled in the history of the Fifth Republic and, indeed, unprecedented in French history since the abolition of the Parlements in the 1790s. Moreover, by many measures it hindered the government's reform campaign even more than the American Supreme Court checked the enterprises of the New Deal administration. The Council overturned more laws dealing with a wider range of political issues, delivered negative decisions over a much longer period and prevented some laws from ever reaching the implementation stage. Furthermore, the Council annulled approximately the same number of important laws that the Supreme Court overturned, and indirectly affected even more through autolimitation.

Second, it is not clear that the Council's approval of the Socialist government's legislation provided a "certificate of authenticity" of much real political significance. Negative rulings by the Council were often front-page news; in contrast, the positive decisions of the Council were generally accorded much less publicity. It is far more evident that the former impaired the government's image than that the latter enhanced it. Furthermore, it is an exaggeration to claim that the positive rulings of the Council made it impossible for the opposition to contest the constitutionality of laws. In the case of the nationalization decision, for example, staunch conservatives contended that intimidation by the Socialists prevented a more "just" (i.e. negative) ruling, and some even portrayed the Council as "pusillanimous" for caving in to such pressure.[44]

Finally, it is not firmly established that the legislation of a French government *requires* "authentication" by a body of constitutional guardians. After all, from the Revolution of the 1790s through the very recent past, parliamentary sovereignty was as generally accepted in the Republics of France as in Britain. The Constitutional Council was not established until 1958, did not attempt to exercise a power of substantive judicial review until 1971 and did not overturn a law central to a government's platform until 1982. What little survey data exists regarding the Council indicates that it has long been a relatively unfamiliar institution of government to the French public. The vast majority (80 per cent in 1983) now claim to approve of its role, and there can be no doubt that many informed citizens appreciate the fact that the Council's rulings since 1971 have instituted a *de facto* Bill of Rights through according "constitutional value" to the texts cited in the preamble.[45] Nevertheless, no careful attempt has ever been made to gauge the degree to which citizens affiliated to a particular party feel it to be legitimate for the Council to overturn a law passed by a government including that party. Until the Council has been generally accepted as legitimate in its current activist mode, it is reasonable to expect that every judicial–political confrontation will provoke widespread demands that the tradition of parliamentary sovereignty be respected and the "government of judges" brought to a halt. It should be remembered that even the American Supreme Court, commonly viewed as the most respected activist judicial body, has often been subjected to harsh criticism when it has challenged the legislative judgement of popularly elected officials.

Although the Socialists stopped short of challenging the Council directly with a scheme such as FDR's "court-packing" plan, they did try to implement one reform that would have enabled the government to circumvent the judges in certain cases. In July 1984 Mitterrand sent to Parliament a bill that, if passed by both houses and approved in a referendum, would have amended Article 11 of the Constitution to allow for referenda on bills dealing with public liberties. In his inscrutable style, the President stated simply that the amendment deserved support because it would "open to our people a vast space of liberty". Critics pointed out, however, that this amendment would provide Mitterrand and future presidents with the only conceivable means of avoiding the jurisprudential constraints imposed at the Palais Royal. Since the Council had ruled in 1962 that it was not competent to review laws passed through referenda, a president fearful of an annulment but confident about the public mood would be able to assure undiluted passage of a controversial law by submitting it to the citizenry. Consideration of this possibility, combined with political rancor, led the Senate to reject Mitterrand's proposal.[46]

Despite the failure of this measure, a number of eminent public-law specialists have argued that it is a sound idea and may come to be viewed as a necessary reform if the Council continues on an activist course. As Loic Philip has asserted, there appears to be an element of danger in the fact that with a *bloc de constitutionnalité* already vast and ever expanding (as the Council introduces more "fundamental principles"), it seems that the judges "can always find arguments to determine that [a law] is contrary to the Constitution". Maurice Duverger has suggested that a viable solution to this problem would be to institute a reform similar to that suggested by Mitterrand but altered so as to require the Constitutional Council to issue an advisory opinion on questions concerning public liberties before they are submitted to the public; such a measure would retain an influential role for the judges, enhance the ability of governments to institute reforms that they feel are vital and leave the final word to the people.[47] It is by no means clear that this form of referendum will ever be embraced, but it is apparent that the trend toward an increasingly powerful Constitutional Council will keep it near the agenda of public debate.

Now that the Socialists' reform era has passed, the Council is unlikely to loom as quite the obstacle it has appeared to be in recent years. Nonetheless, it should continue to be a much more important and visible institution than it was a decade ago. Every law of consequence is now routinely referred, and laws must now be carefully formulated to wend their way through a legal web of unprecedented density. Through a sort of jurisprudential ratchet effect, the precedents set by successive Council decisions serve to make that web ever more dense and problematic. For example, Jacques Chirac's proposed reform of the legislative electoral laws reinstituting single-member constituencies will need to be drafted with concern for the principle established with the 1985 New Caledonia decision. The Council's significance for the *cohabitation* period and beyond was implicitly acknowledged by President Mitterrand when, in February 1986, he appointed one of the most capable Socialist officials – Minister of Justice Robert Badinter –

to serve as President of the Constitutional Council through 1995. Under such leadership, with a new political orientation (four of the nine *conseillers* are now Socialist appointees), and emboldened by the activism of the past, the Council can almost certainly be counted upon to make its mark in an important if unpredictable fashion.

NOTES

1 Louis Favoreu, "Le Conseil constitutionnel et l'alternance", in *La Constitution de la Cinquième République*, eds Olivier Duhamel and Jean-Luc Parodi (Paris, Fondation Nationale des Sciences Politiques, 1985), pp. 434-37.

2 François Luchaire, *Le Conseil constitutionnel* (Paris, Economica, 1980), p. 31; Barry Nicholas, "Fundamental Rights and Judicial Review in France", *Public Law*, (Spring 1978), p. 84; L. Favoreu and Loic Philip (eds), *Les Grandes décisions du conseil constitutionnel* (Paris, Sirey, 1984), pp. 598-9.

3 The lesser duties of the Council include supervising presidential elections, parliamentary elections and referenda (68% of the Council's 988 decisions from 1959-83 dealt with such matters), certifying the incapacity of the President, advising the President on the exercise of emergency powers and ruling on the constitutionality of parliamentary regulations. The Council also reviews all organic laws and referred treaties.

4 As mentioned in note 3, the Council also has the power to review *all* organic laws. Important though this power might seem, it has been exercised rarely (1.6 times per year on average from 1959-83) and has normally involved rulings on minor technical issues; see Conseil Constitutionnel, *Controle de constitutionnalité et délimitation des compétences: table analytique des décisions 1959-1984* (Paris, Conseil Constitutionnel, 1984), pp. 751-60.

5 Luchaire, *Le Conseil constitutionnel*, p. 112; the few rights and liberties of citizens cited in the text appear in Articles 2, 3, 4 and 66; for the founders' view of the status of the preamble, see the comments of Raymond Janot (the government's speaker on this issue during the drafting process) in Louis Favoreu (ed.), *Cours constitutionnelles européennes et droits fondamentaux* (Paris, Economica, 1982), pp. 212-13.

6 For a list of the first five Article 61.2 decisions, see Conseil Constitutionnel, *Controle de constitutionnalité*, pp. 751-52; for the comments on the 1962 decision, see *Le Monde*, (8 Nov. 1962); and François Mitterrand, *Le Coup d'état permanent*, 2nd edn (Paris, Juillard, 1984 - originally published in 1964), p. 137.

7 Jean Chatelain, *La Nouvelle Constitution et la régime politique de la France* (Paris, Berger-Levrault, 1959), pp. 183-84.

8 Burt Neuborne, "Judicial Review and Separation of Powers in France and the United States", *New York University Law Review*, 57, 3 (June 1982), p. 392; Jacques Robert, "Propos sur le sauvetage d'une liberté", *Revue du droit public*, (Sept.-Oct. 1971), pp. 1171-205. On the "revolution . . . made in four words", see Rivero's comments in Favoreu, *Cours constitutionnelles*, p. 520; for the Left's reaction to the 1971 ruling, see *Le Monde*, (1-2 Aug. 1971).

9 Loic Philip, "Bilan et effets de la saisine du conseil constitutionnel", in Duhamel and Paradi (eds), *La Constitution*, p. 421; for the Left's view of the 1974 reform, see *Le Monde*, (10 Oct. 1974) and *L'Humanité*, (19 and 22 Oct. 1974).

10 Favoreu and Philip (eds), *Les Grandes décisions*, chs 29, 34 and 37; Michel Charasse, "Saisir le Conseil constitutionnel", *Pouvoirs*, 13 (1980), p. 90.

11 *Le Figaro*, (26 Aug. 1981); *La Croix*, (29 Oct. 1981); *Journal des finances*, (12 Nov. 1981).

12 For discussions of the political orientations of Supreme Court justices serving during FDR's first term, see William E. Leuchtenburg, *Franklin D. Roosevelt and the New Deal* (New York, Harper and Row, 1963), p. 143; Alfred H. Cope and Fred Krinsky (eds), *Franklin D. Roosevelt and the Supreme Court* (Boston, D. C. Heath, 1962), pp. 1-2.

13 Leuchtenburg, *Franklin D. Roosevelt*, pp. 145-46; Malcolm M. Feeley and Samuel Krislov (eds), *Constitutional Law* (Boston, Little, Brown, 1985), pp. 183 and 186-9.

14 Laurent Habib, "Bilan de la saisine parlementaire du conseil constitutionnel de 1981 à 1986", *Pouvoirs*, 13 (June 1986), pp. 197-206; Olivier Duhamel, "L'Histoire extravagante du conseil constitutionnel", *L'Express*, (4 July 1986), p. 56; on the New Deal era, see Robert A. Dahl, "Decision-making in a Democracy: The Supreme Court as a National Policy-maker", *Journal of Public Law*, 6, 2 (Fall 1957), pp. 286-7.

15 FDR as cited in Robert H. Jackson, *The Struggle for Judicial Supremacy* (New York, Random House, 1941), pp. 341 and 344. On the Court's "judicial arrogance", see Daniel Novak, "Economic Activism and Restraint", in *Supreme Court Activism and Restraint*, Stephen C. Halpern and Charles M. Lamb (Lexington, MA., (D. C. Heath, 1982), pp. 91-5.
16 Dahl, "Decision-making", p. 287; Ellis W. Hawley, *The New Deal and the Problem of Monopoly* (Princeton, Princeton University Press, 1966), pp. 130-1; Leuchtenburg, *Franklin D. Roosevelt*, p. 161.
17 Louis Favoreu, "Le Droit constitutionnel jurisprudentiel en 1982", *Revue de droit public*, (March-April 1983), pp. 340-1.
18 François Luchaire, "Doctrine, necessité ou poésie?", in *Nationalisations et constitution*, ed. Louis Favoreu (Paris, Economica, 1982), p. 65; François Luchaire, "Le Conseil constitutionnel d'hier et d'aujourd'hui", *Après-demain*, (Feb.-March 1985), pp. 17-18. The three important decisions not discussed here concerned the financial liability of union activists for damages caused by strikes (October 1982), the electoral law for assemblies in the overseas departments (December 1982) and the electoral college provision in the higher education law (January 1984).
19 *Le Monde*, (19 and 20 Jan. 1982); *Le Matin*, (18 Jan. 1982); *Quotidien de Paris*, (18 Jan. 1982); *Les Echos*, (18 Jan. 1982).
20 Favoreu (ed.), *Nationalisations et constitution*, esp. pp. 45-7; Favoreu and Philip (eds), *Les Grandes décisions*, ch. 38; Didier Linotte, "Les Nationalisations de 1982", Revue du droit public, (March-April 1982).
21 *La Croix*, (24-25 Jan. 1982); *Le Matin*, (20 Jan. 1982); *Le Monde*, (19 and 20 Jan. 1982); J. Rivero, *Le Conseil constitutionnel et les libertés* (Paris, Economica, 1984), pp. 116-21; Favoreu and Philip (eds), *Les Grandes décisions*, pp. 559-61. For a comparison of the French and Italian decisions on nationalization, see Gustavo Zagrebelsky, "Opinion", in *Nationalisations et constitution*, ed. L. Favoreu pp. 87-90.
22 *Le Monde*, (19 Jan. 1982).
23 *L'Humanité*, (19 Jan. 1982); *Le Monde*, (20 and 23 Jan. 1982); *Quotidien de Paris*, (20 Jan. 1982); *Le Canard enchaîné*, (20 Jan. 1982).
24 *Libération*, (20 Jan. 1982); *Le Monde*, (27 Jan. 1982); *Le Figaro*, (20 Jan. 1982).
25 *Le Monde*, (3 Feb. 1979).
26 Daniele Loschak, "Les Hommes politiques, les 'sages' . . . et les femmes (à propos de la décision du conseil constitutionnel du 18 novembre 1982)", *Droit social*, (Feb. 1983), pp. 131-7.
27 *Le Monde*, (21-22, 24 and 25 Nov. 1982); *Quotidien de Paris*, (22 Nov. 1982).
28 *Le Monde*, (16 Dec. 1983; 12 Sept. 1984); on Hearst, see Leuchtenburg, *Franklin D. Roosevelt*, p. 152.
29 *Le Monde*, (15 Feb; 12 July and 14 Sept. 1984).
30 *Le Monde*, (11 Oct. 1974).
31 *Le Monde*, (13 Oct. 1984).
32 *Le Monde*, (13 and 15 Oct. 1984); *Le Monde*, (3, 23 and 24 Oct. 1984); *La Croix*, (9 Nov. 1984); Luchaire, Le Conseil constitutionnel, p. 18.
33 *Quotidien de Paris*, (9 Aug. 1985).
34 *Le Monde*, (1 June 1985; 4-5 Aug. 1985).
35 *Le Monde*, (10 and 14 Aug. 1985).
36 *Le Monde*, (7, 10, 14, 23, 25-26 Aug. 1985).
37 The term "autolimitation" was coined by Louis Favoreu.
38 Louis Favoreu, "Actualité et légitimité du contrôle juridictionnel des lois en Europe occidentale", *Revue du droit public* (Sept.-Oct. 1984), p. 1196; interview with Guy Carcassonne (a former legislative assistant for Gaston Defferre) in July 1985.
39 André G. Delion and Michel Durupty, *Les Nationalisations 1982* (Paris, Economica, 1982), pp. 78, 84, 161; interviews with Duhamel and Carcassonne.
40 Favoreu and Philip (eds), *Les Grandes décisions*, pp. 570-571.
41 *Le Monde*, (25 Jan; 9 Feb. 1984).
42 *Le Monde*, (14, 22-23 July 1984).
43 See Olivier Duhamel, "Les Logiques cachées de la constitution de la Cinquième République", in Duhamel and Parodi (eds), *La Constitution*, p. 18.
44 *Le Figaro*, (4 Feb. 1982).

45 Olivier Duhamel, "Les Français et la Ve Republique", *Opinion publique: enquêtes et commentaires 1984*, eds. O. Duhamel et al. (Paris, Gallimard, 1984), pp. 113-14.

46 *Le Monde*, (14, 15-16, 17, 21, 27, 28, 31 July 1984).

47 Loic Philip, "Le Développement du contrôle de constitutionnalité et l'accroissement des pouvoirs du juge constitutionnel", *Revue de droit public*, (March-April 1983), pp. 417-18; Duverger in *Le Monde*, (31 July 1984).

IV
Reforms and French Society

Introduction

The Left experiment was full of paradoxes. In its first months the new Left government moved full steam ahead to implement the most controversial reforms in its program – nationalizations, decentralization and the Auroux Laws, among others. The economic policy about-face of 1982-83 obliged it to retreat from further reform, however, and changed the meaning of many of the reforms which it had already legislated. From this point on, the entire focus of the Left began to shift towards preparing industrial France to assume a more successful position in the international market, a far cry from "rupture with capitalism". This movement culminated in the period of "modernization" starting in 1984.

In all this the meaning of Left reform to different social groups fluctuated wildly. French organized business, discussed by Suzanne Berger, had every reason to fear the worst and ultimately was pleasantly surprised. In contrast to business, labor was designated as one of major beneficiaries of the Left's stay in power, hence the Auroux Laws and myriad smaller measures taken in labor's favor. Yet persistent economic crisis, internecine union rivalries and the effects of government policy turnabouts left labor even weaker and more disoriented in 1986 than it had been in 1981, as George Ross concludes. The Left did manage to preserve the Fench Welfare State more or less intact, however, no small accomplishment. Intellectuals had always been an essential element in the French Left. Yet, coincident with the Left's 1981 victories the long-standing alliance between the progressive intelligentsia and the Left came to the end of the road. This coincidence proved to have very serious implications for the Left and for French political life more generally, as Diana Pinto shows.

The relationship between Left policies and French society can also be analyzed through the biographies of the Left's different reforms themselves. Arguably the notion of *autogestion* – self-management – had been the Left's major and most innovative mobilizing slogan throughout the 1970s. Governmental decentralization, "*l'affaire du septennat*" in the words of François Mitterrand, was a change of great magnitude. It was also the reform where one might have expected *autogestion* to have been most at issue. Yet what turned out to be most interesting about decentralization, as Catherine Grémion and Yves Mény explain, was how much it ultimately reflected a pre-existing consensus rather than bearing any particularly *Left* trademark. If *autogestion* was forgotten in Left reformism, the old-fashioned Republican quest for laïcité in education was not. As Antoine Prost shows, the Left's nostalgic search for *laïcité* eventuated in a major and costly fiasco over the issue of school reform.

Industrial policy was another key target for Left reformism. Jean-Louis Moynot discusses the evolution of Left industrial policy – nationalizations and planning – in the key high-technology area of electronics. The Left's record was controversial in another essential area, that of electronic media, as Jean-Marie Guéhenno demonstrates. Here, inheriting a limited, highly politicized state monopoly, the Left, perhaps despite itself, ultimately opted for large new measures of decentralization and commercialization, laying the foundations of a veritable explosion of decentralized and privatized new media activity which the Right was only too happy to extend after March, 1986.

10

French Business from Transition to Transition

SUZANNE BERGER

Five years after the Socialist victory of 1981, business faced an environment different in every critical respect from that of the past two decades. The improvement in the overall economic outlook, the decline of the unions, profound shifts in public attitudes toward private enterprise, and the triumph within all major political parties of new views on business–government relations had created an unprecedented opportunity. The broad acceptance of the value and legitimacy of private enterprise that French business had not achieved even during the *trente glorieuses* seemed within reach. At the same time, the representatives of the *patronat*, long accustomed to the contempt of a public that considered them nothing but agents of the narrow interests of big capitalists, now appeared as the standard-bearers of a liberal vision of the common good.

For the first time in the post-war period, French business contemplates the possibility, although hardly the certainty, of a world in which the importance of both unions and the state might be greatly reduced. Whether business organizations should pursue this vision of the promised land and how to pursue it are the questions at the heart of the debates today within the *patronat* and between it and the parties. In this novel situation, how best to consolidate the shifts of the recent past? How to exploit the spoils of the recent Center–Right legislative victory without endangering the new gains? As French entrepreneurs, in firms and in the organizations of the *patronat*, begin to explore the new terrain and reconsider old practices, strategic options that in the past appeared undesirable or Utopian now acquire plausibility. To understand the stakes in these debates, we need to consider, first, the changed environment, for the roots of the new prospects and also of the new dangers are both entangled there. We then speculate about the impact of these changes on the character of the political demands of business and on the internal cohesion of business organizations.

ECONOMIC REVIVAL

The first years of Socialist government coincided with the worst troubles French business had experienced in the Fifth Republic.[1] In 1982, one-fifth of all French companies ended the year in the red.[2] Profits collapsed, and indebtedness climbed with the decline of the ratio of savings to investment from 76.1% in 1979 to 51.2% in 1982.[3]

The Socialists' mistake in attempting to relaunch the economy on a growth track at a time when the other European economies were retrenching and in heaping new taxes and social security contributions onto overburdened enterprises surely worsened matters, but these errors had especially disastrous impact because they continued previous trends that had already weakened French business badly. Fonteneau and Muet have shown how from 1973 to 1983 profits continued to fall (with only brief exception) in response to declining productivity, deteriorating terms of trade and rising social security payments.[4] The continuities between the Giscardian years and the Socialist policies are especially striking with regard to the increases in *prélèvements obligatoires* (taxes plus social security contributions) which rose about as rapidly from 1973 to 1981, from 35.7% of the *gross national product* (GNP) to 42.9%, as during the first years of Socialist government, when they climbed from 42.9% in 1981 to 44.7% in 1983 and 45.5% in 1984.[5]

The trends have now been largely reversed, and the underlying dynamics that had propelled the economy down the slope to the depths of 1982–3 have been halted. From 1983 on, as Fonteneau and Muet show, profits began to revive.[6] With productivity rising more rapidly than real wages, with the halt and slight reduction of fiscal pressures and with the erosion of the inflation differential between France and its principal trading partners, firms by the end of 1985 faced brighter prospects than they had known since the end of the sixties.[7] Over this rosier picture, many shadows still hover. One in particular should be signaled, for it is critical to understanding the constraints and temptations that are shaping the relations of the *patronat* with the Center-Right parties.

The novel feature in the current economic environment that complicates relations between the *patronat* and the "natural" parties of business is the widening range of disparities within the private sector. The universe of business has never, of course, been a homogeneous one, but the impact of the crisis and then of the current economic revival has been to magnify substantially preexisting cleavages, to create new ones and to reverse old patterns. A 1983 Credit National business survey, for example, found that while the average French firm in 1982 experienced a decline of 11% in its cash flow and had lowered its investments by 4%, in contrast, 40% of French firms, compared with 31% the year before, had had an increase in their cash flow and 49% of the sample (in contrast to 44% in 1981) had increased their investments by more than 10%.[8] There were good and bad performers to be found in all parts of the economy, although such sectors as the metal-working and textile industries had, as was to be expected, a higher proportion of firms in trouble.

The uneven impact of the crisis on different industrial sectors is at the origin of another set of disparities, that between regions with firms established during the first and second waves of industrialization and regions with more recently developed industries. The boundaries between the two Frances, which once cut between a richer, more productive, and more highly developed East and a poorer, more backward West, still stand. But the balance of advantage has shifted, and now the areas of old industrialization in the East are suffering from higher rates of unemployment, firm closings and economic decay, while the West, with more recent industrial implantations and activities based on new technologies and products, is prospering.[9]

Within the organizations of the French *patronat*, tensions that crystallize differences in interest and perspective of firms of different sizes have been virtually a permanent source of internal conflict and disruption. Periodically, these internal conflicts have broken out in secession movements, with the dissidents mobilized as much against the main business organization, the Conseil National du Patronat Français (CNPF), as against the state. The attacks on the CNPF of the Poujadists in the fifties, of the organization of small and medium businesses, the Confédération Générale des Petites et Moyennes Entreprises (CGPME) over most of the past thirty years, of the Comité d'Information et Défense – Union Nationale des Travailleurs Indépendants (CID-UNATI) in the seventies, and most recently, of the Syndicat National du Patronat Moderne et Indépendant (SNPMI) have posed major problems for the main organization.[10] As the SNPMI organized mass rallies against the Socialist government and against what the SNPMI's leader, Gérard Deuil, called with heavy sarcasm the "nationalized council of the French *patronat*", (i.e., the CNPF, whose largest members were, in fact, as of the 1982 nationalization laws, public-sector firms), another set of members, including forty or so very large private companies, also regrouped outside the CNPF, in the Association Française des Entreprises Privées (AFEP). Ambroise Roux, the speaker for these large firms, charged that the CNPF's new president, Yvon Gattaz, lacked the experience and perspective that would make him an effective defender of big business. Gattaz was in fact a self-made man who had founded his own medium-sized enterprise, Radiall, and still runs it together with family members and so was very different from the big industrialists and graduates of the *grandes écoles* who had previously headed the CNPF.[11]

By 1986, Deuil had been discredited, and the SNPMI was in an advanced stage of decomposition. The AFEP still existed but functioned more as a club with powerful connections than as a representative organization. But the new economic lines of cleavage within the business world were generating new conflicts within the CNPF. Many firms – larger ones with greater financial resilience, with better-than-average profitability; smaller and medium ones without unions or with a greater autonomous capacity to deal with the unions in their own plants – are coming to see membership in the territorial federations of the CNPF as more burdensome. They are pushing for greater decentralization of the organization and for a range of services different from those the association provided in the past. At the same time, firms that have been slower to recover and others with insufficient resources, sometimes because of size, cling to the old patterns. There are cleavages between private-sector firms and public-sector firms. Caught between the demands of the majority of CNPF members – that the opposition parties commit themselves to denationalizing companies incorporated into the public sector after 1981 – and the pressures of the government and of the public firms – which contribute a substantial part of the CNPF's resources – Gattaz changed horses several times before rallying to a demand for all-out privatization.[12]

Finally, and perhaps most important, the business universe has become more heterogeneous and difficult to organize because of a growing tendency toward reorganizing firms around the specific "culture of the enterprise", toward refocusing the firm on a core set of activities, identified as the firm's special *métier* and retreating from the diversification, mergers and expansion of the previous decades.[13] This tendency converges with the emergence of an enterprise-based trade unionism (see below) and both together make firms less dependent on the structures of representation and collective negotiation that traditional business organizations provide. The diffusion of these tendencies is extremely uneven, so the CNPF increasingly confronts a clientele that is differentiated, not only by size and by sector, but by forms of organization of production that make firms more or less capable of negotiating and defending their own interests without reliance on patronal associations.

The widening range of interests and situations within the membership makes it more and more difficult for the CNPF to provide substance to flesh out the generic demand for liberalism. Once one moves beyond the generally agreed-upon demands for an end to price and exchange controls and for the right to fire workers without administrative authorization, and more generally, for greater flexibility in the hiring and use of labor, other concrete projects for reform begin to raise serious difficulties for some part or other of the *patronat*. The divergent interests of public and private firms in the denationalization debate is only one of these divisive issues. Another is the fate of the subsidies, credits, tax relief and administrative fiats that buttress the *aménagement du territoire* program. These forms of state assistance, once interesting above all for industries locating in regions of new industrialization, have come to be critical in the zones of old declining industries, where they serve as incentives to attract new firms. Yet another hurdle on the road to freedom is the Royer Law, which limits new supermarket openings and expansion and so in liberal theory should be a prime target for repeal. Yet anticipation of the wave of protest from shopkeepers that would follow any attempt to rescind it has effectively removed this obstacle to free market economics from the agenda of liberalization. How many booksellers, the FNAC and the Centres Leclerc excepted, wish a repeal of the Lang Law?

The problem for the CNPF on these questions is not so much that of inconsistency - although in a political climate dominated by liberal zeal and ideology, this is not a negligible consideration. Rather the issue is how to define a liberal program that is something other than a list of *ad hoc* demands. Long experience with the leaders of the Center-Right in their previous roles as Prime Ministers and President of the Fifth Republic has taught the CNPF how difficult it is to negotiate with those of "one's own religion", as a leader of the *patronat* put it. The chances of committing the opposition to a program of liberal reform are best before it returns to government. And yet the conflicts within the CNPF that arise out of differing economic stakes and divergent political conceptions (see below) made it virtually impossible, even on the eve of practically certain victory, to define a coherent program. Thus a situation has been created in which different leaders and parties within the Center-Right pick up different pieces of business demand and fuel internal competition within the patronal world.

PUBLIC OPINION

Values and attitudes toward private enterprise have changed more radically than any other part of the business environment. A decade ago, Jean Boissonnat explained to an audience of *patrons*, come to listen to the Socialists defend their program at a time when the victory of the Left seemed imminent (1976), that, however bitter the medicine, nationalizations had to be understood as a remedy to a long-standing and unresolved malady in French life, the illegitimacy of private enterprise.[14] The cluster of public attitudes associated with a refusal to accept the legitimacy of the exercise of authority within private firms or to acknowledge the public goods that result from an economy based on the market and private enterprise has been variously attributed to the strength of aristocratic values, to ruralism, to Catholicism, to Jacobinism.

Whatever the explanation, the rapidity with which these attitudes apparently vaporized after the Socialist victory in 1981 is truly confounding. Already by 1983, a national survey found a sharp decline in positive responses to the term "socialism" while "liberalism", "profit", and "competition" all rose in public esteem.[15] Another survey of the same year asked about solutions for the economic crisis. Three-fifths of the respondents (62%) thought the first priority should be the "health of firms" and only 23% called for giving priority to raising the standard of living.[16] By 1985 a national survey found the French equally divided (42% on each side) between those who do and do not have confidence in *les patrons*. This marked a major shift from the results only three years earlier, when the same question elicited a negative response from 60% and a positive response from only 26%. Indeed business comes out far ahead of political parties and the unions in the 1985 survey, for only 13% of the respondents expressed confidence in the parties (72% registering a lack of confidence) and 26% had confidence in the unions.[17]

Simultaneously – hence not (yet) in response to changes in public attitudes – a new productivist language appeared both in the arguments of the CNPF and in parts of the Socialist Party. Yvon Gattaz, the new President of the CNPF, centered the program of the organization on a defense not so much of property but of entrepreneurship and the enterprise.[18] The themes that Gattaz emphasized as President of the CNPF had already been laid out in two books he had written in the seventies. In them he had pleaded for a change in public attitudes toward entrepreneurs. He castigated the "*bureaucratie de bonne foi*" for interventions that distort the market and attacked the idea that modernization requires ever bigger firms. The so-called industrial imperatives that led the governments of de Gaulle, Pompidou and Giscard d'Estaing to pump state funds into large firms and to starve start-ups and smaller companies completely misunderstood the nature of economic growth, according to Gattaz. Perhaps the most original note was the exaltation of the creation of a company as an act of adventure and independence calling forth a kind of superhuman dynamism and energy.[19] The notion of entrepreneurship as creative invention and romantic adventure is at the heart of much of the media treatment of firms in the eighties and becomes an important component in the Socialist discourse on enterprises after 1983, most strikingly in Mitterrand's last television appearance before the March 1986 legislative elections.

The Socialists would pick up not only Gattaz's reorientation of the defense of business around the heroic figure of the creator/entrepreneur, but also the notion of the enterprise as the source of national wealth. Gattaz wrote in his second book: "The patron is a citizen, and so is the firm, even though it does not vote. It participates directly in economic and social life; in fact it is the principal actor in it. Our private companies support most of the French population, and this performance gives them civic and national rights and duties.''[20] Within the Socialist camp, the same Saint-Simonian themes were struck by Jean-Pierre Chevènement, then Minister of Industry and Research:

> To revalue industry means that we can no longer allow the prices of services to rise more rapidly than industrial prices; it means that we must channel savings towards industry; we must pay skilled industrial labor better; it means recognizing professional conscience and the value of initiative at all levels. It means finally giving industry the respect it has always been begrudged in our country – as if the bourgeoisie in 1789 had taken over not only the lands of the aristocracy, but also its prejudices against industrial work. More profoundly, whereas the former majority for the sake of electoral survival had to protect all sorts of rents, privileges, parasitisms, or simply outmoded economic structures, the new majority has a clear interest in carrying out an audacious industrial policy, for this reflects the needs and aspirations of its social base.
>
> [On employment] In fact, industry supports all the rest. People say that one job in industry creates three in other sectors. It would be more exact to say: one industrial job pays for three others.[21]

These changes, then, in public opinion, in the language of business organization and in Socialist views, developed at the same time and by the end of the first two years of the Socialist government constituted a sort of bloc of mutually reinforcing sentiments and symbols.

For the *patronat* scrutinizing its future, the resilience of this bloc to the shocks of political transition is a major issue. There is, to start with, a cynical view: that a public opinion capable of rallying under social democratic banners in 1981 and under liberal ones so rapidly thereafter is intrinsically too fluid to constrain the political class. But even for those inclined to believe that the new liberal attitudes reflect deep and permanent changes in France, there still remain questions. To what extent are liberal sentiments a specific response to socialism and their vitality contingent on the Socialists remaining in power? For the opposition politicians, liberalism provides the broadest possible platform from which to launch a campaign to return themselves to government. But once the Socialists are out, what constraints will play to keep the new government to its promises? Indeed, even in the preelectoral pronouncements of the opposition leaders, nuances and quarrels over the scope and timing of denationalization, for example (All the firms incorporated into the public sector in 1982? All the public sector companies including those that date to 1936? Immediately? Gradually? – and so forth) already suggested to the *patronat* that politics after the Socialists might be less an instauration of liberalism than a restoration of the status quo ante 1981. Indeed, as the discussion above suggested, there are many groups within the *patronat* itself whose enthusiasm for liberalization translates concretely into no more than a demand for higher prices and more flexibility in the use of labor.

UNIONS

By the end of 1985, the place, dimensions, and relative scale of the trade unions, all of which had seemed fixed features of the French scene, now appear in a changed perspective as up for redefinition, perhaps at the end of a historic role with no new function clearly in sight. Though the *patronat* dare not yet openly proclaim that the last days of trade unions are within view, the notion is clearly in the air. For business, the most significant change has been the precipitous decline of the Confédération Générale du Travail (CGT), which lost at least a quarter of its members over the three-year period 1980–3.[22] The CGT's efforts to launch major mobilizations in plants that had been strongholds of syndical activism have failed, most strikingly, in the recent Renault strike. The fears that if ever the Communists left or were forced out of government they would be able via the CGT to bring the economy to its knees have vanished. And in retrospect, the series of concessions that the Center–Right governments of the Fifth Republic made to the unions in order to ward off anticipated labor unrest begin to appear to the *patronat* as largely unnecessary.

Not only have the two unions most feared by business, the CGT and the CFDT, suffered major falls in membership and capacity to mobilize, but at the same time these two confederations' share of the unionized work force has been slipping relative to that held by Force Ouvrière (FO). From the perspective of French business organizations, this is a positive shift. True, André Bergeron has shown even less inclination than the others to make concessions on the minimal liberalization program of the *patronat*, i.e., on flexibility. But FO is a "nonrevolutionary" organization, Bergeron is believed to be simply shrewdly awaiting the best moment to make a deal with the new government, and in any event, given the weakened state of the unions, a consistently liberal government will be able to put through the changes in labor legislation that are needed.

The real question is to what extent in the future French business need take account at all of the trade-union movement. Fueling this kind of reflection, aside from the evidence of the decline of the unions precisely at a time when they were expected to have expanded, that is, with the Left in power, is a new approach to industrial relations. This approach relies on an eclectic body of examples that demonstrate the possibilities and benefits of direct contacts between management and workers that bypass the old union channels. Even before the passage of the Auroux Laws, the *patronat* had developed an original and highly successful program of instruction that taught middle-level managers and foremen how to organize discussion groups around the problems of shopfloor life and production.[23] The Auroux Laws provided an enormous incentive for further experimentation and diffusion of results along these lines.

At the same time, a new semipopular literature presents the unions as narrowly corporatist in their demands and defending an archaic and self-destructive system of industrial relations. The books of François de Closets, *Toujours plus!* (1982) and *Tous ensemble: pour en finir avec la syndicratie* (1985) are exemplary in this regard. *Tous ensemble* goes from an analysis of the dysfunctions of unions in the current system to description of firms in which workers and managers negotiate agreements that enlarge the common pie and the shares of each and every one. At best, the unions in these cases stand aside and let the productive elements get on with the negotiations. At most, the unions are acknowledged to provide some undefined sense of security, a kind of fallback position that reassures the workers that if all else fails, they still have the old card left to play. But the basic image of unionism that emerges in this literature is that of a relic of the bygone days of "primitive" industrialization, of an organization with no significant role to play in the new world.[24] As Michel Crozier has put it: "Once an indispensable counterweight to an all-powerful and exploitative *patronat*; then a useful conservative force in the times of rushed technocrats; today unions are becoming a source of regression in our open and changing world . . . The mechanism of old trade-union practices and habits is not only archaic but absurd and increasingly counter productive.[25]

The stirrings of new ideas about the role of unions within enterprises are to be found, not only in the camp of those fundamentally antagonistic to unionism, but within the union movement itself. In part, the new tendencies toward enterprise-based trade unionism reflect continuing high levels of unemployment. In a context in which the only plausible alternative to employment at one's current job is unemployment, workers are likely to see themselves as lifetime employees of the same firm and to develop greater loyalty to their enterprise. Together with the generalization of such other shifts as plant assemblies (Auroux Laws), quality circles, and new management styles associated with the "culture of the enterprise", these responses to the economic crisis are promoting the emergence of an enterprise-based trade unionism.[26] Even aside from the changes in attitudes provoked by high levels of job insecurity, there are other fundamental shifts at work – in the occupational distribution of the work force, in educational endowment, in the mass entry of women into the work force, in the expansion of public sector and services, in the culture and aspirations of young workers – that are putting intolerable strains on the old union system. The exhaustion of traditional patterns of trade unionism, wittily and brilliantly dissected in *Les Cowboys ne meurent jamais* by Jean-Paul Jacquier, has created a space within which new conceptions are beginning to appear.[27] Many of these, too, start from the notion of a unionism recentered within individual firms.

Within the new majority as well, there is division over the role that unions should play in the future. On one side voices call for circumventing and limiting the participation of the unions within firms and within the political system broadly, but there are also more cautious views. As Raymond Soubie, who had served as an advisor on labor matters in the seventies under both Chirac and Barre, warned recently: "We have unions that are essential for collective negotiation. It would be dangerous to disperse or weaken them, for that would arouse habits that one day could turn into leftist or demagogic behaviors. We are at the beginning of a revolution in economic organization and social relations. The stakes are too high to be compromised by new ideologues or brilliant *sabreurs*."[28]

Its desires in the matter aside, the *patronat* is undecided about the future of its *frères-ennemi*, the unions. And while the organizations of the *patronat* clearly lack the power to determine whether or not there will be unions and of what sort, still they do have a chance to weigh in on the outcomes both at the level of individual enterprises and nationally. The tensions within the CNPF over negotiating with the unions within the framework of the proposed law on flexible work hours reflected two options: that of the leadership which retreated from negotiation and apparently placed its hopes for a better deal on the anticipated change in government, and that of groups within the *patronat*, like the Union des Industries Métallurgiques et Minières, which was more favorable to negotiation.[29] The indecision and internal dissent over the legitimacy of its partners also shows up in the debates over whether to press the government to change the system of union representation that accords a monopoly in works' committees to the union that wins the most votes (hence gives disproportionate weight to the CGT) and whether to press for reforming the decree that accords recognition to only a limited number of representative unions.

PARTIES

Other chapters in this volume describe the great transformation that has taken place since 1981 within both Left and Right on the question of the place of private enterprise within French society and the proper scope of state intervention in the economy. Here we consider only the impact of these changes on the political strategies of business. The first years of the Socialist government coincided with a change at the head of the CNPF, from a leader (François Ceyrac) inclined to understand the role of business in French society in a broad and political fashion, to a leader who believed that the role of the organization of the *patronat* should be a defense of economic interests, defined relatively narrowly.[30] It was obvious from the start that any leader of the CNPF would have to find some language with which to negotiate with the new rulers. And for this reason, the retreat of Ceyrac, who had made public statements in support of the Center-Right in 1973 and in favor of Giscard between the two rounds of balloting in 1981, was inevitable. Indeed, as one of the leaders of the *patronat* commented in retrospect, the head of the CNPF is condemned to collaborate with whomever is in power.[31] What is certain is that the language that Gattaz found to defend the interests of business in those early years facilitated some kind of dialogue between the government and the *patronat*, and that Gattaz's own predilection for frequent and well-publicized meetings with the Socialists also contributed to the impression of a rapprochement between *le patron des patrons* and the government.

This impression was reinforced as Socialists themselves moved away from their early open hostility to business. At the October 1981 Valence Congress the Socialists had voted a motion proclaiming that "the hopes for change lie within firms. It is there that the class struggle is being played out and there that the political battle will be won." By the end of 1983 this radical rhetoric had long since been buried under a flood of enthusiasm about the economic virtues and "nobility" of private enterprise.[32] The recognition of the failure of the policies of the first year, the loss of the hope that public-sector enterprises would be locomotives that would propel the rest of the economy into greater rates of investment and growth, progressive discouragement about the various industrial policy strategies – *reconquête du marché intérieur, filières*, and so forth, growing acceptance of the idea that obstacles to flexibility (administrative approval of firing, threshold effects of the numerical cutoffs for *comités d'enterprise* and union delegates) were in fact blocking hiring – all of these discoveries brought the Socialists closer to the positions that the *patronat* had been pushing on it.

Perhaps others might not have gone as far as Gattaz did in his dealings with the Socialists or might not have eschewed as ostentatiously as he did all contacts with the opposition politicians, on the grounds that politics was no part of the defense of economic interests. In any event, by the time (fall 1984) that Gattaz reversed course and proffered support for the opposition, "rejoicing sincerely", for example, that the economic program of the Rassemblement pour la République (RPR) "goes in the direction of the liberalism that we have supported for so many years" it was too late.[33] Gattaz appeared too compliant and moderate in his relations with the Socialists to survive. Even before the legislative elections, one of the CNPF Vice-Presidents had resigned (Jean-Louis Giral, head of the powerful public works federation), ostensibly to protest the "omission" of the demand for an end to the system of administrative authorization of firings from a CNPF "proposal for a new economic policy", in fact opening the first round in a battle to depose Gattaz.[34] The resignation of Yvon Chotard, the longtime rival of Gattaz, soon after the election and the battle among various groups within the CNPF that is being carried on virtually in public made it impossible for Gattaz to reassert his authority within the organization. In the summer of 1986, he announced he would not seek re-election.

CONCLUSIONS

Whatever the difficulties and costs of dealing with the Socialists, relations with the natural parties of business, now in government, are hardly likely to be easier. First of all, the Center-Right parties, although rallied under the banner of liberalism, remain deeply torn over the practical modalities of this cause. As suggested above, these divisions are manifested in views on denationalization, on the role of unions, on the role of the state in regional development, in sum, on the full range of issues of concern to business. These divisions do not correspond neatly to party lines but seem rather almost matters of personal style, of pragmatic or ideological temperament.

However maximalist the liberalism of the economic program that Jacques Chirac presented to the new National Assembly, the practical embodiments of this liberalism are far closer to the policies of previous governments of the Fifth Republic. The selective satisfaction of the demands of certain vital or volatile groups within the population (farmers, landlords, those who paid the new wealth tax) are a return to "a classic management by the State of a society segmented into electoral categories".[35] In this context, the chances for a rapid and radical liberalization of the economy appear far weaker than might have been imagined a year before the election.

It is, however, not only the Center-Right parties' commitment to liberalism that is likely to crumble over the next few years; it is business support that seems likely to crack along lines of fissure that were once plastered over by common opposition to the Socialists but now are increasingly visible. The experience of Socialist rule aroused a set of emotional and political responses from the business world that drew on various sources. In part the responses reflected the ascendancy of new ideas about enterprises and markets; in part the responses reflected new realities of the workplace. But the unifying element and the one that generalized the support for liberalism far beyond those *patrons* who were genuinely drawn to the idea of operating in an environment less regulated and less protected by the state was an old set of antistatist ideas that had been dominant in the Third Republic. The organizing norms for state-economy relations in the Third Republic, as Richard F. Kuisel and others have explained, were those of noninterventionism in the internal decisions and organization of the firm, on one hand, but a high measure of protection against external challenge, on the other.[36] In the depth of the post-war revulsion against the economic stagnation, social decay and political fragility that had produced defeat in war, this Third Republic legacy had been swept under the rug. It is this stock of ideas that has reemerged over the last five years and that has rooted the new forms of support for liberalism to old and still vital traditions.

United under and against the Socialists, these different impulses toward the state are likely to move along separate trajectories under a government of the Center-Right. These conceptions of liberalism, each potentially the core of an ideology that might reorganize the defense of business, are not necessarily mutually exclusive. But they do appeal to different segments of the *patronal* universe, and these segments, for the reasons laid out above, have less and less in common. The prospect, then, is for weaker and more divided business organizations. The organizations of the *patronat*, which were the main forces of opposition in the first years of the Socialist government, when the Center-Right parties were still weak, dispersed, and without a program, are now likely to be more dependent on the parties. Businesses are in far stronger shape in 1986 than at any other point in the past two decades; business as an organized political interest is, for reasons of internal division and political conjuncture, on the wane.

NOTES

1 Two attempts by economists to assess the economic situation of France at the time of Mitterrand's victory and to evaluate the choice of policies at that point stand out as especially valuable: Alain Fonteneau and Pierre-Alain Muet, *La Gauche face à la crise* (Paris, Fondation Nationale des Sciences Politiques, 1985), which is a sympathetic account; and Jeffrey Sachs and Charles Wyplosz, "Mitterrand's Economic Policy", in *Economic Policy*, 30 (1986), which is more critical. For a lively account of the politics of economic policy-making over the period 1981-85, see Philippe Bauchard, *La Guerre des deux roses* (Paris, Grasset, 1986). For a highly critical view of Socialist policies and their impact in the early years, see the essays, in particular that of Bertrand Jacquillat, "L'Entreprise et l'état prédateur", in *La France socialiste*, ed. Michel Massenet (Paris, Hachette, 1983).

2 *L'Expansion*, (Dec. 1983), p. 5. On that year, see also Elie Messeca, "Les Résultats des entreprises industrielles en 1982", *Economie et statistique*, 159 (Oct. 1983).

3 From calculations by the Commission des Comptes de la Nation, reported in *Le Monde*, (21 June 1983).

4 See Fonteneau and Muet, *La Gauche face à la crise*, ch. 1. They do note a slight upturn between the end of 1976 and 1979.

5 Figures from Jacquillat, *L'Entreprise et l'état*, p. 234 and *Libération*, (29 Feb. 1984).

6 See Fonteneau and Muet, *La Gauche face à la crise*, ch. 5, especially pp. 321 ff.

7 On success in bringing down inflation rates to the Common Market average and to that of its main trading partners, see *Le Monde*, (28 Sept.; 13-14 Oct. 1985).

8 Cited in Jean Saint-Geours, "Les Entreprises performantes . . . et les autres", *Le Monde*, (14 May 1983). He goes on to note that in a group of firms that received more than 2 million francs in credit in 1983, the top-quarter best performers had increased their cash flow by more than 30% the previous year, while the bottom quarter had suffered a decrease of at least 20%.

9 See the map of the evolution by region of the salaried work force from 1976 to 1983 in *Le Monde*, (16 Oct. 1984).

10 On the SNPMI, see Suzanne Berger, "The Socialists and the *Patronat*: Dilemmas of Co-existence in a Mixed Economy", in *Economic Policy and Policy-making under the Mitterrand Presidency*, eds. Howard Machin and Vincent Wright (London, Frances Pinter, 1985). On the earlier organizational battles, see Suzanne

Berger, "D'Une boutique à l'autre: Changes in the Organization of the Traditional Middle Classes from the Fourth to Fifth Republics", *Comparative Politics*, (Oct. 1977).

11 See Bauchard, *La Guerre des deux roses*, pp. 203-16, on the centrifugal pulls on *patronal* organization after Gattaz's election in 1981.

12 See for example the exchanges reported in Eric Hassan, "A Quoi joue donc Yvon Gattaz?" *Libération*, (8 Oct. 1984).

13 On the spread of the management practices associated with the "culture of enterprise", see the articles by Alain-Charles Martinet, Daniel Zumino and Jean-Marie Peretti in the special issue, (entitled "Dix ans qui ont changé l'entreprise"), of *Revue française de gestion*, 53-4 (Sept.-Dec. 1985).

14 Jean Boissonnat (ed.), *Les Socialistes face aux patrons*, (Paris, *L'Expansion*/Flammarion, 1976), pp. 21-6.

15 *Le Figaro*-SOFRES survey cited in Jérôme Jaffré, "Le Retournement de l'opinion", *Le Monde*, (1 Jan. 1984), p. III.

16 Survey carried out by Brulé Ville Associés for *L'Expansion*, (1-5 Oct. 1983), reported in Jacques Fontaine, "Les Français ont viré leur cuti", *L'Expansion*, (Oct. 1983), p. 247.

17 The results were presented by Alain Lancelot, (21 Jan. 1986), in a conference at the Fondation Nationale des Sciences Politiques.

18 See Berger, "The Socialists and the *Patronat*".

19 Yvon Gattaz, *Les Hommes en gris* (Paris: Robert Laffont, 1970) and *La Fin des patrons*, (Paris: Robert Laffont, 1980). See also a newsletter edited by Gattaz et al., *Les Quatre vérités*, which commenced at the end of 1973 with these new themes as well as the publications and papers of the Institut de l'Entreprise.

20 Gattaz, *La Fin des patrons*, pp. 121-2.

21 Cited in *Le Monde*, (15 Sept. 1982).

22 *Le Monde*, (19 Nov. 1985).

23 The IRPOP (Director, Bertrand Hommey), an agency associated with and financed in part by the CNPF, invented this program and carries out training sessions in individual plants on contracts with management.

24 For an article that picks up these themes and presents cases in which the new harmony between workers and managers already reigns and unions are absent, see Vincent Beaufils, " 'Un Syndicat chez moi? Jamais.' Répression? Non: imagination et communication", *L'Expansion*, (8-21 Nov. 1985). See the response of Alain Minc, "Eloge du syndicat", *L'Expansion*, (22 Nov.-5 Dec. 1985).

25 Michel Crozier, "Le Syndicat-roi est nu", *Le Figaro*, (12-13 Oct. 1985).

26 Perhaps the single most informative work on this subject in France is Jean-François Amadieu, "Le Développement du syndicalisme d'entreprise", doctoral thesis, Université Paris IX-Dauphine, 1986.

27 Jean-Paul Jacquier, *Les Cowboys ne meurent jamais* (Paris, Syros, 1986). Jacquier is a CFDT national secretary.

28 Raymond Soubie, "Une Politique sociale pour l'avenir", *Le Monde*, (22 Oct. 1985).

29 See *Libération*, (21 Nov. 1985).

30 See the interviews with Ceyrac in 1976 in André Harris and Alain de Sédouy, *Les Patrons* (Paris, Seuil, 1977), pp. 233-44; in July 1981 in *Le Monde*, (3 July 1981); and in 1982 in Jean-Gabriel Fredet and Denis Pingaud, *Les Patrons face à la gauche* (Paris, Ramsay, 1982), pp. 97-106. The latter book also provides a good sense of the differences between Ceyrac and Gattaz.

31 Interview, November 1985. The analogy drawn in this interview was between Renault, "obliged to collaborate with the Germans during the war" and Gattaz. Interesting in more than one respect, the comment reveals a widely held view that Gattaz has been too implicated in his dealings with the Socialists to survive a change in government. Who will be found to play the role that Villiers, also evoked in the same interview, performed for the CNPF after the war?

32 Cited in Fredet and Pingaud, *Les Patrons face à la gauche*, p. 36.

33 On the comment and its context, Olivier Biffaud, "Flexibilité de l'emploi: le roseau CFDT rend Gattaz plus cassant", *Libération*, (5 Nov. 1984). On the government's response, *Le Monde*, (9 Nov. 1984).

34 "M. Giral, prépare-t-il l'après-Gattaz?", *Le Nouvel économiste*, 514, (8 Nov. 1985).

35 Jean-Marie Colombani, "Questions de temps", *Le Monde* (24 April 1986).

36 See Richard F. Kuisel, *Capitalism and the State in Modern France* (New York, Cambridge University Press, 1981); and Robert Delorme and Christine André, *L'Etat et l'économie* (Paris, Seuil, 1983).

11

From one Left to Another

Le Social in Mitterrand's France

GEORGE ROSS

In virtually all industrial societies the Left has been associated intimately with constructing and expanding the Welfare State, humanizing industrial relations and strengthening the power of labor. The French Left had taken important steps in these directions in the Popular Front and Resistance–Liberation periods. Progress had been shut off abruptly in 1947, however. A very long backlog of new proposals had therefore been accumulated. In its programs, then, the Left which came to power in 1981 thought that the French Welfare State needed to be expanded and that France's backward industrial relations system needed substantial reform. Given the centrality of these proposals to the Left's program and identity, how the Left in power dealt with such matters lies at the very heart of evaluating continuity and change in Mitterrand's France.

The pre-1981 setting, which we will review in the first part of this chapter, did not allow the Left simply to beef up the Welfare State and grant new powers to labor against capital. Given the times, the new government could not avoid confronting the problem of reconstructing France's economic position in the international division of labor. Moreover, there were good reasons to suspect that tackling this problem seriously might be detrimental to rebalancing France's domestic social compromise in favor of labor, the poor and the weak. By the 1980s, debate in many other countries had turned towards questioning how much of existing post-1945 domestic social deals could be salvaged in the face of new international economic constraints. The second and third parts of the chapter review different stages of the Left's efforts to reconcile its programmatic pledges with the huge constraints created by France's difficult international economic situation. Our title betrays our conclusion. The Left which came to power in 1981 was one which still focused primarily on renegotiating France's domestic social compromise upward. The Left which lost power in 1986 had become primordially concerned with adapting the French economy to a new international situation.

SOCIAL SETTINGS

After a complex, but relatively successful, history after Liberation, the French Welfare State – family allocations, healthcare programs, pension systems, unemployment compensation, etc. – began to face troubling trends in the 1970s.[1] Demographic projections – the end of the baby boom plus increasing longevity – became threatening. The ratio of contributors to beneficiaries began to decline – for pensions, for example, the ratio was 3.55/1 in 1973 and fell to 2.71/1 by 1980, with further deterioration in the offing.[2] Healthcare expenditures as a percentage of GDP more than doubled between 1950 and 1980 (3.0% in 1950, 4.0% in 1960, 5.7% in 1970, 7.5–8.0% in 1980), again with no foreseeable end in sight. The cost of the entire package of Welfare State/social service expenses in France rose from 19.2% of GDP in 1970 to 27.4% in 1980 (France, in this respect, fell very close to the EEC average). The percentage of GDP going to government more generally through combined social insurance contributions and direct taxation, which was 32.2% in 1960, rose to 35.7% in 1970 and 42.5% in 1980, making France the leader of the six largest OECD economies.[3]

Even with strong economic growth, demographics, rising healthcare costs and other factors would have created serious problems for the French system. Stable, predictable economic growth came to an end in the mid-1970s, of course. By itself this change had dramatic enough implications for financing and ultimately maintaining the French Welfare State. In addition, however, it brought a shocking increase in unemployment (from a low 2.2% between 1964 and 1973 unemployment rose to 6% in 1979, again with no end of increase in sight). Rising unemployment accentuated the ever more unfavorable demographic ratio between contributors and beneficiaries and placed vastly greater demands on unemployment compensation funds which, in France, were relatively well endowed to begin with, given France's historically low jobless rate.

Political circumstances in the 1970s provided the final, and somewhat unique, factor structuring the situation which the Left would face. Valéry Giscard d'Estaing won the 1974 Presidential Election by a miniscule margin, and the Left's electoral strength continued to grow after this. Thus while unprecedented economic crisis closed in it was dangerous electorally to engage in serious cutbacks. As a result, costs continued to rise at a moment when general levels of growth no longer came anywhere near covering them. This, in the context of an intensifying profits squeeze on French capital, was of particular importance for the French Welfare State given the relatively large proportion of contributions to it which came from employers (in 1981, for example, French employers paid 56% of the bill for social transfers, with wageworkers paying 22.64% and the state budget 18.47%, an employer contribution rivaled only in Italy and best compared to that of West Germany at 38.8%).

The industrial relations setting was likewise affected in the later 1970s by economic changes. Crisis had many of the same general effects in France as elsewhere. French industry as a whole was threatened by downturns in international trade, while vulnerable "smokestack" areas – coalmining, steel, shipbuilding and textiles, where French labor had been traditionally strong – were particularly hit. Here, as in Welfare State matters, the French Center-Right faced a setting in which managing politics and managing economics had become unusually contradictory. It therefore felt obliged to refrain from serious economic and social surgery. One important consequence was a clear deterioration in France's general economic position and a worsening of the financial and other difficulties lying just beneath the surface of French industrialism.[4]

The economic and social policies of the Giscard-Barre regime thus did little to help French capital out in a newly difficult context. The union movement suffered as well, however. Changing economic circumstances – rising unemployment, regional dislocations, deindustrialization, inflation – brought a swift end to the period of increasing union influence which had begun in the early 1960s. With economic crisis came declining union membership, finances and mobilizing power, processes which were accentuated by the workings of competitive trade-union pluralism. The major union Confederations – the CGT, CFDT and FO – had historically fought tooth and nail with one another over ideology, politics, trade-union strategy and, most fundamentally, over rank-and-file support. Such combat, leavened occasionally by tactical alliances like the "unity in action" agreements between the CGT and CFDT after 1966, had worked to the labor movement's advantage during the boom conditions of the 1960s and early 1970s. This was to change during the crisis which followed.[5] By the end of the 1970s French unions were more divided than they had been since the early 1960s. Moreover, in the cases of all three major unions, strategic revisions had been worked by the later 1970s which posited the continuation of the Right in power, at least through the medium term.

THE LEFT TRIES POWER: UNAMAZING GRACE

In power the Left initially responded to the problems of the French Welfare State with the same optimism which colored its responses to other important issues. In Year I, the year of radical optimism, it actually *expanded* Welfare State benefits and enacted almost all of the social policy commitments which François Mitterrand had made in his election manifesto. Family and housing allocations were raised substantially. Old-age pension minimums were raised dramatically (62 per cent over two years). The retirement age was reduced to 60, a measure which also demonstrated the Left's concern to keep unemployment rolls down. The only small negation of this general *largesse* involved slight contribution increases for social security funds related to cost increases in health care in November 1981.[6]

This Welfare State package contained no profound reform of social policy and exposed no new grand schemes, a lack of creativity which was often decried from within the Left.[7] For this approach to work the Left counted on the success of its macroeconomic policies, and in particular of its demand-stimulation program, to promote new growth (3 per cent was projected). New growth would refloat the old system and minimize its various cost problems. The Left's first Minister of National Solidarity, Nicole Questiaux, symbolized this euphoric, if brief, moment of *largesse* when she announced that she was "an activist, not a Minister of Accounting". The gamble was great, however. In the absence of the projected growth and without reform the Left's generosity might intensify problematic financial tendencies, and possibly anti-Welfare State ideological trends, which existed before its arrival.[8]

We need not go into great detail about the macroeconomic policies of the "state-of-grace period", which was connected to the Left's initial industrial relations goals. Through redistributive measures aimed to benefit lower-income groups, the Left stimulated domestic demand. It focused on worksharing and job creation, in addition to growth, to prevent new unemployment, through various measures like lowering the retirement age, extending paid vacations to five weeks, diminishing the length of the workweek (pledging to lower it eventually to 35 hours), promoting jobsharing and collective bargaining in the *contrats de solidarité*. It promoted other active labor-market policies like youth employment and apprenticeship programs, public-sector hiring, careful administrative controls over layoffs, particularly in the public sector, supplemented by efforts to keep dying firms afloat in critical sectors (steel, shipbuilding, coalmining, engineering). In time the Left envisaged these short-run measures being supplemented by additional new growth generated by a predicted international upturn. By then by the positive effects of astute industrial policy choices made in France through newly nationalized industries to "reconquer the domestic market" and build new international economic strength would also be felt. The ultimate message in all this was that Keynesianism and *Colbertisme* in one country would restore boom conditions and, by altering the labor market in labor's favor, affect industrial relations positively.

The Socialist–Communist government hoped that by implementing this macroeconomic package, it would consolidate labor support for the Left for a long time to come. Even before this hope was shattered there were difficulties, however. The major problem was that "labor" in France came in multiple forms. While the government wanted to consider labor as a privileged ally and essential negotiating partner – a situation which had really not existed in France since 1947 – it had to be even-handed and avoid giving undue advantage to any one union over the others. This was especially true because the CGT, CFDT and FO had renounced none of their fierce fraternal rivalry because of the Left's victory. Each was eager to see the government promote its chosen policies, but quite as eager to get ahead of its union comrades thereby. The CGT, a hostage to Left government policies as long as there were Communist ministers, hoped to gain through skillful use of its intimate ties with the government itself.[9] The CFDT, which supported the Left, but less completely and overtly than the CGT, hoped to use its margin of independence to overtake the CGT as France's number-one union. FO, which had been gaining slowly on both the CGT and CFDT in the 1970s, hoped to deploy its patented apolitical unionism to win advantage over the two "Left" unions which were compromised in one way or another by their support of the government.

In the absence of any *one* privileged union interlocutor the government tried to give all unions "equal time". Alas, structurally compelled to listen to everyone and favor no one, the new government gave unions the general impression of soliciting their wisdom and advice in ways which had few direct consequences. André Bergeron of FO noted early on that *la concertation ne sert pas seulement à bavarder. Bavardage* notwithstanding, the government had to make policy. And here, because of the need to combine extensive *concertation* with unions and the need not to favor anyone too much, the government tended to fall back onto Civil Servants and technocrats. All of the unions perceived this quickly and all held it against the government.

Quite as important, policy-making often confirmed one union's positions over another's. The CGT favored nationalizations and strong Keynesianism more than the CFDT and FO, for example, and used its power inside the government to overrule the CFDT's position on workweek reduction and work sharing. The CFDT, in contrast, predominated in the definition of the Auroux Laws, which the CGT would have liked to have made stronger and which FO opposed altogether (fulminating characteristically about the dangers of "Soviets"). FO also propagandized incessantly, with almost complete disregard for the facts, about the dangerous "boring from within" which the Communist ministers were carrying out. Even before the economic roof fell in, then, and even if the Left government was clearly more pro-labor than any France had seen in decades, it was obvious that the Left was not likely to be able to make any dramatic changes in Left–union relationships. The union movement was simply too divided to welcome any such changes.

In its efforts to consolidate union support for its endeavors and for Left politics the Left in power faced a Catch-22 situation, then. To be sure, it was somewhat statist, technocratic and Jacobin in its approach to mass organizations. But this merely made the dilemma worse. The fact that the CGT was tied to the PCF and thus to support of the government incited the CFDT and FO to take distance from the government. In turn, the CGT, even if its loyalty to the Mauroy government was impeccable until later in 1983, felt obliged to generate rhetorical flourishes critical of certain governmental policies.[10] Edmond Maire of the CFDT for his part quickly perfected his media-centered, *deuxième gauche "coup de gueule"* method of criticizing the government for its economic naïvete and unwillingness to promote greater "new solidarity" in work sharing.[11] FO quite ostentatiously played its tough, nonpolitical "pure and simple" union role to the hilt. In time this complicated system of union–government relationships created the impression that the unions, whatever they were actually up to, were constantly carping about the government. Since the unions, or at least the CGT and CFDT, were in fact the Left's major base of support, this impression fueled the widespread sentiment which succeeded the brief 1981 "state of grace" that the Left government was not much loved by anyone at all.

Whether this situation got better or worse depended upon two very important things. The first, of course, was the success or failure of government economic policies. The second was the effect of government efforts to reform the industrial relations situation. The centerpieces of these efforts were, of course, the Auroux Laws (plus the complementary legislation for the democratization of the public sector).[12] Auroux Law I – here the Laws are numbered in chronological order of their passage by parliament – gave increased resources and power to union sections at firm level, union and personnel delegates and *comités d'entreprise*. It also extended the coverage of union sections to firms with less than 50 employees and established new "group committees" to cover an entire industrial complex. Law II contained provisions for obligatory annual firm-level wage bargaining and a clause which allowed majority unions to veto the implementation of minority union signed contracts, in addition to refining the 1950 law about branch-level collective bargaining. Law III amalgamated formerly separate works committees on health, safety and working conditions and endowed this new combined committee with greater powers. Law IV discussed workers' rights in the firm, defined the legal scope of internal work rules (*règlement intérieur*) and established new shop-level "rights of expression". The public sector, in general, benefitted from even stronger versions of the same changes, plus new provisions for the election of workers' representatives to boards of directors.

The Auroux Laws were a clear attempt to bring France's backward industrial relations system up to date. With unions and workers strengthened at firm level and stronger incentives to decentralized collective bargaining – away from the industrial-branch focus of such bargaining as France had been able to generate prior to 1982 – there would theoretically be more negotiations around workplace issues. In the best of all possible worlds it would then follow that employers and unions would gradually learn to treat each other with more tolerance and respect and, in consequence, be able to assume more collective responsibility for what happened in the world of work. As this occurred, both the *patronat* and the unions would become less prone to resort to politics and the state for redress of grievance, ultimately making the workplace less politicized.

RIGUEUR AND MODERNIZATION: THE OTHER LEFT APPEARS

The flaws in the Left's initial macroeconomic policy scenario, upon which almost everything else depended, were not long in appearing.[13] Radical reformism lost out in two installments – June 1982 and March 1983, leading to *rigueur*. Policy and the effective political balance within the Left government shifted towards the center. Devaluations, exchange controls, tax increases, incomes policies, price increases for public services and new budgetary stringency were introduced to cut inflation, lower French purchasing power and correct the massive trade imbalance. France hurriedly, if belatedly, joined the international deflationary club, at the very moment, ironically, when other countries, buoyed up by the Reagan recovery, began to loosen up their own austerity. French growth was to be notably slower than that of other countries for most of the rest of the Left's tenure in power.

The "account balancing" approach of Jacques Delors' *rigueur* was nonetheless carried on in the name of "solidarity". If everyone was obliged to sacrifice, sacrifices were to be shared out proportionately. In 1981 the Left had pledged to keep unemployment from growing, a pledge honored during *rigueur*. The shift to "modernization" in 1984, however, meant abandoning this commitment in favor of a healthy dose of fashionable neo-liberalism. Priority was to be given to making French industry more competitive in international markets. This meant clearing the decks for aggressive business activities in France while giving French industry a new push towards adopting advanced technologies and a rejuvenated international prominence. One corollary of this was that remnants of the old industrial past, in particular economically unjustifiable jobs in "smokestack" industries, could no longer be retained.[14].

The coming of modernization was the turning point of the Left experience. The Left had come to power in 1981 ambivalently straddling social democracy and a peculiarly French version of more radical leftism. If these trajectories differed, and if the differences were important, both were designed to alter the terms of the domestic social compromise which France had developed during the post-war boom. Modernization, in contrast, was not primarily about visions of a new domestic compromise. Rather it was about working towards a new balance between French international competitiveness and domestic social arrangements. What this balance would ultimately turn out to be was unclear. But it would obviously involve major changes away from post-war-boom formulations of domestic social compromise.

Trimming the Welfare State from the Left

Awakening after its sweet and unrealistic economic dreams the Left found itself with large social policy problems to face. And as it had in the realm of general economic policy, here too the Left turned to methods which weren't remarkably different from those of its predecessors and international peers. Mme Questiaux was removed from her "non-accounting" office in June 1982 when her newly "rigorous" colleagues found her proposals for reforming the social security system much too generous. Pierre Bérégovoy was assigned the task of facing the facts and was to prove much more successful as "Minister of Accounting".

Social policy *rigueur* came in several installments between June 1982 and late spring 1983. To balance health insurance funds a 20 franc/day deductible payment was applied to hospitalization, a much larger deductible percentage was applied to reimbursable pharmaceuticals, doctors' fees were frozen for a time, the accounting base for hospital financing was shifted from a patient/per diem method (which overencouraged hospitalization) to an annual budget, and the income from new indirect taxes on alcohol and tobacco (plus new levies on the advertising expenses of pharmaceutical companies) was channelled into the system. Ceilings on employer contributions were raised slightly as well. In the area of unemployment compensation the government initially had hoped that financial problems would be resolved through peak-level collective bargaining between employers' associations and unions. Employers refused to play the game, however, in protest against ever-rising payroll taxes (the French system placed unusual emphasis on employer contributions of this kind in ways which had clear disincentive effects in the crisis). In consequence, the government decreed a 1.2% raise in contributions divided 60/40 between employers and unions and asked parliament to vote for a 1% "solidarity" tax on the gross income of Civil Servants to last until December 1984 (Civil Servants, with their statutory employment protection, did not participate in the regular financing of the unemployment system). Finally, the government pared 10 billion francs in benefits from unemployment plans (mainly by cutting out certain categories of eligibility altogether, putting restrictions on the rights of those looking for their first jobs and stretching out prebenefit delay periods for those eligible).

Generosity excepted, given the stinginess of the times elsewhere, there had been a lack of originality in the Left's first approach to the Welfare State after 1981 – boosting benefits and hoping for economic growth. Little more originality came with *rigueur*.[15] There were new, more serious, efforts at cost control, particularly in health care. Actual and projected budgetary *trous* were plugged in multiple ways, by nibbling around the edges of benefits and coverage, by raising the contributions of all principal contributors (workers and employers), by funneling new general tax revenue into the systems ("budgetizing" parts of the problem), and by tapping new constituencies to contribute in the name of "solidarity". All of these measures, and others, nonetheless proved reasonably effective remedies for unbalanced social policy account books – after its first year the Left was to demonstrate considerable managerial talent. But these measures were to have immediate costs as well (particularly for the unemployed, many of whom began to run out of benefits in 1983).

In general, from 1982 onwards the Left dealt with the Welfare State by maneuvering from year to year, "muddling through". Perhaps most important, however, the patching and trimming which it did to make ends meet were carried on without calling the general principles of the system into question. Increasingly after 1983, however, there was a shift within these parameters as the government acknowledged publicly that promoting profitability was an important thing, an admission which did have certain consequences. Tried and true methods of balancing social program budgets by increasing employer contributions became less and less desirable. One important dimension of this was President Mitterrand's pledge to cut back *prélèvements obligatoires* (social service payroll taxes plus general taxes) in general by 1%.

Pursuing such ends the government levied a 1% additional income tax on everyone to finance projected social security deficits, a step which observers expected would lead towards greater "fiscalization" of Welfare State expenses (as opposed to financing by potential beneficiaries) but which was cancelled in the 1985 budget, largely for preelectoral reasons. In addition there was a varied package of contribution increases for the pension system, weighing rather more heavily on wage earners than employers. Simultaneously the growth in purchasing power equivalence of social service benefits (which had risen by 6% a year in 1981–82) was cut back substantially (2.2% in 1983 and 1984) with the figure for pensions falling even lower as benefit growth retreated significantly once the aftereffects of the *largesse* of 1981–82 had worked through the system.[16] The most important change which occurred in this period was a recasting of the unemployment compensation program in 1984. After this point unemployment benefits were split into two types, those which came from the insurance funds – "professional" solidarity from wage earners to wage earners (earlier the unique source) – and those which came from the state budget in the name of "general" solidarity.[17]

By the time the government turned towards its full-fledged "modernization" commitment in 1984, budgetary problems in basic social service programs had been taken in hand and movement away from taxing employers – to obliterate "red ink" – was well underway. This was a good thing in at least one important area. "Modernization" might have been a serious threat to the unemployment compensation scheme had not changes been made to the system, since the government's new willingness to allow layoffs and employment-costly industrial restructuring cost the jobs of many tens of thousands of workers. Still, the Socialists, governing alone after July 1984, were not willing to leave the newly unemployed completely to their own devices. Thus what ensued was a new "social" treatment of unemployment, the *ad hoc* creation of a set of public policies to alleviate the worst difficulties caused by industrial restructuring. The worst-hit areas – steelmaking Lorraine, shipbuilding and coalmining localities among others – became "conversion zones" where special efforts at new job creation were encouraged, along with early retirement, relocation payments and special "conversion leaves" for retraining purposes. Elsewhere other kinds of job-creation aids were implemented along with broader retraining programs. Perhaps the most innovative of these new programs, the Travail d'Utilité Collective (TUC), was directed at young people who were given part-time work at subminimum wages in various public-works and service activities.

With the 1986 elections approaching the Socialist government adopted more and more the dimensions of a fashionable, neo-liberal stance. Industrial "modernization" was only part of this. The 1985 budget, pointing towards the elections of 1986, among other things cut taxes, dropped the earlier 1 per cent social security tax, cut taxes on employers and cut the deficit. At the same time the government raised the costs of a number of public services (telephone, gasoline, public transport), thereby taking back much of what it had just given away. It had also become more neo-liberal on key labor-market issues such as "flexibility", in ways which promised even higher employment insecurity in coming years. But there was little new to report in the social service area.

Industrial relations: rigueur and false promises

Beginning with the *rigueur* period the Left initiated a number of retrenchment-oriented macroeconomic policy measures affecting workers and unions that its Center–Right predecessors had been much too timid to initiate. A wage–price freeze followed by well-enforced wage-growth guidelines effectively deindexed wage growth to cut inflation. From 1982 until 1985 the purchasing power of virtually all wage earners declined, excepting only the poorest (whose situation stagnated), primarily because wages, first controlled and then deindexed, began to fall behind the level of inflation. The workings of the tax system meant here, though, that the higher one's salary, the more purchasing power one lost, relatively.[18] The Left also began to trumpet the need for new entrepreneurial energy and for the profits necessary to encourage it, determining in consequence to limit the state's annual budget deficit (to 3% of GNP) and to reduce overhead costs for business. Thus *rigueur* policies also began a decline in the share of wages in GDP (from 76.3% in 1982, a historic high, to 75.2% in 1983) while profitability in manufacturing started upwards for the first time in a decade.[19] Quite as important, however, the coming of *rigueur* dramatically attenuated the government's progressive first-year efforts at income redistribution – from capital, the wealthy, middle-income earners (including better-paid skilled workers) – to poorer groups.

Despite all this, however, the "rigorous" Left did continue to show great determination to control the effects of austerity in at least one area, unemployment, at least until 1984. In most national contexts, such a large deflationary shock would have engendered a sharp increase in unemployment. The Left government sought to minimize this, at least until 1984, using a battery of labor-market programs, its control over public-sector employment and its administrative power to limit private-sector employers from laying people off.[20]

Since most unions disliked the government's austerity package, the new period brought increased strain on union–government relationships, which had been tenuous even during the "state of grace". Prompted by acute trade-union competitive pluralism, each major union accentuated its own specific response to the Left's policies in the new period – "Yes, but do more more quickly" from the CGT, "Yes, but don't do it that way" from the CFDT, and "It is not really our business, but no" from FO. This vocal union complaining undoubtedly helped nurture the Left's electoral and public-opinion decline which came with *rigueur* and from the failure of major reforms to make much positive difference.

As long as there were Communist ministers in the government, the CGT was obliged to remain a solid "interest-group" supporter of the Left experiment (indeed, perhaps the most loyal of such, until 1984). Both to maintain its rank-and-file credibility and to help prod the Socialists towards the policies which it (and the PCF) preferred, the CGT nonetheless felt obliged to complain against government policies it didn't like. To "make change succeed", the CGT claimed it was necessary to struggle "against the Right and the *patronat*", and the "managers of crisis" in the Left who were seeking to divert the process of change. With *rigueur* this became more urgent, because the CGT stood in ever-greater danger from its status as "hostage to a friendly government", hence its more vociferous complaining, intensified nationalist Keynesian rhetoric and aggressive talk about "soaking the rich".

The CFDT likewise intensified its "Second Left" critical commentaries on government actions. To the CFDT, "Old Left" statist and bureaucratic ways, even those of *rigueur*, led into a cul-de-sac. Only the initiation of a "new type of development", which recognized the seriousness of the crisis, could work. The CFDT derided the Keynesian and public-sector industrial policy dreams of the CGT, advocating instead social mobilization "from below" to formulate "new social solidarities". Against *rigueur* the CFDT complained that balancing accounts resolved no real problems and that the new policy had been bought at the expense of work sharing (little more was to be heard of the 35-hour week) about which the CFDT felt strongly.[21]

Force Ouvrière, the other major union player, had felt no obligation to support the Left government's policies from the outset in 1981, given its "pure and simple" unionist posture. With *rigueur* it could feel even freer to oppose retrenchment with "paycheck" rhetoric and, in the process, to gather in as much antigovernment labor support as it could, in particular from Right-leaning segments of the work force (FO became rather more friendly with the RPR at this point than it had ever been before).

One of the most important consequences for unions of the Left's tenure in power was already clear by the October 1983 social security elections. Trends towards significant change in the relative strengths of different unions had already been visible in 1981. As it turned out, not only had the Left in power done little to halt these trends, but it had actually helped to accentuate them. The balance of strength between France's three largest unions had been rather substantially "reequilibrated", as table 11.1 shows. In this "reequilibration" the unions which supported the Left did worst. The CGT, in steady decline since the second half of the 1970s, declined, if anything, even more quickly with the Left in power, perhaps because of its support of the government until 1984. The CFDT, which had long aspired to displace the CGT as the leading union in France, saw this goal fall further away, again probably because of its leftist image. FO, the only one of the three which maintained a politically independent posture, continued to gain steadily on the others, even making the CFDT "number three" in the social security ballot. In all, the Left's stay in power – for the above tendencies persisted through *rigueur* into later "modernization" – moved France

Table 11.1 Relative union strengths

| | *Professional election results – % of total votes (all colleges)* | | | | | |
	1974	*1975*	*1978*	*1980*	*1982*	*1984*
CGT	42.8	38.1	38.6	36.5	32.3	29.3
CFDT	18.7	19.4	20.4	21.3	22.8	21.1
FO	8.3	8.4	10.0	11.0	11.7	13.9

| | *Prud'homme elections 1979 and 1982 (%)* | | |
	1979	*1982*	*Gain/loss*
CGT	42.5	36.8	− 5.6
CFDT	23.1	23.5	+0.4
FO	17.4	17.8	+0.4

| | *Social security elections, October 1983 (%)* |
	1983
CGT	28.29%
FO	25.17%
CFDT	18.38%
CGC	15.93%

Note:
The social security electorate, and to a lesser extent the Prud'homme electorate, included large numbers of occupations which did not ordinarily vote in professional elections to works' committees. In addition, the social security election was conducted by a mail ballot rather than in the workplace.

even further towards a situation with three major unions of roughly equal strength, away from the earlier post-1947 model in which the CGT was roughly as strong as the others put together.

Unions against modernization

Rigueur shook, but did not destroy, Left union support for the government. "Modernization" had more profound effects. *Rigueur* had been justified as a necessary interlude when reform and change had to be put on hold. Modernization, which rejected Old Left-style change and reform, in contrast, was a decisive break with the political thought which had led to 1981. France's new priority was to build an industrial economy which could survive and compete internationally. Overstaffed industries were allowed to trim their work forces while "restructuring". Bailouts were henceforth to be avoided, whatever the employment costs, as the bankruptcy of Creusot-Loire demonstrated. Brutal reorganizations were encouraged in firms in steel, automobiles and shipbuilding. To achieve the goals of modernization, entrepreneurial activity, profit and the market were deemed central. One consequence of this was, of course, a reorientation of macroeconomic and other policies to provide incentives to business. Earlier Left promises and policies to cap unemployment growth were abandoned. An almost inevitable political result of all this was that the Communists, after louder and louder protests against modernization and *rigueur* inside the government, finally left in July 1984.

Changes in the CGT's attitude roughly paralleled those of the PCF. CGT rhetoric about not "giving in to the Right and the *patronat*" intensified, beginning in 1983. With the Talbot conflict of winter 1983–84 and the government's April 1984 decisions to "modernize" the steel industry, CGT "critical support" gave way to ever more strident criticism. The departure of Communist ministers in July made the CGT's line shift official. For some time, however, CGT injunctions to *descendez dans la rue* to protest declining living standards, deindustrialization and managerial betrayal, were more talk than action, reflecting the timidity of CGT leaders (Henri Krasucki, among others) who were afraid of the consequences of adopting the new anti-Socialist course being urged on them by the PCF. Such foot-dragging, in turn, caused internal conflict between pro-PCF hard-liners and "realists", similar to conflicts within the PCF itself. Indeed, in spring 1985 the CGT and its general secretary were taken to task at a PCF Central Committee meeting for their failure to attack "*le pouvoir socialiste*". By this point, however, hard-liners had seen to it that more action would occur around deindustrialization, PS "efforts to undo what had earlier been begun" and the PS's new affinity for "the bosses and the Right". The CGT's resistance to "modernization" at loss-making Renault was more than symbolic. Proposing "new criteria of management" and behaving in an old-fashioned job-defending way, the CGT rapidly lost many of the *de facto* codetermination powers which it had held at Renault for decades.[22] Mobilizational difficulties due to unemployment and the crisis plus the obvious sectarianism of the new line made such CGT actions into minority ("commando") movements – as at SKF in Ivry and Renault. Once again the CGT was being deployed by the PCF to undertake quasi-political mobilization tasks, perhaps to follow the PCF's own path to decline.[23]

The CGT's shift rather ironically brought it closer in terms of many of its stated positions to FO, even though FO's phobias about the CGT and PCF ruled out any common action. FO protested the decline of living standards and government neo-liberalism almost as loudly as the CGT, even if it took few practical steps to back up its protests. The FO leadership had different strategic purposes from the CGT, however. It wanted to build a situation in which it could resume its pre-1981 position of privileged interlocutor with the *patronat* and the foreseeable post-March 1986 Right government. Here, ironically, FO's very successes prior to, and under the Left, presaged future internal tensions. FO had been penetrated by ultra-leftists over the years. And during the years of Left power it had also attracted considerable support from the Right (the RPR in particular). With its extremely powerful leader André Bergeron on the verge of retirement, serious strategic disagreements between such widely divergent groups seemed quite possible.

Even the CFDT took its distance from modernization, if, typically, it did so in a maverick, *deuxième gauche* way.[24] The CFDT was willing to admit that something like "modernization" was needed, but claimed to reject a definition of modernization which involved "neo-liberalism, even with a social face". Restructuring, to the CFDT, ought not to be imposed on workers by the state and/or the *patronat* but rather should be the product of negotiations in which unions "proposed rather than submitted". Underneath this was a CFDT sense that unions would have to give up certain *acquis* – parts of labor law in the case of the unsuccessful "flexibility" negotiations of 1984–85, for example, to gain some influence over the shape of future change. Here the CFDT expressed attitudes which looked like Anglo-Saxon "give back" concession bargaining. In the CFDT's response to modernization there was also more than a hint of a new desire to supplant FO as trade-union *interlocuteur valable* for a new Right government. In a union which had earlier taken a long turn towards radicalism such positions did not go unchallenged, however.

By 16 March 1986, then, additional conclusions about the effects of the Left experiment on unions were glaringly obvious. First of all, if it had been the Left's, and more pertinently the Socialists', desire to recast relationships between trade unionism and Left politics in less idiosyncratic and more social democratic ways, next

Table 11.2 Trade-union memberships (millions)

Year	CGT official	CGT Kergoat	CFDT	CFDT active	FO
1974	2.34	1.72	1.01	—	.87
1976	2.35	1.69	1.15	1.07	.9
1978	2.19	1.49	1.12	1.05	.98 (est.)
1980	1.92	1.17	1.03	.96	1. (est.)
1982	1.72	.98	1.04	.96	1.1
1984	1.4	—	—	.9 (est.)	1.1

Note:
The CGT Official and the first set of CFDT figures include retired members. The CGT Kergoat figures are estimates of actual CGT members once retired members and CGT overinflation are subtracted, as done by Jacques Kergoat, see "CGT: un recul . . .", *Le Monde*, (19 Nov. 1985). The CFDT active column substracts CFDT retired members from the first CFDT column. FO membership statistics are few and far between. See Alain Bergounioux, *Force ouvrière* (Paris, Que-sais-je, 1982), for a discussion of this.

Table 11.3 Number of days lost in strikes 1962–84

Year	Days lost (millions)
1962	1.9
1964	2.5
1966	2.5
1968	150.
1970	1.7
1972	3.7
1974	3.4
1976	5.0
1978	2.2
1980	1.7
1981	1.5
1982	2.3
1983	1.5
1984	1.3

to nothing had been accomplished. The CGT was, if anything, even more devoted to the PCF. The CFDT was further away from the PS than it had perhaps ever been, having profited little from the Left in power. FO had been marginally rewarded for consistently resisting any and all temptations to move closer to the PS. Divisions among the three were as deep as they had been in 1981. All that had changed were the justifications for the animosity. Next, if the Left in power had hoped to strengthen the unions its record here was quite as dismal. The CGT, and to a lesser extent the CFDT, had been declining in terms of membership and financial support since the later 1970s and, if anything, the period of Left power accelerated this, as tables 11.2 and 11.3 show. FO had done better in such terms, although mainly by maintaining a steady state. The level of unionization in France as a whole was declining. Perhaps a better index of the effects of trade-union division, economic crisis and the Left's policies after 1982 were the figures for strike action, which show the mid-1980s as the calmest years since the early 1960s.

The Auroux reforms were, of course, the Left's major initiative to rebalance the French industrial relations system in labor's favor. Qualitative and quantitative indicators gathered during their first three years could only review the establishment of new procedures and habits rather than the workings of finished institutions.[25] Still, several things were clear initially about the new "rights of expression". Workers themselves, perhaps because of the crisis and shifts in government policy, were timid and skeptical about them. Problems arose because of the lack of information available to workers, uncertainty about the roles of *cadres* in the process, excessive formality in the proceedings themselves and disbelief that "expression" could have serious consequences for the firm. There was some enthusiasm about positive effects of the new "expression" on intrafirm communications and "climate".

The first years of firm-level "obligation to negotiate" on wages and working conditions brought mixed results. There was more negotiating, probably a good thing. But since there was no "obligation to reach agreement" in the new law, negotiations often ended without agreement, and almost as often in agreements which favored employers. Beyond these things, shop committees (and new group committees) were getting more economic information about their firms and using such new resources to build up greater knowledge about firm decision-making. Eventually such knowledge might be used in innovative "propositional" ways.

Legislation can only partially manipulate industrial relations practices, of course. The final outcomes of reforms like the Auroux Laws depend on the relative strengths and intentions of labor and capital over the long run. Ironies nonetheless accumulated in the reforms' first years. Employers' associations had initially opposed the new reforms in vigorous terms. But the obligation to bargain with labor when it was historically weak and when little existed in company coffers to concede posed fewer problems than anticipated. Moreover, new obligations to consult with workers meshed well with new firm-based managerial strategies of the "quality circle" type. By dealing directly with workers, employers in many cases used "rights of expression" to cut out unions on the shopfloor and to increase productivity. Evidence also suggests that the reinforcement of representative institutions in the workplace has enmeshed already overtaxed union militants in deeper levels of bureaucracy.

In all, the Auroux Laws were disorienting.[26] Unions initially gained little from them, even if the laws had originally been passed to help them. *Patronal* hatred for them, logical if they were intended to strengthen labor, had rapidly turned into benevolent neutrality and sometimes enthusiasm. The laws did seem to move capital–labor relationships towards one of their objectives, the decentralization and "deglobalization" of industrial relations towards a new focus on firm-level issues. But rather than giving unions a greater foothold at firm level, the laws seemed to become a part of a new *patronal* armamentarium of "deregulation", pressuring unions and workers to assume greater responsibility for firm success even, in some cases, at the cost of undermining national labor law. "Flexibility" in working time, for example, spread rapidly at firm level – often through firm-level negotiations – despite laws against it. As of 1986, the unintended, and pro-business, consequences of the Auroux Laws were perhaps more surprising than their failure to strengthen the unions. But the jury will remain out for some time.

CONCLUSIONS: FAILURE OR *FAUTE DE MIEUX?*

The Left coalition which began governing France in May–June 1981 brought with it the most radical program seen in any advanced capitalist nation in a long, long time. This new French regime had committed itself not only to maintain, but to expand, the French Welfare State when elsewhere many other governments were trying to find ways to cut back, if not dismantle, their own. In industrial relations workers would be granted a "new citizenship" in the enterprise itself, with unions being strengthened and empowered in economic decision-making in the process.

The social policy debate of the 1986 election revealed how far the Left had fallen short of its Welfare State aims. Having themselves danced around the edges of serious change year by year in order to balance the books, but without taking radical steps to reformulate the logic of the system, the Socialists posed as protectors of *les acquis sociaux* and of the principles of solidarity which underlay them.[27] The Communists, now in opposition, assumed an "integralist" position and accused the PS of having already begun the dismantling of *les acquis sociaux*, an accusation which, given the important cutbacks which the PS had undertaken (most of them while the PCF had been in government), was not completely inaccurate.[28] The Left had split, of course. The party which counted most, however, the PS, had moved from advocating radical optimism in 1981 to announcing that "things would have been much worse without us". Indeed, "smart" centrist opinion, which echoed inside the PS itself, had begun to favor basic changes in the principles of the French Welfare State away from universalistic "solidarity" towards a "Franco–American" approach of universal programs for part of the population – the poorer part – and private insurance schemes for the rest.[29]

The French Left in power, if it failed to fulfil its promises to rejuvenate the French Welfare State, at least did not act in any dramatic ways to destroy it. The nature of its performance in this respect was basically similar to those of most of its European contemporaries, if marginally better in some areas. Ultimately, however, the fact that it was a government of the political Left did not make that much difference. Muddling through may turn out, in the near future, to have been a prelude to larger, more coherent and concerted efforts to unravel, undermine and recast the French Welfare State. It may also turn out to have been a sound strategy for warding off such efforts. We simply cannot say yet.

In the industrial relations area the *bilan* is clearer. The Left wanted first to change the relationships between workers, unions and employers to labor's advantage and then to change relationships between labor and politics. Neither goal was achieved. In some ways despite, in some important ways because of, the Left's tenure in government, the French working class has been weakened substantially. Deindustrialization, unemployment and other effects of the economic crisis have broken its back in "smokestack" industries – accentuating a process of sociological decomposition with little recomposition in sight. Parallel to this the organized labor movement, which had been divided and weakened already in the years immediately prior to the Left victory, has become substantially more divided and weaker since. The Auroux Laws, undertaken during the first year of radical enthusiasm, have thus far probably helped employers more than workers, if, as we noted, the jury is still out. And the Left government's turn to "modernization" after 1984, involving much greater tolerance for unfettered hiring and firing and greater labor-market mobility ("flexibility", as the French call it), has worked in the same direction. Whatever one thinks of the likely effect of such changes on France's future economic performance, their immediate effect in further fragmenting and demoralizing French workers has been great. And here, perhaps more than on Welfare State issues, the Left has opened new doors to the Center–Right to go much farther.

Parcelling out praise and blame to the Left is considerably less interesting, however, than speculating about the deeper meaning of what happened between 1981 and 1986 for the Welfare State, workers and unions. For it may be that very great change is in the works, facilitated by trends which became clearer during the Left's moment in power. For generations a "certain leftism" was characteristic of the French working class, the leftism which had created the 1981 Left Program. Anticapitalism, strident radicalism and somewhat Manichaean "antibourgeois" attitudes lasted longer in France than elsewhere. The supports of this leftism over the years had been the PCF, the CGT, to a lesser extent, the SFIO/PS, joined beginning in the 1960s, by the CFDT, with these political and union organizations aided and abetted enthusiastically by many French intellectuals. What became clear in the early 1980s was that this once-powerful array of organizational and social forces supporting France's "certain leftism" was collapsing. The demise of the old-style left-leaning intellectual has been discussed widely, including in this volume. The PCF's dramatic decline began before 1981, but it occurred in large part because of the politics which brought the Left to power in 1981 and continued apace thereafter. The PCF's decline was paralleled by the CGT in the trade-union realm. The CFDT had begun to move away from radical leftism prior to 1981 but this movement had become a headlong retreat by 1986. The most spectacular changes occurred in the PS, whose leftism simply collapsed in the face of the contradictions of governance, and most especially in response to the constraints of France's international economic situation. What would ultimately take the place of this "old leftism" in Socialist politics was not completely obvious as of 1986, but it would clearly involve a new technocratic realism which placed primary emphasis on developing France's competitiveness in the international division of labor rather than on radical projects for recasting France's domestic social compromise.

One Left won the 1981 elections. A very different Left lost the 1986 legislative elections. Evaluated on its performance in the two areas discussed above the "first Left" would not get very high marks. It is probably too soon to know even what criteria to use in evaluating the "next Left". But one outcome is already evident. The Left in power presided over, and to a degree facilitated, a set of important changes in the strength and outlook of those very organizations which had historically been the strongest forces in favor of extending the Welfare State and increasing the power of workers and unions in French life. Such changes will weigh heavily in the future.

NOTES

1 For history see Henri Hatzfeld, *Du Pauperisme à la sécurité sociale* (Paris, Armand Colin, 1971) and for institutions see Pierre Laroque (ed.), *The Social Institutions of France* (New York, Gordon and Breach, 1983).

2 IRES, *La Protection sociale* (Paris, Institut de Recherches Economiques et Sociales, 1983), p. 61.

3 CERC, *La Croissance et la crise: les revenus des Français* (Paris, La Documentation Française, 1985), p. 36.

4 For a most interesting overview of this, see Alain Lipietz *L'Audace ou l'enlisement* (Paris, La Découverte, 1984), part I.

5 This story of CFDT/CGT relations in the 1970s is recounted in George Ross, *Workers and Communists in France* (Berkeley, University of California Press, 1982), ch. 10. For standard reviews of French unionism see Gérard Adam, *Le Pouvoir syndical* (Paris, Dunod, 1983); René Mouriaux, *Les Syndicats dans la société française* (Paris, Fondation Nationale des Sciences Politiques, 1983); and Hubert Landier, *Demain, quels syndicats?* (Paris, Pluriel, 1981).

6 For a detailed description of all this see *Bulletin Social Francis Lefebvre*, (1982; 1983). See also Alain Fonteneau and Pierre-Alain Muet, *La Gauche face à la crise* (Paris, Fondation Nationale des Sciences Politiques, 1985), pp. 97–130, for a macroeconomic assessment of these measures.

7 See Jean-Michel Bélorgey "La Politique sociale, carrefour ou impasse!" *Projet*, (May-June 1985), for example.

8 Alain Lipietz in "Crise de l'état providence", *Les Temps modernes*, (Nov. 1983), skillfully reviews the French debate on the future of the Welfare State and proposes his own "regulation school" solutions.

9 It is a well-known fact that Henri Krasucki of the CGT and Pierre Mauroy, who was endowed with a large amount of old-school workerism, dealt with one another often and, for the most part, well. The notoriety of their regular meetings did little to reassure other unions about governmental propensities.

10 The CGT published a major evaluation of the first 18 months of Left government which, if tinged by the Confederation's growing bitterness in 1983, is still a good source for its views. See CGT *Rapport annuel sur la situation économique et sociale de la France, (10 mai 1981–décembre 1982)* (Paris, CGT, 1984).

11 Here the best source is Hervé Hamon and Patrick Rotman, *La Deuxième gauche* (Paris, Ramsay, 1982). See also CFDT, *L'Année sociale 1982* (Paris, CFDT 1982) for a volume roughly comparable to the CGT's cited earlier.

12 On the coming of the Auroux Laws see Jean Auroux *Les Droits des travailleurs* (Paris, La Documentation Française, 1981); "Les Nouveaux droits des travailleurs", *Le Monde, Dossiers et Documents* (June 1983); and the excellent "Les Autres et les droits nouveaux", *CFDT-BRAEC Dossier*, 22 (Oct.-Dec. 1982), which details the positions of different unions on the reforms.

13 For overviews see Michel Beaud, *Le Mirage de la croissance* (Paris, Syros, 1983); Lipietz, *L'Audace ou l'enlisement*, ch. 7, and Fonteneau and Muet, *La Gauche face à la crise*, ch. 2. In English see George Ross and Jane Jenson "Political Pluralism and Economic Policy", in *The French Socialist Experiment*, ed. John Ambler (Philadelphia, ISHI Press, 1984).

14 The best political history of these shifts is found in Philippe Bauchard's *La Guerre des deux roses* (Paris, Grasset, 1985).

15 The exceptions were commitment to reimburse abortion through social security, for example, and the repeal of most of the 1967 social security decrees.

16 Fonteneau and Muet, *La Gauche face à la crise*, p. 332.

17 For a good overview of this in English see Jean-Pierre Jallade "Redistribution and the Welfare State: An Assessment of the French Socialists' Performance", *Government and Opposition*, (Summer, 1985).

18 CERC, *Constat de l'évolution récente des revenus en France, 1980-1983* (Paris, La Documentation Française, 1984).

19 OECD, *Perspectives économiques*, (July 1984), p. 59; Ministry of the Economy, Finances and Budget, "L'Economie Française début 1986", *Les Notes bleues*, (3-9 Feb. 1986), p. 7.

20 For a general overview of labor-market policies in this period see Aude Benôit *La Politique de l'emploi* (Paris, La Documentation Française, 1984). For an econometric history of their working see Fonteneau and Muet, *La Gauche face à la crise*, ch. 4.

21 See CFDT, Secteur Emploi, Secrétariat Economique, "La Politique économique en question", internal document dated 13 Sept. 1984, for a detailed discussion of the *rigueur* policies.

22 Despite its self-confident bluster, the CGT was as puzzled as any other union about how to cope with the effects of economic crisis. On the one hand there was considerable "modernist" discussion about "new criteria for management" and trade-union propositions and counterpropositions about matters such as investment patterns and economic policy. Here the *documents de base* were PCF economist Philippe Herzog's most interesting book *L'Economie nouvelle à bras le corps* (Paris, Messidor, 1984) and the economic review series *Analyses et documents economiques* put out by the CGT research center. On the other hand was the time-honored job-protecting defensiveness which had been the lifeblood of all trade unionism, including the CGT's, during the long post-war boom. When one superposed PCF strategic desiderata on such internally generated strategic conflict, the possibilities for confusion and inefficacity were great. For the CGT's official analysis of the Socialists' turn to modernization see CGT, *Rapport de la CGT sur la situation économique de la France, 1983-1984* (Paris, CGT, 1985).

23 Here see Jacques Kergoat, "La CGT: un recul . . ." in *Le Monde* (19 Nov. 1985).

24 See Edmond Maire's two articles in *Le Monde* (2,3 Nov. 1984) for a good outline of this.

25 For an overview of the application of the Auroux Laws see Commission des Affaires Culturelles, familiales, et Sociales de l'Assemblée Nationale, *Rapport d'information*, (Paris, CACFS, 1985), document 2681, submitted to the National Assembly early in 1985; also Anni Borzeix, Danièle Linhart and Denis Segrestin, *Sur les traces du droit d'expression* (Paris, Centre National Des Arts et Métiers, 1985) for a series of skilfully done case studies.

26 See Michele Millot and Jean-Pol Roulleau, "Les Relations sociales depuis les lois Auroux", in *Projet*, (Nov.-Dec. 1985), for a very good overview.

27 *Nouvelle revue Socialiste*, (Dec. 1985) has a long discussion of PS campaign positions on the Welfare State.

28 See the "Dossier sécurité sociale", in *Cahiers du Communisme*, (Sept. 1985).

29 In this respect the interview of Simon Nora by Edmond Maire - "Sécurité sociale: de l'impasse à la réforme", *Le Débat*, (Sept. 1983) - is very interesting.

12

The Left, The Intellectuals and Culture

DIANA PINTO

To speak of the Left, intellectuals and culture[1] in a discussion of "continuity and change in modern France" is to describe a major "sea change" whose repercussions transcend the Mitterrand experiment and constitute one key dimension for reflection about the potential pluralist transformation of France. It is one of the supreme ironies of the Socialist years that evolution away from initial ideological certitudes towards a pragmatic, pluralist understanding of French reality should have been triggered as much by hostile domestic and international economic actors, turned into positive interlocutors, as by a traditionally supportive intelligentsia, which turned a deaf ear to the siren songs of the Left and embarked on a "sea change" of its own.

The Socialist victory of 1981 marked the end rather than the high point of a long historical marriage between the French intelligentsia and the political Left. Two centuries of near symbiosis between the militant consciences of humanity and the universal forces of revolution trickled down to a Socialist political triumph without major intellectual engagement. There followed a ballet of misunderstandings, a "silence" based on incompatible world views, open clashes over the meaning of culture and, finally, indifference. In the end no common ground could be found between a newly defensive intelligentsia bent on redefining its *raison d'être* in a historically relativist and critical antitotalitarian light, and a political Left at first imbued with a cultural/political triumphalism, whose identity later floundered as it sought to construct a more pragmatic and realistic profile.

In many ways the Socialists' itinerary with respect to the intelligentsia paralleled their evolution in the economic sphere. From ideological certitudes and a radical will to alter reality to a more humble, pragmatic adaptation, the Socialists had to face an intellectual context which was no longer open to old left-wing credos, and above all negated the classical symbiosis between politics and culture, revolution and ideas. This confrontation was to prove far more traumatizing for a Socialist identity than embracing the principles of economic reality. Intellectuals were supposed to be a solid Left bastion, a motor driving its world views. Distancing themselves from the Socialists in power could only be construed as a betrayal and an anomaly which had to be remedied. Once in power the Socialists sought the active support of the intellectuals without ever winning it, while paradoxically finding new economic interlocutors and even partners. The Left's relationship with intellectuals thus became a desperate search for a lost unity of purpose which was destined to fail because the very paradigms of intellectual life had changed.

Beyond personalities, media coverage and journalistic debates, the saga of the Left, intellectuals and culture from 1981 to 1986 can be seen as a Sophoclean play whose tensions and clashes were predetermined by events which took place before the curtain rose in May 1981. The clash between the Left in power and the intelligentsia was, in reality, a clash between two cultures. Both were children of 1968, crystallized in their separateness in the 1970s, but unaware of the gulf that separated them until the political triumph of the Left. The slow discovery of the rift occurred with the help of the media (acting as Greek chorus for the occasion). The discovery–play had three acts: the state of restless grace, the era of suspicion vs the big upheaval, and indifference vs recycled resignation.

A TALE OF TWO CULTURES

The new Socialist Party was born in 1971 at the Congrès d'Epinay – the year of the centennial of the Paris Commune – proclaiming full allegiance to the revolutionary traditions of the Left and its own incarnation in the people. Avoiding the murky waters of social democracy, the PS, from the outset, sought links with the Communist party stressing shared revolutionary ideals, common patrimony in the Resistance, and opposition to capitalism. Clearly defined in opposition to the Right, the political Left on the early 1970s also adopted a strong anti-Americanism based on the United States' domestic injustices (racial tensions, inequalities), capitalism and above all its international imperialist role (most visible in Vietnam but discernible elsewhere as well). Militantly Third Worldist and disaffected with revisionist models, the Socialist Left embodied a strong Jacobin heritage with a clearly defined interventionist mission premised on the universality of French culture.

The French intelligentsia took a different tack in the post-1968 years. It was interested above all in dismantling cultural certainties and was ready to reveal the hand of repressive, centralized, Jacobin authority in the name of *autogestion* (part of the popular success of Michel Foucault's writings stemmed from association with this 1968 current). Delving into the underside of French history – collaboration, French anti-Semitism, Vichy – this intellectual Left harbored a far less glamorous view of the French past precisely when revelations about the Gulag obliged head-on confrontation with Soviet totalitarianism and inspired comparisons with the French Revolution itself.[2] Seeing the consummate totalitarian evil in the Soviet Union, the intellectual Left could not have differed more from the Socialists in its perceptions of the Communist Party, and in its reexamination of much of revolutionary Communist cant. Old Left vs Right divisions began to crumble as many intellectuals embraced liberal democratic tenets formerly cast as rightist as the height of the cold war.[3] Because of their condemnation of the Soviet Union, their recasting of the French past in a less exalted light, antiauthoritarianism and opposition to centralized power, many members of the French intelligentsia were no longer sure of France's mission. They were far more concerned with demystifying their past in an antitotalitarian context, and were unable to condone the left-wing brotherhood that the Socialists were trying to forge with the Communists.

There were also major differences regarding the United States which the intellectuals perceived (especially after Watergate) as the center of a new spirit of dynamism, a true democracy where checks and balances prevented creation of any central power authority, and, above all, as the nemesis of Soviet totalitarianism. (This type of pro-Americanism was best exemplified by the tone of newspapers like *Libération*).[4]

Advocating power from below in the tradition of the *deuxième gauche*, seeking to separate intellectual pursuits from political engagement and criticizing the excesses of revolution in the name of democratic change, higher-level French intellectuals took the opposite tack from the middle and low-level intelligentsia who had found meaning in Marxist and Socialist engagement. Intellectual militants of this latter type populated the Socialist Party throughout France, and in 1981 became the new deputies in a National Assembly rebaptized by some critics as, "the Republic of professors" (of the *secondaire* this time around).[5] Solzhenitsyn's Gulag revelations in 1974 slowly filtered through the French media[6] and merged with revelations on Cambodian atrocities, the Vietnamese boat people and the Soviet invasion of Afghanistan to create an intellectual climate in France which was more than wary of the traditional Marxist, revolutionary postures on national liberation movements. The French higher intelligentsia had thus converted to formal bourgeois liberties as the best guarantee of democracy precisely when the political Left, celebrating the virtues of "the eternal Left", moved toward power. In May 1981, then, the situation was ripe for major misunderstandings between the intelligentsia and the political Left.

The potential for conflict was exacerbated by the fact that both groups shared a commitment to words and symbols (as opposed to facts, around which there might be *entente* with enemies of the Left, such as economic elites). Thus, the Left in power was to engage in a passionate dialogue, based on hope and denunciation, with an intelligentsia vacillating between malaise and indifference towards the Left. The struggle over symbolic words – such as the people, cultural imperialism, the state, society and culture – reflected two radically different ways of perceiving political and intellectual commitment along wholistic or pluralist lines. But it was over the meaning of culture that these two currents came to a head.

Between 1981 and 1986 there were three distinct periods in the relationship between the intellectuals and the Left. The first "wait and see" phase from May to December 1981 (ending with the Polish coup) one might call the "state of restless grace". In the second phase (from December 1981 to June 1983) the higher intelligentsia entered an era of suspicion *vis-à-vis* a Left intent on carrying out *le grand chambardement* (roughly, the big upheaval). The Left's intellectual crusades were met with increasing silence until the imposition of *rigueur* and the government's fundamental change of orientation. Phase three involved indifference of the intellectuals and recycled resignation on the Left, which was searching for new cultural interlocutors to replace a definitively lost intelligentsia. The cultural "creator" became this new interlocutor, with the very vagueness of the concept constituting one of its major assets in an era emphasizing pragmatism and efficiency. Characteristically, changes made by the Left to appease its opponents and detractors did not produce the desired effect. Even though Socialist cultural policy was more in keeping with the concerns of the intelligentsia after 1983, the separation of intellectual and political spheres made it impossible for the Socialists to reap any of the desired benefits. The old conceptual unity of the political and intellectual Left was broken.

THE STATE OF RESTLESS GRACE: MAY–DECEMBER 1981

The Left came to power determined to impose its own cultural and intellectual symbols as a way of asserting its lofty identity and sense of universal mission. Mitterrand's presidential inauguration was a carefully orchestrated celebration of France's leftist past as well as of its cultural future. Roses in the Pantheon and Beethoven in the streets set the tone for an inaugural during which foreign writers and intellectuals (Gabriel Garcia Marquez, William Styron among others) confirmed Socialist France's position as an international leader, as the country of civilization and culture. The support of French intellectuals was implicit for the Socialists; foreign guests were symbols of Socialist France's desire to export her intellectual/political symbiosis to countries whose cultures were stymied or repressed by the two superpowers. It was no accident therefore that one of the first symbolic acts of the Socialists was to grant French nationality to two prominent exiled writers, Julio Cortazar from Latin America and Milan Kundera from Czechoslovakia. France transcended the East–West divide to embrace the cause of the South, placing itself at the head of those countries and peoples repressed by superpower collusion. Socialist France formulated its international vision in several ways: Mitterrand's Cancun speech, in which an imperialist United States loomed as the major international threat and Latin America as a victim;[7] Jack Lang's call for a new *latinité*; and a new policy toward Africa, symbolized by the nomination of Jean-Pierre Cot to the Ministry of Cooperation. Above all, "culture" was to transcend its own limits to encompass all other policy spheres in a vision that could best be described as "everything is cultural" or "cultural is political". It was against just such a transcendental backdrop that the French intelligentsia was rebelling. Jack Lang's actions on behalf of actors, writers, artists and poets lost much of its intellectual support because of the deliberate confusion of the two spheres.

By remaining faithful to its 1970s vision of national liberation and struggle against imperialism, the geopolitically oriented cultural policy of the Socialists was out of step with the new views of the French intelligentsia. The eyes of the latter riveted on Soviet transgressions of human rights; French intellectuals were far more concerned with the emergence of Solidarity in Poland and with East European dissidence in general, than with developments in Nicaragua and El Salvador. For them, American interference or clout in Latin America was easy to condemn. The true test of Socialist commitment to human rights would be over Soviet totalitarianism, its conquests and repression.[8] For the intelligentsia it was essential not to put the two superpowers on the same plane; Soviet domestic and international behavior posed a far greater threat to freedom and culture than America's transgressions.

More than anything else, this divergence in world views was to condition the state of restless grace of the French intelligentsia after the Socialist victory. The presence of Communist ministers, the call for unity of the people of the Left against the Right and an international analysis based largely on old-fashioned left-wing views (which did not give priority to human rights in an antitotalitarian context) as well as its economic voluntarism, were so many clouds in the Socialist sky for an intelligentsia fearing that reality might be less easy to manipulate than the Socialists believed.[9] For the higher intelligentsia, the Left was no longer sacrosanct. Given its past views, guilt and tolerance of Soviet totalitarian terror in the name of revolution, the Left had to prove itself in practice.[10]

On a more concrete level, Jack Lang's Ministry approached French culture and intellectual life with protectionist and Colbertist reflexes. He fused culture with national grandeur, not individual accomplishment. In so doing, Lang satisfied corporatist grievances (i.e., the Lang Law which prevented the discounting of books and thus protected small booksellers from the FNAC; the permission to amortize taxes on writers' royalties), and gave in to professional pressure (as evidenced by the creation of the Maison de l'Ecrivain and the Collège de Philosophie, directed by Jean-Pierre Faye). Such cultural Colbertism went profoundly against the grain of an intelligentsia which looked askance at state intervention (with political implications) in the intellectual sphere. The new intelligentsia preferred to separate politics and intellectuality and to seek its influence within civil society.[11] The Eastern bloc was after all rife with state-sponsored publishing houses and projects for artists and painters. In particular, few intellectuals were willing to become the new "organic" intellectuals of a Socialist Party in power.[12] Socialist voluntarism did not have an automatic audience in an intelligentsia no longer willing to follow leftist projects simply because they were of the Left. Cultural paternalism was no longer appreciated as a lofty ideal even for the best intentions. The state, it was argued, should not be a substitute for the intellectuals themselves. Intellectuals thus became increasingly vocal in their criticisms of Socialist initiatives, especially in the economic realm.[13] The state of restless grace lasted only for a few months. Intellectual criticism and detachment grew and the cleavage between the Left's two cultures became increasingly evident.

THE ERA OF SUSPICION VERSUS "THE BIG UPHEAVAL": (DECEMBER 1981–JULY 1983)

Intellectual suspicion of the Socialists grew around two cardinal reference points: Poland (and behind it the Soviet giant), and the United States. Different reactions and emphases brought out entirely different perceptions of what intellectuals out of power and the Left in power should be doing with respect to human rights and in the name of culture.

The Polish coup

The December 1981 outlawing of Solidarity and the imprisonment of its leaders broke the state of grace. In the space of a few weeks, French intellectuals saw their worst fears of leftist/statist behavior confirmed. The Socialists reacted weakly and hesitantly to the Jaruzelski coup. Claude Cheysson's instant declaration, "Of course we won't do anything" and Pierre Mauroy's signature of the Franco-Soviet gas pipeline accords in early January (when he stressed that there was no point in adding the suffering of the French people – potentially without heat – to that of the Poles, the mere comparison was insulting) did not reassure the intelligentsia. The Socialist Party's initial hesitation over joining the major protest march on behalf of Solidarity in late December 1981 and Jospin's last-minute rallying, combined with the CGT's condemnation of the protest movements, destroyed many of the remaining ties of affinity between the intelligentsia and the political Left. Jack Lang's spectacle at the Opéra de Paris on behalf of Poland was too much of an effort at co-optation to be convincing.

The CFDT under the leadership of Edmond Maire, one of the pillars of the *deuxième gauche*, emerged as the only institution of the Left whose behavior was judged beyond reproach by the intellectuals. The two cultures of the Left came out in broad daylight. On one side, the Socialists, draped in the justifications of *raison d'état*, but buttressed by an implicit affinity with the Third World – as opposed to Eastern Europe – seemed to be aligned with the CGT in their responses to the Polish crisis. On the other, the Left – which gave priority to freedom and antitotalitarianism, to society over state and to human rights over national liberation movements – rallied around the CFDT and felt closer to other protesters of the liberal Right than to the CGT. The last efforts to present a unified Left disappeared. Thus shortly after the Polish crisis some very important intellectuals – Michel Foucault and Pierre Bourdieu, for example – participated directly in reflections of the CFDT on the Left.[14] The only interlocutor was to be found in society, not within the state, even if it was in Socialist hands.

The United States and cultural imperialism

The second major cleavage separating the intelligentsia from the Left was the interpretation of the United States. In a curious display of differing priorities, French foreign policy and cultural policy stressed different postures at different times. When Mitterrand had four Communist ministers in his cabinet he felt the need to reassure the United States on foreign policy and France's commitment to the Western Alliance on defense policy and security more specifically. During the same period Jack Lang inveighed against the United States for its cultural imperialism, economic clout and the ravages wrought by its popular culture throughout the world, where weaker states could no longer defend their national cultural identities against the onslaught of cheap commercialism. The first sign of France's new official line occurred when Lang chose to boycott the 1981 Deauville Film Festival stressing that it was not his job to help American media penetrate French culture. The strongest accusations, however, came in August 1982, when Lang used a UNESCO address in Mexico to encourage countries to fight American cultural imperialism. French intellectuals were outraged by the fact that in such a speech there would be no reference to Soviet transgressions of human rights.[15]

Furthermore, Lang chose to visit Castro in Cuba during the same trip and was photographed in a fraternal (socialist) embrace with Castro while on a lobster-fishing spree, and even proclaimed Cuba to be a courageous country. This gesture could not have been better chosen to alienate the most important members of the French intelligentsia. Cuba, the French intellectuals' pet country during the Third-World phase of the 1960s, had become no more than a tropical Gulag for the newly antitotalitarian intellectuals. Castro, the "Brezhnev of the Caribbean", was the last person with whom a Socialist minister advocating human rights should be seen.[16] Official French cultural policy thus seemed clearly at odds with the values and concerns of its high intelligentsia. Intellectuals no longer condoned national liberation movements which did not explicitly favor civil liberties, and laughed at politicized anti-American barbs. The Socialist government subsequently justified Lang's trip by the Cubans' release of a well-known poet, Valladares, who had been a political prisoner for 20 years. This outcome did not cancel out the negative reactions of the French intelligentsia to Lang's cultural policy, however.

Many of the intelligentsia's objections to Lang's actions were connected to his ridiculously inflated language assailing the United States, its cultural imperialism and influence. Debates surrounding banal soap operas such as "Dallas" assumed a highly symbolic value, for example. Was French culture being attacked, or was France inherently less brilliant than in the past for letting such American products enter French popular culture? Worse yet, was American commercial culture endowed with qualities which the French had to learn? To Jack Lang there was a distinct enemy out there to be fought off. It was as if American cultural imperialism stemmed from a central will. The intelligentsia labelled the whole battle ludicrous. No one was ready to die to oppose "Dallas" and some of the United States's deepest traits, hitherto condemned as "base" by cultivated French intellectuals, were now perceived in an entirely different light. Part of the Copernican revolution of the French intelligentsia consisted precisely in praising United States's pluralism, flexibility, openness, perpetual motion and change and the very fact that society was not restrained by a central authority that legislated on all matters.[17] In this context, Lang's crusade seemed to combine ideological barbs left over from the 1970s with new public-relations gimmickry for getting media headlines – the exact opposite of the new low-profile attitude desired by a more modest intelligentsia.

The high point of incompatibility between Socialist cultural policy and the intelligentsia took place in February 1983 when, under the auspices of François Mitterrand (who actually attended one session in regal pomp) and Jack Lang, a major international colloquium was held at the Sorbonne on the theme "Creativity and Development". Celebrities – ranging from Sophia Loren, movie producer Volker Schlöndorff, Ettore Scola, Sean McBride, the founder of Amnesty International, the exiled South African poet Breyten Breytenbach, numerous African cultural figures (including Léopold Senghor), and an American group flown in on the Concorde (including Susan Sontag, William Styron, John Kenneth Galbraith and an assortment of New York University professors) – flocked to Paris to discuss the future of the world and how creative people could aid development. This "Versailles of the Mind", a glamorous extravaganza that Socialist cultural policy gave itself, implied that Socialist France was at least appreciated by foreign intellectuals, if not by its own. Indeed, the absence of most big names in the French intelligentsia was striking. In their place one had guru-like groupies of Socialist power. Left culture in power and the culture of ideas of the Left were never so physically distant as during the Sorbonne festivities.

A *Wall Street Journal* writer suggested ironically that perhaps French culture was attempting to hide its current "nullity" (the fact that it no longer had writers and poets of world significance) behind such international extravaganzas. Lang immediately seized upon this article as a major American attack, leading to countless debates and commentaries of the validity of French culture. Once again the response of intellectuals was much calmer and more even-handed than the Socialist "culture machine" would have wished.[18] No one felt like picking up the glove that Lang had thrown in the hope of generating a major conflict between the United States and France on the issue of the latter's cultural brilliance. It seemed as though the intellectuals were busily working on their own projects and had no desire to take public stands, much less to make argumentative challenges against a putative insult. After General de Gaulle's famous defense of France's cultural grandeur, the Socialist reply may have sounded too much like a farce for an intellectual milieu with new, more important, antitotalitarian and democratic preoccupations.

The lukewarm reception of Socialist cultural efforts in intellectual circles matched a wider refusal on the part of the intelligentsia to militate actively in favor of the Socialist policy in the wider realm of politics and economics. Its failure to carry the Socialist torch, and to criticize an increasingly vocal Right (perceived by the Socialists in power as a hostile ideological bloc), which by 1983 was already regaining confidence after the municipal elections, became another burning issue for the Socialists.

Max Gallo, the government spokesman, wrote an article in Le Monde in July 1983 on "Le Silence des intellectuels de gauche" which accused French intellectuals of having betrayed the Left in power by their refusal to defend its policies.[19] What had happened to the glorious image of the committed intellectuals? Why were they no longer defending the left-wing cause, especially at a time when the communists were generating their own left-wing critiques of the Socialists in power? Gallo intended to begin a debate, and indeed for the month that followed, there was scarcely a day when Le Monde did not include an article on the topic by practicing artists, professors, socialist militants and activists. Even if the subject of the articles, the intellectuals, was difficult to isolate as a genre, their contribution was once again conspicuously absent.[20] Put bluntly, Socialism in power was not perceived as the incarnation of a universal ideal. The intellectuals felt that the no-longer inexorable cleavage between Left and Right was more important. Both sides of the divide, provided they worked in a democratic setting, had full *droit de cité*. Socialist arguments that "their" intellectuals had to take the torch and fight for Socialist stands were simply rebuffed in the name of a more tolerant and pluralist allegiance to democracy.

It is therefore no accident that the Socialists in power bemoaned the silence of the intellectuals and engaged in cultural anti-Americanism during their preparations for the Sorbonne colloquium, while France's leading intellectuals were reflecting on the link between society and the state, the market economy and the necessary foundations of democratic pluralism.[21] The work of Tocqueville, strangely absent from French debates but central to American social science, finally appeared in all its importance to French intellectuals who had grown up believing that he was of the Right. In this context there was no more revealing a sign of the times than the success of Raymond Aron's *Mémoires*, a virtual best-seller. It was as if with time Sartre had lost the political debate to his old Ecole Normale Supérieure comrade. In the reflections of intellectuals, the very notion of the Left paled in comparison with the issue of democracy. The era of suspicion was slowly giving way to one of total indifference.

INDIFFERENCE VS RECYCLED RESIGNATION: SUMMER 1983 TO THE PRESENT

With the new policy of austerity and *rigueur*, 1983 marked a major turning point. The voluntarist euphoria of the first year gave way to a new realism. Economic and technological considerations which had been relativized during the first voluntarist phase, now dominated a Socialist message which sought to become pragmatic and future-oriented and no longer Utopian. The spirit of Cancun gave way to the spirit of Silicon Valley. Mitterrand's trip to the technological haven was light-years away from the original Latin orientation of Socialist culture.

The Socialist cultural message was indeed transformed and now resembled more closely the world view of the intelligentsia. Yet there was no great reconciliation. The debate around "the silence of the intellectuals of the Left" was in itself symptomatic of the major changes the Left had made in 1983, and it marked the last attempt by the Socialists to reconquer "their" intellectuals. Max Gallo replaced Jack Lang for this battle. Lang's demotion to the rank of junior minister in the third Mauroy government seemed to herald the end of a political line which placed too much emphasis on "everything is cultural". Gallo tried to lure the intelligentsia by stressing that the Left needed them to confront the new challenges of modernity. All references to France's universal mission, ideological support for national liberation movements and American cultural imperialism were dropped. The message was domestic. Yet the intelligentsia turned a deaf ear to Gallo's claim that the Right was once again a menace on the horizon. In his alarm over the fact that the Right was debaptizing streets named after Salvador Allende in newly won municipalities or firing cultural organizers, it saw a caricature of what the Left had stood for originally.

Accepting the fact that there was no way of recapturing a "lost" intellectual audience, the Socialists, in keeping with the new spirit of the *septennat*, turned to more economically oriented cultural partners. Jack Lang and the entire Socialist cultural apparatus in effect "recycled" themselves by concentrating on the role of orchestrators for France's "creators". They promoted French products, arts and culture by emphasizing their modernity and economic "payoff". The United States and its cultural, technological spin-offs were no longer condemned as forces of cultural imperialism, but were imitated, copied and improved so that France's cultural presence in the new technological age could be affirmed. Videodiscs, computerized art, furniture design, comic strips and rock groups replaced Third World speeches. Art and mundane concerns for France's balance of payments were suddenly conjugated in a new pragmatic vision which stressed France's need to be competitive if the country was to keep its international rank. Culture became another way of presenting France on the international economic scene, and no longer embodied the essence of France's universal mission. Jack Lang's reference "culture and economy: one struggle" in his Mexico UNESCO speech was ironically reversed. With a more restricted vision of his role, and deprived of political declarations, Jack Lang attained great popularity, if not with the intellectuals, then with his artistic constituencies and the general public. He was restored to the rank of full minister in July 1984 in the Fabius government.

As of 1983, France's cultural image had lost its previous confidence and intentions. Lang's highly symbolic voice in 1981 and 1982 was supplemented by the sometimes cacophonous voices of other members of Mitterrand's closest entourage. This could be seen as proof of the loss of any clear Socialist identity. Max Gallo, the government spokesman, had already spearheaded the debate over the silence of the intellectuals. Jacques Attali, one of Mitterrand's closest aides, was responsible for the emphasis placed on technological modernization, computers and Silicon Valley "spirit". Laurent Fabius, especially after becoming Prime Minister in 1984, set the tone for a pragmatic notion of modernity in the daily life of industries, schools and offices. Despite assigning top priority to modernity through an ambitious program of placing one computer in every French elementary school, Jean-Pierre Chevènement, the Minister of Education, represented the voice of the Left's traditional values. His educational reforms endorsed classical learning methods based on discipline and hard work rather than experimental student-generated projects, thus pleasing cautious and often conservative parents, not left-wing teachers and militants. Chevènement also implemented the Socialists' attempt to consolidate a new, less ideological non-Communist identity with roots in the Republic.[22]

In the realm of foreign policy, Régis Debray set the tone with a new, more independent French line which marked an end to the more anti-Soviet, pro-American honeymoon of the first Socialist years.[23] With the Euromissile crisis over, and no remaining Communist ministers, the Socialists could return to a more Gaullist stand and slowly begin, in tandem with the United States, less frigid relations with the Soviet Union (while still expelling Soviet spies and maintaining a very strong sense of national purpose). A new much more pro-American policy with respect to technological, cultural, social and even economic orientations went hand in hand with a less pro-American foreign policy.

All of these tendencies took shape, however, in an intellectual/cultural context, irrespective of geographic localization, which seemed to present only one universal value, that of human rights. Eastern European cases made the headlines not just with Solidarity and classic Soviet dissidents (such as Sakharov), but also with the *rocambolesque* story of the exiled Romanian writer Virgil Tanase's "kidnapping", orchestrated by the French secret services to preempt a Romanian murder squad. Interest was also aroused for Chinese artists and dissidents. The new message was that France's human-rights record was exemplary for all other countries.

Perhaps the greatest irony of the Socialist interlude was the entrepreneur achieving a quasi-heroic status – portrayed as leader, creator (of jobs and products for foreign trade), and as cultural role model (witness recent metro advertisements that show young men saying, "*J'abandonne les boîtes* [*de nuit*] *pour créer la mienne*", a play on words meaning "I'm giving up nightclubs to start my own business"). The old anticapitalist, revolutionary certitudes which were still present in May 1981 evaporated amidst a cultural metamorphosis that may remain the greatest (probably indirect) accomplishment of the Socialist political experience.

By changing its political tack – espousing a more open cultural attitude toward the United States; taking greater interest in human rights; recognizing the totalitarianism in some societies; acquiring a more reserved interpretation of Latin American events and wanting to spread flexibility and more open society as well as a more competitive and modest role for France - France's Socialists seemed to have learned from their initial mistakes and to have gradually adopted many of the new credos of the French intelligentsia. But with the thematic *rapprochement*, all illusions of recreating the historical symbiosis between the Left and "its" intelligentsia disappeared.

Absorbed by their own work, in search of greater philosophical rigor and studying political culture, the intellectuals adopted universal values only with respect of nonpolitical themes such as racism, human rights and justice (witness the interest for nonpolitical organizations such as SOS Racisme and the new search for eternal themes and the cross-fertilization of cultures in manifestations such as the "Month of Judaism" around Marek Halter). These themes conceded little importance to the daily political show or the coming elections. The supreme value was democracy; all those who played by its rules and values were henceforth legitimate in a worldview which eschewed revolutionary or anticapitalist visions and condemned only nondemocratic currents, whether Communist or extreme Right. In this context the Socialist was only one democratic voice among many.

A major watershed has thus occurred in France. Intellectual and political spheres have been separated by a noncombative vision of democratic politics which no longer pits a universal Left against a reactionary Right where the intellectuals must make the difference. By addressing problems pragmatically, focusing on future needs and technologies and abandoning eschatological ideological left-wing categories, the Socialist Left underwent a major transformation which forced it to accept the separation of spheres, something which the intellectuals had already espoused by the late 1970s.

The glory of intellectual life and engagement may have suffered in comparison to the days when Saint-Germain-des-Près ruled the international consciences of progressive intellectuals. The great victor, however, has been a more prosaic but more balanced pluralist democracy sheltered from the shrill cries of ideological certainties. This "sea change" of the intellectuals, the Left and culture could only have occurred with the Left in power. Its implications, however, transcend the Left's tenure in office and will provide the perfect litmus test of France's evolution toward a less ideological pluralist democracy. While in office the political Left learned its lesson the hard way due to two key factors: the constraint of economic reality and the silence of the intellectuals. It will now be up to the Right to show that it too has learned the lesson and can bury primary anti-leftist sentiments. Could it be that the "golden" political silence of the intellectuals helped spawn a new French political maturity?

NOTES

1 For a more complete presentation of this theme, see Diana Pinto, "Le Socialisme et les intellectuels", *Le Débat*, (Jan. 1982); and in English: "Mitterrand and the Intellectuals", *Dissent*, (Sept. 1982).

2 F. Furet, *Penser la Révolution Française* (Paris, Gallimard, 1978); and the movement of the "nouveaux philosophes" whose two most visible books (in terms of the media) were André Glucksmann, *Les Maîtres*

penseurs (Paris, B. Grasset, 1977) and Bernard-Henri Lévy, *La Barbarie à visage humain* (Paris, B. Grasset, 1977).

3 Cf. the work of Claude Lefort, *L'Invention démocratique* (Paris, Bernard-Henri, 1981); and the writings which stemmed from the review *Libre* at the crossroads of social anthropology, political theory and political economy, one of the reviews in which the "opening" to Tocqueville took place for the 1968 and post-1968 generation.

4 See D. Pinto, "De l'Anti-américanisme à l'américanophilie: l'itinéraire de l'intelligentsia française", *Commentaire*, (Autumn 1985).

5 Régis Debray, *Le Pouvoir intellectuel en France* (Paris, Ramsay, 1979); and *Le Scribe: genèse du politique* (Paris, B. Grasset, 1980). For an analysis of the new Socialist militants, Jacques Julliard, *Contre la politique professionnelle* (Paris, Seuil, 1977).

6 For a thorough and damning account of this chapter of French intellectual history see Pierre Grémion, *Paris-Prague: la gauche face au renouveau et à la régression tchécoslovaques 1968-1978* (Paris, Julliard, 1985), pp. 272-92.

7 The Cancun speech cannot be found in F. Mitterrand, *Réflexions sur la politique étrangère de la France* (Paris, Grasset, 1986), but its spirit is reflected in a speech given just before in Mexico on 20 October 1981, (pp. 313-20).

8 This fear of the Soviet Union was best reflected in books such as Cornelius Castoriadis, *Devant la guerre* (Paris, Fayard, 1981).

9 This mood of worry *vis-à-vis* the Left was epitomized in Jean Daniel's *L'Ère des ruptures* (Paris, B. Grasset, 1979) and in his editorials in the *Nouvel Observateur* in the month that followed Mitterrand's victory in May 1981.

10 As witnessed in a special issue of the review *Esprit* carrying the highly significant title, "La Gauche pour faire quoi?" and devoted to a critique of the implementation of many ideological reforms in the Socialist Program which were not compatible with France's modernization.

11 The Lang Law on book prices had its left-wing critics, opponents of corporate interests and pleading the cause of the consumer, see *Libération*, (1 Dec. 1981).

12 One such "organic" intellectual was Catherine Clément, a journalist/author who left her job at *Le Matin* to take on a position of responsibility in artistic exchanges at the Quai d'Orsay. Her views on Socialist cultural policy were stated in Clément, Catherine, *Rêver Chacun pour l'autre: sur la politique culturelle*/Catherine Clément, avec des participations de Costa Gavras et al.; et des réponses du Président de la République et du Ministre de la Culture, (Paris, Fayard, 1982).

13 See D. Pinto, "Left-wing Criticism and the End of *L'Etat de grâce*", unpublished paper, Dec. 1981.

14 One of the concrete published outcomes of this interaction was the interview of Edmond Maire by Michel Foucault in *Le Débat*, 25 (May 1983).

15 When asked to explain his silence over Soviet transgressions, Lang stated that "there was not enough time to mention all in one speech" and that the Soviet Union could not be accused of multinational cultural imperialism. The reactions in the press were forthcoming and fierce: B. H. Lévy, "Anti-américanisme primaire", *Le Matin*, (3 Aug. 1982); Guy Konopnicki, "A des Années lumière", *Le Monde*, (7 Aug. 1982), for two hightly symptomatic attacks on Lang.

16 Gilles Anquetil, "On s'est trompé de scandale", *Les Nouvelles littéraires*, (5-18 Aug. 1982); Pierre Daix, "La curieuse croisade de Jack Lang dans les Caraïbes", *Le Quotidien de Paris*, (6 Aug. 1982).

17 See D. Pinto, "De l'anti-américanisme".

18 *Le Matin*, *Le Figaro*, *Le Nouveau journal*, and *Le Quotidien de Paris* all carried special dossiers on the state of French culture in the days that followed the Sorbonne Colloque of 13-16 February 1983.

19 In *Le Monde*, (26 July 1983).

20 The "intellectuals" did not write but they let themselves be interviewed by a journalist, Philippe Boggio, who wrote a two-piece article for *Le Monde*, "Le Silence des intellectuels de gauche", "victoire contretemps", *Le Monde*, (27 July 1983); "Les chemins de traverse", *Le Monde*, (28 July 1983). In one of these interviews, the historian Emmanuel Leroy Ladurie spoke of the necessary "cure de silence" the French intelligentsia had to undertake after having spoken out strongly for wrong causes in the post-war period.

21 Among the 1968 generation, see Pierre Rosanvallon, *Le Moment Guizot* (Paris, Gallimard, 1985); and Marcel Gauchet, *Le Désenchantement du monde* (Paris, Gallimard 1985).

22 Diana Pinto "Vive la République!" *Partisan Review*, (Fall 1985); in French, *Intervention*, 10 (Jan.-March 1985).

23 Régis Debray, *La Puisssance et les rêves* (Paris, Gallimard, 1984); *Les Empires contre l'Europe* (Paris, Gallinard, 1985).

13

The Educational Maelstrom

ANTOINE PROST

Although the creation of a *"service public unifié et laïque de l'Education Nationale"* (which seems to imply the nationalization of the private schools, subsidized by the state) figured prominently in the program of François Mitterrand, it did not play a large role in the presidential and legislative campaigns of 1981. The Catholic hierarchy had also refrained from taking a position on the issue. Today calm reigns again in this domain. By the time of the televised debate between Laurent Fabius and Jacques Chirac on 27 October 1985, if the question of manpower training arose, the education issue did not come up at all. Between 1981 and 1985 however, there was a veritable tempest which brought about the departure of the Minister of Education, Alain Savary, and the Prime Minister himself (14 July 1984). Without reviewing the details of these events, we would here like to do two things. First, we want to demonstrate the parallels between quarrels about schools and pedagogy and understand the links between them. Then we want to show why the Left ultimately suffered a double defeat.

THE SCHOOL QUARREL

The secular tradition of the French Left is widely known. Therefore it was not surprising that the Socialists tried, in keeping with their views, to modify the educational *concordat* imposed by Michel Debré in 1959. The Right itself had already amended it for its own purposes with a 1971 law and the 1977 Guermeur Law, which allowed the private school directors (rather than the state's recteurs) to appoint teachers in the private schools. Over the years, however, the French people had grown accustomed to direct state financing of private schools and the ranks of partisans of strict *laïcité* had thinned. Only 23% of the French population favored subsidies to private education in 1946, as compared with 46% in 1951. In 1974, only 23% opposed subsidy. Indeed, only 40% of François Mitterrand's votes were against any subsidy, versus 36% in favor of complete financing and 19% for partial state financing of private schools. The scholastic status quo was therefore largely accepted, even within the Left.

The Socialists after 1981 were thus forced to choose between abstaining from raising the school question directly or approaching it very prudently. Even before the elections, Mitterrand had chosen the second route, affirming that the *grant service public* should result from "negotiation and not from a unilateral decision" (letter of 1 May 1981).

The Minister of Education, Alain Savary, adopted the same attitude, discreetly discussing the topic, and avoiding rash statements.

It became apparent very quickly that the "united and secular service" that a personal advisor had included in the President's election program could not be realized. It would have led to a costly and intolerable power struggle. The abandonment of this crucial proposal, the fundamental point for the laïcs, was decided before the summer of 1982. Careful observers would have noticed that, on 4 August 1982, the cabinet did not use the "united . . . service" expression a single time when reporting on ongoing discussion about educational policy. From then on, Savary's goals were to organize the progressive reconciliation and coordination of state and private education, with the latter to be subjected to the same rules as the former regarding size and school calendar.

Catholic education constitutes more than 90 per cent of private education. The Catholic hierarchy, therefore, was a powerful voice. Conscious of the historical impact which a peace treaty concerning education signed with a leftist government would have, it negotiated cautiously and firmly, but with a clear desire to conclude. The proposed law finally adopted by the government on 8 April 1984, met with its approval excepting only one provision: the option for those private-sector schoolteachers who so desired to become Civil Servants. It was confidentially made known to the Elysée, however, that the prelates would not oppose this point if its implementation were discussed.[1]

The supporters of secular education rejected the compromise. It is obvious that they were not aware of the state of public opinion on the question. For example, certain officials of the National Committee on Secular Education questioned the accuracy of an IFOP opinion poll requested by the Minister on this subject in April 1982.[2] Perhaps it was personally too costly for them to recognize that their ideal was no longer possible. But the fact remained that the government could not have scheduled a vote on the Savary Bill without having overcome their resistance. The laïcs were believed to be committed to the Savary Bill, therefore. Then, on 22 May 1984 Prime Minister Mauroy accepted Socialist amendments to stiffen the bill in a laïc sense which shattered the consensus. What followed is well known: the massive 24 June demonstration (blessed by three bishops), the obstructionist tactics announced by the senators and the final withdrawal of the bill by Mitterrand (12 and 14 July 1984).

When all was said and done, the real stakes of this complex negotiation were limited. The principle of academic freedom was not questioned at all, nor was state financing of private education.[3] However, what took place was an unprecedented mobilization marked by huge rallies like the one in Versailles on 5 March 1984, which involved one million participants. Private school Parent–Teacher Associations (PTAs) generated a movement that went far beyond their rather restricted circle. The opposition parties poured themselves into the movement. This was politically sound, of course, but the movement was out of their control as well. Various polls show that in June 1984, 55 per cent of the French people thought that the Savary Bill infringed liberties and 56 per cent approved the demonstration of 24 June.[4] How can we account for the vast size of this mobilization?

Undoubtedly, religious allegiances played a role locally (in Brittany, for example). On the whole, however, they did not matter much. Approximately 7% of the French populace are practicing Catholics and only 16% of school children attend private schools. Yet more than half the French condemned the Savary Bill. Given these statistics, many French people without religious conviction apparently support a type of school to which they would not send their own children. Moreover, close to half of the parents of public-school pupils, 47% to be exact, disapproved of the bill.[5] Conversely, parents did not send their children to private schools primarily for religious reasons. According to the April 1982 IFOP poll (which confirmed previous results),[6] religious education was only the sixth most important reason for selecting private schools. The revived war of the schools in 1984 differed from preceding ones, then. Catholics were no longer the first to defend their faith.

In truth, parents were defending their children's future. The 1982 IFOP poll states this fact eloquently: among those selecting public education, 85 per cent favored retaining the option to choose between public and private education, and 58 per cent saw private education as a possible recourse.[7] With the reforms of the Fifth Republic, public education became a vast bureaucracy with little pity for those who did not understand its inner workings. To enroll a child in the primary school of one's choice was impossible: each school had a precise zone of recruitment, a "sector". This "sectorization" also determined enrollment in secondary school. Then followed "orientation", a complex procedure which definitively decided the assignment of students to a particular section, and, as a result, to more or less prestigious future prospects. It was a rigid system, disliked by many parents, particularly those parents whose children were denied attendance in the desired section's schools and those who quite simply did not understand the way enrollment worked and felt helpless.

The private school therefore became a second chance, the best recourse against an undesired assignment or orientation. The proof of this was the large number of students transferring from public to private schools, especially those students at critical transition points such as the beginning of the *sixième* and the *seconde*. In 1980, 10 per cent of students in the *seconde* of private institutions had come from public schools. The vague discontent aroused by the educational bureaucracy, amplified by the new wave of antistate liberalism, was without doubt the essential reason for the mobilization favoring instructional freedom. It was a demand for deregulation.

THE PEDAGOGICAL DEBATE

The 1983–84 education war differed from preceding campaigns in another way: it was accompanied by widespread questioning of the quality of public education. Until recently, it was generally acknowledged that the best instruction was to be found in the lycées and public schools. They offered a better qualified faculty, recruited through very competitive examinations, and a more rigorous screening of pupils before promotion to the next grade. With the exception of certain schools maintained by prestigious religious orders, private education could not rival that of the state.

It is quite different today. For one thing, the faculty in private schools has been massively upgraded since the Debré Law, which allowed the recruitment of teachers who had the same background as those in the lycées. In addition to being equal in ability, they have the reputation for caring more about their pupils. Pedagogical reasons play a determining role in the choice of a private school; in fact, the reasons mentioned most frequently in the 1982 IFOP poll substantiate this claim. Respondents mentioned the following order of priorities: private institutions provide not only instruction, but also education (92%); both discipline and the quality of the faculty are superior to those of state schools (90%); and relations between parents and teachers are more fruitful (86%). Next in line was the possibility of receiving religious instruction (64%) and innovative pedagogical methods (59%). Proximity to home was mentioned in only 37% of the cases. Another survey carried out in northern France in 1976 placed better human and moral training as the first reason. Christian education was next, followed by the belief that "they take better care of our children".[8]

As unkind to the public schools as the picture drawn by these polls appears, it does seem to be confirmed by the unequal satisfaction of parents with one or the other type of school. Sixty-two per cent of parents of privately educated children were very satisfied with the schools, 37% were quite satisfied: a total of 99% positive opinions. Parents of publicly educated children are only 76% satisfied and, among them, only 25% are "very satisfied".[9] The dissymetry is striking.

In this context, the policies of Alain Savary, which aimed to reduce the difference between the two forms of schooling, might be perceived as risking the degradation of supposed "good" teaching. Why propose aligning good private teaching with a public rival not up to its standards? Opponents of the Savary Bill defended the right to "difference" in private education: 35% felt that private education should not be required to follow the same rules as public.[9] More generally, currently fashionable ideas were transferred to education: the state's performance, by definition, would be worse than that of private enterprise. Consequently, in order to improve education, it ought to be freed of state supervision. Posters and flyers displaying a birdcage were widely distributed in May 1984, and they went so far as to proclaim, "Free the school", implying that the schools were as bad as Gulags.

Paradoxically, the strictly pedagogical reforms undertaken by Savary did not benefit from this climate. The authors of the principal reports guiding the minister's action (André de Peretti, Louis Legrand and Antoine Prost) disregarded the polls mentioned above, but nevertheless were sensitive to the effects of the bureaucratization of the educational system. In order to train teachers better and revitalize the schools or lycées,[10] they proposed a decentralization of the system which would bolster the initiative of individual institutions. They hoped that each school would embark on its own educational project. They advocated better supervision of each pupil's work through a tutorial system. Their proposals did not require tremendous upheaval, but moderate evolution affecting the methodology of teaching in the system more than its structures. This orientation probably responded to the needs of the moment for it rested on sound documentation. Moreover, teachers themselves endorsed the proposals widely. In 1985, 77 per cent of teachers favored greater autonomy for educational institutions.[11]

Far from being supported by general opinion, however, this new pedagogical policy prompted a chorus of criticism. This pedagogical quarrel, which became increasingly widespread, in turn reinforced the private schools quarrel. The chronological overlap between these two opinion campaigns merits note. Louis Legrand delivered his report on secondary education (*collèges*) in December 1982, at the very moment when the Church hierarchy was refusing to discuss the initial propositions of the Minister of Education. A wave of protest arose immediately against the idea of instituting a "tutorial" for school pupils. In the winter of 1983-84 several books denounced lowered educational standards and pedagogical laxity.[12] In recognition of their large readership, these topics became the subject of a debate on the television program "Apostrophes" on 3 March 1984, exactly two days before the Versailles demonstration.

This wave of criticism originated from two distinct sources. The conservative Right held that individual supervision of pupils' work was an attempt at gaining an ideological or moral hold over children. This mobilized parents against the tutorial that would "take away their children". In keeping with tradition, this position advocated authoritarian education where students had only to do what they were told. The vehemence of these criticisms was so excessive as to be suspect. For example, in *Le Point* (21 May 1984), Jean-François Revel stated that "all education in the proper sense is from now on positively forbidden" in elementary schools, while Michel Debré asked the Minister of Education if it was true that it was henceforth forbidden to learn to read.[13]

More surprising, at least at first glance, was that the Right's viewpoint was supported by part of the Left. The Trotskyite tendency of the FEN (the Fédération de l'Education Nationale, the teachers' union) which split in 1984 to join Force Ouvrière, resurrected the positions of the intransigent defenders of secularism. It fought against an educational renewal that seemed to it to weaken the image of teachers and learning and to abandon administrative uniformity and therefore to threaten the equality of citizens and the unity of the nation. These criticisms were reiterated by many Parisian intellectuals who, from 1965 to 1968, had themselves been followers of the most dogmatic Marxism and were often doctrinaire Socialists. These voices joined those of the Right in calling for pedagogical "restoration". They also indisputably found a receptive audience among teachers, especially those with the most advanced degrees, the oldest and those teaching in the better lycées.[14]

This campaign was unjustifiable. In fact, the pedagogical "restoration" that it called for had been happening since the mid-1970s while the audience for liberal educational methods had continued to diminish. To criticize pedagogical innovation was therefore like finishing off a badly wounded soldier. Careful examination of the facts[15] showed that selectivity had been strengthened in the schools and lycées for more than ten years, and that the famous "standards" were certainly rising. None of this mattered much for the media which orchestrated the campaign. Instead they repeated *ad nauseam* that students knew nothing and that teachers no longer taught. In the end, the public began to believe it.

THE FAILURE

In July 1984, therefore, the government confronted double waves of opposition to the Savary Bill and to any educational reform. It might have faced up to it, of course. At the time, some people believed that it had resolved to do so. But in the end the government preferred to abandon its plans. The bill on private education was withdrawn, purely and simply. Mitterrand hinted at it on 12 July and announced it explicitly on 14 July. Like everyone else, Savary learned of the decision while watching television. Apparently he still cannot understand it.[16] In fact, it is difficult to understand why, when a historic compromise was on the verge of succeeding, the President of the Republic did not oppose the Socialist amendment which cast doubt on it. Why, later, after having hardened his stand, did he suddenly back down? Less ambitious texts, drafted by Savary's successor and adopted in the fall of 1984, subsequently settled some of the disputes that existed between the state and the private schools. But they did not chart any middle course. What happened was an armistice, not a peace treaty.

This change on the private schools question did not necessarily imply an about-face on the pedagogical question, of course. The choice of Jean-Pierre Chevènement as Savary's replacement settled this additional issue, however. The first words of the new Minister were interpreted as the blow of the whistle ending recess, hinting that efforts at educational renewal had not been serious. Insisting on the scientific competence of teachers, on the solidity of the knowledge to be transmitted and the indispensable effort and work of students, without mentioning the equally critical need to adapt instruction to the actual needs of students and to appeal to their interests, Chevènement accepted an opposition between learning and students that one would have believed outdated, siding with the "scholars" and not the "teachers". This speech was also greeted with enthusiasm by those considered the most reactionary inhabitants of the university, the Société des Agrégés and Union Nationale Interuniversitaire.[17] The right-wing press did not spare its praise, either.

Subsequently, the Minister's speeches became more balanced. On more than one question he pursued the policies of his predecessor, in the reform of collèges, for example. But the new programs and instructions for elementary schools, divided by disciplines, were marked by their encyclopedism and insistence on the primacy of teacher initiatives. The activities of students appeared, in their light, to be the teacher's job. It probably was appropriate to reestablish a certain balance following the overemphasis on student "awakening" in 1969. The programs of 1977, 1978 and 1980 had already attempted to redress things, however. By 1984 the pendulum had gone well beyond the point of equilibrium.[18]

The public was elated. On 2 September 1985 Le Point commented on a poll in which lycée students rated their teachers. The number one criticism of their teachers was the lack of communication (30%), ranking well ahead of professional incompetence (21.8%). Being able to interest students in learning (21%) came before competence (19.5%) in the definition of a good teacher, and indifference came just after incompetence in that of the bad teacher (16.1% and 17.6%). Le Point's headline ran: "Profs reinstated" with the subtitle: "What a revolution! The end of the 1968-style dilettantism."[19]

CONCLUSION

The place which state education holds in the French democratic tradition is well known. The Republic was basically universal suffrage plus free, obligatory and secular schooling.

As far as matters of schooling were concerned, the Left traditionally pursued three objectives: democratization, secularism and teaching methods focused on the student. These three features characterized the work of Jules Ferry. But Ferry, as Minister, was not only responsible for the bills on free, compulsory, and secular primary schooling, but he also mentioned active teaching methods and active school and lycée curricula, in opposition to the authoritarian methods ascribed to the Congreganists who were men of dogma. Ferry hoped "to dictate the lesson to the child as a judgment no longer, but to make him find it . . . to excite and awaken the spontaneity of the child . . . instead of imprisoning him in rules already made".[20] These three features surfaced again in the major text serving as a reference for the Left from 1945 to 1968, the - unrealized - Langevin-Wallon plan (1947).

With respect to these objectives, where did the recent Socialist experiment stand? It definitely honored democratization (in the wider sense of distribution), in particular with Chevènement's recent goal of 80 per cent of the youth earning the *baccalauréat*. On *laïcité* things are less clear. The adversaries of secularism were incontestably at the center of the movement that swept away the Savary Bill. Its withdrawal was therefore a defeat for the secularists. But one cannot forget that they contributed to this final defeat. On the whole they preferred compromise on the official existence of subsidized private education, rather than run the risk of progressive unification which might introduce pluralism into the very bosom of the state school.[21] In a way, both the secularists and their adversaries refused an evolution in which their identities would have been at risk.

The attitude of the *laïcs* may be interpreted either as fidelity to their tradition or rigidity in so far as their ideal proved inapplicable in present-day society. It must therefore be concluded that the Socialists were the victims of the vast international trend of antistate liberalism, of a hostility to regulations reinforced by the bureaucratic evolution of the school system and of their own refusal to modernize their reform plans.

The same ambiguity was found in pedagogy. In a sense, the restoration answers the very conservative demands of a population anxious about order, security and the newly unruly behavior of youth. If the schoolmaster "on high" is reinstated, it is to control students better and instill in them a respect for authority. Praise for authoritarian teaching here serves the moral order.

The Left assuredly contradicts itself in this dogmatism. But not *all* of the Left. A certain Jacobin tradition leads parts of the Left directly to such dogmatism. Despite their political roots in this tradition, the teachers are divided. The decentralizing discourse of Savary obliging them to face their responsibilities toward students upset them. Chevènement's discourse reassured them, in contrast, by absolving them of responsibility for their students' failure and reaffirming their identity as specialists in a discipline. Even if such teachers are not a majority, many adhere to this vision of their function.

More profoundly, French society is today settling some of the issues with its schools which were raised in 1968. Among teachers, the divisions provoked by the "events" of 1968 have not been forgotten. Some have been seeking revenge. Others have been converted to 1968 ideals. Still others, having become teachers, have repudiated the earlier identities which they had held as students at the time. Passions are, therefore, quick to flare up.

Outside the teaching profession few have forgotten that the explosion of 1968 came from the universities. This fact conjures up a vague danger to be averted. A door through which unforeseeable demons might one day enter should be kept tightly closed. A minister of the Left like Savary, despite his caution and reason, seemed, to the Right, to open that door by his liberal initiatives. A more authoritarian leftist minister could, on the contrary, avert the peril on a lasting basis: Chevènement chased away the shadows of 1968. Because of this, and because economic crisis and unemployment constitute effective antidotes to generous Utopias the Right in power doesn't fear such demons.

NOTES

1 Alain Savary, *En toute liberté* (Paris, Hachette, 1985), p. 96.

2 Ibid., p. 127.

3 Complete text of the bill, ibid., p. 220.

4 Polls published respectively by *Paris-Match*, (8 June 1984); and *La Croix*, (22 June 1984).

5 Poll published by *La Croix*, (22 June 1984).

6 Cf. a poll carried out by the IFOP in 1978 and the Catholic weekly *La Vie* which cited the following situation regarding the reasons behind choosing private education: the seriousness of the studies (25%), religious education (21%), which was equal to discipline and supervision of the students. Also Robert Ballion, "L'Enseignement privé, une école sur mesure", *Revue française de sociologie*, (April–June 1980).

7 Alain Savary, En toute liberté p. 125-6.

8 Poll cited by the *Cahiers de l'actualité religieuse et sociale*, 15 February–1 March 1982, p. 182.

9 Poll published in *Le Matin*, May 30 1984.

10 André de Peretti, *La Formation des personnels de l'Education national* (Paris, Documentation Française, 1982); Louis Legrand, *Pour un collège démocratique* (Paris, Documentation Française, 1983); Antoine Prost, *Les Lycées et leurs études au seuil du XXIe siècle* (Paris, Centre national de documentation pédagogique, 1983).

11 Poll from *Le Monde*, September 10, 1985.

12 Among others, see Jocqueline de Romilly, *L'enseignement en détress* (Paris, Julliard, 1983); Maurice T. Maschino, *Voulez-vous vraiment des enfants idiots?* (Paris, Hachette, 1984); Jean-Pierre Despin, Marie-Claude Bartholi, *Le Poisson rouge dans le Perrier* (Paris, Criterion, 1983); M. Jumilhac, *Le Massacre des innocents* (Paris, Plon, 1984). Jean-Claude Milner's *De l'école* (Paris, Seuil, 1984) came a little later along with Hélène Huot's *Et voilà pourquoi ils ne savent pas lire* (Paris, Minerve, 1985). See also the special issue of *Le Débat*, September 1984.

13 Written question.

14 The *Le Monde* poll which we have already cited clearly shows this phenomenon.

15 We tried this in our own report and, more recently, in *Eloge des Pedagogues* (Paris, Seuil, 1985), supporting our points on the age of students, the evolution of the rate of failure and international studies.

16 Alain Savary, *En toute liberté*, p. 179-80.

17 See the reaction to the press conference of the Minister at the 1984 rentrée.

18 Ministère de l'Education nationale, *Ecole élémentaire, Programmes et instructions* (Paris, Centre national de documentation pédagogique, 1985).

19 The poll at issue was done in collaboration with *Phospore*, a magazine for *lycéens* which commented upon it somewhat differently. See *Phospore*, September 1985, which also published an interview with the Minister in which students are very important.

20 Speech to the pedagogical congress, April 2, 1980 in *Robiquet*, Volume III, p. 320.

21 I agree here with Jean-Marie Mayeur, "La Guerre Scolaire", *XXe siècle, revue d'histoire*, January–March 1985, p. 107.

14

Decentralization in France

A Historical Perspective

CATHERINE GRÉMION

A CHEQUERED HISTORY

For the past ten years, innumerable commentators have written that the Left in France is reversing a political tradition by implementing reforms to decentralize the country.[1] According to them, decentralization was an idea thought up by the Right, then awkwardly adopted by the Left. No matter what your point of view, this way of encapsulating history is unsatisfactory. A more dispassionate look at the history of this ideological and political issue shows the astounding continuity of certain themes of decentralization discourse. What is also striking is the degree to which decentralization partakes of France's common political heritage, no matter which group claims paternity for it. Decentralization has been much more than an ideological issue: it has been a passion of those in opposition.

A closer look at the political pronouncements of the nineteenth century shows a continual overlapping of three polemics. The first merged decentralization and grass-roots democracy, the latter of which in turn was joined to an elected executive and representatives, each exercising executive and legislative power over local affairs. The second concerned local administration. It is widely believed that decentralization is a contemporary solution to the encroachments of Parisian bureaucracy and a way to rationalize administrative circuits, but this is simply not true. As far back as the first half of the nineteenth century, Tocqueville expounded on the theme of decentralization, identifying some very modern-sounding advantages: first, proximity makes for good communication and the rapid spread of information; second, in a system where every decision has to be referred to Paris, the capacity for taking initiative and assuming responsibility is diminished. Needless to say, the line between decentralization and "deconcentration" is rather fuzzy in this approach.

The third polemic dealt with what could be called "natural communities". It is here that those who claim decentralization is a right-wing idea find their ammunition. It is obviously true that, well before the Revolution, a traditional school of thought lauded the merits of the ancient provinces and communes. After 1789, this school rallied around a common hostility to the new administrative districts, the *départements*, whose boundaries they wrongly criticized as being artificial.

This hostility was indeed openly and essentially antirevolutionary. By referring to the land and the strength of historical boundaries, there was diametrical opposition

237

to the political concepts of the Constituent Assembly which lauded individualism, rationalism and universality. Despite this, Republicans – and later, certain Socialists – did not hesitate to play on the heartstrings of childhood attachments to the village square. This sentiment continued right up to the 1981 election.

The three instances mentioned above roughly depict the way of thinking of those supporting decentralization. The first two themes, however, can hardly be considered the exclusive property of any particular political tendency. Only the appeal to the blood-ties of community and the land is a right-wing theme, but even here not exclusively. Decentralization is a fundamental element in the French national political heritage.

While the Republic of the eighteenth century was itself on the side of centralization, the *ultras*, under the Restoration, pleaded the cause of decentralization, which they hastened to abandon upon coming to power. The Liberals picked up the torch and increasingly declared themselves to be for decentralization. The Second Empire got under way by taking a number of steps to reestablish, though only partially, the centralized system of Year VIII. The opposition vigorously and almost unanimously defended decentralization against this display of authority. The liberal empire took this into account, and the first fifteen years of the Third Republic, with the 1871 and 1884 acts, saw the conversion of all Republicans to this idea. Louis Adolphe Thiers realized that the only way to counterbalance the revolutionary fervor of Paris was to rely on the basically conservative provinces. The Radicals were late to convert, and did not try to build a political base in the countryside until the early 1880s, when Paris had swung to the Right and was brandishing the threat of Boulangism. It was at that point that Gambetta spoke of the "new radical social strata that would furnish local society with its new elites".

In 1903, both Republicans and Monarchists proclaimed their allegiance to decentralization. Times had changed: those in power were now giving top priority to the consolidation of the Republic, which needed to stand up to Monarchists as well as Caesarists. The fight for the Republic had to go hand in hand with the fight against the Church, which was also clamoring for a strong state. These ambiguities are reflected in the following passage of Clémenceau: "For us, decentralization means the establishment of centers of freedom. For them [the Monarchists], it means the creation of Roman enclaves, bastions against the liberating law of the French Republic."

It is tempting to see in decentralization merely an opposition passion, which grew stronger as the state became more authoritarian or as the time out of power grew longer. It followed that such a passion was destined to diminish quickly once the opposition came to power. This explanation is nonetheless an oversimplification. It overlooks both the frequency of minor reforms dotting the modern history of France and especially the discreet changes in institutions, the corps of Civil Servants and administrative practices. With the new Socialist reform, decentralization is once again a burning question.

Post-war moves towards decentralization: technocrats,
notables and the new elite

After the successive shocks of World War II, Vichy and the Liberation, the grass-roots politico-administrative system was shaken by contradictory tendencies. Upheavals in national politics, however, led to the reestablishment of pre-war routine. The same *notables* returned to power, backed by institutions that remained unchanged. Soon, though, plans for renewal began to germinate, fostered by newcomers to the political scene: technocrat–planners, zealots of *aménagement du territoire*, and advocates of changing local elites. Such different groups represented a new approach to decentralization marked by a desire to modernize the country.

The philosophy of Maurras, incorporated into the counterrevolutionary regime of Vichy, led to a corporatist regional reform plan that paradoxically proved slightly ahead of its time. The plan proposed the representation of organized interests within the framework of an active regional administration oriented towards economic development. In many ways, it prefigured the reform that was to come. The fact that the plan was ahead of its time and was voted down after the Liberation blocked debate for years to come. No one at the Constituent Assembly defended the regionalist cause, but some, like General de Gaulle at Bayeux, did speak of new forms of socioprofessional representation. Their suggestions were not heeded, however. The general climate was dominated by the desire to return to democratic representation, and the idea of giving the regions an economic function that would organize various interest groups must have seemed like heresy. Popular opinion held that only duly elected representatives should have the right to speak in the name of the nation.

The first step toward decentralization took shape with the 1950 policy of *aménagement du territoire* launched by Minister of Town Planning Claudius Petit. It was to come into its own during the governments of Mendès–France and Edgar Faure. For the first time, those actually involved in productive work, who until then were incredibly underrepresented in the local power structure, found a way into decision-making circuits. For the first time, a public body did not operate according to the rules of the traditional *notables*. Despite this innovation, the government and political parties proved incapable of formulating a doctrine that clearly defined local and national jurisdictions. They were faced with too many conflicting pressures. Fresh thinking about decentralization was to come from those who, by necessity or choice, were outside the *notables'* sphere of influence.

The early sixties witnessed a proliferation of plans for a complete overhaul of the country's territorial administration. They were the fruit of discussions involving enlightened technocrats at the Commissariat Général au Plan, the DATAR (Délégation pour l'Aménagement du Territoire et l'Action Régionale), as well as leading nonaffiliated figures generally on the non-Communist Left, and other groups outside political circles or on their periphery.

At the Socialist Party convention in Grenoble, Michel Rocard attracted attention by combining the theme of democracy with that of economic efficacy. He stressed that a centralized state created cumulative disparaties in economic development which prevent well-balanced growth. Here, too, there is a remarkable similarity between the ideas developed by governmental experts of the time and left-wing innovators. The DATAR spoke of the "growing industrial desert", of "social costs", and of "external diseconomies", whereas the Parti Socialiste Unifié incriminated "unequal exchange", the "confiscation of added value", and the "colonization of the provinces". Both sides were talking about the same thing, however. One group wanted "integrated" economic development while the other spoke of "development centered on each locality". Roughly speaking, the remedy was the same. Each local community should be able to refashion its economy and master its own development. That was all very well, but it was no match for resistance from the traditional network of *notables*.

There is no need here to describe in detail the legal changes that slowly gave municipalities and departments more autonomy, designed instruments to promote groupings of communes and created the regions. Suffice it to recall the attempts at reform during the Fifth Republic by various governments that had no intention of destabilizing the entire local politico-administrative structure. Even so, they were met by the determined resistance of the provincial establishment, which succeeded in completely watering down any and all new bills.

There was a second type of resistance to the reforming tendencies of the sixties. The departmental establishment progressively took over the regional centers of decision-making. In the face of demands for greater community autonomy, the Gaullist state preferred a "regionalizing" approach that would strengthen the "periphery" by making the regions an echelon for negotiation and study. The regionalization law of 1972 clearly reflected this political choice by giving regions the status of mere public establishments specializing in economic planning. This approach made it impossible to question the authority and power of the local *notables*.

The regionalization law of 1972 tacitly acknowledged the failure of General de Gaulle's 1969 referendum by turning the regions into federations of departments. They would be responsible for distributing funds equitably rather than promoting independent policy. For Georges Pompidou, this approach was not a renunciation but rather a political plan: the idea was to entrust the traditional power networks with the task of absorbing the shock of industrialization.

Until the early 1970s, the Left was as badly prepared as the Right to propose a coherent innovative plan for decentralization. It was content to join the chorus of protest whenever the government tried to group communes together or institute regional planning. There was no one within the narrow confines of the established political organizations – which were themselves weakened from within by local officials on the defensive – to goad the Socialist Left to action. It was outside these circles, in the Groupements d'Action Municipale (GAM), that modern reformers found the social movement they needed to propose a real alternative.

The birth of the GAMs can be traced to the realization by the Left that it was time for collective action, not only in the limited sphere of the workplace, but also in the "daily reality of alienation". Translated into ordinary language this meant a movement that would grapple with such practical matters as housing, public transport and education. The GAMs attracted "nonpolitical" people as well as activists from various political organizations who felt the need for direct action, or at least for something practical to do. These grass-roots discussion and action groups proved to be an optimal form of collective cooperation for the Left. The success of these groups gave the Left new hopes for decentralization. Speakers for the new Socialist Party talked of creating another type of municipal government by setting up extramunicipal committees. The only way to "change our cities" was outside the normal channels, bypassing institutional roadblocks.

Paradoxically, by the time the Socialists came to power in 1981 leading a coalition of old-fashioned politicos and modern movements for self-management, this type of proposal for a model local administration was already running out of steam. It is not easy to keep ordinary citizens participating actively for any length of time. Imperceptibly, where such administrations had come to exist, an intermediate layer of professionals or regular activists took over, acting as a screen between the managers and voters. Since no one seemed to notice for some time, the shock was all the more brutal for mayors like Hubert Dubedout or Françoise Gaspard when they lost the 1983 municipal elections.

One thing was clear throughout this progression: the Left - for traditional, intellectual and political reasons - was definitely on the side of decentralization. These reasons, unfortunately, did not coincide, but since the Left was forever in opposition, it did not matter. The Bonnet Bill, proposing the transfer of more responsibility to local institutions, remained under discussion. However, left-wing members of Parliament continued to vacillate in their opinion of the bill, giving their critics an ideal opportunity to denounce them.

SOCIALIST DECENTRALIZATION: HOW THE 1981 REFORM CAME INTO BEING

The kind of decentralization that was in fashion in May 1981 was neither the self-management nor the reformer-planner type. This is clear from the choice of title for the ministry created to organize the process: the Ministry of the Interior and decentralization. Logically, jurisdiction should have gone to the Minister of State for the Plan and *Aménagement du territoire*. Gaston Defferre, the new Minister, was first and foremost a local *notable*. Like the Prime Minister, he was mayor of a major regional metropolis (Marseilles) and was prepared to defend the rights of big cities. "What we locally elected officials find intolerable," he stated, "is that someone else decides for us what our cities need." His goal was clear from the outset: direct management of city affairs without the intolerable control of the prefect. The basic principles of the new system would be institutional autonomy and its corollary, legal responsibility. This was in sharp contrast to the earlier Bonnet reform, which tried above all to set up structures for cooperation to fit the needs of the small communes.

The Prime Minister's counsellors on decentralization were two local technocrats: Michel Delebarre, General Secretary of the Municipality of Lille, and Pierre Marnot, who held the same job at Nantes. Thus, managers of big cities - Lille, Nantes and Marseilles - were in charge of the reform. At the Ministry of the Interior and Decentralization, Gaston Defferre found that the ministerial department in charge of local communities was accustomed to this type of thinking, for it had prepared the bill that the preceding government had discussed at length in the Senate. Ready to take action, Defferre proclaimed the Ministry's Director, Pierre Richard (originally appointed by Giscard d'Estaing) to be competent and asked him to stay on.

On the whole, the situation was quite favorable for Defferre's grand plan. In Paris, the Minister had the President's full support and the backing of an exceptionally large majority in the National Assembly. In the provinces, the Left was in a very strong position: both the 1977 and 1978 municipal and departmental elections and the 1981 parliamentary elections were successful. The Left found it could control the regional councils thanks to the newly elected deputies, who were legally members of the councils. The new Socialist majority thus dominated 13 regional councils out of 22, 12 of which were in the hands of the Socialist party alone. What more could one have asked for when trying to consolidate one's gains on the local level?

Defferre was determined to push through his decentralization plan and wanted it to bear his name. Thanks to his extensive administrative and parliamentary experience, he persuaded the government to agree to a series of reforms in successive installments, involving institutions, apportionment of responsibilities, financial and human resources and, if necessary, reform of the election law. Defferre's primary goal, however, was the transfer of executive power from the prefect (departmental or regional) to the president of an elected regional assembly. The first part of the reform was to include institutions (i.e. issues of tutelage and the respective powers of the state and local communities). An irreversible situation had to be created as quickly as possible.

In less than two months the reform plan was completed, and the Council of Ministers adopted it on 2 July 1981. The reform did not choose between *de facto* competitors; the communes, departments and regions all received the same autonomy and structure based on that of the communes. The plan, in order to counterbalance the new freedom of these elected officials, did give new power to the judges of the administrative court, regional *chambres des comptes*, and national *cour des comptes*. The prefect, therefore, lost some of his authority, which was in turn carefully distributed among the various interested parties.

Ministers in the opposition

The first and most serious difficulty that the Minister of the Interior and Decentralization encountered was adding financial provisions to his institutional reform. By making the infrastructural subsidies through block grants, the state would have to hand them over to local communities, which would give the latter greater freedom of action. On the other hand, this move would also deprive the national political and administrative agents of their power to guide the use of these funds, thus curtailing their ability to create policies and not just orient the rules and regulations.

It is not surprising then that Defferre met with the combined opposition of the ministries which relied on those subsidies, as well as the Ministry of Finance and the Budget. For once, they were all on the same side of the fence; Deferre's plan was a threat to their autonomy. Despite their past history as ardent promoters of decentralization, ministers began to change their stance. Laurent Fabius led the troops to battle against an excessive transfer of state funding to local authorities, and most ministers refused to give up such a large part of their arsenal.

The parliamentary debate

The key man at the National Assembly is the Chairman of the Law Committee. Two of Michel Rocard's followers held the job successively: Alain Richard, member of the Conseil d'Etat and mayor of Saint-Ouen-l'Aumone; and Jean-Pierre Worms, a sociologist specializing in analyzing the local system who had frequented the Parti Socialiste Unifié and the Club Jean Moulin and landed in the Socialist Party at the time of the 1972 Left Common Program.

The parliamentary session opened on the floor of the National Assembly with the government's bill – the first test of strength for all the political parties in 20 years. Decentralization was to be the proving ground for coexistence of the new majority and opposition forces in the legislature. Even though the Left had won control of the Assembly, the Senate was still in the hands of the Right.

On the occasion of the session, both chambers of Parliament started a new tradition which continued through all stages of the decentralization process. Each chamber systematically refused to examine the bill that the other chamber had submitted for approval. Thus, the Senate debated its own bill and not, as is the rule, the government bill amended by the Assembly. In similar fashion, the Assembly only conducted a second reading of its own bill on almost every disputed point.

Real confrontation between the government and the opposition was in fact limited to a few questions, in particular the order and rate at which the reforms were to be adopted. In the National Assembly, Olivier Guichard, who before 1981 had been responsible for the then government's decentralization program, argued that the Socialists were putting the cart before the horse by allowing discussion of a bill defining the rights of each echelon of local representation to precede the definition of its jurisdiction. The leaders of the opposition, who had only the power of words left, all took up Guichard's argument.

The opposition in the Senate, conversely, held two trump cards. It controlled the agenda and, more importantly, could propose the bill of Defferre's predecessor, on which it had already done a great deal of work. Therefore, when the Defferre Bill came before the Senate, the senators were ready with a counterproposal and could, as Guichard suggested, put the horse before the cart. The senators were ready to discuss simultaneously both the statutes and the powers of the local institutions. They amended the bill to include two new subsections on the powers of local institutions, as well as a third, stipulating creation of a body of local Civil Servants, and a statute for locally elected officials.

The stakes were high. Both sides sought credit for decentralization; the opposition was trying to grab it away from the government by passing its own bill through the Senate. The opposition tried to do exactly the same thing in 1982 when the government bill on the division and attribution of powers came up from discussion.

Nevertheless, real grounds for dispute between the government and opposition were not all that numerous. Two essential points continued to divide the two chambers until the end of the debates: the role of the prefects and local aid to business and industry. The Senate refused to accept the complete dismantling of the prefects' authority over local governments. The senators of the opposition expressed the concern of the mayors of small communes who preferred postponing responsibility for decisions until the prefect had checked them and assured the senators of their legality. The importance of the tutelage of the prefect was clearly expressed at the mayors' convention, which questioned the principle of responsibility on which Defferre had built his plan. Defferre stood his ground and the opposition appealed to the Constitutional Council, which condemned parts of the bill without really shaking the foundations of the reform.

The senators were reluctant to compel communes financially and juridically to come to the aid of companies in trouble. Since senators generally hold a local office in addition to their national duties, they understandably wanted strict legislation allowing them to resist local pressure groups capable of forcing more and more mayors into excessively risky situations.

The other items on the decentralization agenda gave rise to technical discussions in both the Senate and Assembly. Even the discussion on basic principles, however, helped to attenuate dissension rather than heighten it; both the majority and the opposition had had practical experience of local problems, and this tended to draw them together. The key to future implementation was thus revealed in the debates.

A delicate balance between freedom of action and responsibility

The criticisms of the opposition more often than not reflected the genuine, though not always verbalized, concerns of the majority. The best example of this was the question of the financial responsibility of local officials. The government bill stipulated that the mayor, as well as the president of the regional general council, could be held accountable before the *cour des comptes* for public expenditures in the communes and the departments. This was a truly revolutionary step. For the first time in the history of France, elected officials would be personally responsible before a nonpenal court for their acts while in office. This was a very big pill to swallow for officials who were used to relative immunity due to the tutelage of the prefectoral system. The Association of French Mayors was quick to express its uneasiness and demanded an advisory mechanism to counsel them, the right to correct their own mistakes and a limit on the penalties that could be imposed.

Members of the former Center-Right majority were apparently totally opposed to the government. Though they had once praised "the development of local responsibility", they quickly came to the defense of the mayors, especially those of the small communes: "Local officials", proclaimed Jacques Toubon, "will be prey to the Inquisition." Others emphasized the unjustness of creating severe penalties for officials, while depriving them of the advice of the prefect to guide them through the labyrinth of governmental rules and regulations.

The majority let the debate run its course, and the government put up only a weak defense. It knew that even the Left would not support it on this particular point. Faced with the lack of enthusiasm of its own majority, the criticisms of associations of elected officials, as well as the obstinacy of the Senate, the government's determination faltered. Gaston Defferre was obliged to concede that the *cour des comptes* would intervene only for "very serious cases". He suggested that technical agencies be created in the departments to offer those communes requesting it the kind of help the prefect had been giving. At the second reading of the bill in the Assembly, Defferre finally withdrew the proposal concerning the legal responsibility of local officials, to the relief of the majority and the applause of the opposition.

Other items met the same fate in Parliament. The question of whether the general council could overthrow its president and resolve the question of several offices being held simultaneously was the subject of lively debate. The debate never became a real battle, however, since no one wanted to fight in it.

With the benefit of hindsight, it is clear that all these compromises and concessions effectively broke the balance between freedom and responsibility sought by Gaston Defferre. From one chamber to the other, from one amendment to the next, members of Parliament nibbled away at the controls implicit in the government bill and limited the risks inherent in the exercise of local power. The juridical concept behind the government's bill on decentralization was slowly replaced by a much more political construct which parliamentarians of all the parties helped build. Could it be that they reacted more in their capacity as locally elected officials than as defenders of the national interest?

An even more illuminating example of the irrelevance of the Right–Left dichotomy was the debate concerning the future of the regions, which the government bill had promoted to the rank of juridically recognized *collectivités locales*. A number of interests and tendencies came to light around the question of the status of the region and the department respectively. The RPR which opposed the election by popular vote of a regional assembly, found itself in opposition to the UDF, which was for direct universal suffrage. On the Left, Mitterrand's followers defended the rights of the departments, while Michel Rocard's followers favored the regions. Rocard would willingly have worked on the government's bill because he had long been involved in trying to reform the system; however, he had very little to do with the preparation of the bill. After the smoke cleared, it was evident that the government bill would pass without any other major changes. The shift from the communes and departments to the regions was thus adopted with minor modifications, as were the principles of the election of an assembly by popular vote, the abolition of prior control and the recourse to a judge.

The last act: heroics vs realism

By an ironic twist of fate, no sooner had the decrees on the transfer of power to the presidents of the *conseils généraux* been promulgated than the Left began to lose its grip over local institutions. During the March 1982 cantonal elections, the Right obtained the majority in 58 departments. Though decentralization was not an issue during the campaign, it seemed it would have a boomerang effect. "I have no intention of changing the bill that was voted," Defferre announced on 22 March, "nor will I make changes in my plans. The others have won and so will benefit before we do from the law on decentralization. I'm sorry it turned out that way, but so much the better for them."

Whereas Defferre may have been inspired to take so heroic a stance in order to have his name go down in history, the same could not be said of his colleagues in the government. They were becoming increasingly alarmed by the holes the law was making in their budgets and jurisdictions. The Ministers in charge of Education, Culture and Town Planning – supported and indeed pushed by the officials of their Ministries – were fighting inch by inch to defend their means of action.

The President of the Republic then stepped in to remind his Minister of the need to be realistic and asked him to "readjust the reform by balancing out the section on jurisdictions". The functional ministers asked for nothing more than this presidential support, and further tampering with the reform decreased noticeably. The Council of Ministers was scheduled to discuss the bill covering jurisdictions on 1 April but the item simply disappeared from the agenda. This new realism on the part of the government was seen by Jacobins of all sorts as a sign of weakness, showing that it was entirely possible to put a stop to decentralization.

The determination of Defferre's team, however, carried the day. With remarkable political adroitness, the Minister of the Interior and Decentralization took advantage of proposals presented by the opposition in the Senate to force the hand of his colleagues and the Parisian administration. In July 1983, the entire legislative package involving jurisdictions was guaranteed to pass; it had taken the determined and skillful Minister, backed by a small team of obstinate technocrats, less than two years to institute one of the most far-reaching administrative reforms that France had seen since World War II.

The risks of diversity

The new system created by the law on decentralization has gone into effect smoothly. Elected officials still favor the law, and disruptions in the acceptance of features such as new jurisdictions, financial transfers and election of regional assemblies by popular vote are rare. A bill to reduce the number of offices that can be held simultaneously has been passed. Citizens' participation in the new system is the only thing to have disappeared. Moreover, politicians – be they past or possible future victims of alternate parties in power – have been attracted to the new and considerable role of President of the General Council.

At this point, it is not our purpose to perform a detailed analysis of the new model. Five trends, however, are worth calling attention to. First, the mode of regulation by a judge, which was created as an alternative to the tutelage of the state, does not really meet the needs of the local administration. Judgements, which deal more often with form rather than substance and are subject to unavoidable delays, are in fact being supplanted at an earlier stage by recourse to negotiated arrangements between the prefect and the local officials. Here, the prefect is gaining back some of the power over financial matters which were lost earlier.

Second, decentralization saw the light of day at the height of the recession, even though it was not planned with the economic crisis in mind. In addition, it was based on what was intended to be a liberating mechanism, globalization of subsidies (block grants). Unintentionally, decentralization now appears to have become a way to "decentralize the recession". The onus of administering the bitter pill of governmental "rigor" has been transferred to local echelons, and individual methods have been adopted in handling this unexpected development. Some pass the problem on to the next echelon, others pare down financial aid to nonprofit organizations that are ill prepared to stand up to elected officials and still others apply for assistance from the next highest echelon, with all the ties of dependency such an action implies.

Third, despite the ostensible similarity of the new structures from one end of the country to the other, their evolution has been quite varied. This can be attributed to the extremely close-knit fabric of overlapping jurisdictions, as well as political and financial ties. Predictions on how the regions and departments will evolve are therefore very tricky. Even though the election of the Regional Council by *scrutin de liste départemental* would seem to favor the departments, it is impossible to anticipate evolutions that are proving to be very varied indeed. The diversity in reaction to the new structure is regulated in part by the relationship between local political machines and national headquarters, which gained importance after the Socialist government came to power. The growth in power of these local politicians has occurred at the very time when political activists were turning their backs on the parties to an alarming degree.

Lastly, the diverging evolution of institutions has been accompanied by differing management practices which have produced – *de facto*, if not *de jure* – gross inequalities based on local affiliations. But are the French ready to accept such blatant inequalities? True, inequalities have always existed, but they at least were not subject to party politicking at the local level and electoral fluctuations at every echelon. Nevertheless, it is highly unlikely that the French will be eager to revert to the impersonal, protective management of the prefects. Decentralization, however complicated and flawed, may well be one major legacy of Mitterrand's France.

NOTES

1 This chapter draws heavily on a large research project, parts of which have already been published in *Le Sacre des notables*, Jaques Rondin (Paris, Fayard, 1985). I am grateful to my colleagues on that project: Philippe Crouzet, Jean-Michel Guibert, Guillaume Hannezo, Jean-Baptiste Hy, Gilles de Margerie and Patrick Molis.

15

The Socialist Decentralization

YVES MÉNY

The French Socialists have already achieved something which neither the "all powerful" Gaullists nor the *notables'* friends, the Giscardians, proved capable of during the first 22 years of the Fifth Republic – decentralization. How can we explain the fact that the main principles of this reform, and indeed most of the detailed dispositions, were passed, with relative ease, in the space of just two years?

The first reason for this was bound up with the political climate of the day. The Socialist government came to power on a wave of popularity unprecedented in the history of the Fifth Republic. This popular support was matched by that of local political elites in major cities and in many *départements* and regions. For the first time under the Fifth Republic, a strong national majority was dominant in cities of over 30,000 inhabitants (two-thirds of which the Left controlled), and in the regions and *départements* (the Left swept many of the most populous and industrialized of these, such as Nord, Isère, Bouches-du-Rhône etc.). Thanks to the single-member two-ballot electoral system and the 1964 municipal electoral law (both Gaullist devices to squeeze centrist and right-wing *notables*), the Left seemed in control of the French political structure from top to bottom.

A second reason lay with the antecedents of the Left – particularly Socialist – politicians. Apart from a few political dinosaurs with fourth Republic ministerial experience, such as Gaston Defferre and Maurice Faure, the vast majority of new parliamentarians had only managed at the local level. Most new deputies rose to power through town halls and *conseils généraux*. The Socialists were skilled practitioners of the *cumul des mandats* (the accumulation of two or more local or national elected offices)[1] and there had never been so many *cumulards* in a National Assembly under the Fifth Republic as in 1981. It was at the local level that Socialists had endured the frustrations of central government controls and checks and the petty vexations of symbolic "guerilla warfare" with prefects. In the Utopian atmosphere of 1981-82, new Socialist deputies were determined to 'liberate' France's local authorities.

A third reason for the success of decentralization in France was the method used by Gaston Defferre – to push the reform rapidly through Parliament, and only then to take the time to work through the details. It is clear that some Socialists, from Mitterrand down, were well aware that the grace period was temporary, and this led them to quicken the pace of reform in the first months of Left power. The two most important structural reforms, nationalization and decentralization, were rushed through in a jubilant atmosphere that recalled the earlier French "Revolution". After 22 years

248

in power, the opposition was still stunned by its defeat. By March 1982 the point of no return had already been reached; the central government *tutelle* over local authorities had been abolished, elected executives were set up (in the place of the prefects) in the *départements*, and regions gained full-fledged recognition from local authorities.

The fruits of both the general strategy and specific tactics have been considerable. With a notary's painstaking precision, the Direction Générale des Collectivités Locales has kept a month-by-month account of the reform's progress: 33 laws and 219 decrees, as well as innumerable circulars (some of them book-length), were issued between 1982 and 1985. This was an impressive record, and it is probably no exaggeration to say that it represented the most important reform in the area of decentralization since the Acts of 1871 and 1884.

Leaving an assessment at that would be both superficial and wrong, however, for the following reasons. First, statute books can also be cemeteries and, as Michel Crozier underlined a few years ago, "society is not changed by decree".[2] Secondly, a policy is always defined not only by the positive measures it contains but also by its "nondecisions". Thirdly, like other countries with interventionist and legalistic traditions, France has a long history of "adapting" rules. Tocqueville's observation in *The Ancien Régime and the French Revolution* that "the rule is rigid, the practice flexible", has lost none of its acuity. In other words, neither the self-satisfied pronouncements of the government nor the criticisms of the opposition provided an accurate evaluation of the decentralization reform. Fourthly, this first assessment of the reform cannot help but be tentative, If certain trends and tendencies are now discernable, many questions are still pending. We shall turn to these areas of uncertainty, and to new challenges to the system, after dealing with the characteristics of the reform and the points which can already be considered as fixed.

CHARACTERISTICS OF THE REFORM

François Mitterrand presented decentralization as the main task of his seven-year term (*la grande affaire du septennat*), and many observers have seen it as one of the most important politico-administrative changes to take place since the French Revolution. The Right, on the other hand, denounced the financial mess which it said would result. In fact, the reform deserves neither excessive praise nor visceral condemnation, and politicians on both sides of the fence modified their assessments as soon as the parliamentary debate was over. The opposition, so critical of the reform in Parliament, rushed to take advantage of its provisions and even condemned the government for the slowness with which its decisions were applied! In short, unlike most of the local-government changes undertaken by Gaullists and Giscardians,[3] the changes introduced by the Socialists met with no serious resistance. The explanation for this may be sought in the characteristics of the reform itself – gradualism, consensus and, in spite of its apparent uniformity, a considerable degree of differentiation between authorities.

Indeed, the Socialists' reform is an excellent illustration of the thesis argued by Douglas Ashford, summed up by the title of his recent study *French Pragmatism and British*

Dogmatism.[4] The changes of 1982-85 were part of a progressive, incremental process in the politico-administrative system which goes against common descriptions of the "heroic style" (Jack Hayward) of French politics.[5]

There is also a big contrast between Socialists' claims concerning the reforms and the reforms' real content. To a considerable extent the reforms took into account developments that had already taken place in a number of localities, especially in major cities, *départements* and the more active regions. The laws ratified *faits accomplis* as much as they broke new ground. The prefect, for example, had already lost the position of preeminent departmental figure in many regions. The heads of state field-offices stationed in a given locality for two or three years were perfectly well aware that they could not hope to challenge the leadership of local bosses like Mauroy in Lille, Defferre in Marseilles, Marcellin in Morbihan, or Chirac in Corrèze - to cite just a few of the most striking cases.

It is worth recalling that the first 15 to 20 years of the Fifth Republic represented, in this respect, a pause in a long evolution in which the *député-maire* of a major city has occupied an increasingly central position. This evolution was already underway during the Third Republic and was explicitly acknowledged by the Constitution of the Fourth. Although the cold war and the fragility of the new regime prevented the application of Articles 87 and 89 of the 1946 Constitution, the practice of consulting the boss of a *département* prior to a prefectoral appointment lasted until 1958. The restoration of prefectoral authority after 1958, and especially after 1962-64, was very effective but lasted no more that 15 years in many *départements*. In this respect, then, the reform returned to an old tradition, rather than bringing about a real break with the past.

The policy was also symbolic, however, and symbols can produce real results. Although change had barely started before 1981, it was precipitated by the reforms, and thus rapidly transformed some quietly disposed *notables*, peacefully reconciled to prefectoral preeminence, into ambitious "political entrepreneurs". In other areas, the "legalization" of current political practice was common. *Tutelle*, in its traditional form, no longer existed outside legal textbooks and Sunday speeches. Financial and technical supervision by the state was much more burdensome and fastidious, and although modified by the reform, it remained decisive. We shall see this below. Similarly, dispositions allowing economic interventionism by local authorities ratified the "administration of the crisis" already underway in the worst-affected municipalities and regions. Pierre Mauroy and Gaston Defferre were merely absolving their pre-1981 "sins" here; this meant allowing themselves (and other mayors) to do openly what they had previously been doing in secret.[6]

Despite its egalitarian appearance, the reform accepted the status quo by allowing the continuation of a two-tiered system consisting, on the one hand, of the communes, *départements*, and regions, all of which possess the necessary resources - human, economic, technical, or demographic - and the local authorities, on the other hand, who lack either the resources or political will to keep up with the pace of change. The two-tiered system is the exact opposite of its predecessor created by the Departmental Acts of 1871 and the Municipal Acts of 1884. These laws, ostensibly "general rules" applicable to all local authorities, flagrantly favored France's rural areas to the detriment of the major cities, which were constrained by tight administrative restrictions and neglected by rural, *notable*-dominated *départements*. It is significant that the only major exception to this rule was the administrative status accorded to Paris. This, however, merely accentuated the inequality in relation to other major cities, placing the capital under direct central governmental control. Here again the prognosis made in 1945-46 was correct, but the administrative status envisaged for big cities by the Constitution of the Fourth Republic was never applied. For all its power, moreover, the Fifth Republic in its Gaullist phase never managed to provide a wholly satisfactory answer to the problem, despite having set up the Urban Districts and later, the Urban Communities.

Defferre's method, in this respect, was diametrically opposed to the Gaullists' attempts to apply particular solutions to specific problems. In accordance with a "republican tradition" which has particularly deep roots in the Left, the Socialists applied a general solution to the problem. In principle, all the communes, *départements*, and regions are placed on equal footing. As far as "liberties" are concerned, equality is a fixed rule and variations are readily perceived as discrimination. Behind this uniform facade, however, exceptions and inconsistencies are abundant. For example, while it is certainly admirable to proclaim that communes, *départements*, and regions will henceforth enjoy the right "to intervene in the economic and social interest of their inhabitants", this right can only be exercised in practice by a few hundred local authorities. Similarly the law provides an escape route for communes that do not wish to take responsibility for issuing building permits (as is the case with most small communes); and bestows this prerogative on the prefect if the commune has no *plan d'occupation des sols* (local land-use plan). Thus, voluntary inaction leads to the maintenance of the status quo ante. In another instance, the government, having created the *dotations globales d'equipement* (block investment grants) in order to increase commune autonomy, decided a year later to restore the old specific project-related grants for small communes. In addition, they were distributed by the Commissaires de la République (the new name for the prefects), "in order to avoid the *tutelle* of one local authority over another".

The two-tiered character of decentralization in France is not, it should be repeated, a new phenomenon. The new system has both positive and negative aspects. Among the positive is the fact that the reform has motivated ambitious local leaders to maximize the assets of their communes. If some medium-sized towns have been caught napping, other small communes have shown a remarkable energy under the influence of vigorous local leaders. One indication of this is the rapid growth of the number of *plans d'occupation des sols* undertaken, illustrating how many mayors want to take responsibility for the planning of their commune. On the other hand, the veil of uniformity cast over a varied and multifaceted reality has enormously complicated its rules and processes.

If the reform was *de facto* gradualist and differentiated, it was also highly consensual. Indeed, it could be called a "Common Minimal Program of the Left and Right". If the wording seems excessive, the general idea may be sustained by several arguments. Firstly, it is clear that the Socialists' ambitious - and in some eyes, even Utopian - reform programs before 1981 were enforced very unevenly. Not the remotest trace of self-management will be found in the 300 or so legislative and regulatory texts which were passed.[7] It was apparently not deemed worthwhile even to mention this magic word as a sort of posthumous tribute. The same could be said of the ambitious plans to reform the local tax system that were proposed before 1981. The local authorities' resources have changed somewhat, but in the direction started by Valéry Giscard d'Estaing as Finance Minister 20 years ago. In addition the *taxe professionelle* (local business tax) is still very much alive, even though Mitterrand criticized it as an "absurd" levy. The Defferre Acts are only socialist because they were elaborated by a Socialist government. As for the rest, they are examples of pure French politico-administrative classicism. Not one voice of the French political milieu was raised in opposition.

Decentralization proved to be consensual in a second sense in that it was grounded to a considerable degree in the experience of previous governments. There was near-unanimous agreement to keep the small communes and *cumul des mandats* (for lack of a better solution) and to nullify prefectoral *tutelle*. For evidence of this consensus one need look no further than the process by which the bills were drawn up: the legislators responsible freely admitted that their starting point had been the project of Giscard's Interior Minister Bonnet, which was amended and modified by the Senate in 1980-81. Moreover, the same men at the Direction Générale des Collectivités Locales (DGCL) prepared both the (aborted) reform of Giscard's term and the successful one of the Socialist government.[8] Gaston Defferre, initially mistrustful of the Civil Service, started by setting up a "cell" of Socialist university professors to prepare the reform for him. As early as September 1981, the professors demonstrated that they were not a satisfactory substitute for the DGCL specialists, and were sent back to their books.

The third indication of the consensual approach was the effort to avoid, as much as possible, obstacles and opposition. The reform was "smooth", and parliamentary debates eliminated its few controversial points (such as the proposal to hold mayors personally responsible for their administrative decisions). In this respect Defferre's strategy was no different from Giscard's, even if his style was distinct. Some years ago this strategy was called the "line of least resistance".[9] In other words, both Giscardian and Socialist governments drew the same lesson from the defeat of the Gaullists: no reform rejected by the *notables* and their most eminent representative body, the Senate, can succeed. As Pierre Sadran observed, "what the reform did not say is as important as what it did".[10] Thus, the law omits any incentive to merge communes, feebly suggests new forms of intercommunal cooperation (which had become a moot issue even before efforts were made to put them into practice) and rejects both changes in regional boundaries and the establishment of a hierarchy between the different local authority levels. The long-standing quarrel between regions and *départements* did not resolve itself and the attempt to tackle the *cumul des mandats* – that cornerstone of French political life – was in effect limited. As much for what it failed to accomplish as for what it achieved, the reform constituted a triumph for the *notables*. The title of the book on the subject, *Le Sacre des notables*,[11] edited by Jacques Rondin, is much more than a clever turn of phrase. It is a correct assessment of political power relations.

THE REFORM'S PERMANENT ACHIEVEMENTS

It was inevitable that among the mass of bills passed over the past five years, a number of intentions would either resist implementation or change rapidly. Indeed, the process of adaptation and variation was practically simultaneous with that of the reform itself. It is impossible to adopt "universally applicable" laws and regulations without providing amendments to deal with the inevitable exceptions. It is clear that some elements of the Defferre Laws are irreversible. We shall not attempt, here, to distinguish between "perishable" and supposedly permanent provisions. We shall confine ourselves to pointing out a few aspects that seem to constitute more durable structural or relational changes due to the culmination of a long and progressive evolution.

The transfer of the *département* and regional executives from prefects to elected presidents was one of the most symbolically meaningful components of the reform. Proposed immediately after the war and enshrined in the 1946 Constitution, this reform was never implemented; the cold war and break with the Communist Party prevented its application. In the meantime, however, powerful elected officials like Mauroy, Defferre, Marcellin and Chaban-Delmas were imposing their authority at the expense of the prefectoral corps, which had reigned as almost unchallenged feudal lords in their local fiefs. It is significant that the prefects – who could scarcely have been overjoyed at the prospect of this parliamentary amputation of their powers – nonetheless did nothing to oppose the transfer. They were acutely aware of the evolution's inexorable character.

If the capacity of an elite to survive depends on its ability to adapt to new circumstances, it is clear that the French prefectoral corps has not resigned itself to the fate of its Italian counterparts. Not only did the Commissaires de la République immediately reinforce their control of ministerial field services, they also seized the new opportunities at the local level. In many cases, this simply meant offering their services to the new "chiefs" of *départements* and regions. The chiefs' status and authority now appear secure. Many of them enjoy – potentially at least – the bulk of local decision-making powers, and as elected officials they command a democratic legitimacy that the prefectoral corps can neither dispute nor compete with. This is a permanent result since it rests on the greater legitimacy of elected officials than Civil Servants, as is common in Western societies. This, however, does not necessarily signify the primacy of elected officials. Many *cumulants* do not have the time or desire to be real administrators or managers. We may thus have a division of power whereby elected officials legitimate decisions which are made by Civil Servants, either at the initiative of the Commissaire de la République or under the leadership of a prefect seconded in order to run services for the region or *départment*. This new configuration seems well established already, confirming the previous transformation of the local politico-administrative scene. It also has much in common with developments throughout Europe, particularly in Napoleonic systems.

The reform of the local Civil Service represents another development that will be difficult to reverse. Until 1983, local Civil Servants were recruited by disparate procedures that allowed elected officials, especially in small towns, to employ a great deal of individual judgement. Moreover, aside from Civil Servants recruited by competitive examination, many others were hired on contract, at the near-total discretion of elected officials. After a while these contract appointees would be granted tenure under pressure from unions or individuals. Reasonably enough, local authorities complained of their inability to recruit high-caliber officers because they could not offer them career prospects comparable to those of the national Civil Service.

The 1983 act rests on two fundamental principles: first, that the status of local officers and the state Civil Service should be equal. Local officers and their counterparts in the national Civil Service thus enjoy the same rights and advantages and are recruited and promoted in broadly the same way. The second principle, made possible by the application of the first, promoted mobility between national and local services. This law is admittedly somewhat paradoxical and certainly belies the alleged Cartesianism of the French. How can a law "decentralize" when it in fact "nationalizes" and standardizes the statuses of the two services? Both the government and the Civil Service unions reply that the rigidity which may result from standardization will be compensated by the new mobility.

This is hardly a convincing argument. Few local Civil Servants are interested in a mobility that compels them to move from city to city, or region to region. One of the dominant attractions of the local Civil Service is that it affords employees the ability to stay in or near their home towns - *vivre au pays*. Moreover, mobility necessitates a place to which one can move. Jobs are extremely scarce in the national Civil Service, and the *grands corps* are certainly not about to throw open their doors to their country cousins. By contrast, mobility in the opposite direction may prove to be extremely attractive to top national Civil Servants. More than a hundred of them anticipated the movement by being seconded to regional and departmental executives as early as 1982.

Several factors explain this one-way mobility. First, local *notables*, *cumulards par excellence*, have always needed *grand vizirs* to manage things while they concern themselves with politics. The job was formerly done by prefects and the need for prefects - in uniform or not - is now greater than ever. A second reason results from the diminution of authority of some state officers (notably the prefect), which has made the management of major local authorities appear more attractive, even at the financial and symbolic levels.

Other considerations bearing on the question of one-way mobility include the Left's long awaited arrival to power after 25 years in opposition and the less attractive career prospects of lower-placed Ecole Nationale d'Administration (ENA) graduates. A detour through local government is an attractive option for a Civil Servant who finds promotion prospects blocked for political or administrative reasons. This becomes even more pronounced since local government is distinctly short on "highfliers". A mere 8 per cent of local Civil Servants have a *baccalauréat*, compared with 30 per cent at the national level.

The local Civil Service reform is likely to have a lasting effect because it will be extremely hard to call its principles into question. The standardization of rules, status and pay is, after all, very gratifying to unions. The reform constitutes a considerable centralizing counterweight to the rest of the Defferre reforms, introduces rigidity factors and favors entry into local government administration by top national Civil Servants. Notwithstanding the necessity of reforming the local Civil Service and limiting some mayoral nepotism and clientelism, could it not have been done differently? It is paradoxical that the law confirms, in new terms, the interpenetration of center and periphery and the implicit and traditional division of labor. The *notables* will go on with their politicking and mediating among voters, interest groups and government and top national Civil Servants will retain administrative power.

AREAS OF UNCERTAINTY

Any reform, whatever its real or supposed objectives, mobilizes actors, initiates strategies, creates expectations – and produces unexpected effects. When the reform is, as in 1981, also laden with symbols and calls into question regulations dating back at least a century, it is hardly surprising if the implementation period is characterized by hesitation and uncertainty. These waverings were further accentuated by the uniform character of the reform, which did not lend itself easily to the diversity of local situations. In other words, the numerous interpretations and uses of the reform have left flexibility in the system, which has been exploited in highly varied fashion. Still, we may note at least two main areas in which the outcome is uncertain. These are the role of the prefect and the respective functions of the four main levels of decision-making and administration (central government, regions, *départements* and communes).

The prefect: town and country

The "demotion" of the prefect is indisputable. This strange animal, which has excited such interest among foreign observers of French politics, has receded into semiobscurity. If it were not for coordination of state field services, the prefect could now pass for an ordinary representative of the central government in the localities. The post has suffered a thoroughgoing shrinkage of power and authority. As a mere *département* and region commissaire, the prefect no longer has the job of preparing and implementing local budgets. The power of *tutelle* has been lost, and despite the verbal reinforcement of powers in relation to the field services, the prefect no longer enjoys the old means of pressuring or influencing such feudal figures as the local representatives of government departments, like, for example, public works (*équipement*) or agriculture. In addition to this real and symbolic diminution of powers, the prefect has also suffered as a result of the reform-produced shift of authority to elected officials. Whereas in the old days, the central government supported the prefects' resistance to the more aggressive *notables*, the balance is now tipped to the side of the elected officials. Those officials who most want to "do something", or have the most vigorous appetites for power, now feel their undertakings are legitimate and have left the prefects clamoring for a return to past practice.

The prefects have not, however, been left without means of retaliation. In the first place, a major source of their power rests in many elected officials' distaste for administration. Moreover, the propensity of major *notables* to stress the political aspect of their office produces an "equal and opposite reaction" from second-rank elected officials, especially mayors and councillors of small communes afraid of falling under party-political domination. This mistrust, which returns some maneuverability to prefects, found expression in the 1984 reform of the investment grants system. Since the mechanisms in place were not appropriate to the needs and problems of small communes, the government reintroduced the old subsidies earmarked for specific projects. These were to be distributed by the prefects "to avoid any domination of one local authority over another". Thrown out the door, prefects have come back through the window, and those elected officials averse to administration would do well to beware of these already apparent forms of "creeping expropriation".

The "country" prefect undoubtedly has more trump cards than the city counterpart in this respect. Nevertheless, even prefects from cities, *départements* and regions are not denied all means of intervention. In the first place, although no longer enjoying the right of *tutelle*, the prefect retains a key position in the monitoring system of local authorities. It is the prefect, after all, who may demand that the (regional) administrative tribunal hear appeals against local authorities. Prefectoral services have been substantially reinforced to cope with the mass of local ordinances that must be approved by the state's local representative. According to interior ministry statistics, nearly three million (2,915,015 to be precise) such acts were submitted for approval in 1983, as well as 327,547 budgets. Only 1,293 cases found their way to administrative tribunals. Two figures, however, allow us to measure the prefect's crucial role: 72,740 "observations" were communicated to local authorities, and half the appeals were settled out of court.[12] In other words, as in the past, albeit under new forms, the prefect still wields real powers of influence and negotiation. The forms of power depend on the ordinances concerned and on the social and political context.[12]

It is here that uncertainties appear. Some prefects prefer to keep a low profile in the current climate (there were zero or one appeals in 15 *départements* in 1983), while others, especially in the most urbanized *départements*, practiced more aggressive policies (74 appeals in Yvelines, 60 in Var, 45 in Bouches-du-Rhône, 39 in Essonne).[13] Going to court thus becomes the prefect's ultimate deterrent, and elected officials hardly like being dragged into a legal process that lasts two years on average (not including further appeals) and involves serious financial risks.

Finally, thanks to the central government's beloved contractual procedures of the past ten years (and reinforced in 1981), the prefect retains crucial control at the interface between central government departments and local authorities. Conscious of the loss of its traditional prerogatives, and of the inexorable nature of this development, the prefectoral corps defends its remaining functions all the more stoutly against field offices and elected officials alike. If their roles as executives of region and *département* are a thing of the past, the resulting diminution of authority does not necessarily correspond to the one suffered by Italian prefects. The "Commissars of the Republic" apparently still possess substantial power. The scope of this power will be determined by the political climate at the national and local level, and by the instability of balances between political and administrative elites. The situation thus remains wide open.

A game for four players

As underlined above, one characteristic of the reform was the absence of a clear distinction between different levels of decision-making. Territorial reform was effectively postponed *sine die*. From the moment the government decided not to favor *départements* over regions, or major cities over small communes (or vice versa), it was condemned to implement a sort of "redistributive justice", that is, it transferred responsibilities and resources to all levels of local authority.

At the same time, the government fixed the functional distribution of rationalization objectives by transferring "blocks" of responsibility to each level. Municipal services such as primary schools and day-to-day land stewardship (*plans d'occupation des sols* and building permits) were to become the responsibility of communes; social policy and school busing were shifted to *départements* and vocational training and economic intervention were absorbed by the regions. This allotment was intended to avoid the outmoded and confusing system of overlapping responsibility for intervention.

In practice, these fine blueprints fell victim to the demands of the real world and the determination of the central government to retain certain key powers. Far from simplifying procedures, the reform complicated them in many areas. Central government employees wanted to retain their (privileged) status, and were merely "loaned" on a temporary basis to the appropriate *départements*. The state, after delegating new responsibilities for libraries and museums to communes and *départements*, retained its right of supervision and oversight. The division of labor in schools, though quite logical on paper, ran up against the complexity of the situation in everyday practice. Primary and secondary schools and lycées exist in the same buildings oblivious to the clear administrative divisions between them. The same could be said of housing and of many other policy areas. The "layer cake" conceived by the interior ministry was thus transformed into a "marble cake".

The uncertainties born of this situation are accentuated by the fact that each level found some satisfaction in the reform. The communes enjoy widened responsibilities and the *départements* are the main beneficiaries of cash transfers (20 billion francs once the transfer process is complete). The regions, which received the smallest share of transfers, nonetheless cherish their enviable freedom of maneuver. They can allocate the bulk of their resources to investment, whereas the *départements* have only marginal freedom of choice in administering policies decided elsewhere. Many local authorities have thus embarked on policies that merely duplicate central government programs or competing authorities, based on a false measurement of their own real autonomy. The *départements* imitated Directions Départmentales d'Equipements (state infrastructure field divisions) by drawing up *plans d'occupation des sols* and processing building-permit applications. Regions have undertaken wide-ranging initiatives which threaten to damage one of their main assets, their low current budget obligations (which represented less than 10 per cent of their total spending in 1981, but rose to 35 per cent by 1984). It is as if the central government left local authorities to fight it out amongst themselves on the principle, "May the best man win". There is nothing new about this attitude in France, where reform is implemented more by addition than substitution, in the hope that the weakest branches will gradually whither away. Clearly this deep-rooted gradualism is costly, and inaugurates a period of uncertainty during which Civil Servants and elected officials are forced to develop defensive or offensive strategies.

NEW CHALLENGES

Even if decentralization does not entirely fulfill the wishes of local elected officials after being sought for so long, it is definitely under way. As Albert Mabileau wrote somewhat ironically, "local authority is facing an ordeal by decentralization".[14] Local elected officials, in other words, are having to handle new responsibilities and challenges. What, after all, are the advantages of decentralization over centralization if the former is not in practice cheaper, more efficient, or more democratic? Any future assessment of the reform will have to address the question of how authorities have met these challenges.

Innovation or mimicry?

Historically, local authorities have often shown imagination and innovation in the formulation of public policy. Many elements of social and cultural policy were initiated at the local level, inspired by either the dynamic and enlightened bourgeoisie, or the interventionist and socialistic Left. Little by little, though, the state absorbed responsibility for implementing these innovations, either because of the local fiscal crisis or a desire to extend to everyone benefits hitherto enjoyed only by a few.

During the 1960s and 1970s, local authorities again displayed admirable initiative by investing heavily, to the point that they accounted for over half of total nonmilitary public investments.[5] However, local authorities very often found themselves forced to "buy" policies elaborated by the central government by means of specific or incentive subsidies, or more *ad hoc* methods such as contracts.

How great is the innovative capacity of local authorities likely to be in the future? Undoubtedly, many hope to use their imagination to find new ways to improve services, or fill gaps in existing services. This declared wish, however, runs up against serious limitations in three areas. First, and despite declarations to the contrary by those who drew up the laws, technical norms imposed by the state remain as constricting as ever. They are, moreover, supplemented to an increasing degree by the technological requirements that the central government imposes on local authorities. For example, it required all cable networks to use optic fiber, a technology which is still at the experimental stage and therefore very expensive. As a result, France paradoxically remains underequipped in cable networks although many local authorities are keen to invest in the audiovisual sector. This is only the most recent example of a situation that has restricted the options of the local authorities.

Innovative capacity is further limited by factors which may be classified as cultural - notably the tendency of local authorities to be steeped in the values and the ways of thinking of the national Civil Service. Local authorities resort to procedures and instruments created by the Civil Service for its own use. This "administrative culture" - a term coined by Sidney Tarrow a decade ago to illustrate a major difference between French and Italian mayors – seems highly resistant to any changes that decentralization might have brought about. The report produced by the Senate committee charged with studying the application and implementation of decentralization policy notes this phenomenon and expresses anxiety about it. It asserts that "decentralization will have been quite useless if the local authorities purely and simply reproduce the state's modes of intervention". "It is apparent", the senators stress, "that the regions are tending, from one area to another, to reproduce more or less the same types of administrative bodies, formulas, and measures."[16]

This propensity to administrative mimicry can only be reinforced by the practice of recruiting top Civil Servants by seconding or through retirement to run the services of *départements* or regions. How can one expect top Civil Servants hired for their experience to do anything other than what they have been doing for their entire working lives?

The prefectoral style could well get the upper hand in the administrative services, as could the style of *équipement* engineers in the technical agencies that have been set up in various places. This raises a number of questions. Is it reassuring that the administration of school policy has been assigned, in a number of localities, to former *inspecteurs d'académie?* Was it really necessary for major *notables* to imitate structures of the central government to the point of caricature setting up a plethora of *cabinets* or by organizing "delegated working parties" in some of the most out-of-the-way places, to cite two examples. Such excesses are inevitable and the extra costs that resulted from decentralization have been very limited on the whole. But it could also be argued that one of decentralization's *raisons d'être* should be to cut down on this type of prodigal expenditure.

What price decentralization?

It appears that local authorities have responded to decentralization with three different strategies, depending on their respective size and the ambitions of elected leaders. Some carry on as if nothing had happened, doing little and using state-supplied resources and personnel to do it. This is chiefly the case among small communes and a handful of medium sized ones. Other local authorities have behaved like political entrepreneurs, launching innumerable new projects, raising taxes and hiring many new employees. This group appears to consist, substantially, though by no means exclusively, of Socialists inspired by the voluntarist ideology of the government during its first two years in office. The third category is chiefly made up of mayors and councillors of the opposition. Denouncing government policy as spendthrift and interventionist, they have sought, as Le Monde says of Parisian Mayor Jacques Chirac, to do local "rough drafts" of their national projects, such as limiting expenditure and public-sector employment and farming out many services hitherto carried out by government employees.

This crude categorization currently tends to be blurred, given the ever-tighter constraints binding local authorities. The decentralization process, in fact, locks state-locality transfers into tighter limits than before. Transfers for social expenditure, for example – the largest single element in the total volume – now consist of fixed block grants; before decentralization, the state reimbursed local authorities with a percentage of a spending total determined by the latter. This was consequently an open-ended grant which permitted elected officials to distribute the monies without taking overall financial responsibility. Today, elected officials are still free to undertake new policies and new spending, but must limit themselves to definite cash amounts. In other words, elected officials are free to innovate by finding ways to save money or to redefine their policies.

In addition, the excessive growth of local taxation (over 15 per cent on average in the last five years) could become intolerable given the somewhat arbitrary methods by which it is calculated. If inflation stays under 5 per cent, local authorities will simply not be able to indulge in tax hikes on this scale, even if the transfer of certain items away from the state budget pushes them in this direction. Local authorities will increasingly have to look for ways to save money, especially on that most burdensome item, personnel expenses. It seems that since 1983 all local authorities have followed a policy of cutting their labor force by nonreplacement of retiring staff members. This is one way of mining what one top Civil Servant called "veins of productivity" - a prudish euphemism for overmanning.

Thanks to an extraordinary capacity for pressuring the various levels of government, local authorities have heretofore been able to win an ever-increasing volume of central government subsidies. The austerity policy of Left governments not only resulted in its becoming less generous than in the past, but also encouraged an uncoupling of as much expenditure as possible from the central budget. Some of that spending will also have to be covered by local authorities. Local government is thus being squeezed between relative financial disengagement on the part of the state and the impossibility of raising substantial extra revenue by tax increases; the criteria used for tax assessment are making rates increasingly unjust and intolerable for localities.

Which type of local democracy?

Finally, the decentralization reform confirms and strengthens the traditional type of relations between citizens and authorities. Those who hoped that participatory democracy under the Socialists would gradually replace the representative form have been disappointed. Different forms of direct democracy and citizen participation have either been systematically rejected or remain no more than pale imitations of foreign practice. Impact study and public-utility survey reforms have been superficial; popular initiatives and referendums have been totally excluded from the area of the reform and Socialist mayors who promised dramatic changes while in opposition have proved every bit as autocratic as their right-wing counterparts. The Socialist "democratization" has consisted of extending classic universal suffrage models of representation and legitimation to regional elections, *conseils d'arrondissement* in Paris, Lyon and Marseilles, minority representation on all municipal councils and elected executives in regions and *départements*.

The quintessential characteristic of decentralization, however, is less "democratization" than the generalization of the "authoritarian executive" model which now totally dominates French institutions. The model has two variants - the mayoral and the prefectoral - at the local level. The mayoral variant has recently been extended to *départements* and regions, turning their executives into genuine local "bosses". Reforms of the *bureaux* (executive committees) of *départements* and regions will change little. Whatever their good intentions, it is unlikely that political minority representation will moderate the autocratic style of major local elected officials. The decision-making process will be rendered more cumbersome – the majority organizing a parallel system of meetings, consisting of unofficial meetings from which the minority is excluded, and an official meeting which the minority merely attends symbolically – but it is feared that the voice of the people will not be heard more clearly.

As it turns out, the main challenge to the *notables* will come less from the base than the summit, in the form of the government's law limiting the *cumul des mandats* to just two elected offices, one local and one national. This reform, while encompassing more than the propositions of Socialist Senator Marcel Debarge, is moderate and balanced. It limits the *cumul* quite strictly, but does not attempt to abolish it. Total abolition would be unrealistic and the *cumul* can fulfill a useful function in the centralized French system, if kept within reasonable limits.

The adoption of the *cumul* reform in December 1985 surprised many observers. They thought that the Senate would block passage of the bill which, according to the Constitution, should be adopted under the same conditions by the two houses.

The success of the Left governmental initative can be explained by several factors. First, the government benefitted from opposition support, particularly that of the former president, Giscard d'Estaing, as well as public opinion, which is traditionally hostile to every form of *cumul*, private or public. In addition, the opposition found it difficult to defend the *cumul* three months before the legislative elections.

Second, the government accepted amendments which rendered the reform more acceptable to the senators without modifying its substance. The reform would only become effective after the 1986 legislative and regional elections, and its full impact would not be felt until those elected voted to waive their right to a third term. Also, the reform did not take into consideration the mayoral term in communes of 20,000 inhabitants or less which allows a considerable number of senators to hold three offices at the same time.

Although less sweeping than many would have liked, the *cumul* reform, taken in conjunction with the adoption of proportional representation for the March 1986 elections and the creation of directly elected regional assemblies, introduced substantial changes. They led to the expansion of the range of elected offices which can be shared out by the party apparatus, the importance of which was thus enhanced.

In an earlier article on the Defferre Laws,[17] the issue of whether the laws represented a reform of society or a reform of elites was posed. The first three years of the laws' application have dispelled none of the doubts expressed at the time. On the contrary, they appear to confirm that only the political and administrative elites were concerned by the changes. True, the election of all decision-makers by universal suffrage has reinforced their legitimacy, but it has not changed the ways in which society controls and participates in local and regional administration.[18] Far from leading to the dismantling of the state, the reform is rather an element of consensual integration which associates local elites with the administration, while marginalizing the most radical nationalist or regionalist dissenters.[19] Instead of bringing the government closer to the governed, as the decentralization's supporters hoped it would, the reform as it exists has complicated administrative procedures by duplicating state services (which have generally been maintained) with new local ones.

In the face of these intrinsic limitations one can already observe new strategies and policies at the level of high Civil Servants and local officials. Some want to take advantage of the reform in order to acquire new positions or expand their influence. New *éminences grises* and political entrepreneurs are already at work. With the limit on the accumulation of offices, new competing elites could emerge and both the pluralism and the professionalism of local elites could gain from it. A final pitfall remains to be avoided, however. It concerns the professional status that the organizations of elected officials are demanding for themselves. If this demand were agreed to, the wheel would have come full circle. Political elites, already recruited far too exclusively from the Civil Service (thanks to the facilities guaranteed by their professional status), would then be able to perpetuate themselves all the more easily due to their new elected official status. Civil Servants would be elected officials, and elected officials Civil Servants, the whole becoming a splendid example of self-reproduction.

NOTES

1 Jeannette Becquart-Leclercq, "Cumul des mandats et culture politique", in *Les Pouvoirs locaux à l'épreuve de la décentralisation*, Albert Mabileau (Paris, Pedone, 1983), série "Vie locale", pp. 207-241.

2 Michel Crozier, *On ne change pas la société par décret* (Paris, Grasset, 1980).

3 Yves Mény, "Central Control and Local Resistance", in *Continuity and Change in France*, ed. Vincent Wright (London, George Allen and Unwin, 1984), pp. 203-14.

4 Douglas Ashford, *British Dogmatism and French Pragmatism* (London, George Allen and Unwin, 1982).

5 Jack Hayward, "Mobilizing Private Interests in the Service of Public Ambitions", in *Policy Styles in Western Europe*, ed. J. Richardson (London, George Allen and Unwin, 1982).

6 Yves Mény, "Local Authorities and Economic Policy", in *Economic Policy and Policy-making under the Mitterrand Presidency 1981-1984*, eds Howard Machin and Vincent Wright (New York, St Martin's Press, 1985), pp. 187-200.

7 Mark Kesselman, "The Tranquil Revolution at Clochemerle: Socialist Decentralization in France", in *Socialism, the State and Public Policy in France*, eds Philip Cerny and Martin Schain (London, Frances Pinter, 1985), pp. 165-66.

8 Jacques Rondin, *Le Sacre des notables: la France en décentralisation* (Paris, Fayard, 1985).

9 Mény, "Central Control", pp. 203-14.

10 Pierre Sadran, "L'Evolution des relations centre-périphérie en France", unpublished paper delivered at the conference of the International Political Science Association, Paris, July 1985.

11 Rondin, *Le Sacre des notables*.

12 Quoted in *Rapport d'information du Sénat par M. Poncelet*, session ordinaire 1984-1985, 177 (19 Dec. 1985).

13 Michel Crozier, "Clochemerle ou la region, il faut choisir", *Projet*, 185-186 (May-June 1984).

14 Mabileau, *Les Pouvoirs locaux*.

15 Groupe de Recherches sur l'Administration Locale, *Les Interventions économiques des collectivités locales* (Paris, LITEC, 1981).

16 *Rapport d'Information du Sénat par M. Poncelet*.

17 Yves Mény, "Decentralization in Socialist France: The Politics of Pragmatism", *West European Politics*, 7 (Jan. 1984), p. 69.

18 See Vivien Schmidt, "Decentralization in France, Past and Present: Myth or Reality?" Paper delivered at the 1985 American Political Science Association Meeting, New Orleans, September 1985. Douglas Ashford, "Decentralizing France", in *The French Socialist Experiment*, ed. J. S. Ambler (Philadelphia, Institute for the Study of Human Issues, 1985). Mark Kesselman, "The End of Jacobinism? The Socialist Regime and Decentralization", *Contemporary French Civilization*, 8 (Fall/Winter 1983-84), pp. 84-103.

19 On problems of nationalism in recent years see J. Loughlin, "Regionalism and Ethnic Nationalism in France", in *Centre-Periphery Relations in Western Europe*, eds Yves Mény and Vincent Wright (London, George Allen and Unwin, 1985), and J. Loughlin, "A New Deal for France's Regions and Linguistic Minorities", *West European Politics*, 8 (July 1985), pp. 101-13.

16

The Left, Industrial Policy and the *Filière Électronique*

Jean-Louis Moynot

The Action Program for the electronics *filière*[1] (*Programme d'Action pour la Filière Électronique*, or PAFE), begun in 1982, was perhaps the most important manifestation of the voluntaristic industrial ambitions expressed at the beginning of the Mitterrand presidency. Subsequent to 1982, economic difficulties, plus the enormous costs of restructuring, reduced available financial resources appreciably. Despite this, ambition in electronics did not disappear completely. Persistent efforts undeniably produced accelerated development and a new strategic concentration of resources, so that by 1986 electronics had become both a symbol of the politics of industrial modernization in France and a measure of the will for European cooperation in the technologies of the future. The chapter that follows will propose a balance sheet of the Left's successes and failures in electronics, as well as its strengths and weaknesses.

Towards a new industrial policy in electronics

In 1981 the French industrial situation was generally poor. Apart from professional, military and telephonic sectors, electronics in France was no exception. It was seriously behind, and more and more threatened by, its international competitors. Many of the corporate groups designated for nationalization by the Left had already incurred heavy losses. The share of electronics in GNP had dropped to 3% against an earlier 5%, comparing quite unfavorably with the United States and Japan. Annual growth rates of 2-3% compared poorly with the 5-7% of its principal international competitors. The commercial balance of electronics was negative (91% of trade covered), and in rapid decline after 1979.

The electronics situation belonged in a more general context. The Pompidou presidency had made strong commitments, with positive results, to industrial change. The Giscard years, in contrast, had neither comparable ambitions nor results. Between 1974 and 1981 industrial policy in electronics was conceived of quite narrowly as the relationship between computers (or telematics) and society. Moreover, this narrow conception was itself not backed by serious and substantial industrial effort. The semiconductor plan of 1977, for example, even though a step in the right direction, turned out to be inadequate.

The Left's policies in electronics, which came to be embodied in the PAFE, began even before 1981 with the reflections of specialists close to the Socialist Party. At the time of the Nora–Minc Report (Paris, 1978–79) and the Computing Society Conference (Autumn 1979) some of these specialists were state administrators, some worked in university-based industrial studies and others were industrialists. The PAFE itself was established in 1982 for a four-year term as part of the Direction of Electronic and Computing Industries (DIELI) within the Ministry of Industry as a continuation of the Farnoux Report of 1981 at the new Ministry of Research and Technology. The program announced a "clear, long-term voluntarist strategy" which would be inseparable from the 1982 nationalizations in electronics and aim to reposition the French industry. At the beginning of the eighties, private-sector industrialists in Europe, in a position of weakness and with an uncertain future, would not have invested spontaneously in research, development, human resources and productive equipment. In order to implement this strategy, then, the government nationalized Thomson, the tenth largest electronics corporation worldwide and third in "professional–military" areas, Bull Computers, destructured by successive reorientations and dependant strategic thinking and the Compagnie Générale d'Electricité (CGE) which was strong in telephonics.

In keeping with the Left's long-standing preference for *filières* (vs *créneaux*), a *filière* strategy was chosen to recompose all linked elements – from components to materials, technologies to markets, industrial and professional products to consumer goods – with the purpose of creating competitive "poles". This strategy was defined to counter the fragility of overly specialized and narrow competitive positions, or *créneaux*. A global four-year growth target (9 per cent per year in volume) for the entire electronics industry was set. The strategy also sought a commercial surplus of 14 billion francs, total investment of 140 billion francs (60 billion provided by the state), 11 billion francs of capital base and investment aid, 45 billion of market and/or research subsidies and 4 billion of support for disseminating and using new research.

The new approach also implied precise aims, a specific program and clear resources for each operational branch of the *filière*. For example, the PAFE proposed increasing the annual turnover in components from 11 to 20 billion francs and doubling French worldwide market share for two-pole integrated circuits. It aimed for 9% of the worldwide market in color televisions, 7.5% of video cassette recorders (VCRs). The PAFE sought to maintain France's third place worldwide in military electronics, improve her position in telecommunications and progress in space markets. The consolidation of Bull Computers was proposed to obtain 35% of the French computer market and improve the productivity of computing service companies. It counted on the CGR to develop new techniques of medical imagery and to penetrate the worldwide medical electronics market. The proposal also included new goals in office automation, scientific instrumentation and industrial robots.

For each sector, the program proposed industrial and commercial initiatives, research and development, financial resources and restructuring (here multiple options were generally offered). Detailed estimates of manpower changes were also projected. Two of the main objectives of the Mauroy government, maintaining employment and reconquering the interior market, were observed. The *filière* strategy, which was designed to make a major contribution to the regeneration of French industry as a whole, envisaged the electronic transformation and revitalization of all French industrial structures. It also sought to move electronics into first place in the French consumer-goods sector, industrial markets and industrial markets of a mass-production kind (components). Strong past performance was the result of government purchases in these areas.

It is also important to underline that the electronics program not only proposed an industrial policy, but also a democratic social project. There was a focus on understanding the social changes implied by the industrial development of the *filière*. In 1979, the Nora–Minc Report had raised the issue of social changes which would likely follow the progress of "telematics". But its problematic was reduced to an "informational" framework, removed from any coherent industrial project (one sign of this was the then general director of telecommunications' fantasy about the use of ten million mini-teleterminals in less than ten years, a projection which was unrealistic both in production and market terms). In contrast, the PAFE discussed policies to broaden and vary utilization; specified sectoral policies towards industrial users, the service sector, the administration and public enterprise; and defined "transversal" actions in manpower training, employment and work organization.

There were some who considered social and economic aspects only as "effects" of changes, and others, technocratic or even totalitarian, who favored predefinition of a complete technology – society project. In contrast to both, the PAFE proposed an interactive policy involving widespread participation. It consistently advocated mechanisms for organizing social debate as a privileged instrument for finding the appropriate paths for technological change, thus complementing, in the manpower and job-shaping area a parallel program of social science research on the theme of "technologies, jobs, labor", whose implementation mobilized scientific firms and unions. Its ambition in the manpower-training area was a prelude to the new importance given to this theme in the "modernization" policies of the Fabius government. More generally, the PAFE published extensively on such matters. In these and other ways this program found its place in the general orientations of institutional, political and social reform legislated by the Left in 1982: specifically decentralization, the Auroux laws, nationalizations.

One final example of the shaping of the electronics *filière* to social questions is to be found in audiovisual communications. From the *plan cable* to television satellites, different technological tracks have been given high priority in French thinking. The opening up of television broadcasting to private channels was also proposed. Such issues remain central to public debate, of course. But in all this, the notion of the necessity of complementary economic and cultural efforts to develop a national programming industry was consecrated. Thus an international center for audiovisual communication was established, funded with substantial resources and directed by one of the people who was most influential in shaping general thinking about the *filière*.

THE 1985 BALANCE SHEET: THE POSITIVE SIDE

A recent BIPE study[2] demonstrated the progress made by the electric and electronics industries and argued that projected upturns would be due to the improved commercial

balance of electronics after 1983. The study forecast that industrial rehabilitation would
continue towards a total surplus of about 30 billion francs in 1989. According to other
recent data, the external deficit in electronics was reduced from 11 billion to 3 billion
francs between 1982 and 1985 and will reach or exceed equilibrium in 1986. The
growth rate in production for the whole of the *filière* was estimated at 8.2% in 1983,
10% in 1984, between 7% and 8% in 1985. The share of electronics in GNP - 3.1%
in 1981 - reached 3.7% in 1984 and continued to progress. The BIPE[3] estimated that
such growth would hold steady even though the *rate* of growth would slow to roughly
5% to 6%. Growth rates in imports and exports were projected to be even higher
(10% to 14% according to the products). The same study emphasized that the actual
component plan, in contrast to its predecessors, had begun to bear fruit and that the
Thomson group, in particular, seemed to be on the right track to become a world-
class component producer.

The financial balance sheets of principal nationalized groups were either maintained
(CGE, CIT, Alcatel), or else restored more quickly than expected (Thomson
and Bull Computers since 1984). Budget and capital allocations, the *contrats de
plan*, as well as the autonomy the shareholder state allowed its managers, all
contributed to this. The only example in the *filière* not conforming to this return
to solvency was the CGCT, whose deficit was inseparable from the difficulties
of the telephone sector itself. In terms of public financing of the *filière*, substantial
progress was made, even though the period of the PAFE program corresponded
precisely to the "rigor" policies. Global public financing exceeded 11 billion
francs in 1984, with funding for markets and scientific research up from 5.6
(1982) to 8 billion francs (1984). This effort was as positive for general research
and development (R & D) activities as it was for specific branches of electronics.
But public financing was much lower than planned originally by the PAFE.
For example, 7 billion francs was provided for R & D instead of the expected
9 billion. This shortfall was distributed unevenly, with planned outlays achieved in
components and telecommunication, less in professional electronics and computing
and virtually negligible in consumer electronics.

Significant progress was made in industrial and commercial positions. The renewal
of 1983 and 1984 helped to support important growth and intensive efforts to raise
productivity and exports in the components area. The gross income of Thomson
Semiconductors reached 2.15 billion francs in 1984 against roughly 1.5 billion in 1983,
while Thomson's position in integrated circuits grew considerably stronger. For its
part, Matra–Harris's semiconductor business grew steadily (345 million francs in 1984
against 175 million in 1983), basing its financial equilibrium on a commercially coherent
line of integrated-circuit products. Both of these companies will, in all likelihood,
progressively acquire an independent research and development capacity in these types
of advanced technologies not to mention industrial *savoir-faire*. Thomson is associated
with the LETI (Atomic Energy Commission) and Matra–Harris with the National
Center for Telecommunication Studies to develop and transform into production the
"submicronic" stages of miniaturizing integrated circuits. The year 1985 was more
difficult, obliging everyone to reexamine strategy and growth perspectives. Nevertheless,
countercylical efforts continued and the two French companies avoided the disaster

which many of their American counterparts experienced. Indeed, Thomson Semiconductors has just bought part of Mostek to enhance its position in the American market.

Among other sectoral success stories, there is also the consolidation of the CGR (affiliated to Thomson, and through it, French advanced medical electronics. CGR restructured and limited reductions of annual turnover and manpower adjustments. Its new 1984 capital base and sustained efforts to finance research permitted it to reposition itself rapidly in the market for imagery by nuclear magnetic resonance (NMR), and to expand its postions on the market for X-ray scanners. CGR's activity and orders are increasing, its commercial balance has been reestablished and the outlook is good.

France's successful defense of its worldwide top ranking in professional and military electronics is well known. This established reputation did not preclude its recent successes, which attracted a great deal of attention. Financing of research in this area has not reached the level PAFE projected. Even though recent successes follow the strengthening of research teams and technological capacities over a long period – 20 years for RITA – they also owe some of their success to recent general efforts favoring the electronics industry. Space electronics is well placed in an industry in full expansion; Ariane-Space has made its commercial breakthrough and the outlook is good; the European communications satellite industry is becoming competitive (TDF 1 is scheduled to be launched in 1986); the European Society of Propulsion is well positioned to compete for the observation of the earth.

The only "good example", Bull Computers, is more remarkable. The press, specialists in data processing and managerial milieux all agree that Bull President Jacques Stern and Chief Executive Officer Francis Lorentz have together formed a remarkable team, cultivating a public enterprise *esprit* with wide industrial responsibilities, as well as managerial independence from the state. Like other public-sector leaders, they asked for tranquility, time and money. Unlike others, they obtained them. Bull Computers is the only nationalized firm which has profited from a pluriannual state commitment for capital endownment and other types of assistance. Taking over an enterprise in crisis, Stern and Lorentz avoided extensive layoffs and rejected alignment to IBM standards. They wanted to preserve work teams, form a corporate culture and shape common motivations in an enterprise whose past was checkered with difficult reorganizations. Bull's strategy aimed at coexistence with industry leaders (primarily IBM), while avoiding the pure dependence which might follow from a strategy of "compatibility" of technological material. Links of European cooperation, broken in 1978, have been reestablished, beginning with joint research with Siemens and ICL. The results have been remarkable. Bull's commercial balance has been restored since 1984, productivity has been rising at 16 per cent per year, financial structures have been reviewed and some new affiliated firms have been created. Regular dialogue with clients and data-processing service companies has been established. The general staff of the conglomerate has been rebuilt smoothly. Even the "look" of the company was remade without internal disruption. Here also, success came at the cost of a controlled short-term loss of market segments and of a limited number (900) of jobs. Technological independence remains to be achieved, however, and many other problems must be resolved. But Bull Computers has returned from afar and is now on the right track.

It is harder to offer such general opinions about the other nationalized electronics groups. For two of them this is in large part because their size and complexity render such generalizations risky. At Thomson, the decentralization of legal and industrial structures and the restructuring of the Thomson Group have worked well according to the 1984 accounts and a recent Senate report. Alain Gomez has become a *grand manager* in the eyes of public opinion and has succeeded at some important initiatives. For Thomson, future stakes are nevertheless very high and success is far from certain in the crucial fields of components and consumer electronics.

The positive results of considerable efforts in manpower training made under governmental leadership must be underlined. Two principal training plans for the electronics *filière* were put into place. One of them, now fully implemented, projected the training of an additional 1,100 engineers, 3,000 technicians and 100 teachers between 1983 and 1985. The other, a plan to accompany the general development of the *filière*, initially projected an annual flow of 3,000 engineering and 1,500 graduate technicians; by early 1985 it had produced 3,200 engineers and more than 2,000 technicians. The distribution of graduates by specialties (microelectronics, data processing, etc.) has improved as well. Concurrently, in four years, more than 400 million francs were invested in the equipment needed for this modernization and expansion of manpower training. the annual training grants of the DIELI (roughly 100 million francs, to which 70 million must be added to finance the materials) were given preferentially to organizations and activities which tied company resources to the training system. Thus multiple "marriages" between industry and schools or universities had been consummated even before they were officially ordered by the ministry of Education in 1984–85. The relationship between the University of Savoie and the local professional electronics organizations is one example. The best model of universities/*Grandes Ecoles*/industry association is to be found in Grenoble's National Polytechnic Institute (INPG). Toulouse and Paris provide other examples (i.e., Paris VI for fundamental microelectronics, and the association of Paris XI-Orsay with Sup'Elec and the neighboring *Grandes Ecoles*).

Important additional manpower training efforts are worth mentioning. A study group on workers and technicians in the *filière* and a group to monitor and project manpower development have been established, along with general reviews of the adequacy of training and placement. All these efforts have been enhanced by the orientations of the Ministry of Education which began in 1985. The "computer plan for all" has devised an efficient and low-cost formula to diffuse technological expertise in the general education curriculum and to permit the greatest number of young people to appropriate new technical tools. A long-term effort was also undertaken to increase the proportion of young persons getting their *baccalauréat*, and to develop specifically technical *bacs*.

Mixed results

A number of restructuring, regrouping and repurchasing operations have been carried out in electronics. Some, like the repurchase of Eurotechnique by Thomson (it had earlier been a *filiale* of National Semiconductors and Saint Gobain), or the takeover of

Telefunken by Thomson General Public, have been successes. Sometimes regrouping success has been achieved even when preexisting conditions were judged to be very difficult. Such was the case for the Bull Group. Other operations have not brought desired results. Perhaps the biggest redistribution of telephone activities was between the CGE and Thomson groups. The conditions under which this was done have often been criticized. Without underestimating the requirements for secrecy in such high-stake transactions, too few people were associated. Because of this, neither the desired redistribution of activities and technical choices nor association of the personnel representatives in decision-making were realized. Thomson was pressured by a reduction of available finances necessary to its recovery in ways which promoted a redistribution that was too favorable to CGE. CGE took over management of Thomson Telecommunications without assuming its losses, for example. More generally, this amalgamation caused many social, industrial and financial problems that had not been foreseen – CGE alone announced the elimination of 4,500 jobs. The state had to absorb a large part of the losses of TTL (telegraphic and telephonic lines) in order to bail it out. Finally, the restructuring operation, which should have "reinforced the worldwide positions of French industry", ran into problems in choosing material and did not produce a clear redefinition of industrial strategy. The management of PTT (Post Office) telecommunications did not appreciate Chief Executive Officer Georges Pébereau's attitude towards employment or his attempt to stake everything on the American market. For such reasons the government in 1985 ordered an acceleration of the restructuring process and a 100 per cent absorption of Thomson Telecommunications by CIT-Alcatel (CGE) leading to a new group, Alcatel-Thomson, which fell totally under CGE control after 1 July 1985. But if a sorting-out of factories and products has been accomplished, the problems have not been resolved. In response, there were numerous social conflicts "in the field".

The French position in telecommunications is largely a function of these difficulties. In 1983 exports increased by 49 per cent, the commercial surplus grew from 1.8 billion to 3 billion francs, public research credits were approximately in line with targets and technological potentialities were great. But the financial situation of the industrial group remained fragile (or bad, as with the CGCT), its international positioning was weak and it had serious industrial relations problems. This was a preoccupation in an international context of deregulation and the multiplication of marketing and technology-sharing agreements between telecommunications firms. Meanwhile, the internal market tightened up because the desired level of telephone equipment had been attained, even if the *plan cable* took more time than planned. In contrast, the diffusion of professional and consumer videotext services occurred rapidly.

On another plane, the evolution of employment in the whole of the filière has not conformed to plans. Because the PAFE was established with a general perspective of growth, the *filière* was assigned a yearly growth target of 9 per cent. Although the actual rate has been 8 per cent the shortfall has statistically reduced employment growth, if in skewed ways. The need for new specialists in new jobs has continued to grow. Simultaneously, however, there have been too many less qualified workers (semiskilled in particular) for the slowly growing number of such jobs. Restructuring, with consequent reduction in manpower needs, has occurred in consumer electronics, certain component activities and professional electronics, in addition to telephonics, as noted already. Nearly all of these cases corresponded to new positionings in markets, product redefinition and efforts to increase productivity and modernize.

It is clear that the future evolution of electronics implies multiple long-run structural modifications. On the one hand, new activities and employment will be created; on the other, some jobs will be lost. The idea of programmed management of employment has been adopted progressively by the nationalized groups, with strategic options for high qualification and training efforts to allow mobility and promotion. The actual practice of these options has been more or less pursued according to the specific conglomerate and industrial area of the *filière*. Drawing up coherent policies for the management of the most qualified human resources (engineers and diverse specialists) has been possible. In other areas there are still too many situations with an excess of available manpower, situations which can only be resolved by a "social plan". This difficulty has led the big conglomerates to develop the activities of "societies of conversion", which, when group affiliates cut back employment, act as consultants and bring financial support to local firms creating new jobs. The principle behind their intervention is to reinforce the coherence of local economic life and to rebalance the local job market in response to problems created by the firm. The workings of these societies of conversion has also raised, in new ways, the issue of the relationship between large, medium-sized and small industries (technological transfers, technical support to smaller firms etc.). Likewise, these societies have focused anew on the use of venture capital to encourage the creation of firms which will have privileged links with the conglomerate. In such areas, few things have yet been done, but attitudes have been changing.

Industrial relations in electronics have evolved likewise. In general, high technology calls for the modern management of human resources and the provision of new incentives for employees, philosophies not always synonymous with progressive social ideals, however. It is nevertheless possible to judge electronics more easily in this realm than anywhere else in French industry. There has been an unanticipated congruence between reforms that employers rejected initially (the Auroux Laws) and the development of more favorable attitudes towards the firm and the economic conditions for its success on the part of workers (and the French more generally). Today, business leaders admit privately that there has been a considerable change, which they owe, in large part, to the Left.

Enterprise-level work relations have therefore changed somewhat. Employer experiments – development of intra-enterprise communications; independent production teams; quality circles; the individualization of management and social matters; the elaboration of enterprise projects and the promotion of enterprise "culture" – have coincided with the application of the Auroux Laws allowing employees much greater leverage over the conditions determining their own work. The creation of "expression groups", the new economic prerogatives of works committees and the obligation to negotiate salaries annually have already paid off in quantitative balance sheets. Debates over the qualitative contents of these balance sheets will continue, of course, since the facts of these new experiences have been ambiguous. It will take much longer to develop new behavior.

Institutional change has gone further in public-sector firms, with the establishment of "group committees" plus the election of "employee administrators" to new boards of directors. Experience demonstrates how difficult it is to alter such managerial functions. Employee group administrators risk being cut off from their base; they were not very well prepared for their new roles and the boards have not really stopped being rubber stamps and intermediate managerial hierarchies have resisted the institutionalization of such new relationships. Nonetheless, strategic information has begun to circulate more and relationships between management and unions have been changing, especially in restructuring negotiations. Changing work relations demonstrate an indirect but real effort at reform. New management in "social affairs" areas has undoubtedly been responsible for an appreciable part of this change. In short, if the nationalized groups have had little influence over the general evolution of business ideas, they nevertheless have been a pilot sector of working reforms which may help after March 1986 to contain the antiunion projects promoted by certain members of the Center–Right before the elections.

Next comes the problem of exclusion. Certain sectors of the *filière* have been left out of most post-1981 changes, whether there were insufficient funds to support their technical and commercial development, or because of strategic choice. This has been the case in the measurement and scientific-instrumentation sector (which is led by American firms) where coordinated European initiatives would have made sense, but have not been undertaken. It is also true in office automation, where French industry is very weak. Results have come slowly in this area (an accord with Olivetti remains limited and no new strategic action has occurred). Other sectors' performances remain uncertain, without having been completely "excluded". Engineering and computing services have maintained their market positions, high growth in turnover and employment, but are experiencing a decline in profitability. Important steps will be necessary to resist an invasion of rival software and a plan for introducing industrial methods into production started late (1984). Here, the only strong French positions are in programmable robots and certain CAD/CAM software. American domination remains overwhelming in the field of industrial calculators.

Strategic problems also play a role. Consumer electronics still lacks a real strategy in very difficult competitive circumstances, for example. The only plausible long-term tactic is an alliance of big European firms. The defeat of Thomson's takeover of Grundig in 1983 was not due to a lack of political will or "preference" for an alternative strategy,[4] but because of the attitude of Philips which, at the time, was unconcerned with finding an equal partner in Europe. The purchase of Telefunken and the agreement with JVC for the European production of VCRs have given Thomson consumer goods a European scale. Industrially, the production of mechanical VCR parts in France and their assembly with the electronic components in Berlin has been a success. The Villingen Laboratory in West Germany, moreover, is potentially an excellent research center for consumer products. The market breakthrough of the personal computer[5] and recent public purchases in this field have also been remarkable successes. But Japanese (and, in the future, Korean) competition is dangerous; most Japanese firms are now establishing themselves in Europe. Despite constant and rapid growth in productivity, French prices, notably for televisions, do not allow profitability and research support in this area. Thus, Europeans are threatened with a fate similar to that of American consumer electronics. The situation calls for important decisions, and soon.

UNCERTAINTIES

Technical progress and product cycles in electronics are extremely rapid. Amounts needed for research and development thus increase constantly, and R & D itself becomes more risky. Market control and profits go to those who arrive first. The American industry is a concentration of considerable power and has the largest market. In competing with the Americans the Japanese have not made a mistake for more than 20 years in their triumphant march forward, as is well known. French efforts are fully justifiable, but the struggle will be hard and the future uncertain. Apart from the problems of the consumer-goods sector, the very unfavorable conjuncture in semiconductors leads one to think that a decisive moment in the concentration of principal semiconductor producers is coming. Alliances are multiplying, like the one between Philips and Siemens in Europe. In order to consolidate returns from the intensive efforts made over the past few years, France must develop a strategy of alliances and of cooperation. And we must make no mistakes in developing this strategy, which does not yet exist. It is at this crucial point that the French electronics industry stands presently.

Buried somewhere in the uncertainties about the success of the electronics *filière* program is the destiny of small and middle-sized firms. Their fragility has often followed from a situation of pure subcontracting or a lack of expertise in product and market evolution. Both the government and conglomerates have undertaken actions to reinforce the technological and commercial capacities of such firms, systematize certain technological transfers, and allow smaller firms to cooperate in research, innovation and marketing. The best of these smaller firms have adopted strategies of participation and cooperation with various partners: French and foreign industrialists, public research centers, universities, etc. But actions of this type have just got underway and final results are uncertain. In particular, French venture capital is still insufficient and of unequal quality.

The future development of communications and its social effects are other major uncertainties. Initially, the government staked a lot on the *plan cable* and the development of local broadcasting companies linked to specific territories. The Direction Générale des Télécommunication (DGT) considered that with cabling and the use of the Telecom 1 satellite France had sufficient means and a technically coherent system. The construction and launching of the TDF 1 telecommunications satellite was then approved, however. And, parallel to delays in implementing the *plan cable*, the government decided again to stress traditional techniques of television broadcasting while reviewing, and finally deciding on, how to open the airwaves to private television. The very large recent regrouping maneuvers of the principal European communications groups have taken place in this perspective. Will France be able to control the pressure of private interests on audiovisual communication and maintain both pluralism and the conditions for a public service?

EUROPEAN NOVELTIES

The evolution of the industrial situation and PAFE have made the development of European cooperation and research programs look more and more crucial. During the early 1980s the Commission of the European Communities began the first phase (five years) of a vast research program (10 billion francs, 50 per cent financed) in data and information-processing technologies. The first group of research projects was launched in 1984, a second in 1985. Today a reasonably clear evaluation of this first phase is possible and the modalities of a second five-year phase (a 1987 start-up) are being discussed. All participants in the first phase of ESPRIT, as the program was called, consider the results to be positive. Etienne Davignon, the last Vice-President of the Commission, emphasized the fact that the part of ESPRIT directed towards small projects was particularly profitable and that the allocation of funds for it should be increased in the second phase. From the point of view of big industrial groups, it is worth quoting Thomson's assessment of its participation:

> Thomson and its cooperating companies participate in 30 research programs, representing 20% of the total amounts of all studies done in the ESPRIT program. Those aspects which will be done by Thomson teams involve roughly 500 million francs. In other words, with 250 million francs of research investments on a five-year basis (and 250 million of subsidy from the Community) Thomson will have access to 1.8 billion francs for research, divided into 30 different projects.
>
> Many projects involving the participation of some parts of the Thomson Group were proposed but not included while still considered excellent by CGE experts. Some of them will be proposed again, after updating, as part of the second ESPRIT phase.

Because experience is important in this field, the success of ESPRIT has been demonstrated by the launching of the much larger and more ambitious EUREKA program, of which an important part lies in the electronics *filière*. Whatever European judgements are of the Stategic Defense Initiative (SDI), it will have had the merit of bringing Europeans, prodded by François Mitterrand, to respond to the technological challenge. Because of EUREKA's extra-EEC scope and its initiatives being divided between governments and firms, we do not yet know exactly what EUREKA will be, but its existence and its importance are now assured. Etienne Davignon considers EUREKA to be a major event because it is the first time that European political and industrial leaders have followed up their industrial policy assertions with actions. Such was not the case five years ago. Davignon further confirms, following ESPRIT, that cooperation is now judged to be systematically essential, not only for big programs, but also for small-scale projects.

Obviously, much remains to be done before one can talk about European industrial construction in electronics. All big European industrialists, whatever sector they are in, insist upon the need for a genuinely unified market. They add that the real obstacle to alliances is the balkanization of national industrial norms. Without this, the addition of two European industrial and commercial forces will always add up to less than their arithmetic total, while alliance between any single European and American or Japanese firm will individually be more advantageous. The consequence of this, of course, will be the increasing foreign penetration of the European market. The size of a real European inland market must correspond to the size and strength of the forces prepared to conquer it.

It is not easy to be excessively optimistic about all this. The reciprocal opening of public markets and European telecommunications has barely progressed. The advantage of research programs in future technologies is that they will develop practices which will create greater trust in cooperation. Here there has been a very clear temptation to circumvent middle-range industrial and commercial obstacles by proposing extremely long-term programs. One example of this was a 1983–84 study for the EEC on telecommunications' infrastructure. By the year 2000, it proposed a transnational system of wide-band transmissions with bands superimposed on each other with optic fibers. Without underestimating the significance of such a perspective (a futurist system of telecommunications "highways"), smaller and shorter steps forward will be more important.

In short, both in France and in Europe, the consciousness and the practice of cooperation, notably in electronics, have progressed considerably in five years. Indeed, such perspectives had barely been sketched out in the 1982 PAFE goals. The French government, and in part French industrialists, have since played leadership roles to encourage this European cooperation. But multiple institutional obstacles still exist in Europe itself. The political will to overcome them does not yet measure up to the difficulties and high stakes at hand.

HALF SUCCESS OR HALF FAILURE?

Our review illustrates successes, mixed results, failures, uncertainties and a few novelties. In a changing world, economic actions often produce results different from those anticipated. The important thing is to understand the reasons for these differences. Some depend on the context and on politics more generally. There is little doubt – a posteriori – that the Left initially sinned through excessive optimism about the capacities of the French economy, in particular those of its industry *vis-à-vis* external competitors. The politics of *rigueur* which had to be adopted subsequently had a generally restrictive effect on growth, specific sectoral effects on electronics (for example, the measures of Poitiers in 1983 on the internal consumer electronics market) and the budgetary effect of reducing planned public financing for PAFE. The Left concluded that its duty was to keep its electoral promises in social matters. But we must at least ask ourselves about the chronology of economic policy: revival, *rigueur*, modernization. In brief, the Left consumed its resources and created difficulties which had to be faced *before* undertaking the actions which it considered decisive. The Left's industrial policies had only been defined by the end of 1982. Their course was then changed implicitly and explicitly, wavering from a voluntarism essentially based on statist means to discourse which came close to economic liberalism. Happily, practice has been more open than discourse and correctly left the necessary strategic and managerial autonomy at the firm level. But at no time did the Left really know how to think about links between governmental action, the initiative of economic forces (private or public) and the movement of social forces by which politics takes on consistency and becomes reality.

The second cause of shortfall between results and ambitions has been the lack of reasoning of PAFE on the real limits of French resources in relation to worldwide competition. The program's ambitions were correct. The real problem was that it had insufficient means to achieve them. Moreover, a serious underestimation of the magnitude of European industrial problems, compared to the worldwide competition, underlay this. The PAFE did not reflect sufficiently upon the issue of industrial alliances. In addition, the resources committed by France have been far inferior to those even of its principal European competitors. To borrow Eric Leboucher's observation, the problem is not in knowing whether the glass is half full or half empty; in reality, the glass is too small. The PAFE was well placed in worldwide competition. But Europe lay between France and the world. And Europe contained the possibility of creative new industrial alliances. This lack of vision has been somewhat corrected *en route*, and the future looks brighter than five years ago.

It is difficult to conclude about a subject in flux. The worldwide electronics industry will certainly see change in the decades to come. The difficulties that many American enterprises encountered in this sector in 1985 demonstrated how uncertain the world of electronics was. There is no doubt, however, that results in electronics will be decisive for industry as a whole. And it is certain that a concentration of effort on research innovation is necessary to ensure the future. Some may think that PAFE was Utopian; if this is the case, it was a very well-reflected and researched Utopia. Despite its limits, PAFE has generally played a leading role. The mobilization that has occurred around it has led to an acceleration of development in French electronics, a beginning of industrial coherence and a movement toward modernization with positive effects for the European context. French electronics faces a new future with the political changes of 1986. PAFE has made this future brighter than it may have been otherwise.

NOTES

1 The *filière* vs *créneaux* argument became the central industrial policy disagreement between Left and Right in the 1970s. The Left advocated policies to retain the complete chain of "affiliated" activities in an industry, from parts to finished products – hence the notion, *filière*. In turn, the Left accused the Right of seeking only international niches – *créneaux* – in specialized industrial areas, as opposed to an entire industry. The core of the Left's argument was about the preservation of French industrial autonomy to avoid international dependency.
2 Bureau d'Information et de Prévisions Économiques. 3 Prévision, Lettre 101, Ministère du Redéploiement Industriel et du Commerce Extérieur, supplément au no. 207, October 1985.
3 Bureau d'Information et de Prévisions Économiques, *Tric-Tronic 85-89: bilan et perspectives pour les industries électriques et électroniques françaises* (Paris, BIPE, 1985).

4 The political will/alternative preference thesis is advanced by Michel Bauer and Elie Cohen, *Les Grandes manoeuvres industrielles* (Paris, Belfond, 1985).
5 An agreement to collaborate on the development of a European standard for personal and micro-computers was signed in September 1985 by Olivetti, Acorn and Thomson Micro-Informatique Grand Public.

17

France and the Electronic Media

The Economics of Freedom

JEAN-MARIE GUÉHENNO

The electronic media, which in France started as a branch of the Post Office (Postes Télégraphe et Téléphone – PTT), have gained increasing independence from the state. In 1959, General de Gaulle set up Radiodiffusion Télévision Française as a governmental agency, granting it a separate budget, but placing it under the authority of the Minister of Information. In 1964, the Office de la Radiodiffusion Télévision Française (ORTF) was created. It was to be an independent agency, placed under the control – but no longer authority – of the Minister of Information. By 1974, the ORTF had become a cumbersome monster, criticized both for its alleged complacency to governmental requests and for wasteful management. President Giscard d'Estaing therefore decided to dismantle the ORTF and created seven agencies: three for the three television channels (TF1, Antenne 2, FR 3); one for radio (Radio France); a production agency (SFP); an agency for the management of broadcasting installations (TDF); and a training and archival agency (INA).

When the Socialists won the 1981 elections, however, the reforms enacted in 1974 were overwhelmingly perceived as inadequate. The seven agencies were not protected from government intervention, since the government appointed their chief executives, and the state maintained its monopoly over radio and television. With the exception of Europe 1, Radio Monte Carlo, and Radio Télé Luxembourg – all three partly or indirectly controlled by the state – no private radio stations existed. A number of entrepreneurs and local groups – many of them leaning toward the Left – were beginning to test the state monopoly, however, by establishing small radio stations, which the police soon dismantled because of their illegality. The multiplication of local radios continued after the Socialist victory, illustrating the ineffectiveness of the monopoly and the intensity of pent-up demand for more diversity. The optimistic mood of 1981 made it seem that the elimination of the old monopoly would be easy; a new *espace de liberté* (territory for freedom) was to be conquered, which in turn would encourage self-expression and increase communication.

Events between 1981 and 1986 sometimes contradicted that optimistic scenario. The electronic media – simultaneously an important industry, powerful political tool and expression of the integrity of a country's culture – have confronted the government with some difficult choices. The government responded by agreeing generally to guarantee the independence of public broadcasting. Beyond this, the state faced serious policy dilemmas.

To begin with, it would have been paradoxical for a Socialist government to forfeit state responsibility for providing the public with quality programming. No government of the Right had ever repudiated the notion of public service behind radio and television, after all. How then was this "public service" to coexist with new independent stations? What would their respective shares be? Would it be appropriate for the private sector to play the major role in the development of new media at a time when some of the biggest French companies were being nationalized? Would market forces work any better than the state monopoly? The "Italian model" – the disorderly multiplication of television stations, avalanche of low-quality cheap programming and the accompanying decline of the Italian film industry – was not the road to take. The audience had to be protected to some degree against greedy private interest, and perhaps against itself. In contrast, such protection could become the new name for dirigisme and state control over the media. A set of rules ensuring the state's disengagement and guaranteeing an *espace de liberté* needed to be established.

Next, the state wanted to maintain some control over the hardware side of the new media, particularly the cabling of French cities, because of the rapid development of new technologies and the Socialist government's emphasis on France's participation in the technological revolution. The risk remained nevertheless that controlling hardware would lead to controlling software, i.e. programming. The abolition of the state monopoly over programming had to be reconciled with the persistence of state control over the technical means of diffusion.

Finally, financing had increasingly become the most crucial issue of the establishment of the new media. Budgetary constraints became more pressing and competing demands for funds made choices more difficult. How much money would be left for programming after the financing needs of cable were met? And, where would that money come from? If the financial support from the state and local governments was to be limited, what portion of revenues could, and should be expected from advertising? Was there a risk of diverting funds at the expense of the written media?

The leftist government did not react uniformly to these dilemmas. Greater reliance on market forces, paralleling changes in overall economic policy, could be discerned, of course. Nevertheless, the initial objectives did not disappear, and a structural framework to achieve them was erected. How much this framework will influence the development of the French media notwithstanding different political majorities is the underlying question of this paper.

THE AMBITIONS OF 1982

Law 82–652 of 29 July 1982, ambitiously called *Loi sur la communication audio-visuelle*, was intended to be much more than a reorganization of public broadcasting. Only one of its five crucial sections is specifically devoted to public broadcasting, in fact. Of the other four, one section states some "general principles", asserting that freedom is the governing principle of "audiovisual communication"; another section establishes the new institutions guaranteeing these principles and creating the Haute Autorité de l'Audio-Visuel; the third sets up the parameter within which radio and television stations and a cable system can be created; the last section reorganizes methods of film distribution.

La Haute Autorité - a French Federal Communications Commission

The Chirac government decided to replace the Haute Autorité with a new regulating agency, which would supposedly be entrusted with more powers. The creation of the Haute Autorité was nevertheless one of the most important decisions made by the Socialists; it started an evolution which cannot be stopped. The Haute Autorité is a long way from playing the role of the Federal Communications Commission (FCC) in the United States, however. It has neither the FCC's technical responsibilities nor its staff and budget. The half dozen *"chargés de mission"* of the Haute Autorité cannot be compared with the FCC's 1,300 employees. Moreover, other agencies within the French government continue to play a key role in determining the future of the media. The Secretary of State for Communication and its legal office (Service Juridique et Technique de l'Information), the Minister of Culture, the Minister of the PTT - not to mention the President of the Republic himself - have retained essential responsibilities in the policy-making process. Technically Télédiffusion de France (TDF) continues to determine which frequencies are available, a responsibility which has been entrusted to the FCC in the United States.[1] Last but not least, the decisions of the Haute Autorité cannot be enforced through the criminal justice system without the consent of the executive branch.

The Haute Autorité nevertheless quickly became a respected reference. Its nine members were appointed for a nine-year term, with no reappointment. One-third of the members were appointed by the President of the Republic, one-third by the President of the Senate and one-third by the President of the National Assembly. Members were to be replaced on a rotating basis in thirds in order to encourage independence. Prior to March 1986 this seemed to have worked. Few, if any, of the decisions of the Haute Autorité - the majority of whose members were appointed by the Left - were criticized as being politically oriented.

In the short run, the most visible role of the Haute Autorité has been to appoint the presidents of the six public broadcasting companies (TF1, Antenne 2, FR 3, Radio France, SFP, Radio-télévision Française d'Outre-mer) for three-year periods. This responsibility, among others, symbolized the Haute Autorité's function as guarantor of the independence of public broadcasting. This was all the more important because the three public television networks were not competing with each other, except for Canal Plus, a pay-television system (see below). The credibility of the Haute Autorité with the general public depended, without doubt, on the degree of independence granted to public broadcasting. The Haute Autorité subsequently enhanced its credibility by selecting, for the six broadcasting companies whose three-year term expired in October 1985, a new set of presidents who generally met the public's approval.

The role of the Haute Autorité in regulating other areas of communication is bound to increase in the long run, but its powers are considerably limited at present. The Haute Autorité shares the responsibility of granting licences to radio or television stations with the state. The state maintains responsibility for authorizing radio stations extending beyond 30 kilometers, and cable-system programmers beyond 60 kilometers. In the original version of the law of 1982, off-the-air television also remained entirely under state control.

The Haute Autorité also depends on TDF for the technical aspects of broadcasting and is limited to authorizing programmers to use specific frequencies. TDF determines which frequencies will actually be available to local radio stations, and installs all transmitters (with power over 500 watts) and master antennas of television cable systems. The Haute Autorité does not have the staff or expertise to challenge the evaluations and decisions of TDF. Both the uncertainty of the number of available frequencies and TDF's traditional secrecy have created some controversy concerning their sharing of information. Local television stations have yet to enter the picture. When they do, the dependence of the Haute Autorité on TDF is bound to become even more controversial since the 1982 law was revised to give the Haute Autorité power to authorize local television stations. However, as with radio stations, TDF would determine which frequencies are available. French broadcasting does not have a big supply of frequencies because of the "public service" principle which gives top priority to equal access for the greatest possible number of citizens. Moreover, the quality of reception is often better in France than in the United States, but this is because of imposed limits on the number of frequencies for new stations and the wider spaces between them. The Haute Autorité may therefore find itself in the uncomfortable position of allocating scarce resources, even if this scarcity is partly due to political factors beyond its control.

These limitations help clarify a major difference between the Haute Autorité and the FCC. The Haute Autorité is not a regulatory commission; it has limited control over the technical and political aspects of the media. Still, somewhere between its inability to make rules and its role as buffer between the government and stations, the Haute Autorité has its own niche. It is the ultimate guarantor of freedom and self-expression in both public and private media; the government, on the other hand, is responsible for creating the conditions of economic health in the media and for defining the goals of public broadcasting. In the perspective of the law of 1982, the Haute Autorité was expected to ensure the prevalence of a cultural perspective, as well as freedom from government intervention or economic constraints.

A cultural perspective

Indeed, the purpose of most rules in the media policy area is cultural rather than economic. Cultural concerns, along with economic considerations, explained, for example, why the government observed the tradition established by its predecessors in deferring to the wishes of the motion picture industry and regulating the broadcasting of feature films. Thus no feature film can be shown on television less than 36 months (12 months for pay-television) after its release. Additional constraints (again less stringent for pay-television) limit the broadcasting of films to Wednesdays, Fridays and weekends. Similarly, the idea that local radio stations are a means of self-expression for local communities led to the ruling that local programming (*programme propre*) must represent 80% of the station's total programming with news constituting a part of such local programming. In the case of cable television, the general franchise agreement, approved only at the beginning of 1985 (Decree 85-54 of 18 January 1985) was much less constraining, requiring that 15% of the system's capacity be reserved for local programming, with 20% of this period reserved for public access. Foreign programs may not exceed 30% of the capacity of the system; programs from the European Community must represent at least 60% of the programs (not of the capacity) and programs originally in French should represent 50% of the programs. In the case of public broadcasting, more specific rules determine the programming grid of each network.

There were economic concerns, of course. The prohibition on advertising on local radio stations was motivated by the fear that the local press would lose important advertising revenues. This consideration for the local press stemmed from political motives, but the rule was never observed, and in 1984 the law was officially dropped. The initial law nevertheless illustrates how optimistic the 1982 lawmakers were about the economic prospects of the media industry: if any economic problems arose, subsidies would be granted. The government, in fact, put a mechanism in place to provide local radio stations with subsidies. The decree of 1 December 1984 appropriated approximately 76 million francs, raised through a tax on television and radio advertising, which were to be distributed to 400 not-for-profit radio stations, provided these stations do not air commercials (except public-interest messages). In comparison, FM radio stations received 300 million francs of advertising revenues in 1984. Funds channelled to the French motion picture industry – thanks to a tax on all theater ticket sales – were increased (see below), and earlier tax programs were extended.

Finally, the circulation and supply of programs among the various cable systems was facilitated by the establishment of an "exchange" for cable television programs. This small agency, the Mission Cable, acts as a public syndicator of noncommercial programs and now boasts more than 2,500 hours available at low prices for cable systems.

The Satellite project and the "global village"

The emphasis on local programming was meant to convey the feeling that cable systems and local radio stations were the electronic equivalents of the old town square, a meeting place for each small community. Complementing this local emphasis was a renewed interest in direct satellite broadcasting. The Giscard administration actually initiated the satellite project, with industrial policy playing a major part in its inception. At stake were the development of an independent satellite industry, the complementary Ariane rocket project and Europe's place as an independent player in the world space industry.

Bureaucratic rivalries were also involved in this. Since the powerful PTT was responsible for the cabling of French cities (see below) and low-power communication satellites, TDF could assert its independence from it by launching a high-power Direct Broadcasting Satellite (DBS). Thus, TDF 1 was to be launched in July 1986, followed in 1987 by TDF 2. These satellites would utilize cheaper, smaller (40 cms) receiving antennas, instead of the bigger dishes required by telecommunication satellites.

The government asked a respected television executive, Pierre Desgraupes, to undertake a preliminary study for the programming of one of the DBS channels. The completed project, Canal 1, proposed a kind of European Public Broadcasting Service (PBS), which could technically reach more than 123 million households, or 250 million people. The Louis Harris Institute estimated that approximately 13.1 million households, or more than 40 million people, would buy the appropriate dishes or be connected to a cable system. Desgraupes recommended that the anticipated cost of Canal 1 - one billion francs per year (of which 75 per cent would be spent on programming) - be covered by some advertising and by sponsoring. The new company would be a joint effort of European television companies, which would share the capital expenses. Public start-up money was considered absolutely necessary and the French government had earmarked 300 million francs to that effect. It remains unclear, however, whether this amount can get the project off the ground.

Whatever the industrial and bureaucratic motivations of the satellite project, Canal 1 added a cultural and political dimension to the DBS project, symbolizing the Left government's desire to foster greater European identity, and create a "global village" - a unifying link between the many local communities.

NEW APPRECIATION OF THE ECONOMICS OF THE MEDIA

The anticipated equilibrium of this two-prong approach to the media revolution has been challenged by economic constraints. On the one hand, there were cost problems, some caused by government policy. On the other hand, the potential for advertising revenues in the media put tremendous pressures on the various players. In many instances the initial local dimension of radio and cable projects has proven to be uneconomical. In addition, the satellite project opened the Pandora's box of Europe's communication policy. At the same time, continuing public demand for more varied programs created a sense of urgency.

The 1982 law had been passed thanks to the momentum created in 1981; its perspective was cultural and political rather than economic. In conformity with French tradition, liberty was seen as a political rather than an economic issue. The evolution of government policies in the media closely follows the pattern which can be observed in other areas, however. In the new framework that was set up to protect and nurture freedom of expression, new actors, raising economic issues, appeared. The administration has had to acknowledge that political liberties could not be insulated from economic liberties - and realities. The Haute Autorité was not primarily designed to be an antitrust commission and economic regulator. But the logic of the evolution set in motion was for the Haute Autorité to take up this new role, even if the administration was not fully prepared for such a change.

Examining how the system of 1982 has adjusted to those economic pressures provides some clues as to how it may evolve in the future, and whether the mechanisms are adaptable. It is noteworthy, at the outset, that start-up costs, both cabling and programming, have been underestimated.

The cabling of France

The government decided to cable France with optic fibers in July 1982 and gave the PTT Ministry the responsibility of program implementation. Contrary to experience in the United States, it was considered more economical to make the same agency responsible for both telephone and cable television lines. The government subsequently decided that the same lines might eventually be used for both purposes, making cable part of the global revolution in communications.

The rapid growth of the telephone industry had diminished after the boom of the 1970s so that French industry began looking for new investment opportunities. Fiber optics seemed promising since the technologies had applications not only for television, but also for the whole range of data transfer. After testing, France could then take the lead in the technology by developing the captive home market. If everything worked, fiber optics would be to the eighties what nuclear energy was to the seventies. Goals were set: 6 million households would be cabled by 1992, and the number of homes newly cabled per year would reach one million by 1987. From 1983 to 1985, one billion francs were allocated to trunk lines, 5 billion francs to local networks.

The actual development of cable has not been as fast as anticipated. According to the Socialist PTT Minister, 2 billion francs were spent in research and development from 1982 to 1985, and the budget would reach 2.8 billion francs by 1986. The number of cabled households would reach 200,000 in 1985, 750,000 in 1986, 1,8000,000 in 1987, and 3,100,000 in 1988. More than 250 local councils, representing 5 million households, have expressed an interest in cable. Eight cities signed a cable agreement by September 1985; a dozen more reached an agreement by year's end.

Delays in development have been generally caused by the high program costs and the reluctance of local councils to assume the financial burden. Faced with this, the government encouraged private-sector participation, aligning the cable industry with the water-distribution, rather than the electricity, model. This also paves the way for future disengagement of the state. Law 84–743 of 1 August 1984, adapted the *sociétés d'économie mixte locale* to the particular case of cable. Only one-third of the capital – instead of 50 per cent for other *société d'économie mixte* - must be public, but the president of the company must be a local official. In the case of Paris, a major part of the capital is controlled by a private company, Société Lyonnaise des Eaux and the President of the Parisian Société Locale d'Exploitation du Cable (SLEC) is an official of Paris.

Many SLECs have discovered that they will not recoup the cost of renting the lines from the PTT if they do not have enough attractive programs for which they can charge a reasonable price to a substantial number of households. They have also discovered that adding the costs of producing or buying programs to the costs of cabling would make profitability even more difficult. Some people doubt the long-term wisdom of the fiber optic choice, and local councils resent the added financial burden.

They feel they should not have to finance an industrial policy choice which reduces the amount of funds available to them for programs. Thus, a conflict came to exist between a national industrial policy goal – a goal widely accepted beyond the Left – and a framework based on local initiative and private financing.

The cost of programming

What was uncertain for radio – whether programs could be produced and financed on a local basis – has proven to be uneconomical for television. While successful existing local radio stations are quickly integrating into *de facto* networks through franchise agreements (sharing formats and arranging joint promotion – a trend that some government agencies have been trying to stop) it has become clear that attractive television programs are expensive and cannot be financed locally. French cable households, in addition, will not be sufficiently numerous in the foreseeable future to attract significant advertising revenues, especially if cable makes a slow start.

Lowering programming costs through some kind of syndicated public-interest programs – an approach favored by the Mission Cable – cannot provide a satisfactory answer. The public seems to like expensive, commercially oriented programs and will not buy cable just for PBS-type programming, something they already find on the three public channels. All market studies show that the French, as other nationalities, favor films, sports and, to a lesser degree, music (videoclips). Except for videoclips – which are inexpensive because they are promotional material – the above programs are expensive to acquire and require large audiences to be cost-effective.

If the costs cannot be lowered, additional revenue sources have to be found either through pay-television or advertising. But as soon as advertising is considered, the number of viewers becomes a crucial factor. Cable or DBS can no longer provide the short-term answer that was first expected from them. Other players have to be introduced and a balance has to be found, so that the older players are not threatened by the new ones. The Left government recognized the problem and tried to make room for new players, while preserving the existing balance.

The pay-solution: Canal Plus

The launching of Canal Plus in the fall of 1984 was the first attempt at broadening the range of available programming, while simultaneously protecting existing channels. Canal Plus was the result of a series of compromises and it uses a television frequency which had been abandoned for years. Canal Plus has greater potential than cable, but has pretended not to compete with cable, since it is pay-television. Having all the appearances of a private company, its major shareholder was, until recently, Havas, a company controlled by the state. Films have been the staple of Canal Plus, but it has carefully avoided offending the movie industry by paying substantial royalties – at least one-quarter of its revenues – and agreeing to a set of restrictions negotiated with the motion picture industry. Furthermore, thanks to a compromise reached after several months of severe deficits, some advertising revenues were authorized, but they cannot compete with the other television channels. Canal Plus, after all, relies on subscription for at least 60 per cent of its revenues.

The success of Canal Plus was doubtful as of early 1985. Prospective customers were turned off by technical problems which affected the unscrambling devices attached to television sets. Also, the programming reflected predictions that the audience would be upper-middle class, when in fact the audience turned out to be more varied. Canal Plus eventually received authorization to suspend the scrambling of promotional programs between 6.30 and 8.30 p.m. to raise a limited amount of advertising revenue (approximately 200 million francs in 1985). Sports events were programmed more often and the number of films was increased to represent 50 per cent of programming (instead of the previous 30 per cent) while the film industry, which at first considered Canal Plus a threat, began to support it.

These changes have attracted new audiences and lowered the Canal Plus break-even point to 670,000 subscribers. Thus, the pay-channel, whose deficit was close to 600 million francs in 1985, could be profitable in 1986. After a slow start, subscriptions picked up; by September 1985, half a million people subscribed with three-quarters of a million projected for the beginning of 1986.

Havas (which, until recently, owned 42.3% of the stock) and its main private partners, Compagnie Générale des Eaux (15%) and L'Oréal (10%), have a vested interest in protecting the privileged position of Canal Plus from undue competition. Since the state determined the economic context of Canal Plus, the initial private investors could ask for compensation from the state if Canal Plus were to face substantially different conditions of competition. Thus Canal Plus has become a *de facto* player in the new private television battle, and no government, whatever its political orientations, can ignore it.

The advertising solution: private television stations

The conditions of competition will change substantially as a result of the beginning of private television station operations in 1986. The president of the Republic himself decided to authorize private television stations in January 1985. At the time, it was becoming clear that cable systems would not be completed as quickly as expected, and Canal Plus was still considered a loser by many. Public frustration grew, and the government – which had committed itself not only to more independent media, but also to increased programming – did not want to disappoint an audience whose expectations had been raised. Still, the President's announcement took almost everybody by surprise, since it seemed to drop cable as the government's priority.

The priority change, however, actually reflected the continued interest of the administration in French media. In the new setting the government was no longer to be held responsible for any delay in new program development, and the private sector could now show what it was capable of. The announcement revealed the difficulty of establishing a stable relationship between public and private television in a country where public television occupied a strong position, which it is expected to keep.

The proposals for new private channels originated in a report by Jean-Denis Bredin on the public/private relationship in television, published in the spring of 1985. (Bredin was a well-known lawyer who had previously studied the French motion picture industry.) The Bredin report set the stage for an interesting debate at the Council of Ministers of 31 July 1985. The announced decision followed the same general pattern which had been followed by SLEC and Canal Plus: private interests were invited to participate in and share with state enterprises in a mix of public and private funds. This union, in turn, was meant to give the public more stability and better service than would result from outright competition between public and private interests.

This new involvement of the private sector might be interpreted as a clever way to prevent the opposition from undoing the policy after the 1986 elections, as well as a departure from the 1982 nationalization policy, but it remains very much in the French tradition. The idea was to create networks of joint interest and to blur distinctions between private and public interests.

Local television stations

The government decided that local television stations, in a significant departure from the law of 1982, would not be created through a *concession de service public*. This was very much in the spirit of the Bredin report. A new law provided that local stations would be created through a license granted for ten years by the Haute Autorité. A local station would be restricted to a broadcast range not exceeding 60 kilometers. In view of frequency availability, 40 to 50 local stations would be eligible for a license.

How would television programs be financed? As in the case of radio, but even more so, local television stations cannot afford to produce all their own programs, and *de facto* networks are likely to appear. The law of 1982 ruled that no company could have more than one license per medium. Nothing, however, prevents a local newspaper from owning the local cable system in addition to the local radio station. Local concentration of ownership was not seen as a threat to freedom, while the creation of a network at the national level was.

The government did recognize that excessive fragmentation in media ownership might limit their development, however. It thus changed the 1982 law to allow the same company to be granted up to three licenses in each medium. The Haute Autorité would have the power to ensure that a local monopoly was not created. Furthermore, no stockholder, whether public or private, could be a majority shareholder. This would prevent a television-station ownership monopoly, while allowing some degree of concentration and the possibility of a programming service for independently owned local stations, precisely what American networks do. One can imagine a network "*à la française*" owning and operating three television stations in Paris, Lyon and Marseilles and providing programming for any number of independently owned stations in smaller markets. This will nevertheless be possible only if the attitude that prevailed in the case of radio stations and cable programs is abandoned for television stations. The relaxation of rules limiting ownership concentration suggests, however, that program regulation will follow a similar pattern and tolerate some degree of networking and franchising.

However, while the government had set up a legal framework that made possible the emergence of a national network in the American sense – a national programmer linked to local stations which it would provide with programs – it did not give priority to local stations because, at the end of 1985, time was of the essence. It was clearly impossible to have local television stations operating before the elections of 1986, even if that would have been more in conformity with economic realities and a political emphasis on local expression.

The two national channels (réseaux multivilles)

The Council of Ministers which convened in July 1985 therefore decided to give priority to the creation of two national channels. This decision followed the recommendation of the Bredin report, which had suggested that only two national channels could be created (unless Canal Plus frequencies are used), and it could be implemented quickly, which was a major advantage for a government eager to influence the organization of private television before the March 1986 deadline. Also, the decisions of 1985 conflicted with the spirit of the law of 1982 and the trend it had started, but not with its letter: the 1982 law actually provided that the government retain the power to grant licenses for national television networks and for the DBS satellite. Privatizing from the top had the advantage – and the risk – of putting the government in the central position, from which it could exert some degree of control over its private partners.

A hot debate ensued over who would get the licenses. Interestingly enough, the opposition did not criticize the priority given by government to national channels over local stations, but only the choice of the licensees.[2] That the Left tried to join forces with the companies most likely to have some sympathies for the Socialists (namely Berlusconi and Maxwell) should come as no surprise. The real issue is not the obvious political choice that was made, but the economic choice of starting with two national channels, whose size was deemed critical to attract advertising revenue and to compete with the powerful existing public channels. From a policy-making standpoint, the most interesting aspect of the July 1985 decision is that it can be seen as a departure from the spirit of 1982, when the "Italian model" was considered with horror and when the Haute Autorité was created.

The dilemma of the Left is the relative weakness of the entertainment industry in Europe; this problem was compounded by the lack of time. The Left had to ally itself with strong players in this small market, and it did not have time to let market forces play within the regulated framework it had just created. This lack of trust in the Haute Autorité may prove to have been a mixed blessing, since it exposed the government to sharp criticism from the opposition.

Only the music channel license has survived without too much trouble. It was granted to a company formed – with varying degrees of control – by the following: Europe 1 (a state-controlled company which was subsequently sold to Hachette) 30%, Publicis 25%, Gaumont 25%, WRJ 10%, and Club Med 10%.

The license of Channel 5 – the nonspecialized network – elicited considerable controversy. It was granted to a company with 40 per cent control by the Italian private television tycoon Berlusconi and 60 per cent by Chargeurs Réunis, a company owned and run by Jérôme Seydoux, a member of the Schlumberger family. The license did not submit Channel 5 to the same constraints that affect the other French television

stations for the broadcasting of films. Eventually, one DBS satellite channel was granted
to a consortium headed by Robert Maxwell, publisher of Mirror Group Newspapers.

The DBS channel and Channel 5 licenses were seen by the opposition as a means
for the Left to preempt the field before the 1986 elections, and the Maxwell license
was actually revoked after the elections, while the Channel 5 license, challenged in
court, was substantially modified – the provisions regulating the broadcasting of films
were annulled.

Yet, the opposition has not challenged the priority given by the Left to the creation
of national channels. If private interests are to be involved, it happens in negotiations
at the top, rather than through the play of market forces. This is in sharp contrast
to the attitude of the first Socialist government, when it opened up the airwaves to
hundreds of local radio stations. It reflects a preoccupation with economic constraints,
and also a certain reluctance to relinquishing all state influence over a medium as
powerful as national television.

This orientation, which aims at transforming the media in a massive and centralized
way, does not address two basic issues which cut across the line dividing Left and
Right: the competition for advertising revenues among the media and the respective
roles of public and private television.

The competition for advertising revenues

Television advertising in France continues to be limited by severe constraints.
Commercials do not interrupt programs, limits are imposed on the overall volume
of advertising allowed on public television and several industries are not permitted
to advertise on television. Consequently, advertising contributes only 25% of the total
public television revenues (3.3 billion francs). In 1983, total television advertising
represented 3.75 billion francs, in comparison with the written press's 9.5 billion;
total advertising expenditures in France were 18.5 billion francs. These figures are
all the more striking when compared with American advertising expenditure. Not only
are advertising disbursements much higher in the United States than in France, even
considering the two countries' difference in size (the entire advertising expenditures
in the United States were $88.08 billion, $20 billion for television in 1984, representing
56% of the world market), but the press's share of the total expenditure is very different.
Advertisement in newspapers is more than 50% of total advertising expenditure in
France, only 35% in the United States.

One could speculate that an increase in the volume of television advertising would
result in an increase in the total volume of advertising, and would not occur at the
expense of newspapers. Unfortunately, this scenario is a little too optimistic.

Most studies indicate that (even if television advertising is on the upswing in Western
Europe) there is a long way to go before reaching the level of advertising in the United
States. The *Livre vert sur l'établissement du Marché Commun de la radiodiffusion, notamment
par satellite et par cable* (a report published by the European Community in June 1984)
suggests that television advertising in the European Community, now at approximately
3.1 billion ECU, might reach 6 to 10 billion ECU, if the British example is followed
and television advertising is completely deregulated. In France, the unfilled order for

television advertising may be as high as one billion francs. Even these high figures are much lower than in the United States, however, and may not be sufficient to finance new media at the pace that was first expected. The problem is compounded by potential conflicts with the local and regional press, which, in France, wield great political power. Even if the increase in television advertising was not at the expense of the press, the relative decline is in itself a source of concern and intense lobbying. The competition may be worsened by the fact that no private local television could exist without advertising revenues from distribution and retail industries. These economic sectors constitute the major portion of advertising revenue for local television stations in the United States. In France, these sectors are excluded from television, but provide newspapers with substantial advertising revenues.

The respective roles of public and private television

Real attempts at change have been made in French television to reach a compromise on public and private interests; state funding through taxes versus private funding through advertising revenues; educating versus entertaining the public and competing for quality or number of viewers. French television officials assumed that these goals were complementary, not conflicting, and this assumption is still, in many ways, a part of the French consensus and its democratic credo. The French probably want to believe that there is no fundamental contradiction between entertainment and "culture". At the same time, however, French television must respond to conflicting complaints. On the one hand, it is criticized for being too "highbrow" and often boring; on the other hand, it is blamed for no longer performing the public service expected from a tax-supported broadcasting system.

According to a recent report by the French director–producer Danièle Delorme, foreign series and made-for-television films broadcast on the three public channels increased from 315 hours to 537 hours between 1980 and 1984. During the same period of time, French-produced television drama declined from 479 hours to 407 hours. The same decline is evident in the number of plays and documentaries, which represent a diminishing share of programming and are no longer broadcast during prime time.

The government has responded to these changes by increasing its support to program industries. The Comité de Soutien Cinématographique, which supports the French motion picture industry through a tax levied on theater tickets, has been expanded into the Comité de Soutien Cinématographique et aux Industries de Programme. It will levy a new tax on the revenues of both public and private television: 1.5 per cent toward the motion picture industry, 4 per cent specifically for television programming. The tax is expected to raise 400 million francs in 1986.

Another important governmental decision is the introduction, for the first time in France, of tax shelters specifically organized for the motion picture and television industries. Law 85-695 of 11 July 1985 and Decrees 85-982 and 983 of 17 September 1985 offer investors very advantageous possibilities, even though they are closely supervised by the Ministry of Finance and Centre National de la Cinématographie. Whether this policy will produce a new wealth of programming or reconcile quality with quantity cannot yet be determined.

The competition for advertising revenues has, however, made public television reluctant to broadcast programs which attract less than 5 per cent of viewers, even if this nevertheless represents a substantial number of people. The creation of private television may have the opposite consequences. It is possible that public television will be forced into more intense competition regarding the number of viewers as a result of increased competition for advertising revenues. Or it may be encouraged to assert its public role, since it has privileged access to public money.

To resolve the public/private television dilemma, the opposition proposed to diminish the hybrid character of French television. According to the opposition's plan, one of the three public television channels, TF1, will be used to rid one of the two remaining public channels of its dependence on advertising revenues. But, is there enough advertising to support a private TF1, two other private national channels reaching 60 cities, a DBS program, 40 to 50 local television stations and a public Antenne 2 partially supported by advertising? Providing more programs means more advertising and public money, rather than a different mix of the two. Although the present hybrid situation is not satisfactory and a more clear-cut definition of the roles of public and private television could improve the situation, it is doubtful whether the French have fully abandoned the ideal of hybrid television: that is, the combination of public and private funding and the reconciliation of entertainment and culture. Whether they want that combination to be changed by decisions made at the top and on a national basis, rather than through local experimentation which would tell what is successful and what is not, is even more doubtful.

NOTES

1 The Chirac government follows the American model and has proposed to transfer to the new Haute Autorité some of the technical responsibilities of TDF.
2 The Chirac government has also given priority to national channels as opposed to local stations, probably for the same reason that the left did so: political control.

V
France in the World
under Mitterrand

Introduction

The five years of Socialist experiment in France were marked by all manner of unpredictable change in the international realm. The Left came to power in the midst of European-wide controversy over the issue of Euromissiles, for example. Moreover, the eighties rapidly became a moment of renewed superpower rivalries in which European countries fell under intense pressure to "support the Western Alliance" and the United States. Trouble-spots in the Third World continued to flare up. International monetary, trade and financial difficulties were rampant.

Despite all this, and despite pre-1981 programmatic good intentions, France's positions in international affairs under the Left demonstrated great continuity. François Mitterrand and the Left steered a steady pro-NATO and pro-United States course, despite small disagreements about international financial and monetary issues, as Stanley Hoffmann's chapter shows. Continuity was again the rule in the realm of nuclear policy, even if, as Jolyon Howorth claims, such continuity involved the postponement of important decisions about the future of France's independent deterrent. Finally, France's Third World policies were perhaps the area in which the Left had the most serious pretentions to change. Prior to 1981 much thought had been devoted to North-South economic issues and many specialists in the Socialist Party were convinced North-South Keynesians. The Left also had strong feelings about minimizing the effects of superpower rivalries on developing societies. The Socialist Party had a long history of *tiersmondisme* and professed little sympathy for authoritarian and militaristic regimes of the Right whose stability was built around pro-Americanism. Closer to home, the Left had also reflected on alternatives to traditional quasi-client ties with Francophone Africa. Here, despite much brave early talk, the hopes and dreams of the Left for new ways of dealing with less fortunate societies came largely to naught as a result of a combination of internal bureaucratic pressures and external realities, as Stéphane Hessel's chapter shows.

18

Mitterrand's Foreign Policy, or Gaullism by any other Name

STANLEY HOFFMANN

THE GAULLIST ORTHODOXY

When François Mitterrand became President of France in May 1981, two questions concerning France's international behaviour could be posed: first, how "Socialist" would his foreign policy be?[1] The answer was easy to predict: not very, since before May 1981 the Socialists had already given up so much of what had been distinctively Socialist in the past, especially in the realm of defense. Second, how far, if at all, would Mitterrand depart from the foreign policy principles of Charles de Gaulle, and how would he interpret those he still wished to observe? Despite noticeable changes by Mitterrand's predecessors – such as Georges Pompidou's lifting of de Gaulle's veto on British entry into the European Community (EEC) and Valéry Giscard d'Estaing's ending of France's attack on the "privileges of the dollar" in the world monetary system or accepting direct popular election of the European Parliament – continuity had marked French diplomacy during the 23 years of Gaullist and Giscardian rule. Yet Mitterrand had been de Gaulle's most persistent opponent and headed a coalition of Socialists and Communists.

Now, six years after the Socialists' triumph, the long shadow of de Gaulle still falls over the French political terrain. Without the Constitution de Gaulle gave to the Fifth Republic, Mitterrand would not have been strong enough to convert his Socialist Party to his new economic austerity policies. In foreign affairs, de Gaulle took a number of irreversible decisions, such as creating the French nuclear force, rejecting military integration into NATO and ending an exclusively pro-Israel policy. Originally these decisions may not have been unanimously approved. But the passage of time has made it materially and psychologically impossible to undo them, as their wisdom or their advantages for France became generally recognized. Moreover, he turned French diplomacy in directions unlikely to be changed, both because they made sense to many French and because they were sufficiently imprecise to give successive governments considerable leeway. Throughout his life the General combined intransigence on certain principles with pragmatism in execution.

As a result, during his presidency and posthumously, de Gaulle made life miserable for the opposition. His critics from the Center – especially the Christian Democrats – denounced his destruction of all the strictures of supranational integration into the

European community (EC) as well as his decision to withdraw from the military organization of NATO. They liked neither his attacks on the United States over issues as varied as the role of the dollar, the war in Vietnam, the Arab–Israeli conflict and the American intervention in the Dominican Republic, nor his promotion after 1964 of the first Western policy of detente with the Soviet Union. When the centrists left the opposition and eventually became part of a right-wing majority, however, they made no attempt to turn back the clock.

The new Socialist Party, when it was created by Mitterrand in 1971, also rejected Gaullist foreign policy and specifically the French nuclear force. Faithful to Socialist tradition, the Party asked for general disarmament and the dissolution of military blocs as well as for radical changes in France's arms sales and African policies. But during its ten-year march to power, the Socialist Party had trouble reconciling various factions around a sensible common platform. Its ranks contained not only a majority of Atlanticists and Europe-oriented Socialists much closer to the centrists than to the Gaullists, but also a powerful minority of rather nationalistic Socialists, a group called Centre d'Etudes de Recherches et d'Education Socialistes (CERES), whose support Mitterrand needed in order to remain in control of the Party. CERES was more eager to denounce an imperial United States than a totalitarian Soviet Union. Yet the importance its members attached to the Union of the Left, the alliance with the Communists, made them closer in foreign affairs to the Gaullists than to many fellow Socialists.

But the Communists, in a spectacular shift in 1977, endorsed the French nuclear force whose destruction they had long advocated. From then on, the Party saw the *force de frappe* as a bulwark of French independence that would prevent both a return to NATO and the establishment of a West European defense system – neither of which Moscow would have liked. The Socialists' movement toward accepting the French nuclear force and away from their earlier emphasis on world disarmament began the following year. Mitterrand and his Party wanted to improve their chance of coming to power by appearing realistic, and their evolution reflected both the prevailing trends in public opinion and their evaluation of international developments, especially the Soviet military build-up in Eastern Europe.

During the 1981 election campaign, Mitterrand strongly criticized as naïve Giscard's decision to travel to Warsaw in May 1980 to meet the then Soviet leader Leonid Brezhnev, at a time when Western allies were trying to define a common policy of anti-Soviet sanctions following the invasion of Afghanistan. Thus what Régis Debray, Mitterrand's former revolutionary friend and advisor, calls socialist orthodoxy – international arbitration, collective security, disarmament – and what he calls the "system of socialist reason" – federalism, legalism and pacifism – have now been discarded as irrelevant or even dangerous.[2] A process that began when the lessons of the 1930s led the French Socialists to abandon pacifism was virtually complete.

Some areas of orthodoxy remained, as well as a general suspicion of the United States in world affairs. Nevertheless, the Socialists shed many more illusions about foreign affairs than about domestic ones. They had thereby also entered the world of Gaullist ambiguities. The first principle of de Gaulle's foreign policy was the refusal of integration both into NATO and into the EEC. However, this position left open two questions. How much cooperation could take place between France and NATO? In other words, was France's exit a step toward a kind or armed neutrality? Or did de Gaulle's policy merely make of France a kind of reserve or rear territory for NATO? Similarly, the Gaullist dogma of an independent defense left room for disagreement on such issues as the respective importance of nuclear versus conventional forces and direct or indirect French participation in arms control negotiations.

Regarding the major powers, de Gaulle's policy had meant resistance to American "hegemony" and a mix of containment and cooperation with the Soviet Union. Toward West Germany, his policy consisted of a combination of reconciliation, close cooperation and preservation of French military superiority. But again, much leeway remained. Should French resistance to the United States be fierce or polite in style, comprehensive or selective in scope? And when the principal risk for France is not the United States's overbearing might but its perceived weakness, should France be supportive or act on its own? How should containment and cooperation be combined toward Moscow? How could the desire to anchor West Germany in the West be reconciled with French refusal of integration and insistence on military autonomy? Another Gaullist dogma was activism. France must play a worldwide role in regional conflicts through arms sales and occasional interventions, in former African colonies through its economic and military presence and through efforts to promote Third World development. Here again, considerable leeway existed on goals and methods. Before May 1981 the Left had remained critical of the military side of such activism.

MITTERRAND'S DIPLOMACY

Under Mitterrand, foreign policy continuity prevailed. The Gaullist dogmas have been preserved, starting with the most basic: presidential control of foreign policy. The Foreign Minister remained under tight supervision from the Elysée Palace, and the Socialist Party's contribution to the process of decision-making in foreign affairs, unlike its contribution to the process of decision-making in domestic policy matters was nil.[3]

Presidential supremacy and the other fundamental principle – national independence – combined most imperiously, or imperially, when Mitterrand declared on television in November 1983 that the core of French deterrence was himself. Nuclear sovereignty has been reasserted: France's nuclear force can be only under French presidential command and must not be included by the superpowers in their arms control negotiations. Indeed, France's decision to equip its nuclear missiles with multiple warheads and to build new mobile, intermediate-range missiles will give the deterrent much greater power. This will to preserve a national nuclear deterrent explains current French worries about the new arms race in space. Should the superpowers build defensive antiballistic-missile systems, only the United States would retain the power to deter a Soviet ballistic missile attack on France. Thus France requested a five-year moratorium on the testing and deployment of antiballistic-missile and antisatellite systems.

Mitterrand's rejection of the Strategic Defense Initiative and his criticisms of damaging American economic policies permitted him to argue that France had not become a docile client of the United States. So did his criticisms of American unwillingness to take bolder measures about the Third World's debt and to cooperate with its industrialized partners on monetary policies, of American reluctance to seek political solutions to Central American conflicts, of American timidity in pushing President Ronald Reagan's September 1982 Middle East peace plan and of American inconsistencies in Lebanon.

Mitterrand's June 1984 visit to the Soviet Union surprised many, even his friends, because the conditions his Foreign Minister had listed as prerequisites for a summit meeting – a change in Soviet policy in Afghanistan and of conditions in Poland – had obviously not been met. Critics wondered how this visit differed from Giscard's trip to Warsaw. But Mitterrand covered himself skillfully by broadcasting his criticism of Soviet human rights practices, especially Soviet treatment of dissident Andrei Sakharov, from Moscow. His visit seemed designed to show that France can pursue a dialogue with the Soviets even when the United States cannot. And, as the gas pipeline agreement of 1982 had shown, France under Mitterrand wanted to expand economic cooperation with the USSR.

When he came to power Mitterrand indicated that he would dissolve the Paris-Bonn axis within the EEC, a relationship that began in the days of de Gaulle and Konrad Adenauer and reappeared under Giscard and Helmut Schmidt (Pompidou distrusted Willy Brandt and sought to play a British card). Yet under Mitterrand that axis became stronger than ever.

Much of France's activism also continued, and not only in the form of frequent presidential visits abroad. The most striking example was the abandonment of Socialist doctrine. Arms sales continued, especially to Iraq. At first, the Iraq sales were justified by the simple necessity of keeping commitments made by earlier governments. But later they were defended as a farsighted effort to help protect Arab states against the Iranian revolution. Only arms sales to South Africa were curbed indefinitely.

The need to maintain French positions in Africa led to the deployment of forces in Chad in order to stop Libyan military intervention and to renewed military intervention after Libya's violation of the disengagement deal made in the fall of 1984 – decisions reflecting the predominance of geopolitical concerns over considerations of domestic popularity. The Socialists had hoped to replace the Fifth Republic's policy of support to often vicious or corrupt pro-French regimes in Africa with a policy promoting not only human rights but also democracy. This last notion was abandoned at once as unrealistic. As Mitterrand's first Minister for Cooperation and Development, Jean-Pierre Cot, wrote, nonintervention in domestic affairs became the new policy.[4] As a result, French ties with President Omar Bongo of Gabon were maintained and relations with the late President Ahmet Sékou Touré of Guinea improved. But Cot himself proved a bit too energetic in the pursuit of a human rights policy and had to resign.

Activism persisted in development assistance as well. A new trade and aid pact between the EEC and a great number of mainly African and Caribbean Third World states was negotiated. France also participated in the ill-fated multinational peace-keeping force in Lebanon, a former French mandate to which Giscard had already offered French military services. And Mitterrand tried to improve relations with both Algeria, with which the French signed a very costly agreement on gas, and Morocco, where France seeks to limit American influence. In Morocco, King Hassan II, newly allied with Libyan leader Muammar al-Qaddafi, helped Mitterrand negotiate an agreement with Libya about the withdrawal of Libyan and French forces from Chad.

Early in his presidency Mitterrand also tried to regain some influence for France in Israel. After 15 years of frosty, and at times even hostile, Franco–Israeli relations, in 1982 Mitterrand became the first French President to visit the Jewish state. He had previously pulled France away from the Venice Declaration, the EC's laborious 1980 attempt to define a just and durable Middle East peace, probably because he found the text too pro-Arab. In Israel, and on subsequent visits to the Middle East, he used the traditional Gaullist tack of declaring what France would consider a just solution to the Arab – Israeli conflict – recognition of the Palestinian's right to a state in exchange for Arab recognition and security guarantees for Israel. At the same time, since 1982 France has twice played a key role in helping Palestine Liberation Organization chairman Yasir Arafat escape from Lebanon.

Within this general framework of continuity, however, there have been several significant changes. French regional activism outside Africa has been gradually curtailed. Israel's invasion of Lebanon put an abrupt end to the *rapprochement* with France. But since June 1982, there has been neither any attempt to revive or revise a West European initiative in the Middle East nor any effort at pushing a French alternative. The Reagan plan was actually praised by Paris. And France did not try to give its force in Lebanon a political mission – unlike the United States government. As a result, despite the heavy losses of October 1983, a French presence that had been described in humanitarian terms remained much more acceptable to the French public than the presence of United States Marines was to the American people and Congress. Moreover, this stance permitted a much more dignified withdrawal of the French soldiers.

Even in the case of Central America, the earlier policy that seemed to put France on a collision course with the United States has been toned down. The Franco–Mexican communiqué of 1981 concerning El Salvador, which was highly critical of American policy, and the 1982 arms deal between France and Nicaragua, were followed by a period of considerable reserve, partly because of misgivings about the evolution of the Sandinista regime. Even the offer to help remove the mines dropped into Nicaraguan waters by the CIA or CIA-supported *contras* was sufficiently conditional not to qualify as a genuine initiative. And in July 1984 Mitterrand received President José Napoleón Duarte of El Salvador. Above all, the Socialists feared doing anything that might ultimately strengthen the Soviets, or even benefit Cuban leader Fidel Castro, whose totalitarian policies find far less favor on the non-Communist Left now than during the 1960s or 1970s.

Mitterrand has been responsible for more major shifts and innovations, most of which center on NATO and Europe. While they have several rationales, they share a key preoccupation with West Germany. For the first time in the history of the Fifth Republic, the President of France has, in effect, asked West Germany to be a reliable and strong ally of the United States. He also urged the West German and Belgian parliaments to carry out the NATO decision of December 1979 to deploy Pershing

II and land-based cruise missiles in Western Europe. Paris's public support for that decision resulted from a conviction that an unmatched deployment of Soviet SS-20s might lead to a decoupling of Western Europe's defense from that of the United States. The fear of decoupling expressed more or less sensibly in terms of the balance of forces in Europe, explains why Mitterrand, who before coming to power had essentially advocated the zero option – neither Pershings nor SS-20s – switched to a preference for a solution "at the lowest level", a formula that would allow at least some NATO deployments of intermediate missiles. Mitterrand also worried about Soviet political blackmail should the SS-20s remain unmatched by NATO. The French were particularly struck by the growth of the West German peace movement. They saw in it both evidence of Soviet success and the risk of West German drift toward neutralism or toward a form of pan-German nationalism that could only serve Moscow's interests. Hence a Franco – American *rapprochement*, derived from a common sense of shock.

The French stand on the NATO decision weakened Paris's argument that France's nuclear force, being purely national and independent, should not be included in the US-Soviet talks on intermediate-range nuclear forces. Indeed, Mitterrand's predecessor had kept his support for the December 1979 decision private partly to avoid this contradiction. France's willingness to take this chance and to preach Atlanticism to Bonn stemmed from two factors. The first was French anxiety about the global balance of power. The tendency in Paris has been to accept the estimates of the Committee on the Present Danger and believe that the biggest peril to world peace and stability was indeed the United States's weakness or inability during the 1970s to keep up with the Soviet military build-up.[5] The second factor was French anxiety about West Germany, heightened by the shift of the West German Social Democratic Party on the missile issue.

Worries about the balance of power and about decoupling are nothing new. From 1960 to 1962 de Gaulle had sometimes feared the possibility of American concessions to the Soviets over Berlin and worried about Soviet leader Nikita Khrushchev's aggressiveness. Then as now, any talk of American efforts to back away from a policy of willingness to use nuclear weapons first in case of Soviet attack, and to do it quickly, was highly unpopular in Paris. Then as now, proposals for denuclearized zones in Central Europe were seen as political traps laid by the Soviets for West Germany. This view was held even when such plans have originated from Mitterrand's fellow Socialists in Stockholm. De Gaulle, to be sure, had never allowed his concern about the balance of power and West European security to turn him into an Atlanticist. But in those days the military balance overwhelmingly favored the United States. In so far as maintaining a balance of power capable of deterring Moscow was always a Gaullist principle, Mitterrand's startling Atlanticist innovations cannot be seen as a fundamental break with Gaullism.

Nor was his pro-American stance such a break. Mitterrand has always been personally more sympathetic to the United States than was the General, but he is no more eager than de Gaulle had been for heightened US-Soviet tensions, which always restrict the freedom of maneuver of lesser powers. Today these tensions could also strengthen pacifist or neutralist currents in West Germany and in the smaller West European countries. A more militant, less prudent anti-Soviet policy in Washington during the next few years would strain United States relations not only with Germany, but also with France, which, like China, wants Washington to be strong but not too strong; not too friendly with Moscow yet not too hostile either. This too is very Gaullist.

In a similar vein Mitterrand's decision to revive the dormant military cooperation provisions of the Franco–German treaty of 1963 cannot be seen as a major departure from Gaullism. This provision had been put to sleep because Bonn preferred to address defense issues in NATO and because Paris did not want to appear to be forcing Bonn to choose between NATO and some kind of a West European defense scheme in the wake of France's pullout from the Alliance's command structure.

Mitterrand's energetic new efforts were aimed both toward greater Franco–West German cooperation in such matters as the coproduction of weapons and the exchange of views on strategy, and toward a reactivation of the West European Union, the only organization besides NATO with a military function in Western Europe. These policies resulted both from his desire to tie Bonn more firmly to the West and from his worries about what the French call neoisolationist tendencies in the United States, including calls for relying purely on conventional weapons to defend Europe, which the French believe might make war more likely.

The French remain convinced that the threat of nuclear war is the only certain deterrent. They do not believe that a conventional strategy is sufficient, nor do they worry much about whether or not nuclear deterrence, based on threats aimed at the other side's nuclear forces or command centers and on the use of vulnerable weapons, becomes provocative rather than deterring. Crisis instability, or launch-on-warning nightmares, do not seem to trouble them. Right or wrong, they believe that the combination of nuclear weapons of any kind and a will to use them if needed, ensures restraint on the part of the potential aggressor.

Moreover, Mitterrand is still bothered by the division of Europe agreed to by Washington and Moscow at Yalta. He probably sees a West European defense scheme as insurance against the chance that the two superpowers will be tempted once more to solve the world's problems through collusion – a recurrent French fear, even if not a very timely one.

The President has in fact gone beyond Franco–German military cooperation, and proposed a *relance* of Western Europe – a new stab at unification, now that the tiresome *contentieux* opposing Britain and the EC has, for the time being, been liquidated. The most innovative suggestions here concern accepting majority rule in the EC in nonvital matters and drafting a treaty of political cooperation based on the so-called Spinelli draft of a treaty for political union endorsed in February 1984 by the European Parliament. This draft would increase the powers of that assembly and of the EEC Commission relative to that of the intergovernmental Council of Ministers. The French have also asked that a permanent secretariat be set up to revive foreign policy coordination. Much of this was incorporated in the agreement reached by the European Council in Luxembourg in December 1985. Mitterrand has talked about common efforts in space as well and launched project EUREKA – so far with more fanfare than funding and substance. Spain and Portugal have finally been admitted into the European

Economic Community (EEC). Again, irrespective of the details, the underlying objective can most accurately be seen as Gaullist.

De Gaulle, generally viewed as a foe of the EEC, enthusiastically used the community's free-trade provisions to modernize French industry and its agricultural policy as a lever on West Germany. Mitterrand also sees the EEC as an essential tool for France's modernization but in thoroughly different circumstances. His refusal to take the franc out of the EMS and his decision to apply the EEC Commission's directives on the steel industry had forced the government to carry out several devaluations of the franc, to impose a policy of economic austerity, and to close down a number of important steel mills in Lorraine and Provence. The EEC's Common Agricultural Policy can continue to function only by becoming less wasteful, for example, by obliging dairy farmers in France and elsewhere to cut down production of milk and butter, which is still heavily subsidized. In other words, modernization now meant genuine pain, measured by both unemployment and the frustration of Socialist hopes.

But Europeanism also served a new function in domestic politics. It allowed Mitterrand to reject the alternative economic policy proposed by CERES, his former ally within the Socialist Party. CERES had advocated leaving the EMS, waging a kind of export war on France's partners with a drastic currency devaluation, keeping foreign goods out through protectionism, and reflating the economy. Not only did Mitterrand fear such a policy would further weaken France's economy but he also rejected a course that would have led to domestic radicalization, forced him to rely more on the Communist friends of CERES and probably ended in a triumphant return of the Right. The departure of the Communists from the government in July 1984 and the return of Jean-Pierre Chevènement, the leader of CERES, into the government on Mitterrand's terms validated his choice.

Mitterrand's *relance* of Western Europe served still another purpose: it was aimed at obliging British Prime Minister Margaret Thatcher to choose between being left out, if she refused to join the drive toward greater unity, or if she joined, transcending at last the petty issues of the British financial contribution to the EEC that had almost paralyzed the community for years.

Conversely, Mitterrand's very willingness to envisage a *Europe à plusieurs vitesses* proceeding toward integration at different paces – a Western Europe of ten or twelve with little coherence, coexisting with a Western Europe of six, seven, or eight with broader functions and less rickety institutions – his endorsement of the spirit of the Spinelli draft and his plea for reducing the scope of the EEC members' veto power, might ultimately leap the barriers against integration that de Gaulle erected. It is too early to tell. Yet even the neo-Gaullists such as the current Prime Minister Jacques Chirac acknowledge the need for greater West European cooperation. Mitterrand's *relance* corresponded altogether to a general conviction in France that the EEC's institutional and financial paralysis cannot go on and that the only way of preventing it from becoming the terminal sclerosis of the whole West European enterprise may well be to launch a new one. Like many, Mitterrand is convinced that the technological challenge of Japan and the United States can only be met by Western Europe as a whole. Mitterrand's EC views were also calculated to appeal to the old integrationist instincts of the centrists, who were then in the opposition and whose support he may need to protect his powers in foreign affairs and defense after the legislative election in 1986. And, of course, tying West Germany to a genuine and effective West European organization, giving West Germany a new mission in Western Europe, is yet another way of preventing a drift to the East or a resurgence of German nationalism.

ROOTS AND PROBLEMS

What made Mitterrand's shifts and initiatives possible? The most obvious factor is, of course, the President's domination of foreign policy decision-making (a domination that did not suffice to prevent such embarrassing snafus as the wretched *Greenpeace* affair, a result of the defense establishment's nuclear obsession, and the Mitterrand–Fabius public split over General Jaruzelski's visit to Paris in December 1985). The most important factors, however, concern the climate of French opinion – the strong antipacifist consensus as well as antitotalitarian sentiment. Pacifism was largely discredited by appeasement in the 1930s. France and West Germany have obviously drawn different lessons from that ghastly decade, and in recent years the philosophical trajectories of the French Socialist Party and the German Social Democrats have led in completely opposite directions.

It may well be, as many French officials have been saying, that the absence of a strong pacifist movement also results from a certain pride in national independence. France has its own nuclear force, no thanks to the United States, and therefore needs no American missiles on its soil, whereas pacifism in West Germany or the Netherlands is partly a revolt against dependence on American decisions in matters of national life and death. The 1983 statement of the French Roman Catholic bishops about nuclear war shows the strong influence of French official arguments about Soviet blackmail and about the benefits of nuclear deterrence. French antipacifism, however, is not the same thing as bellicosity. According to poll results in the newspaper *Le Figaro* on 1 December 1983, more than half of the French people believe that if the Soviets invade their country, the President should negotiate immediately with Moscow. Only 6 per cent want him to use nuclear weapons.

Antitotalitarianism is the cement that bonds traditional anti-Soviet and anti-Communist Party politicians and intellectuals of the Right, ex-Communist or ex-leftist intellectuals and journalists who have discovered the evils of the empire in Moscow only in recent years – and now often sound like American neoconservatives – and leftists revolted by the invasion of Afghanistan, the crushing of the now-banned independent trade union Solidarity in Poland and Soviet violations of human rights. The French bishops' letter stresses the totalitarian peril much more strongly than the American bishops' letter, perhaps because on the intellectual Left, Marxism and sympathy for the Bolshevik Revolution had remained for so long an obstacle to recognizing facts about the Soviet regime. Aleksandr Solzhenitsyn's *Gulag Archipelago* has had much greater impact in France than in the United States. Antitotalitarianism, in turn, has also made the French much more pro-American and especially more pro-Reagan. And this attitude has rendered a dialogue between French socialism and West German antinuclear activists or socialists extremely difficult. Of course, antitotalitarianism has had its domestic functions, too. While it helped the Right denounce the "Socialo-Communist" government of former Prime Minister Pierre Mauroy, it also helped the Socialists isolate the Communists. Mitterrand's Atlanticism, Europeanism, and pro-Bonn policies obviously did not please Communist Party leader Georges Marchais and his colleagues, but even when they finally decided to withdraw from the government they preferred to criticize only Mitterrand's unpopular economic and social policies.

The fact that Mitterrand's diplomacy had a solid popular base, and that the opposition itself attacked it more for an alleged lack of coherence or for imprudent declarations than for its fundamentals,[6] does not mean that it was problem-free. Three flaws stand out. The first is a problem of rationale; antitotalitarianism is clearly not enough. Socialism is obviously not the most profound inspiration of Mitterrand's diplomacy either. The rationale of de Gaulle and his successors was simple: France's greatness. But Mitterrand used to denounce Gaullist policies as anachronistic and often mean. The most interesting attempt at finding a new rationale is Debray's. But whatever is substantial in his brilliant *La Puissance et les rêves* is, quite extraordinarily, Gaullist. His only compass for diplomacy is the national interest in a Hobbesian world of states. He writes that both idealism and ideology can be harmful because they elevate passions over interests and adds that a wise foreign policy must be protected from public opinion and bureaucrats. But when Debray tries to distinguish his left-wing *realpolitik* from the right-wing variety promoted by former Secretary of State Henry Kissinger, he becomes nebulous – and tells readers to wait for the next volume, which unfortunately provides no answer.[7]

The second problem is France's defense policy. Here, the Gaullist tradition of military autonomy and nuclear priority, upheld so often by Mitterrand, collides with the new approach toward West Germany and a West European defense system. The President reemphasizes that the French force will serve only France's vital interests, under his exclusive command. Of course, preventing a Soviet conquest of West Germany ought to be seen as a vital French interest. Does this policy mean, as was suggested by Schmidt in a speech on 28 June 1984, that France should provide a nuclear guarantee for West Germany in order to prevent a conventional defeat of NATO in West Germany? No, say French officials. France's nuclear force, even modernized, would not be credible for such a role, and such a commitment given in advance would violate French military autonomy. The growing French tactical nuclear arsenal might be used during the battle for West Germany but mainly for the protection of the French forces stationed in the south-west of that country, and to deter an attack on France. It is difficult to see how this arsenal could be very attractive to Bonn or contribute to what is referred to as a European nuclear component. Conversely, West German suggestions about the need for at least a "nonexplicit" West German "right of say" (Schmidt's words) on French nuclear weapons situated on or aimed at West German soil were not well received in Paris.

And yet the French realize that the credibility of their nuclear force is greatest only against the least likely Soviet threat – a nuclear attack on France – and that in an age of nuclear plenty and parity, deterrence in Europe requires combining the residual risk of a conflict becoming nuclear with conventional forces strong enough to deny a quick victory to the Soviets. Indeed, what most West Germans want from France is not a nuclear guarantee – after all, as many have asked, if the United States guarantee is no longer credible, how credible would France's be? Instead, West Germans want an effort in the conventional realm. The French have acknowledged this sentiment and created a non-nuclear Rapid Deployment Force that could be sent quickly to the battlefield in Central Europe. Tactical nuclear weapons would be reserved for deterring an attack on France alone. To be sure, this force of 47,000 troops is an innovation, a clear indication of a willingness to rejoin NATO or rather to take part in forward battles if needed. But it is a halfhearted innovation. The separation between the nuclear-armed French army in West Germany – destined to stay where it is as a kind of immediate glacis protecting France – and the Rapid Deployment Force shows the difficulty of fully reconciling a collective NATO strategy with the stress on French national defense.

Moreover, the total French force that could be engaged in West Germany is not much increased by the new force. The French army in West Germany will bear a sizeable part of the 35,000-troop cut in French forces decided in 1983, partly because of the rising costs of nuclear modernization. Finally, there is some question about the military effectiveness of a Rapid Deployment Force that is not going to receive heavy military equipment and that is envisaged for use in African jungles, Middle Eastern deserts and West German plains as if all combat theaters were alike. For the time being, Mitterrand has warned the French military that the imperatives of austerity will not spare the defense budget.

Those French who ask for a West European defense scheme remain remarkably vague. Or, like Chirac, they pull back as soon as they realize that the logic of such a plan would either mean giving Bonn the right to become a nuclear power or to share decisions about the uses of the French force, or would require abandoning France's nuclear priority, spending more on conventional forces and assigning a major role to them in NATO. Further, the French may discover that their anxiety about West Germany is excessive and in particular that their fear of German reunification is based mainly on a French tendency to believe that West Germans must want reunification since French citizens would in similar circumstances.

The third problem is another kind of contradiction – between France's foreign policy and its domestic base. This problem has three quite different aspects. First, global activism and turning Western Europe into a major, cohesive pole of influence require a vast coordinated effort by West European governments and business in the new technologies of the third industrial revolution. There is no conflict between French aspirations for high-tech socialism and West European integration. France's domestic economic base is simply too small to provide sufficient capital or markets. But not even a European political *relance* and the introduction of majority rule in the EEC can be expected to produce the grand, collective industrial policy that appears necessary. Many French industrialists prefer alliances with American firms to West European combinations, which are often far more cumbersome and less profitable.

Moreover, coordinating the more *dirigiste* and the *laissez-faire* oriented West European national bureaucracies will be extraordinarily difficult for governments. If French alarm about Western Europe's technological decline is right, and if West German complacency is wrong, what Western Europe needs is something that few in France believe realistic enough to propose: a genuine federation with greater powers in industrial matters than the United States government enjoys. The Gaullist framework would have to be broken completely, not just stretched or bent.

A second aspect is the contradiction between France's ambitions and her external debt. There is disagreement about its size – more than $56 billion in March 1984 according to the finance ministry – but there is no doubt that repayment will weigh heavily on both the national income and on France's possibilities in the world. The debt problem has been eased by falling interest rates, and will be lightened further if France's trade balance improves and domestic austerity boosts investments and lowers prices. But those resources that reimburse creditors will be unavailable for defense or economic aid to developing countries. Moreover, France's traditional remedy for trade problems – arms sales and heavy equipment exports to developing countries – will be complicated by shrinking markets in debtor states and intensified competition among suppliers. Such contracts already fell off by 20 per cent in 1983.

In his endeavor to reshape French foreign policy through moves that often met with great public skepticism at first, de Gaulle had also relied on his broad domestic base. Even when his majority in the country shrank, he could count on the demoralization of the Socialist opposition throughout the 1960s and on the curious relationship of hostility in domestic affairs and partial connivance in foreign affairs that he had with the Communists. Mitterrand, despite the powers of the presidency and the Socialist absolute majority in the National Assembly of 1984 could not help but be handicapped abroad by his domestic unpopularity. The Left suffered losses in all the elections since fall 1981, most grievously in the European Parliament election of June 1981 in which Communists and Socialists together obtained barely one-third of the votes. Despite his political skills, his domestic freedom of maneuver has been limited. Mitterrand's position in the months preceding the legislative elections of March 1986 might have become even more vulnerable because France's allies and adversaries had reason to believe that during the next few years domestic political, constitutional and social battles would absorb French energies and that the sturdiness and stability of the Fifth Republic could well be severely shaken. However, there was sufficient consensus between the Socialists and the Right in the realm of foreign policy and defense to prevent a dramatic decline of French diplomacy in the long preelectoral period and complete deadlock afterwards.

NOTES

1 This chapter is a revised version of an article published in *Foreign Policy*, 57 (Winter 1984–86), pp. 38–57.
2 Régis Debray, *La Puissance et les rêves* (Paris, Gallimard, 1984).
3 See Samy Cohen's *La Monarchie nucléaire* (Paris, Hachette, 1986).
4 Jean-Pierre Cot, *A l'Epreuve du pouvoir* (Paris, Seuil, 1984).
5 Cf. Raymond Aron, *Les Dernières années du siècle* (Paris, Julliard, 1984), *passim*.
6 Gabriel Robin's fierce and witty onslaught, *La Diplomatie de Mitterrand ou le triomphe des apparences*, (Paris, Editions de la Bièvre, 1985), has not been well received, even by the Right.
7 Régis Debray, *Les Empires contre l'Europe* (Paris, Gallimard, 1985).

19

Of Budgets and Strategic Choices

Defense Policy under François Mitterrand

JOLYON HOWORTH

INTRODUCTION: THE PRICE OF CONTINUITY
AND THE PRESSURES FOR CHANGE

When Louis XIV asked one of his generals what he needed in order to guarantee military success, he was told, "Three things, sire. Money. Money. And money." This anecdote might serve as a political epitaph for the ministerial career of Charles Hernu, but, more generally, it has become the principal factor arguing for the impossibility of continuity and the inevitability of change in French defense policy. For a brief period of 15 years, Gaullism allowed the French to have their defense on the cheap (and to believe, at the same time, that it conferred upon them something they call *"grandeur"*). This was indeed the best of all possible worlds, but it simply could not last – for various reasons, not the least portentous of which was the fact that the historical circumstances which allowed Gaullist defense policy to exist at all were exceptional and fleeting.[1] Perhaps the greatest irony attending the fortunes of the Socialist government has been the fact that men like François Mitterrand and Charles Hernu finally donned the Gaullist mantle at precisely that moment in history when defense on the cheap (with *grandeur*) was no longer a viable option, either financially or strategically. The story of the last five years has been the story of the Socialist government's not very convincing attempts to come to terms with (or to sidestep) that unpalatable truth. It is not yet a success story.

The advent of the Mitterrand presidency and especially the arrival at the Defense Ministry of Charles Hernu were proclaimed in knowledgeable defense circles as implying continuity rather than change, consensus rather than confrontation. So much has been written about the so-called defense consensus that it seems almost heretical to question its foundatiions. And yet, the fundamental ambiguity on which the Gaullist consensus always rested has continued as an unresolved and constantly worsening double tension at the heart of France's defense policy. At a strategic level, that tension involved the relationship between France's declaratory nuclear "independence" (nuclear sanctuarization or *le refus de la bataille*) and her contractual and actual need to bolster Western Alliance solidarity by preparing to participate alongside NATO in any conflict in the Central European theater. Under the special historical conditions obtaining at the time of de Gaulle, this tension was an abstract one and the priority of priorities was the nuclear sanctuary. Under Valéry Giscard d'Estaing, it became a strategic policy dilemma, pitting the guardians of the Gaullist temple against Giscard's efforts to redress the balance in favor of Alliance solidarity. That strategic dilemma contained within it a resources dilemma which, under the Mitterrand presidency, has become crucial. In an age when the cost of sophisticated high-technology weaponry (both nuclear and conventional) is rising much faster than the rate of inflation, and when world and national recession call for major economies, France simply cannot afford both a credible nuclear strategy and a meaningful conventional role in Europe and throughout the world.

On the face of it, there are three main reasons why one might have expected a Socialist administration in Paris, faced with these strategic and financial problems, to have made bold choices in favor of strengthening Alliance solidarity and channelling resources primarily into the conventional sphere. First, Socialist opposition to nuclear weapons had been vociferous and fairly relentless from 1955 to 1978. Second, the Socialist defense heritage, reaching back to Jaurès if not further, has always stressed the notion of the citizen in arms, the collective and "democratic" or "republican" organization of *territorial* defense. Third, the vast majority of the Socialists have always been Atlanticist and Europeanist, especially in their relations with West Germany.

I have examined elsewhere[2] the complex web of explanatory factors that allows us to understand a Socialist defense policy which, on the surface at least, seems to have opted for continuity (and continuity with Gaullism rather than with "Giscardism") rather than change, for a major reassertion of nuclear sanctuarization, and an attempt, mainly on paper, to bolster Alliance solidarity. Briefly, those factors are connected with the dominant personalities of Charles Hernu and François Mitterrand, both of whom assumed the Gaullist mantle with obvious delight; the deep and lasting divisions with the Socialist Party itself, which have kept its defense options in utter confusion; the all-pervasive nature of the "Gaullist myth" which guaranteed popular support for continuity even as the historical and strategic foundations of such a course were crumbling; and the partisan watchfulness of the opposition which (despite its own clear policy shifts in the direction of Alliance solidarity) was only too keen to feed the government the rope of continuity with which it could gradually hang itself.

In what follows, I wish to outline very briefly the main features of the Hernu/Mitterrand/Quilès defense budgets (primarily encapsulated in the *Loi de programmation militaire 1984-88*) and then look in more detail at what I would argue are the three main problems (interlocked and inseparable though they be) which face the French government today and for the foreseeable future: an intractable resources problem, leading to the urgent need to make painful strategic choices at a time of rapid historical change, especially when faced with a massive technological challenge from the superpowers.

THE SOCIALIST GOVERNMENT AND
THE MILITARY WHITE PAPER OF 1983

The centerpiece of Socialist defense policy was the White Paper of 1983 - the *Loi de programmation militaire 1984-88*. Although not all of the programs I shall be discussing in the following pages were set down in the White Paper, it serves well as a symbol of what the government was trying to do. Broadly speaking, the Socialists carried out the programs inaugurated under Giscard d'Estaing in the late 1970s. In carrying them out more in a Gaullist rather than Giscardian spirit, they were led to make certain adjustments which tended to increase rather than dissipate the ambiguities inherent in that original Gaullist scenario.

At the level of strategic nuclear planning, Mitterrand honored the 1979 decision (made by Giscard, but only under intense pressure from the RPR[3] to order a sixth nuclear submarine (SNCE)). This vessel, *L'Inflexible*, was launched on 25 May 1985 and is equipped with the new M-4 multiple-warhead missile whose planning history dates back to 1972. The projected refitting of four of the five existing SNLEs with the new M-4 missile is in hand and work will begin next year. The first SNLE – *Le Redoutable* – which will be withdrawn from active service in 1995, will be replaced by what is often referred to as the seventh SNLE. This will be a vessel of an entirely new generation (quieter, faster, deeper-diving) for which research and development (R & D) work is in progress and for which a firm, budgeted order is due to be placed in 1986.[4]

Giscard's intention of developing a still more sophisticated MIRVed warhead (the M-5) and engaging R & D for a mobile land-based missile (the SX), were early victims of Hernu's shrinking resource problem. In any case, the imponderables of the Strategic Defense Initiative (SDI) have now hung a large question mark over the usefulness of land-based ballistic missiles (even mobile ones), and all parties are currently reconsidering this option. In a speech to the Institut des Hautes Etudes de Défense Nationale (IHEDN) on 12 November 1985, the new Defense Minister, Paul Quilès froze any decision on SX until at least 1990, and intimated that France may well decide to opt instead for long-range supersonic cruise missiles.[5] Meanwhile, the fixed silos of the Plateau d'Albion have been hardened and their previous contents (the 2,750 km, 1 × 150 kiloton warhead S-2 missile) have been replaced by the new 3,000 km S-3 carrying a single one-megaton warhead.

As for the airborne element of the strategic "triad", the old Mirage IVs of the original *force de frappe* will, beginning in 1986, gradually be replaced by the Mirage IVP and especially the Mirage 2000 both of which will be equipped with the new air-to-ground medium-range nuclear missile (ASMP). Essentially, these new systems will be reassigned to theater role. Again, all these developments were in the pipeline before Giscard left office. On the other hand, no decision was taken on a new strategic bomber, and the future of the airborne element of the strategic triad was, to say the least, ambiguous.[6]

As for tactical nuclear systems, there are few real surprises. The *Hades* truck-launched short-range missile – the replacement for *Pluton* – is on schedule for deployment in 1992. Its projected range has been increased to 350 km (from the original Giscardian intention of 200 km), and it has been decoupled from its former First Army command structure and placed under a new separate authority directly commanded by the Chief of the General Staffs. Both of these decisions were the object of significant criticism from the opposition parties and I shall return to them shortly when considering the matter of strategic choices. Although no governmental announcement was forthcoming on the deployment of the neutron bomb, an article in the army journal published by the Ministry of Defense, *Armées d'aujourd'hui*, indicated officially that *Hades* is being specifically designed and constructed to enable it to carry neutron warheads.[7]

The pursuit of all these new sophisticated programs had inevitable repercussions on the operating budgets of the conventional wings of the armed services. The land army has been reduced by some 10,000 troops, with an additional 10,000 to go before 1988. Those remaining have been asked to tighten their belts in various ways. The situation is regarded in some areas as so serious that even General Jeannou Lacaze (faithful servant of the Socialist government as Chief of the General Staffs until his retirement in August 1985) commented in his parting speech to the IHEDN that if things continued in this way, they could not fail to "compromise the operational capacity of the armed forces".[8] More ominously still, the commanding officer of the First Tank Division based in West Germany, General Philippe Arnold, was dismissed by Paul Quilès for having complained to visiting journalists that the French battle tank, the AMX-30, is a generation or two behind its American, West German, British, or Israeli counterparts. The Arnold affair led to angry exchanges between the Defense Minister and a former Giscardian Chief of the General Staffs, General Méry, who took up Arnold's complaint and accused the government of running the land army down through inadequate resources.[9]

As for the navy, despite a slight increase (17 per cent to 18.4 per cent) in the proportion of the defense budget allocated to it, its operational situation actually worsened. This was largely due to the fact that the lion's share of the extra money was funnelled into one or two prestige projects: the new SNLE and the nuclear-attack submarine program. The long-delayed decision to commission a nuclear-powered aircraft carrier to replace the rapidly aging *Clemenceau* was taken, in principle, shortly before the resignation of Charles Hernu, although it will not figure in any budget until 1986. When it does, the cost of 10 billion francs is going to have to be met from somewhere. Meanwhile, the Chief of the Naval General Staff also felt the need to write an article in *Défense nationale*, warning of the dire consequences of inadequate funding for the conventional elements of the navy. His plea was no doubt heard by Quilès who, in his first speech to IHEDN on 12 November 1985, announced that the navy would henceforth be on top of the government's defense priority list.[10] The implications of that, however, were far-reaching, since the Minister spoke of the government's determination to build not just one, but two nuclear-powered aircraft carriers.

In view of all this, it will come as no surprise to learn that two air force generals (including the Commander in Chief of the air force, General Bernard Capillon) also wrote of the urgent need for crucial and possibly cruel choices in procurement policy, given the rapid evolution of the technology of air warfare.[11] While the Socialist government more or less respected the calendar for the entry into service of the Mirage 2000, little else was accomplished. No decision was taken on the purchase of AWACS or the development of a long-distance transport plane. Moreover, there was a growing controversy over the number of combat aircraft in service; the aim is 500, the realistic target is 450, but some voices insist that the actual figure in 1985 is nearer 425. In addition, the number of hours flying-time of these combat aircraft has been reduced because of rising fuel costs, and the average minimum training-hourage "in the cockpit" of France's fighter pilots has been maintained at the already low level of 15 hours per month only by a drastic reduction of the hours flown by reservists. Here again, equipment priorities, largely in other services, imposed painful reductions in operating costs with inevitable consequences on morale.

One must conclude this brief survey of the main outlines of Socialist defense policy by noting that, within a diminishing resource base, the government gave priority to sophisticated new high-technology programs at the expense of the operational budget of the armed forces. Moreover, virtually all of the programs completed in the last five years had been launched under Giscard d'Estaing, and nothing of any significance was ordered (with solid budget backing) in the way of new material. As of 1986, the problems for France had become crucial and some extremely tough decisions must be made within the coming years concerning the types of weapons systems France can afford and realistically expect to require for the coming decades. These decisions will depend directly on the threefold constraints I outlined earlier: resources; strategic choices and the challenge of new technologies.

THE RESOURCE PROBLEM

The debate on the military budget in November 1985 was the occasion for the opposition parties (seconded, on some points, by the PCF) to launch a vigorous attack on the government's overall record on defense spending. The attacks were all the more virulent in that, when the sums were calculated in 1983 for the 1984–88 White Paper (an estimated 705 billion francs, 1983 value, rising to 830 billion, 1988 value) the government promised a full review of these projections in the 1985 budget debate. In the event, the review which was tabled in the National Assembly in late June restricted itself to a self-congratulatory report to the effect that the totality of the objectives of the White Paper for 1984 and 1985 had been met. There were no new programmatic decisions or attempts at budgetary revision for the remaining period. It is a fact that no government in the last ten years has actually been able to meet the resource implications of its own programs. According to the Cour des Comptes, the 1976–81 Giscardian defense White Paper undershot its resource estimates by some 48 billion francs.[12] By the time the Socialists came into power, there was almost a two-year delay in the implementation of that program, which allowed Hernu to avoid drafting a new White Paper until 1983. He first contented himself with completing the existing program.

Nevertheless, according to closely calculated opposition statistics, the previous government did manage to increase the proportion of the GDP devoted to defense (from 3.36% in 1974 to 3.85% in 1981), whereas, it was claimed, it had slipped to 3.73% under the Socialists.[13] Furthermore, the percentage of the overall state budget allocated to defense remained steady at around 17% throughout the Giscard years but fell after 1981 to what some claimed was an all-time low of 14.9% in 1986.[14] Finally these same calculations showed a steady growth in the pre-1981 defense budget of around 5%, whereas they claimed there had been zero growth under the Socialists.

Whatever the precise truth about this "war of statistics" (and it is too soon to know with any certainty), it is undeniable that the defense resource problem under the Socialists was worsening steadily. A recent calculation suggests the possibility of a shortfall of 35 billion francs by the end of the period covered by the Loi de Programmation Militaire 1984–88.[15] Bearing in mind the following – the world recession; the fact that the Socialists budgeted virtually no new programs for the year 2000; costs of sophisticated high-technology weaponry rising far faster than inflation (research and development for these systems has risen from 10% of the overall cost only a few years ago to 30% in 1986 and is still rising); and a massive new shopping list for military hardware which was being pressed upon the government by the various service chiefs – one begins to get some idea of the dimensions of the resource problem. The "Arnold affair" was only the tip of a huge iceberg, but, given shrinking resources, it brings us logically to the next major issue: strategic choices.

STRATEGIC CHOICES AND THE BATTLE OVER MILITARY DOCTRINE

For approximately a decade, France has been attempting to have its cake and eat it too. Exclusive priority was given to the nuclear deterrent under de Gaulle, and the General was not unhappy to see the problematic army (of Algeria) cut quite massively. Giscard d'Estaing made an effort to redress the balance in favor of the conventional armed forces since there was the growing need for France to display some concrete form of solidarity with the European allies. Hence, the Giscardian notion of the "*sanctuaire élargi*" and the "*espace stratégique européen commun*".[16] But his Gaullist allies were not yet prepared to break with orthodoxy and so, despite Giscard's clear preference for France to play down great-power posturing in favor of battlefield cooperation with the NATO allies, he found himself obliged to try to do both. Under François Mitterrand, we witnessed the curious and seemingly paradoxical spectacle of governments actually reducing global defense expenditure while attempting, at the same time, to intensify programmatic and declaratory policy with regard to both France's "nuclear sanctuary" and her conventional role in Europe and abroad.

As far as the strategic nuclear role is concerned, there was a noticeable intensification of Gaullist great-power posturing, in terms of the President's own nuclear self-image as well as the declaratory priority attached to nuclear doctrine; as 1986 approached it was especially noticeable in terms of symbolic public-relations visits to the increasingly beleaguered nuclear atoll of Mururoa in the South Pacific.[17] Although the only strategic innovation between 1981 and 1986 was the launch of *l'Inflexible* in May 1985, there can be little doubt in the public mind that France today is more of a consciously self-styled nuclear power than in the days of Giscard d'Estaing. The Euromissile crisis certainly helped foster this image, but the problems for the credibility of France's strategic nuclear "deterrent" are unlikely to find an easy solution.

Let us leave aside the entire, quasi-theological question of how credible a counter-city deterrent is against a nuclear counterforce capability and conventional/chemical weapon superiority. Let us ignore questions of submarine detection or minor irritations like arms control. Let us simply ask how many SNLEs are essential to ensure deterrence.

The original FOST (Force Océanique Stratégique Nucléaire) program foresaw a minimum of five vessels (no maximum was ever stated), of which two would constantly be at sea deploying 32 single-warhead missiles. Charles Hernu stepped up the servicing facilities on the Ile Longue with the result that, from 1983, three vessels have been constantly at sea, deploying 48 single-missile warheads. With the entry into service of *l'Inflexible*, the total number of disposable warheads on France's SNLEs has more than doubled, and the number at sea at any one time almost trebled. When all of France's SNLEs scheduled to be refitted with the M-4 missile are operational, there will be as much as a sevenfold increase in available warheads.[18]

This would appear to be sufficient for the PS and UDF.[19] But for the Gaullist RPR, the definition of nuclear sufficiency varies constantly. During Chirac's presidential campaign of 1981, his arguments were based on proposals formulated in a policy document of 1979,[20] and called for 15 SNLEs by the year 2010. In the RPR *Proposition de loi* drafted by Yves Lancien in 1983, the figure of nine SNLEs was given as an optimum objective.[21] In the 1984 document, *Libres et responsables* (which called for an increase in the defense budget to 5 per cent of GDP – a proposal which was rapidly laughed out of court[22] – this target was reduced to seven[23] and in the most recent RPR proposals, four SNLEs permanently at sea is urged as "a goal to be attained as soon as possible",[24] although no overall number is cited. Other authors, such as Pierre Lellouche, have insisted that five SNLEs permanently at sea is the minimum number for credibility.[25] Much of this resembles the old medieval debate about angels on pinheads, and is based on inspirational guesses rather than meaningful calculations. The bottom line is that a single SNLE costs somewhere between 8 and 10 billion francs. The number regarded as essential therefore depends on what else is viewed essential.

One of the most potentially vital developments in France since 1981 is the shifting nature, function and purpose of the tactical nuclear systems. The label *arme nucléaire tactique* (ANT) covers both the *Hades* and ASMP programs and developments in these areas have direct repercussions on the various armed forces destined to deploy them: the army (*Hades*), navy, and air force (ASMP). The nature of these weapons has shifted considerably under the Socialists. Whereas the *Pluton* had a range of 20–120 km and carried either a 15 or 25 kiloton warhead, *Hades* has a range of 350 km and will carry either a "regular" nuclear warhead of anything between 20 and 60 kilotons, or a neutron warhead. The carrier-based or air force tactical bombers, which used to carry free-fall AN52 bombs (one per plane) with a 25 kiloton warhead over ranges of 600 to 700 km, will shortly see their range and power extended considerably when they are fitted with the ASMP, which has a 150 kiloton warhead and a range of 100 to 300 km, depending on launch height.[26]

What is controversial about these weapons is less their nature than their function and purpose in Socialist defense doctrine. In accordance with its pseudo-Gaullist image, the new Socialist government made a great show of reasserting presidential political control over tactical weapons.[27] This implied that they had been given over into the generals' hands for battlefield use under Giscard d'Estaing, a charge which is certainly an exaggeration, but not entirely devoid of truth. Over and above the reassertion of political control over ANT, however, the Socialist government went to the lengths of decoupling *Pluton* (and eventually *Hades*) from its First Army command, and placing it under a special command headed by the Chief of the General Staffs. In order to reemphasize the old declaratory notion that the firing of a tactical nuclear weapon would represent an ultimate warning shot signaling the imminence (in the event of continued aggression) of a strategic nuclear strike to an aggressor, the tactical weapons were renamed "prestrategic" weapons. This is where the controversy began, not least among the opposition parties themselves.

For the RPR, which was never particularly sold on tactical weapons, this qualitative and quantitative boost to tactical weapons made little or no sense. In the event of a war in Central Europe, in which (in both governmental and RPR scenarios) France would not necessarily be on the front line, some Gaullists failed to see what France's tactical nuclear systems would contribute to the destructive power of the thousands of existing NATO weapons. It is scarcely conceivable, they argued, that France, which would theoretically be uninvolved in the first battle, would cross the nuclear firebreak before the United States or the other NATO forces (which would actually be in the thick of the fighting). If, on the other hand, the NATO forces were broken and the adversary were moving in on the Rhine, a warning shot would probably be redundant.[28] The Socialist defense spokespersons liked to point out that the new tactical systems (*Hades* and ASMP) were complementary weapons, the latter capable of striking enemy tank concentrations or fixed infrastructure positions well behind the front line and the former able to take out first-wave assault forces.[29] Leaving aside the fact that this sounded more like battle fighting than "prestrategic" battle deterrence, one might ask, along with RPR defense specialist François Fillon, why so many tactical weapons are needed merely to prevent the enemy from concentrating its positions. In a word, the Gaullists viewed the priority afforded to tactical systems (as opposed to strategic) by the Socialists within that section of the budget allocated to nuclear weapons as a serious mistake. Their arguments were not without force.

The Giscardian UDF, however, was upset about the Socialist policy on tactical weapons for totally different reasons. It was pleased about one point of Socialist policy; the increase in expenditure for tactical weapons (+ 50 per cent in 1984; + 30 per cent in 1985). However, the UDF was strongly critical of both the increased range of Hades and the decoupling of the ANT from the First Army. It saw the increased range as unnecessarily extravagant since, in its view, the ideal position for these weapons should be the front line. By the same token, it considered that the more the tactical systems were decoupled from either the First Army or the Rapid Deployment Force (RDF) the less credible they become in the eyes of an enemy. Moreover, the UDF felt that this decoupling would lead to incoherence and confusion as between the different commands, and vigorously denied that its own preference for "sending these weapons into battle" implied any weakening or relaxation of presidential control over their eventual usage. For the UDF, therefore, tactical weapons were to be considered virtually as battlefield weapons and should be deployed liberally on the front line, both with the First Army and with the Rapid Deployment Force.[30] They should also include the neutron bomb which the UDF saw as a more effective deterrent, precisely because its usage was more likely.[31] The UDF did not hesitate to play with nuclear fire, and was all the more determined to put French tactical weapons in the firing line because it suspected NATO of moving rapidly towards a no-first-use stance.[32]

There was a major contradiction at the heart of the UDF position on tactical systems, however. On the one hand, it argued in favor of the multiplication of these weapons in a battlefield situation;[33] on the other hand, it continued to insist that the deterrent value of such weapons was primary. The logic behind this position was the belief that, faced with a French army bristling with such weapons, an adversary would back off. If this latter argument was the true explanation, then the Gaullist questions about the need for more than a few tactical weapons required an answer. If, however, the UDF really favored battle fighting with tactical weapons, it then needed to explain what French weapons would add to existing NATO ones; it also needed to read the literature which argued that once the nuclear firebreak was crossed, there would be no controlling the resultant escalation. The debate about the use and purpose of tactical nuclear weapons remains the most significant, and certainly the most instructive, of all defense debates. It clearly explodes the myth of the consensus, since the four major parties hold widely divergent views on the matter.[34]

The role of ANT, as well as the purpose and credibility of French strategic weapons was, of course, intimately connected to the other major security issue of the day: relations between France and its European partners in the Atlantic Alliance. This was where the Socialists seemed, at least on paper, to have produced some elements of innovation. The creation of the *Rapid Deployment Force* in 1983 was at the time (and to some extent still is) the subject of intense interpretive speculation. Its precise military functions, assuming that they are retained by the new right-wing government, could very easily change with a new political majority in Paris. The one seemingly incontrovertible fact about the RDF was that it was conceived above all as a politico-military gesture towards West Germany. Whichever way one looked at the evolution of European defense thinking – whether one favored a "Euro-pillar" of NATO, a more autonomous integrated European defense, or even stronger bilateral links between the two major continental military powers, France and West Germany – it was by 1981 increasingly vital for France to dispel what Pierre Lellouche has called the "myth of neutrality" with regard to West Germany. Gaullist orthodoxy had held that it was impossible for France ever to give a formal guarantee to come to West Germany's defense in the event of an attack (which France was, incidentally, and still is contractually obliged to do by the terms of the Brussels treaty of 1948). The minimum price to be paid by Paris for any progress at all in European defense cooperation was a clear statement to the effect that the French government no longer regarded the territory of West Germany as a (potentially expendable) glacis. In other words, what was urgently required was a statement that the security interests of Paris and Bonn were the same if not identical.

That clear statement, despite the symbolism of the RDF, was in fact a very long time coming. A joint Franco–German defense commission was established in October 1982 and has met at regular quarterly intervals since. The RDF was launched in May 1983 with a succession of nervous disclaimers as to the automaticity of its engagement alongside the West German ally. With predictable regularity, Hernu, Lacaze, Mitterrand and others constantly insisted that the decision to engage the RDF or not remained a presidential prerogative. Clearly, the Socialists did not feel confident, either *vis-à-vis* the electorate or the opposition, about the repercussions of too unambiguous a line on Franco-German military cooperation.[35] Only very gradually, as both the RPR[36] and the UDF[37] began to make overt noises about a new commitment to the European allies, did the Socialist government dare to stray marginally outside the realms of Gaullist orthodoxy. It was not until 20 June 1985 that Charles Hernu, in a speech at a joint Franco-German military exercise, went so far as to state unambiguously that "the Federal Republic of Germany is our closest ally in all respects; France and the Federal Republic share common security interests."[38] Even then, no sooner were the words out of his mouth than he felt the need to reassert presidential prerogative in engaging in any military action. This mini-disclaimer notwithstanding, Manfred Woerner, the German Defense Minister who was present, publicly thanked Hernu "for having said that the Federal Republic is not simply a glacis for France".

It was not entirely coincidental that this new development came only days after the conclusion of a major poll taken between 11 and 17 June 1985 which showed that, for the first time since the World War II, a majority (57 per cent) of French men and women felt that France should automatically commit itself to the defense of West Germany. An even larger majority felt that the reunification of Germany would now be a legitimate development.[39] Yet despite this public upturn in support for an automatic French engagement on the Eastern front, the Socialist government continued to stick to the old orthodoxy. All thought of using the strategic nuclear weapons to extend the sanctuary to the Elbe was expressly and repeatedly ruled out. As we have seen, the ANT was pointedly divorced from the fighting units of the army.[40] The relationship between the fighting units (First, Second and Third Armies and RDF) and the ANT remained shrouded in ambiguity, but the implication was always that tactical nuclear weapons would not be used in the battle for West Germany.[41] All that the Socialists did, therefore, was to remove five divisions from the existing fighting units and create a Rapid Deployment Force which may or may not be used in the event of war in Central Europe. Poor returns for years of discussion about Franco-German solidarity!

The opposition parties attacked this ambivalence with greater or lesser degrees of enthusiasm and sincerity. Both the UDF and RPR criticized the way in which the RDF was constructed ("unclothing Peter in order to clothe Paul") and argued that the main effect has been to deprive the First Army of key elements of mobility (helicopter units) without adding anything to its military potential. In addition, the opposition parties claimed that the RDF itself was too small a force to be effective and that the entire operation had considerably weakened France's conventional potential by dividing it into two bits (*la stratégie des Curiaces*).[42] What did the right-wing parties propose as an alternative?

The Gaullists were not yet ready with an answer. After floating various trial balloons over the years,[43] most of these amounted in one form or another to a vague proposal that France replace the United States nuclear umbrella, the most recent document refers to the "need to consider and resolve the problems of our defense in the spirit of close solidarity with our partners and European allies". But alas, the document has nothing more concrete to offer than a proposal that the defense cooperation clause of the Franco-German treaty of 1963 be implemented "for example, to proceed by having negotiations on the employment of nuclear tactics".[44]

Discussions with the West Germans about the use of ANT were also at the heart of the UDF proposals, which went much further than those of the RPR. Indeed, the UDF specifically stated on numerous occasions that France must declare unequivocally that, in the event of war, it will fight alongside its allies on the front line.[45] The Giscardians actually proposed, in this regard, that France should once again take its place in NATO's planning committees[46] and there were broad hints that France's opposition to flexible response was misguided.[47] Above all, the UDF launched a frontal attack on the old dichotomy between dissuasion and defense, which it reflects as a "false debate".[48] With no small amount of political courage, the UDF asserted that "it is wrong to say that the defense of France is independent . . . that our nuclear arms guarantee our independence",[49] and devoted detailed attention to the issue of how to engage in concrete collaborative projects with both the West Germans and British.[50] There is no doubt whatever that, of all the French political forces, the UDF made by far the greatest mileage – both in intent and in fact – in the direction of an integrated European defense capability.[51] To be sure, the UDF covered itself politically from time to time by quoting de Gaulle[52] or pleading presidential prerogative on military engagements.[53] Also, it never went so far as to suggest that a French army should take up a permanent position on the Elbe, as Pierre Lellouche has recently done.[54] His study, uninhibited by the political complexities of the defense establishment, seems to me to take the logic of the UDF position to its ultimate conclusions. It is quite clear that it is the Giscardian party which came closest to making a radical break with Gaullist orthodoxy, although prior to March 1986 its status as an opposition party allowed the luxury of avoiding the types of painful stategic choices which are clearly imminent. In its most recent defense policy document, construed as much as an attack on the Socialist government as an alternative governmental program, its own implied military shopping list was comprehensive and indicated no areas for reduction of expenditure. Yet, the UDF was aware that it was politically unrealistic to propose anything more than a 4 per cent target for the defense budget/GDP ratio. So concerned was it, indeed, about the resources problem that its defense spokesman in parliament, Jean-Marie Daillet, launched the idea of a special defense loan to cover the immediate needs of the next decades.[55] Implicit in the Giscardian proposals was a downgrading of strategic nuclear weapons in favor of conventional weapons and tactical nuclear systems, but everything clearly hung on the future shape of European defense collaboration, which might help to some extent in solving the resources problem. Even the UDF was reluctant to make any revolutionary proposals for defense spending rationalization, however, despite its own lucid perception of the implications of the new technological dawn which was peeping over the horizon.

It is to this problem of new technologies and their impact on French (and European) defense planning that we must now turn to complete our review of the problems facing the French government.

STRATEGY AND THE NEW TECHNOLOGY

As we have seen, France is currently faced with a bewildering variety of potential claims on its scarce defense resources. Most of them enter into the category of sophisticated high-technology systems, but are at the same time highly vulnerable to parallel developments in science and technology. The following list comprises only a few of those systems which have been brought into the public domain as a result of existing programs. It does not begin to tackle the problems posed by the next generation of weapons systems.

Research and development into the new generation of nuclear submarines is in progress. Although it is unlikely that any major breakthrough in submarine detection will occur in the next 10 to 15 years, it is not inconceivable that by the time the first new generation SNLE is launched in the mid-1990s, it will already be threatened by imminent obsolescence, either through advances in detection or through Soviet developments in SDI. With the latter in mind, the former Socialist Defense Minister, Paul Quilès, spoke of the need for France to engage in research into a new "radar-resistant" reentry warhead.[56] Assuming, however, a best-case scenario and the continuing credibility of the SNLE, France is already conscious of the need for a military observation satellite to assist in targeting both its submarine-borne and *Hades* missiles. This poses the vast and uncharted question of space technology, a field in which among the Europeans, France is making most of the progress in the face of a marked lack of enthusiasm or even cooperation from her major partners.[57] I shall return to the EUREKA project shortly since it is in some ways a separate problem. We have already seen how the specter of SDI prompted a freeze on any decision on the projected mobile land-based missiles (SX), but it seems likely that if ballistic missile defense becomes a major priority for the USSR, France will be tempted to go in for long-range supersonic cruise missiles.[58] Either way the cost will be collossal.

As far as ANT is concerned, research and development is well in hand for *Hades* and ASMP, although by early next century the delivery systems for these weapons may well be on the verge of obsolescence. It is clear, in addition, that resources will need to be pumped into new aircraft technology. Here the French are already aware of the advantages of European cooperation and recently had to climb down from an intransigent nationalist position on the matter of the European fighter plane.[59] Another item on the aircraft shopping list is some form of radar detection system for low-flying enemy aircraft. The UDF proposes buying AWACS (another 10 billion francs),[60] the RPR still seems to be keen for France to develop its own system, while the Socialists in government tried to negotiate some deal with the United States, either involving substantial industrial compensation in exchange for a straight purchase or some form of rental of NATO information.[61]

I have already mentioned the proposed order for two nuclear-powered aircraft carriers. It is clear moreover, that the Socialist government attached high priority to the nuclear-attack submarine program. Both these developments testify to France's determination to hang onto a world role, in addition to nuclear status and a major contribution to European defense. But keeping up with the superpowers involves not only nuclear but also conventional technology. Indeed, advances in this field have probably been more spectacular over the last decade than in any other. The development of "emerging technology" (ET) weaponry has already produced a significant shift in NATO strategic doctrine. The implications of these developments for French (and European) weapons procurement policy – and indeed for the entire armaments industry – are very far-reaching if France and Europe are not to become totally dependent upon the United States.

Technological advance may well be outstripping current procurement programs. A good example of this is the new battle tank (whose absence prompted General Arnold's indiscretions). So far, about 2 billion francs have been devoted to research and development on a new generation of battle tanks to be deployed in the early 1990s.[62] But, even as this money is being spent, it is increasingly evident, even to the most conservative strategist, that the battles of tomorrow will rely far more on helicopters and anti-tank weapons than on tanks as such. And, in the current climate, that implies ET, "smart" weapons and a whole new range of technological gadgets which are hardly even being discussed in France.

Behind all these headaches about how to outguess the advance of technology and its security implications, there lurks the gigantic shadow of SDI. It is quite possible that SDI will come to represent as radical a break with the past as the explosion at Alamogordo did 40 years ago. The consequences for France and Europe are potentially so far-reaching that no clear response is yet possible. The implications of SDI fall into two separate but related spheres; security and industry. The implications are still unclear on the security front, and many French commentators on SDI still cling valiantly to the faint hope that there will always be a role for nuclear deterrence. But the cost of maintaining credibility is likely to be enormous; and the risk of obsolescence is ever present.

On the industrial front, SDI has posed a challenge that, as usual, has left the European nations in disarray. The Socialist government was consistent in its hostility to the American scheme, and Mitterrand took a lead in promoting the European response, EUREKA. He has had unexpected success in selling EUREKA to the European allies, despite the determination of some nations to keep a finger in the SDI pie as well.[63] However, the new governing parties are, for the moment, hostile both to the Socialists' rejection of SDI and to EUREKA. Both RPR and UDF favor French participation in the American scheme and both harbor illusions (in my view) about Europe being able to influence the course of American research.[64] At the same time, both parties are strongly in favor of a French lead in space research and technology. It is also not hard to imagine that, once they abandon electoral point-scoring over these issues, they too, in government, will put energy and resources into a coordinated European space-cum-high-technology industrial research project. But the costs of such a project are astronomical and everybody is fully aware that the idea can only even be entertained on a joint European level.

CONCLUSION: FRANCE OR EUROPE OR FRANCE AND EUROPE?

This is where we return to our starting point. A combination of forces is urging France to recognize that, in the age of "Star Wars", national defense is increasingly illusory, if not meaningless. For political, economic, technological, military and cultural reasons, France cannot divorce its fate from that of Europe. Nowhere is this clearer than on the security front. And yet the stumbling blocks remain enormous. Perhaps the major problem remains the role of France's independent nuclear deterrent. The Socialist government was fully conscious that West Germany is less than enthusiastic at the prospect of being brought under a French nuclear umbrella, even though the holes in the American one seems to grow wider every day. The UDF speaks loosely of stationing large numbers of tactical nuclear weapons on the battlefront in Central Europe, but (in my opinion) drastically underestimates the difficulties which would be involved in discussing an agreed firing policy for such weapons with the West Germans. For the moment, one fears that the RPR attitude may well be summarized by the comment made to me by a leading RPR defense specialist: "Either they defend themselves properly in whatever way they see fit, or we'll do the job for them, but then they shouldn't complain if they end up carbonized."[65]

The Socialists, in my opinion, were correct in sensing that cooperation on European security must, in the first instance, be conventional. But, in order to be successful, much more in the way of resources will be needed and some deeply entrenched traditional attitudes will need to be exorcised. This brings us back, once again, to priorities and so, yet again, to nuclear weapons. The nuclear capabilities of France and Britain can be conceived in three different ways: first, as being exclusively for last-resort national protection; second, as in the Ottawa declaration of 1974, as an undefined contribution to the peace of the region (these first two are not incompatible); third, as a coordinated European deterrent force with the backing and agreement of all European nations. The latter is inconceivable in the foreseeable future. The Ottawa scenario is highly problematic in terms of European security cooperation since its virtue lies precisely in its vagueness: any attempt to lay down precise guidelines for crossing the nuclear firebreak, in consultation with the West Germans or anybody else, is a Pandora's box of infinite sensitivity and complexity. The national option is a major obstacle to European defense cooperation. As long as France continues to see its contribution to the common defense as being primarily in the nuclear field, the prospects for cooperation do not look good.

Overall, the problems facing France's defense establishment currently are enormous. She cannot afford nuclear superpower status (even of the second rank), and a meaningful contribution to the conventional defense of Europe, and a trouble-shooting world role in Africa, Latin America and the Pacific.[66] But France's great-power self-perception is so deeply rooted and all-pervasive that it will have great difficulty in bringing itself to abandon any one of these roles. An act of uncommon historical imagination is required if France (and Europe) are not to be overtaken by external forces. Throughout this chapter, we have examined the question from within the parameters of the French defense debate itself. That debate is predicated on the assumption that bloc confrontation in Europe and the world will go on forever. Elsewhere in Europe that assumption is increasingly being questioned, and a quest for a trans-European security settlement, within the context of a historic healing process at every level is beginning to take shape. France, for a whole host of reasons, is ideally suited to play a major role in such a process. But so far, there are no signs from within France that this alternative could be the imaginary way out of an increasingly impossible bind.

NOTES

1 By 1980, the technical, diplomatic and military conditions which had allowed "Gaullism" to exist had all disappeared. See Pierre Lellouche, "France and the Euromissiles", *Foreign Affairs*, 62 (Winter 1983-84).

2 Jolyon Howorth, "Consensus of Silence: The French Socialist Party and Defence Policy under François Mitterrand", *International Affairs*, 60, 4 (1984), pp. 579-600; and "Defence and the Mitterrand Government" in *Defence and Dissent in Contemporary France*, eds Jolyon Howorth and Patricia Chilton (London, Croom Helm, 1984), pp. 94-134.

3 Admiral Paul Delahousse, a senior member of the UDF defense commission told me, in an interviw in Paris on 10 December 1984, that Giscard was given an ultimatum by Pierre Messmer that the Gaullists would not vote for the defense budget unless the sixth submarine, which the new President had scrapped, was reinstated forthwith.

4 The green light for R & D was given in the 1986 defense budget: see *Le Monde*, (17 Sept. and 13 Nov. 1985. See also Paul Quilès, "L'Avenir de notre concept de défense face aux progrès technologiques", *Défense nationale*, (Jan. 1986), pp. 17-18.

5 Quilès, "L'Avenir de notre concept de défense". See also Jeannou Lacaze, "L'Avenir de la défense française", *Défense nationale*, (July 1985).

6 See, on these matters, Patricia Chilton, "French Nuclear Weapons" in Howorth and Chilton, (eds) *Defence and Dissent*, pp. 135-72; and David S. Yost, *France's Deterrent Posture and Security in Europe* (London, IISS, 1985), Adelphi Papers 194 and 195.

7 *Armées d'aujourd'hui* (Sept. 1985).

8 Speech published in *Défense nationale*, (July 1985), quote p. 17. See also "Le Général Lacaze sonne l'alerte", *Le Point*, (1 July 1985), p. 49 and René Imbert "Le Choix des armements: un arbitrage entre présent et futur", *Le Point*, (June 1985), pp. 11-22, and *Le Monde*, (7-8 July 1985), p. 16.

9 See Jacques Isnard, "La Grogne de certains officiers", *Le Monde*, (28 Nov. 1985); also Paul Quilès, "Réponse aux gognards", *Le Nouvel observateur*, (8-14 Nov. 1985).

10 The Chief of the Naval General Staff's *cri de coeur*: Admiral Yves Leenhart, "Réflexions pour une stratégie navale d'avenir", *Défense nationale* (Aug.-Sept. 1985), pp. 11-34. See also special report "Objectif mer", *Le Monde*, (28-29 July 1985); the Quilès decisions in *Le Monde* and *Libération*, (13 Nov. 1985).

11 Bernard Capillon, "L'Armée de l'air d'hier à aujourd'hui: le fait aérien: une nouvelle dimension de la défense", *Défense nationale*, (June 1985), pp. 23-30; and Michel Forget, "Le Changement dans la troisième dimension", *Défense nationale* (June 1985), pp. 31-40.

12 This was reported by Charles Hernu himself in "Une Défense moderne et crédible", *Le Monde*, (12 July 1985).

13 For the moment, it is impossible to know what the exact figures are. The UDF calculation is in *Redresser la défense de la France* (Paris, UDF, 1985), annexes, p. 20, tableau 7; the RPR figures in *La Défense de la France: 4 ans de gestion socialiste. Propositions pour le renouveau* (Paris, RPR, 1985), pp. 5-6. On the controversy over precise budget statistics, see, in defense of the government's resource record, Frédéric Tieberghien, "L'Effort de défense depuis 1981", *Défense nationale* (Nov. 1985), and Jean-Yves Le Drian, *Assemblée nationale*, 2365 (10 Oct. 1984), and the comments by David Yost in "Radical Change in French Defence Policy?", *Survival* (Jan./Feb. 1986), pp. 53-68.

14 Provisional figures suggest that this may have risen again to 15.4% in 1986. See Tieberghien, "L'Effort de défense", p. 32.

15 Jacques Isnard, "Le Plan militaire 1984-1988 en question", *Le Monde*, (3 July 1985); "Le Général Lacaze", p. 49.

16 Guy Méry, "Une Armée pour quoi faire et comment?", *Défense nationale*, (June 1976), pp. 11-34. Giscard d'Estaing's speech to the Institut des Hautes Etudes de Défense Nationale in *Défense nationale*, (July 1976); and also in *Le Monde*, (4 June 1976).

17 On 16 November 1983, François Mitterrand made his famous statement to the effect that "the cornerstone of France's deterrence strategy is the head of state, that is to say me; everything hangs on his determination".

See *Le Monde*, (18 Nov. 1983). Mitterrand visited Mururoa on 13 October, as did Fabius and Quilès on 24 October 1985.

18 Prior to 1985, there were, in services, 5 SNLEs with 16 single-warhead missiles (80 in total) but in fact only 2 SNLEs (32 missiles) and then, from 1983, 3 SNLEs (48 missiles) were at sea permanently. *L'Inflexible* alone carries 16 missiles with 6 warheads each (96 warheads in total). When all four of the SNLEs currently scheduled to be refitted with M-4s have been so refitted, the total will rise to 480 warheads, and if the "seventh" (in reality sixth) SNLE carries the same complement, the total will rise to 576 warheads, a sevenfold increase over the pre-1985 situation.

19 The UDF states openly that five or six SNLEs *in toto* are sufficient, as long as three can be permanently at sea, in UDF, *Redresser la défense*, p. 147.

20 RPR, *Réflexions sur la défense*, présenté par Michel Aurillac (Paris, RPR, 1979), pp. 39–40.

21 "Proposition de loi portant définition des principes d'organisation de la défense", *Assemblée Nationale*, 1454, (1983), p. 35.

22 RPR, *Libres et responsables* (Paris, Flammarion, 1984), p. 129. The 5% proposal was regarded as so unrealistic that Pierre Messmer succeeded in having the book withdrawn from circulation. The RPR defense speaker in Parliament, Yves Lancien, resigned over the issue, claiming that he had not been consulted before the drawing up of the defense chapter of this publication. See *Le Monde*, (9 Nov. 1984), and interview granted to the author by Yves Lancien on 20 December 1984.

23 RPR, *Libres et responsables*, p. 131.

24 RPR, *La Défense de la France*, p. 87.

25 Pierre Lellouche, *L'Avenir de la guerre* (Paris, Mazarine, 1985), p. 284.

26 In May 1986 the converted Mirage IVPs of the strategic bomber force began to deploy the ASMP.

27 This "reversal" of doctrine became a constant in all government pronouncements on the tactical weapons, beginning with Pierre Mauroy's first speech to IHEDN on 14 September 1981, "La Cohérence d'une politique de défense", *Défense nationale* (Oct. 1981).

28 These awkward questions were, interestingly enough, openly formulated by the current Gaullist parliamentary defense speaker, François Fillon, "A quoi sert l'armement nucléaire tactique?", *Le Monde*, (10 Nov. 1984). However, in a series of interviews with leading Gaullist defense experts, I was given very different accounts of the role of ANT. The most important development seems to be Jacques Chirac's recent shift towards the UDF line – *Le Monde*, (28 Feb. 1986).

29 Lacaze, "L'Avenir de la défense française".

30 UDF, *Redresser la défense*, pp. 75–6, 81–3, 120–3.

31 Ibid., pp. 122–3.

32 This fear that the generalized doubts about nuclear strategy which have swept through NATO recently will lead to a reluctance to cross the nuclear Rubicon is implicit throughout the UDF defense documents and forms a central argument of Pierre Lellouche's book, *L'Avenir de la guerre*. It is for this reason that the UDF is keen to put the "nuclear risk" back into the overall strategic equation.

33 In an interview with Jean-Marie Daillet, president of the UDF defense commission and UDF defense speaker in Parliament, on 10 December 1984, I was told that the UDF considers tactical weapons as battlefield weapons to be used in the early stages of an engagement.

34 The PCF is dubious about all tactical weapons and is virulent in its refusal of the neutron bomb. See Jean Combasteil, "Non et renon à l'OTAN", *Le Monde*, (10–11 Nov. 1985).

35 See the PS parliamentary speaker, Jean-Yves Le Drian in *Le Monde*, (10 May 1983); Hernu, in *Le Monde* (18 June 1983); J. Lacaze, in *Défense nationale*, (June 1983), p. 21; Mitterrand's press conference of 16 November 1983, p. 8.

36 Jacques Chirac, in a controversial speech to the Konrad Adenauer Foundation in Bonn on 17 October 1983, appeared to be proposing the extension of French nuclear protection to West Germany. His speech caused such a storm of protest back home – see *Le Monde*, (20, 21, 28 Oct. 1983) – that in a subsequent speech to the Royal Institute of International Affairs on 30 November 1983, he was obliged to backtrack somewhat. But the fact remains that, for the head of the RPR, the notion is no longer unthinkable.

37 In their important publication of March 1984, *Défendre l'Europe* (Paris, UDF, 1984), the UDF explicitly demands the immediate forging of a unified European defense capability.

38 *Le Monde*, (22 June 1985. The question of precisely what agreements have been reached in the Franco-German commission remains very unclear. François Heisbourg sees important progress on agreements over the use of tactical nuclear weapons – see "France–Allemagne: une synergie nouvelle", *Le Monde*,

(7 May 1986). But Karsten Voigt, the SPD defense speaker told me on 16 May 1986 that the main value of this agreement is psychological. For him, what the West Germans really want from the French is still not being offered: namely, serious conventional solidarity.

39 See the major opinion poll survey in *Le Monde*, (28 June 1985).

40 See Jacques Isnard, "Le Point sur la réorganisation de l'armée de terre", *Le Monde*, (19 Dec. 1984).

41 Most defense statements on this issue nevertheless stress that the Soviet Union, in "taking on" a nuclear state like France, would have to measure the risks and possible consequences. See Lacaze, "Concept de défense et sécurité en Europe", *Défense nationale*, (July 1984), p. 20.

42 François de Rose, *Contre la stratégie des Curiaces* (Paris, Julliard, 1983).

43 As early as 1979, Alexandre Sanguinetti and General Buis, floated a trial balloon proposing that France share her nuclear capabilities with West Germany, see *Le Nouvel observateur*, (20 Aug. 1979). See, on the subsequent controversy, Jacques Isnard, "Une Passe d'armes académique", *Le Monde*, (31 Aug. 1979). In 1983, Michel Aurillac implied something similar in his article "De la Fin de l'Atlantisme au réveil de l'Alliance Atlantique", *Cahiers*, 89, 12 (July/Aug. 1983). We have already referred to Jacques Chirac's comments in Bonn later that year (note 36 above).

44 RPR, *La défense de la France*, p. 89.

45 UDF, *Redresser la défense*, pp. iv, 25, 45, 46-7, 50-1, 52, 108, 113, 119-22.

46 Ibid., p. 124.

47 Ibid., p. 44.

48 Ibid., p. 45.

49 Ibid., p. 52.

50 Ibid., pp. 130-42.

51 See UDF, *Défendre l'Europe. Propositions de l'UDF*, Paris, UDF, 1984.

52 See, for instance, UDF, *Redresser la défense*, p. 47, quoting de Gaulle's speech to IHEDN on 15 February 1963 as the source of the integrated European defense idea.

53 UDF, *Redresser la défense*, p. 107.

54 Lellouche, *L'Avenir de la guerre*, p. 281.

55 See Thierry Bréhier, "M. Quilès á la poursuite de l'impossible consensus", *Le Monde*, (10-11 Nov. 1985).

56 Paul Quilès, "L'Avenir de notre concept de défense", pp. 11-24.

57 West Germany has so far refused to collaborate either in the military satellite project (SAMRO) or in the Hermes space shuttle project - see *Le Monde*, (16 Jan. and 30 Oct. 1985). See, on France's space options, Jean-Yves Leloup and Pierre Cazalas "Les Options spatiales françaises", *Défense nationale*, (Feb. 1986), pp. 133-40. On the overall question of high technology and French defense capabilities, see Pascal Boniface and François Heisbourg, *La Puce, les hommes et la bombe. L'Europe face aux nouveaux défis technologiques et militaires* (Paris, Hachette, 1986).

58 The SX is costed at a minimum of 35 billion francs. Chirac and the new government seem prepared to try to go ahead with this project, but the Socialist opposition is vigorously opposed.

59 See *Le Monde*, (3 Sept. and 10-11 Nov. 1985).

60 UDF, *Redresser la défense*, p. 161. On the debate about AWACS, see "Sans AWACS, l'aviation restera borgne", *Le Monde*, (10-11 Nov. 1985).

61 The RPR proposed the creation of a French AWACS-type system in RPR, *Réflexions sur la défense*, p. 56, but does not seem to have raised the matter again since. On the Socialists, see Hernu, *Défendre la paix* (Paris, Lattes, 1985), p. 89. However, during the 1986 budget debates in November 1985, Paul Quilès stated that purchase of AWACS was out of the question for financial reasons and that France would try to develop her own, less costly system.

62 Quilès, "Réponse aux grognards", p. 26.

63 See, on this, Henri de Bresson and Philippe Lemaitre, "Le Financement du projet Eureka progresse", *Le Monde*, (7 Nov. 1985). In fact, despite the "optimistic" tone of the article, it is not at all clear whether any country other than France has yet put any substantial amount of cash into the Eureka kitty.

64 UDF, *Redresser la défense*, p. 150; RPR, *La Défense de la France*, pp. 88-9. But it is clear that there are quite considerable divergences of opinion within the right-wing - and within the RPR - on "Star Wars" research. Giscard d'Estaing and Jean-Marie Daillet argue strongly in favor of European priorities going to the American SDI scheme - *Le Point*, (11 Nov. 1985) and *Le Monde*, (10-11 Nov. 1985). Raymond Barre seems highly suspicious of SDI and fears that Europe will merely become a subcontractor to the United States (interview in *Politique internationale*, 27 [Summer 1985]). François Fillon argues that there shall

be no question of France selling out to the United States – *Le Monde*, (1 Aug. 1985), but Jacques Chirac sees France's refusal to cooperate with SDI as "une grâve erreur".

65 Pierre Viaud, general secretary of Club 89, in an interview with the author on 10 December 1984, quoting Michel Aurillac.

66 See, on this, Jacques Fontanel and Ron Smith, eds, *L'Effort économique de défense* (Paris, Ares, 1985); and Malcolm Chalmers, *Paying for Defense* (London, Pluto, 1985).

20

Mitterrand's France and the Third World

STÉPHANE HESSEL

For the past 25 years governments and sophisticated public opinion in France have considered French policy towards developing countries as the most progressive of all the major industrial powers. The term "Third World" was itself coined by French writers[1] as a reminder of the Third Estate, an underprivileged majority imbued with a right to equal status. French thinking on development did not identify developing countries and their common fight for a new economic order with nonalignment, the choice of a "third" economic and social system, or a "third" political position at equal distance from the "Free" and the "Soviet" worlds. Instead the French saw the strength of the Third World's claim in the fact that the prevailing "order" has been decided upon by two groups of privileged countries, the industrialized West and East, with little regard for the needs of the vast majority of human beings in Asia, Africa and Latin America.

After considerable reluctance in giving up imperial rule, France gradually acquired a high degree of competence in working closely with more than 20 newly independent countries and their governments. As early as the Bandung Conference (1955), the wisest leaders of the Fourth Republic expressed the view that the future of democratic industrial societies would be conditioned by a trusting partnership with the masses of Asia, Africa and Latin America. Their accession to higher standards of living through better use of insufficiently explored and exploited natural and human resources would eventually provide an incentive to production and trade similar to the increasing purchasing power of the proletariat in nineteenth- and twentieth-century Europe or the United States.

Every president of the Fifth Republic has pressed for a better organized international community, in which mutual respect and appreciation of widely different cultures were expressed in more equitable monetary, trade and financial systems. Such expressions often met solid skepticism from critics who saw them as mere lip service to lofty ideals while concrete decisions revealed a France clinging to neocolonial attitudes, closing markets to competition from developing countries, using its influence to promote exports including the sale of arms and curbing multilateral programs to concentrate on clients it could control. France has nonetheless been unable to save its closest partners in Africa from hunger and hardship, strife and the encroachment of deserts. Still, as the bitterness of decolonization faded away, the idea that France should concentrate on the river Corrèze rather than the vast African river Zambezi receded in the sixties. Even to those who attached prior importance to European cooperation and integration, partnership with the South was revealed as an indispensable dimension of the foreign policy of this half-Atlantic half-Mediterranean, demographically modest and intellectually ambitious, "nearly great" power.

THIRD WORLD POLICY BETWEEN 1962 AND 1981

Once having decided to replace colonial rule wherever possible by active economic, cultural and, if necessary, military cooperation with the newly independent countries, France devoted considerable amounts of overseas development aid (ODA) to Africa,[2] both north and south of the Sahara. Much of this, of course, enabled governments of those countries to keep French teachers in their schools, French engineers in their technical services, French scholars in their research institutes, etc. Such a policy was readily accepted by governments in sub-Saharan Africa which had decided to keep French as their official, national language, and where transition from colonial to independent status had been smooth. It required much more tactful handling in countries like Tunisia and Morocco whose national language was Arabic and whose fight for independence had been much harder.

The most delicate partner in this was Algeria where a seven-year long struggle had caused terrible hardship and great resentment on both sides. Equating independence with cooperation for Algeria was a formidable challenge for both partners[3] and resulted in a major step forward in French development thinking. Many of the experimental procedures developed in sub-Saharan Africa in the early sixties had to be reshaped to meet Algerian requirements. Thousands of young Frenchmen, allowed to fulfill their military obligations as technical assistants overseas, acquired feeling for the problems and tasks of the developing world during their year in Algeria.

By 1964, when the first United Nations (UN) Conference for Trade and Development was convened, France had become an experienced champion of forward-looking policies in a field where neither the 77 member countries from Asia, Africa and Latin America, nor the Eastern or Western industrialized countries had as yet a clear idea of how to organize their future cooperation. André Philip, who headed the French delegation, could implore all industrial nations to transfer 1 per cent of their GNP to least-developed countries (LDCs) without aiming higher than the actual performance of his own country (a situation which had ceased to exist by the end of that decade).

Meanwhile, a commission headed by Jean-Marcel Jeanneney published a report, drafted by Simon Nora, which analyzed French development cooperation, and made a number of policy suggestions. First of all, in order to make its full contribution to the worldwide fight against underdevelopment, France should actively promote – in its capacity as founding member of the UN and permanent member of the Security Council – the work of the specialized agencies and programs of the UN, making use of multilateral channels to exercise its influence in all developing countries. Second, as a prominent member of the European Economic Community, France should increase the commitments of the then six nations towards the associated countries in Africa, which were mainly Francophone at the time. Third, in its bilateral relations with individual developing countries, France should give priority to its former colonies or protectorates, but – without neglecting its cultural (i.e. teaching) responsibilities – put greater emphasis on investments in such fields as mining, industry, transport and agriculture. Finally, the report hinted at, without elaborating, a reshaping of governmental structures which would have made development cooperation more autonomous, entrusting it to an administration which would pursue long-term objectives independent of conjunctural political relations with various governments.

Neither this report nor the one drafted four years later by Yves Roland-Billecart (for a commission chaired by Georges Gorse) was fully implemented. Sub-Saharan Africa retained a special status under de Gaulle, who entrusted the political responsibility of relations with Francophone heads of state in Africa to a special unit reporting directly to him. Economic and cultural relations were delegated to a separate Ministry (rather inappropriately called Ministère de la Coopération) while expanding programs of development cooperation with North Africa, the Middle East, South and Southeast Asia and Latin America were administered jointly by the Ministries of Finance and Foreign Affairs.

Georges Pompidou was on the verge of bringing change to this development picture when he died prematurely. Michel Jobert, his Foreign Minister, incorporated the services of the Ministry of Cooperation into the Foreign Ministry, increased the geographical area of privileged cooperation to include Anglophone and Arabophone Africa and joined forces with Algeria in the UN General Assembly in support of a new international economic order. Simultaneously, enlarging the European Economic Community led to renegotiation of agreements between the now nine countries and their much larger number of developing trade-partners known as the ACP (African, Caribbean and Pacific countries). The commissioner in charge of that negotiation, which led to the Lomé Convention in 1974, was Claude Cheysson.[4]

By this time Third World leaders – even those who had taken the firmest positions against France during the decolonization period – had begun to rely on France to support many of their causes. With regard to the oil problem, for example, France appeared to hold positions quite different from those of the United States. France had likewise refused to become a member of the International Energy Agency and had taken sides with the Group of 77 in the UN in favor of a new international economic order to be arrived at through global negotiations. Finally, France continued to press its European partners to increase their transfers to developing countries.

In this respect, the election of Valéry Giscard d'Estaing initially appeared as a return to more traditional positions. The Ministry of Cooperation was restored to the same geographical boundaries and administrative independence as before Michel Jobert's changes. Personal relations with Francophone African heads of state were taken up at a higher level than ever before, causing a fair amount of criticism.[5] An attempt was made to harmonize French policy towards OPEC with the United States and to involve Washington in a new round of global negotiations. Pierre Abelin, Minister of Cooperation, published a new report on French Cooperation Policy in 1975 after a series of contacts with France's African partners to find out to what extent the policies pursued met their actual needs and wishes. Much of what needed correction was analyzed in this report, and a number of suggestions were made which came close to the criticisms made by the Socialist opposition of the time.

France played an active role in multilateral fora in other respects, attempting throughout Giscard's presidency to draw conclusions from the obvious new international importance of the Third World. The first oil shock, growing competition from the newly industrial countries, alarming debt problems, erratic exchange rates and the plight of the least-developed countries all underlined the growing interdependence of developed and developing economies and called for common action. Giscard was eager to play a prominent role on the world scene by taking a lead in addressing such problems. Realizing how difficult it was to discuss major oil and trade questions within the UN, given the presence and maneuvers of the Soviets, he skillfully negotiated the convening of the Conference on International Economic Cooperation (CIEC) in Paris in December 1975. The composition of this meeting was quite unusual and its agenda was wide open, though France, the host, elegantly deferred and allowed the European Economic Community (EEC) to speak on its behalf. Lasting until June 1977 the conference failed, by a small margin, to agree on a complicated package in which OPEC countries would have joined major industrial powers to keep energy prices at an acceptable level, in exchange for assurances of continued support for their own industrialization and a fair share of trade and development for the rest of the Third World.

The co-chair of the Conference, Manuel Perez-Guerrero (former Secretary-General of the UN Conference on Trade and Development [UNCTAD]) did all he could to bridge the gap between the 18 LDC delegations and the United States and Japan at a moment when the effects of the first oil shock were gradually wearing off. The EEC, under much pressure from France, would have gone much further towards meeting at least some formal Third World demands for reconsidering post-World War II trade and financial institutions whose functioning had been undermined by President Nixon's decisions in July 1971. Nonetheless the conference fell far short of French hopes.

The failure of CIEC provided Giscard with a new orientation about development cooperation. There was to be new concentration in the UN on the plight of the least-developed countries and the stabilization of major commodity prices for them. Additionally, however, an attempt was to be made to involve France's European partners, her African protégés, and the oil-rich Arab countries in a new kind of dialogue in which cultural and philosophical aspects would at least balance, if not outweigh, economic and financial objectives. Using the rather awkward term "trilogue" to define this venture, Giscard tried to enlist Arab support through a Middle East policy somewhat closer to the Palestinians than to Israel. Trilogue remained in the realm of words and seminars, however, while the interest of OPEC in African development faded even before the financial and monetary effects of the second oil shock had disappeared.

Giscard's policy was more effective within the UN. An integrated program for commodities (IPC) had been drafted by the UNCTAD Secretariat. At UNCTAD IV in Nairobi, Jean-François Poncet overcame the reservations of most of his "industrialized" partners to the creation of a Common Fund to stimulate the conclusion of international commodity agreements and to support all developing countries eager to promote added value and effective trade in their most important agricultural mineral commodities. In the years following Nairobi, French diplomacy devoted a lot of energy in the UN to transforming the "principle" of 1976 into a full-fledged treaty subject to ratification in 1979. Even after that text, with its innovative aspects regarding voting power, was adopted in Geneva, ratifications were slow to come in. The change of administration in Washington in 1980 made United States ratification even more unlikely.

With reference to the LDCs, many of them Francophone African nations, the drafting of the New Substantial Plan of Action intended to overcome some of the most serious internal and external obstacles to their survival, and eventual development was actively supported by France during the last years of Giscard's term as President. It resulted in a French government offer to hold a UN Conference on the LDCs in Paris in 1981.

SOCIALIST CRITICISM OF FRENCH THIRD WORLD POLICY IN THE 1970s

Generally speaking, the Left in France had led the fight in favor of decolonization, kept in touch with national liberation movements and pressed for solidarity with the people of newly independent nations. Yet when one reviewed Left participation in governments, the record was more ambiguous. The old SFIO had been largely responsible for the Indochina and Algerian wars. The Communists, while denouncing capitalism and imperialism as the causes of underdevelopment, had been reticent about most postcolonial governments in the South, including Algeria. The Radicals recruited many of their supporters among the former colonists of North Africa. Only the Parti Socialiste Unifié (PSU) and the *gauchistes* clearly aligned their message with the worldwide craving for a less hierarchical, more natural and convivial society, where the human values of African and Asian cultures would counterbalance an all-too-consumerized Western model. How deeply this message touched the young generation in France was made clear by the explosion of May 1968.

A pioneer in this field, as in many others, Pierre Mendès-France had given expression as early as 1955 to a strategy in which France, relying on its overseas experience and democratic tradition, would mobilize in the UN for a common effort to eliminate underdevelopment, including a thorough revision of the international monetary system. However, after the first years of the Fifth Republic (during which the left-of-center parties pressed for speedier action along the path being followed by General de Gaulle) they found little to object to in the Third World policy implemented by successive governments. It took until the mid-1970s for the newly rebuilt Socialist Party to make a determined effort to analyze, evaluate, criticize and present alternative proposals to the official French Third World policy.

Much of what the Socialists had to say can be found in the writings of François Mitterrand himself, but its most coherent exposition came under the direction of Lionel Jospin, Party coordinator for external relations at the time, in an official collective volume published in December 1976: *Les Socialistes et le tiers monde*. After a particularly thorough, courageous and lucid analysis of the realities of underdevelopment, the plight of the less-developed countries, the failure of development assistance and its dramatic ramifications for the world economy as a whole, the book outlined a policy which a future government of the Left should pursue, and to which it should give high priority regarding foreign relations objectives more generally. Its basic principles had already been incorporated in general and very similar terms in the *Programme de gouvernement du parti socialiste* (1972) and the subsequent Programme Commun signed with the Communist Party in summer of 1972.

Les Socialistes et le tiers monde started from the assumption that a Socialist government must put "cooperation" at the heart of France's international policy. To begin with, this meant that France's presence in the elaboration of a new international economic order should be increased. The relatively limited international weight of France ought to be used fully to press for a more coherent organization of production and trade, in order to avoid the iniquitous play of market forces. More specifically, France should work to stabilize commodity prices, to help poorer countries compensate for shortfall in export revenues, and to extend the generalized preference system. To reform the international monetary system it ought to promote increases in financial transfers primarily through international financial institutions, and debt rescheduling. Joint exploration and exploitation of the resources of the seas and a concerted industrialization of the developing world would go hand in hand, the book noted, with serious structural adjustments to the industrial policies of the developed nations. France ought also to promote more effective policies for development cooperation between the EEC and the Third World, particularly with its partners in the Lomé Convention. To that effect, France should overcome the resistance of some of its neighbors to government-oriented industrialization and to policies less dependent on American positions in such fields as commodity trade and a new international division of labor. Finally, France should maintain a strong bilateral component in development cooperation policy. To that end French official development aid (ODA) should reach the internationally agreed target of 0.7 per cent of GNP within five years, concentrating on the promotion of rural development and effective technology transfers. France should also grant development aid on a long-term (five-year) programmed basis and refrain from substituting French citizens for nationals in traditional forms of technical cooperation.

The document then insisted that France should select those with whom constructive and frank dialogue was conceivable from among existing privileged partners and then engage them in true "cooperation contracts". Where the basic interests and philosophy of each were respected both parties would know what to expect from each other. Such an effort would require a thorough mobilization of public opinion and the active participation of the public and private sectors. As part of the package, fairer deals for African migrant workers in France and recognition of the value of Third World cultures in enriching France's own were proposed.

To what extent did the Socialist party condemn the Third World policy of the Giscard era? A cautious distinction was made between Giscardian words and deeds. Some speeches were deemed acceptable, but the objectives actually pursued by the government were condemned. Instead of promoting democracy and efforts at self-sustained development, France clung to reliable political constituencies mainly in

Francophone Africa and showed complacent solidarity with some of their least commendable leaders, a good example being Emperor Bokassa and his coronation ceremonies. Grants and loans essentially served to support exports of French equipment with no regard for their detrimental effects on the financial stability of the recipients. Cultural and technical assistance was aimed at perpetuating France's influence through teaching French and promoting its cultural models, which were often incompatible with indigenous social and economic development. All this would have to change.

FRANÇOIS MITTERRAND'S APPROACH IN 1981

When Mitterrand replaced Giscard d'Estaing in May 1981 the attention of the world was focused on the Euromissile crisis. The most striking aspect of Mitterrand's foreign policy was, of course, the firmness with which he favored deployment, despite the inclusion of four Communist ministers in the Mauroy government. In the area of North–South relations, Mitterrand faced a difficult situation. France stood out as the single Western power still believing in the need for early global negotiations and denouncing the danger of the excessive indebtedness of developing nations and the inappropriateness of the monetary system. France had also invited the UN Conference on the Least-Developed Countries to Paris, amidst great skepticism in Europe and a strongly defensive attitude in President Reagan's Washington. What more could a Socialist government do than continue along the lines followed by its predecessor? And yet the developing countries which had attentively followed the French presidential election could not avoid interpreting Mitterrand's victory as an encouragement to rely even more confidently on French diplomacy. Moreover, French public opinion was well prepared for more outspoken attitudes of solidarity with the Third World and a commensurate reshaping of French policies.

In these areas Mitterrand made a number of important decisions illustrating his willingness to differentiate himself from his Western allies, particularly the United States. To begin with, he confirmed the invitation to convene the UN Conference on the LDCs in Paris, opening the session with an eloquent statement urging industrial powers to help themselves out of crisis by helping the Third World. The French delegation to the conference, headed by Jean-Pierre Cot, the new Minister of Cooperation and Development, was instructed to press for clear commitments from all participants, haves as well as have-nots, who all agreed. Next, Mitterrand, on his way to the Cancun summit, made a joint declaration with President Lopez Portillo denouncing the situation in El Salvador and insisting on the need for greater justice in Central America and the Caribbean, clearly taking sides with Third World countries and blaming the attitude of the Americans. Third, he did not conceal his disappointment with the feeble results of the Cancun summit, deploring that it had led neither to the resumption of global negotiations in the UN nor to the creation of a new World Bank affiliate for energy. Then he engaged in a novel kind of negotiation around natural gas with France's most important partner in the developing world, Algeria, which gave the Algerians an "adequate", above-market price for one of its major commodities, a distinct sign of France's belief in a world trade system subjected to concerted governmental agreements and not only to market forces.

Mitterrand also declared to the Development Assistance Committee of the OECD that France would no longer include its aid to overseas territories in the calculation of its official development aid, thus bringing the figure of that aid down from 0.72% of GNP, to 0.38%. At the same time he pledged to reach the internationally agreed-upon target of 0.7% by 1988. This apparently procedural move was in fact an important sign of President Mitterrand's readiness to fight for high principles and worldwide solidarity and to reach into the pockets of French taxpayers to allow for a more generous policy than the one pursued by his predecessors.

Finally, Mitterrand chose Jean-Pierre Cot for the position of Minister-Delegate of Cooperation and Development, a most significant choice. Well known as a militant *tiersmondiste*, Cot quickly embarked on new initiatives to create a fresh image for the new administration. When Cot was asked four years later to comment on the emphasis put on the Third World by the government of Pierre Mauroy after 1981 his response was most interesting. Three imperatives, he explained, were at the root of the new policy. First, he argued for the conviction that the destiny of a world caught in serious economic crisis depended on developing the resources of the Third World. Therefore lucid and determined support of nonalignment was the most suitable stance for a government of the Left. Next came a need to provide compensation for the militant Socialists, pacifists and ecologists concerning the deployment of Pershing missiles. Here the argument was that stress on solidarity between France and the suffering peoples in the LDCs would lead leftists to downplay the costs of North Atlantic solidarity. Third came the will to maintain, in very pragmatic ways, French influence in a number of countries in the Third World.

Nobody was more conscious than Cot of the obstacles to profound change in France's Third World policy. In his 1984 book, *L'Epreuve du pouvoir*, he very accurately described the spirit in which he addressed his mission and the major results he had hoped to achieve. In his foreword, he writes:

> For eighteen months I have been charged, by the President of the Republic, and by the side of the Foreign Minister, with directing and renovating our cooperation policy. We have tenaciously worked for change – some will say obstinately – convinced that it was the only way to preserve and increase the influence of France. Some reforms have been put into effect. Others have been merely outlined and shall be either pursued or given up by my successors.
>
> Decolonization and the Third World are themes which have long been variously approached and analyzed in militant visions, economic research, theoretical reflection. This book endeavors to show how these viewpoints have been combined to define a policy . . . To analyze the situation as we found it, to describe the problems, to explain decisions made means also not to hide the weaknesses or the contradictions which have been overcome with widely varying degrees of success. My ambition has also been to allow the actors in the struggle for development – technical assistants, members of non-governmental organizations, officials of foreign service administrations – to benefit from the experience and thinking accumulated in the exercise of governmental responsibilities in a field that had until then inspired mainly the works of militants or scholars.
>
> I hope that all those working for development will not be discouraged by this frank description of facts, obstacles and contradictions. I want them to find here new tools

for thought and new reasons to pursue their task, notwithstanding an indifferent and skeptical environment and regardless of the newly fashionable Eurocentric moralism spread by those who, having been hurt by the fights they didn't fight and the ideological frenzies of the past, shout with horror or sigh and shrug their shoulders when the problems of the Third World are mentioned.

Although admitting that many Socialist objectives had had to be put aside, Cot prided himself on the trust and friendship of Third World leaders gained by a dialogue free of complacency which clearly stated the type of development assistance France was interested in giving. He was satisfied with the substantial increase in French financial support going to the most efficient multilateral programs and that the sphere of privileged assistance had been extended to include additional African and Caribbean nations. He found comfort in the coincidence between the theses developed in the Organization of African Unity's 1980 Lagos Plan and those of Michalet and Grjebine (Cot's favorite French economists) on "independent development" giving decisive preference to autonomous accumulation over extroverted industrialization. The outspoken support given to the OAU by the new French government, which manifested itself in experiments to achieve a higher degree of self-sufficiency either nationally or through regional cooperation, was also a far-reaching innovation. In general, France intended to discuss development strategies with its partners and not be drawn into counterproductive forms of assistance.

Cot also made a serious effort to incorporate respect for human rights into France's African policy, fully aware of the shaky ground on which he was treading. It was said at the time that his attitude in such matters led to his dismissal. Some of the more conservative or autocratic African heads of state no doubt resented this, but on the whole Cot did not lose, at least in this respect, the President's support. Cot also innovated by his greatly increased support of voluntary associations and nongovernmental organizations. Their proliferation and simultaneous lack of adequate resources had long troubled many Third World militants attempting to address the problems of the LDCs in more concrete and human ways than formal intergovernmental agreements and conventions. In his book Cot underlined the positive results of this latter policy as well as the impact of decisions to extend active cooperation to new sectors, manifest in the creation of an international institute for sanitary and social development in Bordeaux, the promotion of industrial cooperation involving small and medium-sized businesses and the extended town and country planning responsibilities of the ACA agency, headed by one of Cot's friends, Claude Alphandéry. Alphandéry was charged with finding solutions for the overwhelming problems of urbanization and the restructuring of agricultural research institutes to support subsistence rather than cash crops.

Intentions, programs and reality

All these tasks were to lead to the expansion of the areas in which France could become a prominent partner for forces in the developing world that understood the imperatives of independent, self-sustained and democratic development. Were these attitudes, innovations and decisions the ingredients of the kind of change that was expected when the Mitterrand administration was voted into office? Could the Third-Worldist militants within the Party have been satisfied? Let us recall the major expectations of the Left's program in the years preceding 1981 and try to find out how many of them were translated into fact:

— A fundamental reshaping of administrative structures to allow the definition and implementation of a coherent new strategy;
— selection of partners would no longer be restricted to sub-Saharan Francophone Africa. Genuine efforts by all developing nations to build democratic institutions and serve the interest of the masses would be taken into account;
— a policy of long-term commitments, including multiannual development "contracts", with a limited number of important LDCs having like-minded leadership;
— replacement of French teachers and technicians with appropriately trained nationals.

Administrative restructuring

At first it seemed as if this part of the Socialist program was being implemented quickly. The independent Ministry of Cooperation was abolished. The Minister for Foreign Affairs was made responsible for all aspects of foreign policy. He then delegated the duties of European affairs and cooperation and development to two colleagues. Nobody could doubt the importance which Claude Cheysson attached to the Third World. He had devoted his whole life – since the days of Vietnam, Algeria and Indonesia, the Commission for Technical Cooperation of sub-Saharan Africa, and finally, as Commissioner for Development in the Commission of the European Community – to these issues. The choice of Jean-Pierre Cot as Minister-Delegate of Cooperation and Development was significant as well. Although his Party position was that of a friend and supporter of Michel Rocard, his relations with the President of the Republic, his status as a first-class politician and intellectual, even the memory of his famous father, all made it obvious that he would play an important role in the Mauroy cabinet. Moreover, the Minister of Finance and Economic Affairs, Jacques Delors, was known for his active commitment to Third World development.

The issue of establishing an independent agency for development cooperation arose immediately. Since all development resources and tools were to be concentrated here, certain operational activities would be handled better by this agency than by ministerial administration. Strong support for this approach came both from within the Party and from the most experienced practitioners of French cooperation (who had witnessed the advantages of such a body for American, Canadian and Scandinavian aid programs). In their view the Ministry should be responsible for overall policy orientation, the negotiation of long-term agreements with individual countries, the positions of French delegations in international debates and the periodic evaluation of development contracts. The financial management of grants and loans, discussion of terms, interest rates and eventual rescheduling should be handled by a development bank structured like the Caisse Centrale de Coopération Economique, whose responsibilities would be extended geographically to include all of the Third World. The agency itself would be accountable for project implementation, field work, recruitment and administration of agents, engineering firms, support for voluntary associations, training and supply of equipment. It would carry out these duties with maximum flexibility to be able to respond to requirements on the spot.

The bureaucracy of the former Ministry of cooperation and the hierarchy at the Ministry of Finance and Economic Affairs both strongly resisted this scheme which would obviously have taken away many concrete responsibilities from them. The agency plan was thus replaced by an agreement to ensure a high degree of coherence, mutual information and cooperation among the various administrations concerned with the definition and implementation of France's Third World policy. In turn, an interministerial Delegate for Cooperation and Development Aid was appointed in the office of the Prime Minister. Equipped with a team of five assistants, the interministerial Delegate was to prepare an annual high-level council which, chaired by the President of the Republic, would draft instructions for the orientation and geographic distribution of French development assistance. He was charged with guaranteeing the implementation of these instructions through personal contacts and interministerial meetings. The system could only work, however, if the powers at the Minister-Delegate's disposal were renovated, strengthened and clearly oriented. Their geographical authority needed to be extended to all of France's partners cooperating with the Third World. Neither of these objectives had been achieved by the end of 1982 when Jean-Pierre Cot withdrew and Christian Nucci replaced him. The interministerial delegation had been phased out even earlier.[6]

Selection of partners

Obviously the new government could not ignore long-term commitments binding France to the newly independent nations of tropical and equatorial Africa, the Maghreb and the Indian Ocean. Even if one had wanted to put more distance between Paris and the more autocratically led of these countries, more time and patience were necessary. Any choice between "moderates" and "progressives" was specious. In addition, the crises in all non-oil-exporting developing countries over the preceding decade had had a particularly strong impact on France's traditional African partners. If Cot wanted to avoid greater hardship for their populations he could not very well lessen the flow of resources to them to find the means for new commitments elsewhere. He might of course have followed the urgent advice of André Postel-Vinay, former President of the Caisse Centrale de Coopération Economique. Postel-Vinay suggested ending the upsurge of loans and commercial credits to finance French equipment exports – to say nothing of weapons – to developing countries which did not need them to increase the purchasing power of their poorer citizens and didn't intend to repay them. French taxpayers, therefore, had to shoulder the burden of this pretense at development aid twice. But at a moment when France was engaged in an intense search for export markets the government would not have followed such advice.

The first high-level council, convened in June 1982, also did not extend the priority area of French development aid much beyond traditional boundaries. It did, however, include the "frontline" countries of Southern Africa, Zimbabwe, Angola, Botswana and Mozambique, at least in principle, as well as Nicaragua and a number of small

Caribbean islands close to the French Antilles. Beyond this, however, neither negative selection (the elimination of former partners because of their undemocratic regimes) nor positive selection (the inclusion of countries such as India and Mexico with which an attempt at concerted codevelopment had been made earlier) had materialized by the end of 1982. The so-called worldwide (or Third World-wide) authority of the Minister-Delegate had therefore lost most of its meaning.

After the *conseil restreint* of June 1982, critical observers such as Marie-Claude Smouts or "Querculus", editor of *Marchés tropicaux*, concluded that François Mitterrand himself remained a staunch defender of the old concept of France's *pré carré*, known to all French pre-war schoolchildren as the shaded pink area on the map of the world where their language was taught and spoken and their history and culture somehow integrated into the environment. This perspective was, of course, strongly repudiated by true French *tiersmondistes*.

Long-term development planning

Among the most important efforts of the restructuring of the Ministry was the establishment of a "development policies department", entrusted with the crucial task of negotiating multiannual programs – to include all aspects of French assistance: personnel, training, food, investment, equipment, balance of payment support, research and industrialization – with individual partner governments. Such programs could have been more effectively coordinated with other aid programs, bilateral donors or multilateral institutions to which France belonged, notably the EEC. Unfortunately, the development policies department remained the weak branch of the Ministry, and the development projects department blocked the overall reconsideration of priorities and results which would have given meaning to long-term programming.

Even if innovation in relations with traditional partners was difficult, more constructive results might have been achieved by long-term cooperation programs with the governments of more or less "like-minded" countries. These nations would have displayed interest in the new philosophy of French development assistance and devoted their own potential to a new type of partnership, somewhat ambitiously termed "codevelopment". Algeria, India and Mexico had all been chosen as possible partners for such an approach and contacts were made, in particular by Michel Rocard when he was Minister of Planning. It would be wrong to underestimate the impact of these contacts or the mutual good will and understanding which they generated. However, except for Algeria, already the beneficiary of a large portion of French ODA, available amounts were not enough to play decisive economic and social roles.

Withdrawal of substitution assistance

It is paradoxical that several thousand French hold teaching, engineering, even administrative positions in independent countries suffering from underemployment of their own national university graduates. Fifteen or more years (beginning as early as the 1963 Jeanneney report) of denouncing this practice has not convinced the recipient governments to dispense with what they considered a guarantee of quality in their schools, universities and technical administrations. Would France under Mitterrand be more determined to impose reason in this area? An excellent report analyzing the situation in North Africa and sub-Saharan Africa was drafted in 1982 by Socialist MP Alain Vivien. This report was different in many ways from its predecessors, but it required equally radical readjustments. Although it is too early to be optimistic, one can hope that the recommendations of the Vivien report will give a new image to what has largely remained a neocolonial type of cultural and technical assistance.

CONTINUITY OR CHANGE?

After this recapitulation, are we bound to conclude that only a small portion of the major changes proposed by the Socialists and expected by Third World militants actually materialized during the Mitterrand presidency? Perhaps these proposals were overambitious? Perhaps the political climate in the North had so deteriorated by the 1980s that a far-sighted and generous policy towards the South was no longer acceptable even in France? Could it be that those attending the spring 1985 Paris roundtable under the auspices of the Fondation Libertés sans Frontières expressed the prevalent mood by sarcastically mocking *tiersmondisme* as an outmoded ideology? Had the worldwide context of crisis come to weigh so heavily in this area – as in so many others – that the French government could not step beyond old-time commitments, procedures and objectives towards radical innovations? Was continuity the most we could have expected from the Left in power?

There can be no doubt that Mitterrand's France has had a distinctly different image from that of its predecessors in the eyes of Third World leaders, perhaps for good reason. In conclusion, let us therefore insist on some of the major elements of change, both in word and deed, which have been introduced to French Third World policy since 1981.

To begin with, Mitterrand and his representatives expressed a coherent vision in coherent language about *mal-développement*,[7] the failure of development policies and development cooperation to overcome the impasse of the vast majority of humankind living in the Third World.[8] This lack of effort seriously threatens the stability and future prosperity of the industrial world and is an even greater challenge than the coexistence of the over-nuclearized superpowers of the East and West.

Next, with greater vigor than any previous French administration, Mitterrand's governments insisted on the need for a new international order, not only in the financial, monetary and trade fields, but also in research, culture and communications. The goal was to create a context for the Third World in which, protected by worldwide respect for its independence and nonalignment, it could find paths toward self-sustained and culture-specific development. Mitterrand's France also firmly resisted purely liberal conceptions of market-bounded development which would create highly unfair competition and strangle the poor. It saw the strengthening of international regulations not as a threat to freedom, but as a requirement in a world of unequal partners.

Finally, even if verbal expressions did not always become deeds, they influenced the thinking and actions of many, both in and out of France. Younger leaders in Third

World countries, in Africa as well as Latin America and South-East Asia, discovered considerable convergence between their own experience and thinking and the analytic principles of French development in the eighties. This seems true microeconomically through the insistence on new experiments in rural development, peasant autonomy, small projects, primary health services and decentralized environmental control. It can also be seen in macroeconomic and political ways in regional, national and international strategies clearly aimed at alleviating the plight of the large numbers of urban and rural poor by subjecting multinational corporations and international trade to limitations and controls.

Simultaneously, the younger generation in France has been attracted by new forms of cooperation with peoples of the South. Participation in operational associations like Médecins du Monde and Médecins sans Frontières is leading to participation in fields other than health. Concerns for migrant communities and public-opinion campaigns are visible in decentralized ventures such as 'Solidarité-Eau, a program through which local French teams are relocated to the poorest areas of the world to work on concrete, manageable projects. The proponents of such initiatives have always claimed that they were not given sufficient governmental support. This claim is still applicable today after five years of Left power, symbolizing the continuity in Third World policies. Yet governments in Mitterrand's France have encouraged and popularized innovative Third World policies and tried to make them part of French civic life more than any of their predecessors.

NOTES

1 Specifically by Pierre Mendès France in speeches to the Economic and Social Council of the UN.

2 Overseaas development aid as defined by the Development Assistance Committee (DAC) of the Organization for Economic Cooperation and Development.

3 Claude Cheysson, who for four years held the position of French Director-General of the Franco-Algerian Office for Industrial Cooperation, played a decisive role in meeting that challenge.

4 It is interesting to note that André Philip, Simon Nora, Claude Cheysson and other proponents of a more active Third World policy had been, in 1954–55, closely associated with Pierre Mendès France.

5 A lucid analysis of Giscard's African policy is to be found in Samy Cohen and Marie-Claude Smouts (eds), *Politique extérieure de V. Giscard D'Estaing* (Paris, Presses de la Fondation Nationale des sciences politiques, 1985).

6 An excellent analysis by Marie-Claude Smouts of this evolution is to be found in *Politique étrangère* (Feb. 1985).

7 So strongly is the need for "coherence" felt by those intent on effective change in areas like tropical Africa that the most biting criticism of Mitterrand's policy (as expressed, for example, by Querculus, "Vingt-cinq ans de relations entre la France et l'Afrique indépendante, " in *Marchés Tropicaux*, June 7, 1985) is that we still lack a coherent "corps de doctrine" for our relations with the African continent. An interesting, if somewhat excessive, claim.

8 Perhaps most eloquently expressed by Pierre Mauroy before the 38th session of the UN General Assembly. Never before had a French Prime Minister used this forum to express France's position in this general debate.

VI
Conclusion

21

Conclusion

STANLEY HOFFMANN

PARADOXES AND DISCONTINUITIES

Rarely have so many books and articles been written, so many conferences held, about a five-year period of recent history – and so soon after (often, indeed, during) the events. Fascination with the Mitterrand experiment sprang from many sources: the first *alternance* in the history of the Fifth Republic, after 23 years of rule by de Gaulle and the Right, the first test of the new Socialist Party built by François Mitterrand, the first experience of Socialist–Communist coexistence in government since the post-war days of *tripartisme* and the rupture of 1947, the prestige the French Left has always exerted on intellectuals and social scientists (abroad even more than in France), etc. This was only the second time in the twentieth century that French Socialists found themselves in a dominant position: *tripartisme* had squeezed them between the Communist surge and the Christian Democratic bloc; 1981 could thus only be compared with 1936, the Union of the Left with the Popular Front. The suspense and expectations were intense.

Five years later, it might well be too soon to present a fair and exhaustive balance sheet. This volume has tried to be fair, if only because of the diversity of its contributions, but it is obviously not exhaustive. I have no intention of filling the gaps, nor of covering once more the story in any detail.[1] But a few concluding remarks may be in order.

Few periods have been more fertile in paradoxes (French political life seems to breed them more abundantly than any other country). The most striking may well be the contrast between the sound and fury of these five years – the inflated rhetoric of supporters and adversaries alike – and the modesty of the actual policies and accomplishments. What is needed, above all, is a sense of proportion, a reminder of Corneille's famous verse: the Socialist experiment deserves *"ni cet excès d'honneur ni cette indignité"*, it has been neither a disaster nor a revolution. As Peter A. Hall and others have shown, France's overall economic performance was close to the West European average; taxation and public spending increased, but less than in 1974–81; even the famous, failed *relance* of 1981–82 was of modest proportions;[2] the redistributive effects of the measures taken by the Socialists appear to have been minimal; the sea change of 1981 produced neither an *Etat-PS* nor a deep transformation in the origins and mentality of the ruling elites.[3] What made the journey interesting was the number of detours taken in order, finally, to get from A to B or C. (France did not move from A to Z.)

A second set of paradoxes concerns Socialist failures and Socialist achievements. One might have expected a rehabilitation of planning; none occurred, largely because a combination of domestic experimentation, lack of control over the external environment and need for micro- rather than macroeconomic measures plays havoc with public planning in times of crisis. One might have expected a strong, *dirigiste* industrial policy; one discovered (not for the first time) that in an economy that is *not* a command economy, state attempts at shaping industrial structures and at imposing priorities collide with the plans and preferences not only of private businesses but of state-appointed managers as well. One might have expected a close and confident relation between the parties of the Left in power and the labor unions – a "neocorporatism" of the Left symmetrical with that which the Right had practiced with the CNPF and the FNSEA. But the divisions among the unions and the very Jacobin way in which the state set policies without bothering about *"concertation"*, the persistent barriers between trade-union leaders and the personnel of the state (the teachers in the Party, the bureaucrats and managers in the public sector), not only prevented any experiment in corporatism but left the unions ultimately weaker. The two parties that competed for the allegiance, and promised to improve the condition, of the working class, left it, in George Ross's words, further fragmented and demoralized.

Other paradoxes characterize reforms that produced unexpected results. The Auroux Laws, aimed at giving more powers and more voice to the workers, and bitterly opposed by the employers at first, appear to have helped them in obtaining the cooperation of workers for the improvement of the firms' efficiency and in strengthening the enterprises, i.e. the level at which French labor unions have always been weakest. The complex reforms entailed by decentralization appear to have provided the state's civil servants with a whole, vast, new field of activity and regulation at the three local levels (communes, departments and regions), and given the ex-*préfets* an ever greater role as necessary mediators and arbiters.

The Socialists' successses were biggest in areas where one would have least expected them. They turned out to be more efficient in managing austerity, in reducing inflation, in squeezing wages, than their predecessors. They rehabilitated competition (including in the public sector), celebrated the entrepreneurial spirit, initiated derugulation (especially in banking) and thus, as Casanova observed ironically, prepared the ground for the return of the Right most excellently. Jean-Pierre Chevènement, as Minister of Research and later as Minister of Education, took steps to reconnect French universities and the research community with industry, something which the Left had bitterly opposed before 1981. Never was the stock market more buoyant; never was public confidence in business higher than at the end of the Socialist era!

Many of these paradoxes point to the somewhat self-destructive nature of the Socialist performance. And yet there is a final paradox: on the day of reckoning – 16 March 1986 – Socialist losses were considerably less than the disastrous results of the European elections of June 1984 and the local elections of March 1985 might have led one to expect. To be sure, the Party lost about five points, in comparison with June 1981. But, as the Lancelots' chapter shows, the legislative elections of 1981 were somewhat anomalous. The electorate, in 1986, punished the defectors – the Communist Party, which lost more than six points, falling from 16 per cent to less than 10 per cent – far more than the rulers – the Socialists, who remain the largest party in the country and in the National Assembly. One may even ask whether the good Socialist performance in March 1986 marks the beginning of a new Socialist tide, just as the Right started to rise again almost immediately after the low ebb of June 1981. The artificially high figures for the Left in June 1981 had helped the Socialists forget how narrow Mitterrand's own victory had been on 10 May, and believe that the Left had been elected for its program, or to carry out the President's 110 Proposals – a program and proposals only experts had read: hence the contrast between the militant *triomphalisme* of the new government's first phase and the fragility of the Left's electoral base (a Communist base already shrunken, a Socialist one temporarily enlarged, not by mass conversions to Socialism, but by what can be called Fifth Republic discipline, i.e. the willingness of the electorate to give a newly elected President the Assembly of his wishes).

Next to the paradoxes, it is the discontinuities that stand out, and make it difficult to deliver any blanket judgement. The Mitterrand experiment was a highly fragmented one – something that is not so surprising if one takes into account the political personality of Mitterrand himself. He has been scrutinized almost to death in a great number of French journalistic accounts;[4] they do not succeed in making him any less elusive and impenetrable. A few things, however, are clear: the tension between partisanship and the (very Gaullian) desire to be a national figure, the President of all the French; between a kind of "leftism" that owes far more to 1848 than to Marxism (and is therefore profoundly anti-Communist) and pragmatism. Pragmatism – or opportunism – takes over the minute one goes beyond Mitterrand's sincere determination to reduce class injustice and inequalities, and his conviction that public enterprises are more capable of serving the common interest than private ones (something which goes back at least as far as the ideas of the Resistance and the Liberation). Equally clear – after so long a period in the wilderness – was what a French poet had called *le dur désir de durer*, a desire that, in a country like France, rules out adventurism (as de Gaulle, Mitterrand's model and nemesis, had clearly understood and masterfully expressed in Bayeux). For such a man, the hated Constitution of 1958 was at least as "accommodating" as for the Founding Father – precisely because it gave him full freedom of maneuver between the two self-imposed limits (no policy that would have given the Communist Party a hold over him or the Left; no policy that would be indistinguishable from that of the Right) – as long as he had control of the Assembly.

And therefore there is the overall heterogeneity, between the areas of continuity and the areas of discontinuity. The former, significantly enough, are on the one hand diplomacy and defense, where Mitterrand practiced Gaullism (which meant, of course, that he adapted it to the circumstances, as de Gaulle would have wanted!) and on the other hand law and justice, where Robert Badinter practiced true liberalism (in the American sense of the word, and in conformity with the tradition of Jaurès and Blum). The abolition of the death penalty and of special courts, the reduction of the excessive powers of French *juges d'instruction*, the improvement of conditions in jails, the tightening of the conditions of identity checks, the granting to individuals of the right to bring violations of human rights before the institutions set up by the Council of Europe, these were the (unfinished and, alas, partly reversible) elements of a "Socialist law and order policy" that was long overdue and hailed even by true Liberals on the Right.[5]

Discontinuity prevailed pretty much everywhere else, even when the same person remained in charge (the Jack Lang whose encouragement to performers and cultural activism earned him immense popularity at the end of the period was not quite the same as the *tiersmondiste*, pro-Castro and anti-Hollywood Jack Lang of 1981-82). There was little in common between the populist, popular, militant Mauroy and the smooth, slick, wealthy and technocratic Fabius. There was little in common between the *relance* of 1981-82 and the *rigueur* of 1983-85, beyond a persistent and moderately successful attempt to mitigate the effects of the unemployment which *relance* could not reverse and which *rigueur* could not but increase. There was little in common between the generous and profligate social security policy of Nicole Questiaux and the retrenchment operated by Bérégovoy. The taxes and social charges raised in 1981-82 were, to some extent, rolled back (at least at the level of the state) later on. Edith Cresson's foolhardy attempt to destroy the cozy symbiosis between the FNSEA and the state was followed by a (tense) armistice when Michel Rocard succeeded her. The early intention to loosen the police controls on immigrants soon yielded to a tougher policy against those who were in France illegally, and to renewed incentives for their return to their country of origin. While there was a continuous trend in removing the maze of controls and interdictions that had kept *l'audio-visuel* under state wraps, there was also a sharp break between the highly regulatory and paternalistic liberalization of 1981-82, and the triumph, later, of what the Socialists had always sneered at: advertising and commercialism. The attempt, thwarted by the Constitutional Council, to "get at" the spider web Hersant had extended over the press, was given up. The new, more "socialist" and human rights-oriented policy toward the Third World advocated by Jean-Pierre Cot was promptly squashed, and "realism", close links with potentates and arms sales (almost) *tous azimuts* prevailed again. The most compounded case of discontinuity is that of education. Alain Savary pursued *both* a highly partisan policy aimed at increasing the powers of leftist unions in universities (the Savary law of January 1984) and at extending state controls over private schools (although with prudence), and an experimental policy aimed at decentralizing and liberalizing secondary education. After Savary's resignation, Chevènement gave up the battle on private schools, but became the champion of law and order in primary and secondary education – thus, incidentally, pleasing the Right on both scores, and, as Antoine Prost points out, appeasing the Jacobin Left (unhappy about its defeat on the Catholic front) with the new clarion call for discipline and traditional curricula.

These abrupt changes cannot all be explained by the dramatic, and largely unavoidable, reversal in economic policy in 1982-83. Can they be accounted for in purely political terms – as an attempt to regain, in the Center, among the "new strata" of middle-class salaried executives and employees, the votes without which the majorities of 1981 would not have emerged, and which the first phase – of drastic redistributive measures at the expense of the upper and middle classes – had squandered? If so, the effort was only partly successful: clearly, the Socialists regained some votes, but between 1981 and 1986, the Left/Right ratio shifted from 55/45 to 45/55, which proved once again that any party or coalition that tries to keep or to regain power by providing a somewhat paler copy of the policy advocated by the opponent, makes the opponent's bed.

Mistakes

Rather than asking whether the Mitterrand experiment was a fiasco or a partial success, I would like to examine some of the errors that were made. (It can be declared a fiasco pure and simple only if one believes (a) that losing power in a legislative election is a necessarily fair verdict; or (b) that the Socialists should have been able to deliver all the goodies promised in the programs drafted during the 1970s, even at the cost of protectionism, or leaving the EEC, or carrying out any of the other economic fantasies that flourished on the far Left in 1982–84; or (c) that the Socialists should have created the nirvana of democratic *autogestion* and people power dreamed of by some intellectuals.)

A comparison with the Popular Front can be instructive. Like the Blum government of 1936, the Mauroy government of 1981 "concentrated almost exclusively on the demand-side of the equation" (Hall), and neglected "supply-side conditions in the private sector"; indeed they took measures that made these conditions worse, by starving profits and investments. Neither government paid enough attention to external conditions. Blum's focused on domestic recovery rather than on the formidable discrepancy between the French higher prices and the prices in countries more badly shaken by the Great Depression. The Socialists in 1981 expected a quick American recovery, i.e. higher outside demand, and got the Reagan recession instead; and they took expansive measures just at the time when all of France's partners were contracting and deflating. The great advantage enjoyed by Mitterrand, over Blum, was the difference between the Constitution of the Fifth Republic and the Third. Blum's was a coalition government, in which the Radicals were torn between financial orthodoxy and New Dealism; Mauroy's coalition had a single driver. Blum had no majority for his own policies, either in the Chamber or in the Senate. Mitterrand had one in the Assembly, and could not be defeated by the Senate. Blum was overthrown after one year. Mitterrand was elected for seven. In other words, the Socialists of 1981 had the time to reassess, and to change course and even to pretend that there was merely a succession of phases, not a turnaround, in their exercise of power!

However, there are three remarkably similar errors at the root of the economic fumbling. One, already mentioned, was the mistake of interpreting a fragile victory as a sweeping mandate: something that can be at least partly explained by the frustration of being "out" so long and by the millennial hopes that build up in opposition (from 1920 – if we start at the Congress of Tours – to 1936, from 1958 – if we start with de Gaulle's return – to 1981). The second error is typical of Liberals (be they reformist democrats or social democrats): a belief that all good things must come together, that there is no incompatibility between, say, the greater social justice obtained by taxing the rich and the corporations more heavily, and the desired rise in profits and investments; or between shorter work and increased production. A third error is typically Socialist: distrust of capitalism, private profit, unregulated competition, dislike for the victory of big sharks over small fish, do not constitute the best preparation for managing a *mixed* economy, and above all an *open* economy, part of the world capitalist system. The desire to minimize the constraints which the latter, and to reduce the injustice which domestic capitalism, impose on the nation, breeds a voluntarism that stands in sharp contrast to the awareness of the structural properties of economic and social systems which Socialists (especially Marxist ones) usually display. It also, as Georges Lavau points out, focuses attention on enemies such as the *patrons* or the IMF, multinationals or speculators. Much less attention was spent examining why previous *relances* (such as Chirac's in 1975-76) and policies favored by supporters of the Right had failed to lift France out of economic troubles. Socialism-in-one-country that remains in the world capitalist economy is a very slippery concept: either one is driven to jumping out, which is almost impossible for a nation that - unlike an earlier France - has become so heavily dependent on international trade and insists on being a leader of a uniting Europe; or else one must concentrate on the kinds of factors that Robert Boyer analyzes in his chapter, factors which are either aggravated or untouched by the kinds of policies that were adopted in 1981-82: *relance* of demand, higher taxes and charges, nationalizations. Between the imperative of competitiveness abroad - the Fifth Republic's obsession - and the nostalgic dream of *"la reconquête du marché intérieur"*, there was an insoluble contradiction.

There were other errors in evaluating the mood of the public (no easy task, it must be said). Diana Pinto has incisively analyzed the failure of the Socialists to understand the evolution of the French intelligentsia - either toward a neoconservative Right or toward a critical, antistatist and revisionist Left. In the country as a whole, on the one hand, a sort of *ras-le-bol* with bureaucracy had been building up for years (paradoxically - again! - it had been one factor in Giscard's defeat, for he was perceived, not - as in his self-image - as a *libéral*, but as a state technocrat). While the nationalizations were initially popular, the hiring of more civil servants, the heavier hand of the bureaucracy in education, (and sometimes its interference with economic management in the nationalized firms), the regulatory mania of the Socialists in the beginning, the way in which the multiplication of levels, bodies and jurisdictions through decentralization, and the attendant rise in local taxes, seemed to provide the French with more government rather than less, all this proved to be far more than an irritant. It fed the "Reaganite" craze that crested in the Right in 1985 (and now troubles the new majority, torn between antistate ideologues and pragmatists). On the other hand, a "liberalism" that protested against state interference with individual initiative went arm in arm with a kind of new authoritarianism, a reaction against the "laxity" of the 1960s and to the various insecurities brought, especially in urban life, by the felt rise in violence as well as by the pace of economic and social change; hence a demand for law and order, for tough anticrime penalties, for better police protection, for the end of experiments in schools. It took some time for the Socialists to grasp this; during that time, Le Pen stopped being an extremist nut and became a "respectable" national leader. Badinter was respected but not popular; Chevènement caught the mood deftly.

One reason why this complex mood was not understood better is analyzed by Steven Lewis and Serenella Sferza in their chapter; it has to do with the nature of the Socialist Party, which they describe as a mix of "internal stalemate and hermeticism", the product of too many clans, cliques, *courants* and *tendances* intent on distinguishing their products, and of clienteles around powerful local *notables* concerned with "administering their new electoral *patrimoine*" rather than with strengthening the Party. The need for tight unity – resulting both from competition with the Communist Party and from presidential dominance – reinforced a weakness caused, from the start, by the orientation of the *Mitterrandistes* in control: the lack of concern for the connections with civil society, with what used to be called *les forces vives*: unions, *cadres*, the women and the young, the voluntary associations and the ecologists. The frustration, isolation and decimation of the *deuxième gauche* ended up by costing the Party dearly.

Finally, there were some more purely political errors that must be attributed to Mitterrand despite his reputation for masterly tactics. One was the decision to keep Mauroy as Prime Minister too long. It is clear that Mauroy, after the failure of the 1981–82 policy, courageously saw the need for austerity and played a major role in persuading the President. It is also clear that he had a better instinct than Mitterrand, when he argued in 1983–84 against the Elysée's preference for massive and quick "restructurations", leading to a huge rise in unemployment in the hope that recovery could then start soon enough before the 1986 elections. But by the beginning of 1984, Mauroy had outlived his usefulness and lost his credibility as a speaker for policy, having had to defend too many shifts and switches while pretending they had all been deliberate. Another error was, in fact, a tragicomedy of mistakes involving the Savary Bill on private schools, its modification under pressure from *laïc* deputies, its withdrawal by Mitterrand, and the episode of the failed proposal for a referendum, predictably killed by the Senate, a move whose benefit for the President remains invisible at least to me.

THE LEGACY

It may be even more imprudent to try to evaluate the legacy of the Mitterrand experiment than it is to establish its balance sheet, but two points and one question mark need to be raised anyhow.

The major contribution of the five years of Socialist rule is a big push toward the "normalization", or banalization, of French political life. Freer television channels and radio stations, more rights for workers in enterprises, more local self-government, more *habeas corpus*, all these changes reduce the "French difference" within Western Europe. To be sure, the rise of Le Pen appears to contradict this assertion, and it does indeed show the persistence of the "Bonapartist", populist, authoritarian, chauvinistic tradition, which goes from Boulangism through the leagues of the 1920s and 1930s to the Front National. It confirms Robert Soucy's argument[6] about the porousness of the borders between the more orthodox Right and such movements: they derive much of their strength from disappointed members of, or voters for, the moderate Right, who find it too sedate and too muffled, as well as from furious, frustrated ex-voters of the Left who switch to movements that speak, at least in part, an antielitist language, rather than to the traditional conservative parties.

Nevertheless, one may hope that the Front National will be the victim, either of a return to the pre-1986 electoral law, or of the traditional dilemma of (basically) antiparliamentary or antiestablishment movements that acquire parliamentary representation and respectability. More important, in the long run, are four changes to which the Socialist experiment has contributed. The first is the consolidation of the Constitution, described by Olivier Duhamel and John Keeler and Alec Stone. It has been legitimized by the way in which *l'alternance* fit into the mold of a system allegedly tailor-made for de Gaulle exclusively, and put into practice by the Right alone before 1981. The current experiment in *cohabitation* may not last, but it has the merit of showing the flexibility of the Constitution: as long as there is a clear majority in the Assembly, the Constitution provides France with strong Executive leadership, either by the President if he controls the Assembly, or by the Prime Minister if the President does not. (The real enemy of the Constitution of the Fifth Republic is proportional representation, which served Mitterrand's interest in 1986, but does not benefit France.)

The second change is the meltdown of the Communist Party. Mitterrand's tactic – unity as a way of reducing Communist power and maximizing Communist strains – is only one of the causes of the Communist Party's decline, and it is difficult to say how important a factor it was. It is a fact that, over the last dozen years, the Party has suffered both when it was *unitaire* – for unity actually helped the Socialists become the locomotive of the train – and when it was not – for it gained nothing from its attacks on the Socialists. Indeed, the Communist electorate has appeared constantly more *unitaire*, and therefore more pragmatic, than the Party's leadership. The decline of the Communist Party results from two trends, both of which go much deeper than the inadequacy of Marchais and the mediocrity of the leadership. One is the disintegration of the old working-class basis of a party which (unlike the Italian Communist Party) was never willing to venture beyond its *ouvrièriste* conception and to build a Gramscian coalition around, but not reduced to the problems of, the working class of traditional industries. The other trend is the fading away of the Communist hope or vision: belonging to the Communist Internationale is no longer a compensation for being isolated at home, once the myth of the Soviet Revolution and the workers' paradise has been thoroughly tarnished.

The third change is the Socialist Party's own *aggiornamento*. The conditions of the Popular Front's defeat made it easy for ideology or eschatology to prevail over realism: there were so many real "enemies" one could blame for the fiasco. Five years in full power turned out to be a sobering experience. In so far as the Socialists had come to power as part of the French post-war consensus on growth and modernization, their "conversion" to profitability, competition and enterprise, their tilt from a mixed economy dominated by the public sector to one in which the market has the lion's share was more like a final push than like a revolution (the symmetrical opposite, indeed, from Jaurès's notion of Socialism as the final push away from capitalism in an already socialized society!). The Socialists have had to understand the constraints of external and internal structures and the limits of voluntarism; they have had to pursue, *à leur corps défendant*, but as persuasively as possible, austerity and industrial reconversion; they were helped powerfully into realism by the desire to remain a, indeed the, major party, by the possibility of staying in the Élysée even if the majority in the Palais-Bourbon was lost and by the evident fact that the electoral chances of a Socialist presidential candidate as well as of the Party as a whole were to be determined at the Center (for there is not much more leeway for gain at the expense of the Communist Party). All these factors have led to the current spectacle of innumerable

Socialist factions flirting with and flitting around a notion that was anathema to them only a few years ago: social democracy. The range of alternatives discussed goes from orthodox social democracy (*à l'anglaise, à l'allemande, à la scandinave*) to grand coalitions of all "progressive" groups against a handful of exploiters and defeatists, as in Chevènement's rather breathtaking reconversion of the now scuttled CERES, and to Rocard's notion of a party that sounds a lot like the Democratic Party in the days of the Rooseveltian coalition! Indeed, the relative success of the PS in March 1986, the popularity of *cohabitation*, and that of Mitterrand as the President in the *cohabitation* experiment, are a kind of left-handed public tribute to the transformation of the Party.

The fourth normalization is that of the electorate itself. It seems far less motivated by ideology than by pragmatic judgements on past performances and present promises (the delicate balance of March 1986 entails both a swing to the Right and a consolation prize for the PS, limited confidence in the RPR–UDF majority and a desire for a cooperation of the nonextremes). Hence a mobility and fickieness, at the expense of those in power, that are characteristic of most other Western democratic publics. As the Lancelots and other students of the French electorate have shown, economic and social categories have become bad predictors of political behavior: the votes result from a mass of individual calculations and personal strategies. This does not mean, as some have argued, that there are no more ideological differences between Left and Right, or that the areas of consensus have spread all over the field of battle. But there *are* important realms of agreement: not only over diplomacy and defense, over economic policy (where choice is indeed limited), over a combination of public and private schools, etc. And many of the disputes are about questions of degree (how much liberalization and privatization of the media and the economy, how much decentralization or "flexibility" of employment, etc.).

A second point concerns continuing weaknesses of the French polity, which the Socialist experiment has put into sharp relief or failed to overcome. One is the structural weakness of French industry, mentioned by Boyer: unlike West Germany, France has "very few industries with a steady and large surplus in international trade"; unlike Japan, it is not highly specialized. Many of its industries are in decline, or depend for survival on trade with developing countries whose own buying capacity is shaky, or on government orders. The main weakness may well be the huge residue of protection and *Colbertisme*: reliance on the state, subsidies and other crutches. State directives and regulations are unwelcome, state help is not, and the reluctance of business to invest when the public climate is not favorable enough – even under a right-wing government – is an extreme yet typical form of such dependence. Part of this comes from the depths of French history; part of it is the French aspect of a West European problem – the gap between national industrial efforts and the dimensions of the technological challenge posed by Japan and the United States, which would require a heroic pan-European undertaking, or else a decision to engage in large-scale joint ventures with the American and Japanese competitors.

A second weakness remains – despite all the changes in society mentioned by Michel Crozier during the conference – the organizational weakness of French society. It is uneven: the case of agriculture is a particularly impressive success story. But the decline of the trade unions, hailed by the critics of *syndicratie*,[7] and beneficial in so far as it helps remove some rigidities in a period of economic stagnation, may also deprive society of important relays and capacities for mobilization in better times. Similarly, the crisis of business unions, analyzed by Suzanne Berger, while it helps (and partly results from) the development of a "culture of the enterprise", may have equally negative effects. Today's more diversified working class, and more heterogeneous *patronat*, are inadequately represented by their traditional union officials; the particular weakness of collective organization, of workers as well as of business, in small enterprises (many of which are in trouble, while others are *à la pointe du progrès*), feeds both sudden, uncontrollable, surge movements and anomie.

Thirdly, this organizational deficiency continues to make the French system of political representation – i.e. the French party system – "fall short of its potential for much of the electorate much of the time". What the authors of this quote call "the unique aspects of the French political culture that de-emphasize parties" are still there, and decentralization, while multiplying local *notables* and generalizing the formula of strong Executives instituted by the Fifth Republic at the top of the state, has done little to improve popular participation or to reduce the stratification which these authors found between "the knowledgeable few" and the mass of the citizens.[8] The withering away of the one party that was also a "counter-society" – the Communist Party – may be a good thing, given the totalitarian features and potential of the Party. However – as in the United States – France's other parties are anything but mass parties or parties capable of mobilizing and harnessing the electorate; and – unlike in the United States – their connections with social movements and organizations are tenuous at best, marked by deep mutual suspicions at worst. As a result, the volatility of the electorate is accentuated; above all a gap persists between the pragmatic and illusionless great bulk of the electorate, and a party-political culture that feeds on inflated rhetoric and *projets de société* even when the ideology behind them is obsolete or sterile;[9] and among that fraction of the electorate that believed in the wordy promises and is disappointed by the contrast with the rulers' performance, sudden explosions of discontent can result in something like the Front National.

The question mark raised by the combination or normalization and continuing weaknesses is that of French distinctiveness or specificity.[10] Much to the regret of many students of French uniqueness, France has become very much more *comme les autres* during and after *les trente glorieuses*, and the Socialists, despite their original hubris and their attachment to models and ideals of the past (so well displayed in their program of 1981 and in Mitterrand's fondness for cemetery or Pantheon rituals), have swum rigorously with the tide after failing to buck it. Normalization has affected the political scene, as we have seen: the Right in the Gaullist years and the Socialists after 1981 have been converted to the realities of Western-style modernization, given up their respective nostalgias and shown a remarkable, convergent ability to learn. De Gaulle, deliberately, and Mitterrand, reluctantly, have been the mighty teachers of transformation. The most intensely ideological party, the Communist Party, is burnt out, and the Front National, while linked to France's troubled right-wing past, can also be seen as a single-issue rather than a comprehensive movement. Thanks to Badinter, French law has lost some of its hard, distinctive edges. The state's prestige and predominance are being questioned. The French intelligentsia, while still not following the path Crozier had wished and prophesied, has moved away, in Diana Pinto's terms, from "the daily political show or the coming elections" and proclaims "universal values only with respect to nonpolitical themes". Economic policy has become, by necessity, remarkably nondistinctive, because of France's vulnerability to the outside. The conversion to European cooperation has affected even the Gaullists, in so far as the RPR is its heir, and even the Left of the Socialist Party has resigned itself to the open borders that prevent free domestic experimentation. Nor is there anything purely French about anti-immigrant and racist sentiment: those who know about the American struggle over racial integration find much familiar material in Le Pen strongholds. French mores show the same mix of individualism, or hedonism, or careerism and "public conservatism" (in educational or penitential matters) as other Western publics,[11] or the same mix of entrepreneurial drives and desires for social security. French mass or popular culture, as it is experienced by millions, or as it is shaped by the media (whose own importance and evolution make them more similar to the media in the United States or in West Germany), is also unexceptional.

There are, however, many features that remain distinctive and they have one thing in common: from the viewpoint of what could be called democratic effectiveness – the stability, competitiveness and continuing success of a modern liberal polity – they are or have become counterproductive. The three weaknesses described above are, so to speak, hereditarily French, and obstacles to economic, social and political health. Another such feature is the monarchic aspect of French authority relations, a characteristic that has become particularly prominent since the fall of the Third Republic. This is partly because of the role of the state (or rather, the bureaucratic, instead of the representative, part of the state) in the reconstruction and modernization of postwar France, and partly because of the Fifth Republic's regime, in which the representative element culminates in an elected monarch, and the bureaucratic and representative elites blend. Does the current apparent consensus on a reduced role of the state – reversing the post-1940 consensus – eliminate this problem? Recent measures of liberalization – as in the *audio-visuel* – may have loosened the grip of this system somewhat; but decentralization, as we have seen, has rather tended to multiply minimonarchs and levels of government. Current *"privatisations"* and deregulation are ambiguous, in so far as the impulse is far from a complete and definitive divestment by the state and is hedged with conditions and controls; and the style of authority in enterprises has not been changed drastically (indeed denationalizations, and the planned new deal in higher education may even decrease the doses of participation introduced after 1981 and 1968 respectively). As the *Greenpeace* affair has shown, the cult of secrecy, the confusion of state action with the general interest, still mark and often mar the French polity. *L'énarchie* has not been demoted by Socialism – there was a revenge of *énarques* in the Fabius era already. The short-lived timid and limited opening of the Ecole Nationale d'Administration (ENA) to a small number of people from the private sector was less effective than a band-aid applied to a major wound.

Another counterproductive feature is the constant tinkering with an educational system that has grown in order to accommodate masses of students, in *collèges* and universities, but without adapting sufficiently its curricula to their mores and needs, and without providing the resources that would allow it to give to its better customers the quality education they deserve as well as adequate opportunities for initiative and research. The separation, in higher education, between the *grandes écoles* and the universities, means that only a very small elite receives the kind of education many more students deserve. The Socialist record, here, has been poor, given the obstacles erected by the educational unions and factions, some of which are far too elitist and reactionary for a system of mass education, and some of which are instinctively hostile to pedagogical innovation. The result is a combination of perpetual surface turmoil – each minister canceling a predecessor's reforms and seemingly obliged to have a plan of his or her own – inadequate slogans (such as Chevènement's "republican elitism"), immobility and waste of human resources.

Another distinctive feature is the Jacobin straitjacket into which the French conception of national identity has been fitted. France, like the United States, has displayed an ample ability to integrate immigrants, to turn aliens into Frenchmen. But the French polity is very different from the American one: the latter is a mosaïc, or a quilt, to which each group of immigrants has contributed its own cultural characteristics; assimilation required only the endorsement of a set of political and economic principles. The French case is more stringent; French pluralism means the right to dissenting opinions rather than the right to retain different customs and cultural traits; assimilation requires the adoption of a whole panoply of values and mores. It means accepting a social system in which there is no cultural pluralism, and in which a radical separation exists between public authority, which is intensely *laïc*, and private behavior, which includes religious beliefs. Thus the integration of aliens, exactly like the social rise of "inferiors", entails an element of conversion, a shedding of the old personality. The crisis provoked by North African (and African) immigration is not new: earlier groups of immigrants were also deemed inassimilable by many Frenchmen. What is new, however, is the clash between those immigrants to whom Islam is a way of life, quite incompatible with the French way, and the French: the latter resist, either with fury or with disbelief, the call made by some for a more pluralistic, "multicultural" redifinition of French identity, while many of the immigrants (fortunately not all) reject assimilation and want to be accepted on their own terms. The Socialists, despite good intentions, never thought through or did much about this thorniest of issues – and thus left the field open to the chauvinists and the hard-liners.

Finally, there is the distinctive feature most startling, or annoying, to foreign observers: the desire for national independence, a national defense, a distinctive role in the world, a national ambition. It is, in many ways, admirable – a deterrent of abdication, a way of reacting against that inevitable "tyranny of the exterior" that used to take the form of a fascination for outside ideologies and models (something the Communist decline appears to have finally allowed France to overcome) and now takes the form of acute dependence on others for prosperity as well as for defense. But the problem, raised in this volume by Jolyon Howorth particularly, is whether France can afford such a stance. Stéphane Hessel told our conference that France was neither willing to have a modest foreign policy nor capable of having an ambitious one. Isn't there now a choice between national policy and national effectiveness? Cannot the goals of the former – welfare, security and a role in the world – be reached only by a West European entity with its own powers of decision? It is a debate that has been going on for a very long time indeed. So far, in diplomacy as well as in defense, the Fifth Republic has tried to have it both ways: to stick to independence and to get the benefits of European and NATO cooperation. But the means for and effects of the former are declining, and the latter, given NATO's structure and "Europe's" limited powers and clumsy institutions, are either uncertain or too meager. And yet no resolution is in sight: to the French, Europe is a reality but not an identity, and in recent years French policies and reactions have often been quite different from those of France's EEC partners (pro-Americanism and anti-Sovietism have become far more intense, and French indifference to arms control has continued).

It is the very magnitude of the efforts the French have undertaken, ever since the fall of 1940 and the humiliation of Vichy, in order to recover rank and power and to stay in the race, which has brought them to the point where national ambition and national identity collide, and where national distinctiveness seems increasingly reduced to features that hamper French performance in the race. The Socialists, in the final analysis, have, after their initial fumbling in economic policy, made a valuable contribution to French modernization and normalization. But that ultimate question, about the functions and dysfunctions of national identity, remains unanswered and, indeed, to a great extent, unasked.

NOTES

1 See S. Hoffmann, "France: the big change", *New York Review of Books*, (25 June 1981), pp. 47-53; "Year one", *New York Review of Books*, (12 Aug. 1982), pp. 37-43; "Mitterrand vs France?", *New York Review of Books*, (27 Sept. 1984), pp. 51-8; "The Odd Couple in France", *New York Review of Books*, (25 September 1986), pp. 66-72.

2 Cf. Jeffrey Sachs and Charles Wyplosz, "The Economic Consequences of President Mitterrand", *Economic Policy*, (2 April 1986), pp. 261-322; and Alain Fonteneau and Pierre-Alain Muet, *La Gauche face à la crise* (Paris, Fondation Nationale des Sciences Politiques, 1985).

3 Cf. Pierre Birnbaum (ed.), *Les Elites socialistes au pouvoir 1981-1985* (Paris, Presses Universitaires de Paris, 1985).

4 Cf. Catherine Nay, *Le Noir et le rouge* (Paris, Grasset, 1984); Serge July, *Les Années Mitterrand* (Paris, Grasset, 1986); Philip Bauchard, *La Guerre des deux roses* (Paris, Grasset, 1986).

5 Cf. Jean-Claude Casanova, "Après trois ans", *Commentaire*, 7, 27 (Autumn 1984), pp. 4444-67.

6 In R. Soucy, *French Fascism: The First Wave, 1924-1933* (New Haven, Yale University Press, 1986).

7 See François de Closets, *Tous ensemble* (Paris, Editions du Seuil, 1985).

8 Philip E. Converse and Roy Pierce, *Political Representation in France* (Cambridge, Harvard University Press, 1986), pp. 786, 785.

9 Public opinion polls continually show very low public confidence in parties.

10 Cf. Jacques Julliard, "Classe politique et société française à l'horizon 1986," *French Politics and Society*, (June 1985), pp. 3-14.

11 Cf. my remarks in "La France face à son image", *Politique étrangère*, 1 (1986), pp. 25-33.

Index